Andrew Liu

Sheffield 2000

From the period of settlement (870–930) to the end of the fourteenth century, Icelanders produced one of the most varied and original literatures of medieval Europe. This is the first book to provide a comprehensive account of Old Icelandic literature within its social setting and across a range of genres. An international team of specialists examines the ways in which the unique social experiment in Iceland, a kingless society without an established authority structure, inspired a wealth of innovative writing composed in the Icelandic vernacular. Icelanders explored their uniqueness through poetry, mythologies, metrical treatises, religious writing, and through saga, a new literary genre which textualized their history and incorporated oral traditions in a written form. The book shows that Icelanders often used their textual abilities to gain themselves political and intellectual advantage, not least in the period when the state's freedom came to an end.

MARGARET CLUNIES ROSS is McCaughey Professor of English Language and Early English Literature and Director of the Centre for Medieval Studies at the University of Sydney. She has published widely in the field of Old Norse–Icelandic studies and Anglo-Saxon studies. Her most recent books include *Prolonged Echoes: Old Norse Myths in Medieval Northern Society* I (1994) and II (1998), and *The Norse Muse in Britain, 1750–1820* (1998).

CAMBRIDGE STUDIES IN MEDIEVAL LITERATURE 42

Old Icelandic Literature and Society

CAMBRIDGE STUDIES IN MEDIEVAL LITERATURE

General editor
Alastair Minnis, *University of York*

Editorial board
Patrick Boyde, *University of Cambridge*
John Burrow, *University of Bristol*
Rita Copeland, *University of Pennsylvania*
Alan Deyermond, *University of London*
Peter Dronke, *University of Cambridge*
Simon Gaunt, *King's College, London*
Nigel Palmer, *University of Oxford*
Winthrop Wetherbee, *Cornell University*

This series of critical books seeks to cover the whole area of literature written in the major medieval languages – the main European vernaculars, and medieval Latin and Greek – during the period c. 1100–1500. Its chief aim is to publish and stimulate fresh scholarship and criticism on medieval literature, special emphasis being placed on understanding major works of poetry, prose, and drama in relation to the contemporary culture and learning which fostered them.

A complete list of titles in the series can be found at the end of the volume.

Old Icelandic
Literature and Society

EDITED BY

MARGARET CLUNIES ROSS

CAMBRIDGE
UNIVERSITY PRESS

PUBLISHED BY THE PRESS SYNDICATE OF THE UNIVERSITY OF CAMBRIDGE
The Pitt Building, Trumpington Street, Cambridge, United Kingdom

CAMBRIDGE UNIVERSITY PRESS
The Edinburgh Building, Cambridge CB2 2RU, UK   www.cup.cam.ac.uk
40 West 20th Street, New York, NY 10011–4211, USA   www.cup.org
10 Stamford Road, Oakleigh, Melbourne 3166, Australia
Ruiz de Alarcón 13, 28014 Madrid, Spain

First published 2000

Printed in the United Kingdom at the University Press, Cambridge

Typeset in Adobe Garamond 11.5/14pt   *System* 3b2   [CE]

A catalogue record for this book is available from the British Library

Library of Congress cataloguing in publication data
Old Icelandic literature and society / edited by Margaret Clunies Ross.
p.   cm. – (Cambridge studies in medieval literature, 42)
Includes index.
ISBN 0 521 63112 2 (hardback)
1. Old Norse literature – History and criticism.   2. Iceland – Civilization. I. Clunies Ross Margaret.
II. Series.
PT7113.O53   2000
839′.609–dc21   00-05980 CIP

ISBN 0 521 63112 2 hardback

Contents

vii

Contents

Contributors

GERALDINE BARNES teaches in the Department of English at the University of Sydney. She is the author of *Counsel and Strategy in Middle English Romance* (1993) and of a number of articles on the development of medieval romance in England, France and Scandinavia. She recently completed an extended study of the 'Vínland sagas' and their reception in nineteenth- and twentieth-century England and America and is currently engaged in an investigation of medieval crime fiction.

MARGARET CLUNIES ROSS is McCaughey Professor of English Language and Early English Literature and Director of the Centre for Medieval Studies at the University of Sydney. She is the author of numerous articles and book chapters on Old Icelandic literature, particularly poetry and myth, and of four books in this field: *Skáldskaparmál: Snorri Sturluson's ars poetica and Medieval Theories of Language* (1987); a two-volume study of Old Norse myth, *Prolonged Echoes: Old Norse Myths in Medieval Northern Society* (1994 and 1998) and *The Norse Muse in Britain, 1750–1820* (1998). She is at present engaged (with others) in re-editing the corpus of Old Norse skaldic poetry, and in research on the contribution of Thomas Percy to Old Norse studies.

MARGARET CORMACK is Assistant Professor at the College of Charleston in Charleston, South Carolina. Her book, *The Saints in Iceland: their Veneration from the Conversion to 1400* (1994), is a survey of the cult of saints in Iceland during the period indicated. She is continuing work on this project, which will eventually extend to the Reformation. She has published a number of articles on women in the Icelandic saints' lives, as well as a partial translation of the saga of Jón of Hólar. Future work includes further study of women as depicted in literature, and annotated translations of the saga of Jón of Hólar and the saga of Árni þorláksson.

KARI ELLEN GADE is Professor of Germanic Studies at Indiana University, Bloomington, and the author of *The Structure of Old Norse* dróttkvætt *Poetry* (1995). She has recently published, with Theodore M. Andersson, Morkinskinna: *the Earliest Icelandic Chronicle of the Norwegian Kings (1030–1157)*. Her research interests are in Old Norse language, literature, culture and history, together with Germanic philology and metrics.

JÜRG GLAUSER is Professor of Scandinavian Studies at the Universities of Basel and Zürich. Among his recent publications are *Isländische Märchensagas* (1998, edited with Gert Kreutzer) and *Verhandlungen mit dem New Historicism. Das Text–Kontext-Problem in der Literaturwissenschaft* (1999, edited with Annegret Heitmann). His research interests include late medieval and early modern Scandinavian literature, especially the history of popular literature, transmission and textuality.

IAN KIRBY was the first professor of English at the University of Iceland, and he is currently Head of the English Department and Professor of Medieval English at the University of Lausanne, Switzerland. His principal publications are *Biblical Quotation in Old Icelandic–Norwegian Religious Literature*, 2 vols. (1976–80), and *Bible Translation in Old Norse* (1986). In the field of Norse studies his current research relates to the generally accepted view that none of the North American runic inscriptions are genuinely medieval.

PREBEN MEULENGRACHT SØRENSEN was, until recently, Professor of Old Norse Literature at the University of Oslo, after having held previous appointments at the University of Aarhus. He is the author of many works on Old Icelandic literature, including *The Unmanly Man: Concepts of Sexual Defamation in Early Northern Society* (1983, first published in Danish in 1980), *Saga and Society* (1993, first published in Danish in 1977), and *Fortælling og ære: Studier i islændingesagaerne* (1993).

GUÐRÚN NORDAL is a specialist in Medieval Icelandic and Editor at the Stofnun Árna Magnússonar in Reykjavík, Iceland. She holds a D. Phil. from the University of Oxford and was the Halldór Laxness Lecturer at University College London from 1990 to 1993. Her first book, *Ethics and Action in Thirteenth-Century Iceland* (1998), has recently appeared and she has another manuscript, *Tools of Literacy: the Role of Skaldic Verse in Icelandic Textual Culture of the 12th and 13th Centuries*, in press.

JUDY QUINN is a Senior Lecturer in the Department of English at the University of Sydney and will shortly take up a Lectureship in Anglo-Saxon Norse and Celtic at the University of Cambridge. She has translated *Eyrbyggja saga* into English and has published articles on Old Icelandic poetics and the female prophetic voice in medieval Scandinavian verse and sagas. Her current project is an electronic edition of the eddic poem *Vǫluspá*.

GÍSLI SIGURÐSSON studied at the University of Iceland, University College, Dublin, and the University of Manitoba, Winnipeg, at the last-named of which he served as a Visiting Associate Professor in 1988. Since 1990 he has been a research lecturer in the Folklore Department of the Árni Magnússon Institute, Iceland, and now teaches in the Department of Folklore at the University of Iceland. His research interests include American–Icelandic, and Icelandic folklore in Iceland and Canada. He has published books on the Gaelic influence in Iceland (1988) and the poetry of the Elder Edda (1998), in addition to a variety of articles.

STEPHEN TRANTER studied Anglo-Saxon, Norse and Celtic at the University of Cambridge and subsequently spent eight years in secondary school-teaching in England before taking his Ph.D. in North Germanic Philology and his Habilitation in Norse and Celtic at the University of Freiburg im Breisgau. He is now Professor of Medieval English language and literature at the Friedrich-Schiller-Universität Jena. He has published *Sturlunga Saga: the Role of the Creative Compiler* (1987) and Clavis Metrica: Háttatal, Háttalykill *and the Irish Metrical Tracts* (1997). His main research interest is the history and development of metrical forms.

TORFI H. TULINIUS is an Associate Professor of French Literature at the University of Iceland. He publishes on French contemporary literature and Icelandic medieval literature. His main interest is in the nature and history of novelistic discourse, and his major publication, *La 'Matière du Nord': Sagas légendaires et fiction dans l'Islande médiévale* (1995), is soon to be published in English.

DIANA WHALEY studied in Durham, Reykjavík and Oxford, and moved to the University of Newcastle upon Tyne in 1978, where she now holds a personal Readership in Medieval Studies, teaching medieval English and Icelandic language and literature and researching in Old Icelandic literature and English place-names. She was President of the Viking Society for Northern Research in 1996–97. She has published articles and books on a wide range of medieval subjects, including Heimskringla: *an Introduction* (1991) and *The Poetry of Arnórr jarlaskáld* (1998).

Introduction

MARGARET CLUNIES ROSS

The aim of this collection of essays is to explore the complex relationship between the development of a new society and a new polity on the island of Iceland during the Middle Ages, and the literature, in the broadest sense, that Icelanders produced in that period. The period we consider stretches from about 870, the beginning of the settlement of Iceland, to about 1400. We ask why and how a materially poor, remote part of medieval European society was able to produce such a rich and diverse literature. We pose these questions, which others have posed before us, within a predominantly social framework, and come up with some new ways of understanding Old Icelandic literature that allow us to make sense of what was, by modern standards, a truly extraordinary suite of explicatory and propagandist mechanisms developed by a small group of people to justify and explain themselves to themselves and to others, in an age well before the existence of such communicative tools as newspapers, mass media and international telecommunications.

We examine what is likely to have motivated Icelanders to preserve and modify the oral traditions that they brought with them when they emigrated in the late ninth century from mainland Scandinavia, especially Norway, and from the Viking colonies in and around the British Isles. We analyse what led to their becoming recognized specialists in poetry, myth and historiography, both of their own society and of others', especially those of Norway and the rest of Scandinavia. We investigate the new literary forms they developed within which to express their perceptions of themselves as members of their own society and in their relationship to the wider world, a relationship that was

1

contemporary but also extended back through time to include both tradtional and Christian history. The new literary genres the Icelanders developed included the various kinds of the *saga* – a new written form with oral roots, as its name suggests – and one that incorporates Norse poetic traditions within a prose base to create a prosimetric medium able to express that combination of the traditional and the exotic, the oral and the written, and the pagan and the Christian, that forged such a distinctive and copious medieval vernacular literature in Iceland.

Although not all contributors to this volume see eye to eye on every point, there is a remarkable congruence about their main conclusions, and many of their major themes overlap, even when they are writing about different literary genres. The book as a whole provides strong testimony of the power of literature in medieval Iceland to affect social life, to alter social and individual consciousness, to promote a national image for a diversity of reasons, and to advance the specific, personal interests of individuals and family groups both inside and outside the country. Equally, and in complex ways, the newly developed Icelandic society itself placed pressure on its component parts to explain and rationalize the past in textual form: to account for the process of emigration and settlement; to justify the establishment of an egalitarian society – at least to begin with – at a time when Europe was ruled by kings and aristocrats, to interpret a pagan society's conversion to Christianity about the year 1000, and, finally, to textualize the loss of independence from outside political domination by writing the narrative of Iceland's capitulation to Norway in 1262–64 as a history whose finer details were determined by rival Icelandic factions acting out their own agendas – though manipulated from Norway – as recorded in Icelandic, and not Norwegian, sagas.

It is now easier to understand the nature of the symbiotic relationship between the distinctive society of medieval Icelandic and the unique character of Old Icelandic literature since the bubble of romantic nationalism has been burst in the later twentieth century. Not only in Iceland itself but also in Europe and other Western intellectual traditions since the beginnings of the rediscovery of medieval Scandinavian culture in the seventeenth century, Old Icelandic literature has been evaluated against a set of changing ideals inspired by modern nationalisms so that it has been difficult to understand it in the context of the society for which it was originally created. The various contributors to the present volume explore contemporary social and intellectual pressures – to the extent that they can be rediscovered – upon medieval Icelandic authors and compilers to produce texts of particular kinds and create new textual genres. They assess the impact of the new textual world of Christian-Latin writings upon medieval Icelandic literary production and show how the vernacular tradition responded to the expanded horizons of Christian culture. They also chart some of the ways in which new literary forms were put to the use of the Church in medieval Iceland.

Many of the chapters in the book accord a significantly greater importance than has been the custom in Old Icelandic studies to the fourteenth century as an age of textual production, in which a majority of the extant medieval manuscript compilations were commissioned by local magnates and religious houses seeking to consolidate their status and power bases through the patronage of literature. From being regarded as an age of literary decadence after the fall of the Icelandic free state, the later thirteenth and fourteenth centuries are becoming recognized as a period when Iceland's textual history was reshaped and as an age in which new literary modes, that also had their roots in the past, took off and flourished. The literature of fantasy and romance, in the form of *fornaldarsögur* and *riddarasögur*, can now be appreciated as appropriate socio-political textual vehicles for late medieval Icelanders rather than as the decadent products of a frustrated society deprived of political independence and sapped of pride in a literary tradition in which realism was always the dominant and superior literary mode.

The thirteen chapters in this volume have been arranged in two broad groupings, introduced by Preben Meulengracht Sørensen's overview of the nature of medieval Icelandic society and its social, political and legal institutions in relation to its literary production, which intersects at some point with every other chapter, though with some more than with others. It offers a succinct and incisive summary of the subject of this book and can be read initially and returned to with profit after having read other, more specialized chapters.

The first grouping of chapters, 2–6, focusses on one of the most important and distinctive aspects of medieval Icelandic literary culture, poetry, though these chapters also deal with a variety of textual traditions, for which poetry was often a medium. There is no doubt that Old Norse poetry was, in pre-literate times, extremely highly developed as an elite, courtly art, especially in royal and aristocratic circles in ninth- and tenth-century Norway. Poets were greatly esteemed and poetry was the vehicle for a good deal of traditional culture, excepting the law and genealogical information of various kinds.

The first grouping of chapters begins with Judy Quinn's overview of the likely character of early Norse oral literature and her assessment of the changes that were involved in transforming that oral culture to the literate textual traditions that have survived to us from medieval Iceland (chapter 2). We then continue with Kari Gade's chapter on poetry, which begins by describing the two major kinds of Old Norse poetry (chapter 3), eddic and skaldic, and their traditional social roles before the development of written texts. Her chapter then traces the developments of skaldic verse in the medieval period and the various ways in which literate writers, particularly historians, used skaldic verse in their texts, and, in some cases, in their lives. Gísli Sigurðsson (chapter 4) next puts a number of the insights offered by Gade's chapter to the test of practical application, with his prosopographical analysis of the knowledge of a single, mid-thirteenth-century Icelandic poet and scholar, Óláfr Þórðarson, as revealed through the poetic quotations in his *Third Grammatical Treatise*. This chapter moves us from poetic practice to poetic and mythological theory.

My own chapter on the conservation and interpretation of pre-Christian myth follows closely on the poetry chapters, for poetry was the traditional vehicle for myth. However, the latter part of chapter 5 addresses the question of the conditions under which Christian Icelanders of the thirteenth century were able to recuperate and assimilate the corpus of Norse myth and it concludes with an appraisal of the mythological dimension of the *Edda* of Snorri Sturluson (*c.* 1225). Snorri's *Edda* is a unique work, incorporating both mythology and poetics. Chapter 6 contains Stephen Tranter's evaluation of a group of learned vernacular treatises on Norse poetics, including parts of Snorri's *Edda*, which assert the high status of Old Norse poetry by claiming indigenous poetics as of equal sophistication to classical poetic and rhetorical traditions.

The second grouping, of chapters, 7–13, is united by its focus upon the new prose genres that were developed in Iceland following the introduction of Christianity in the year 1000. It begins with Diana Whaley's chapter on historical writing in medieval Iceland, for historiography was, arguably, the vernacular genre in which Icelanders first developed extended prose narratives, though these often incorporated poetry in a mixed medium known by the Latin term *prosimetrum*. Some historical writing was undertaken by Norwegians, but it was the Icelanders who became specialists in this area, offering their services to the rulers of various parts of Scandinavia. Whaley investigates why this should have been so, and tackles the question of the social purposes of historiography for the Icelanders themselves.

Jürg Glauser follows her with a chapter on the medieval Icelandic literary genre that is best known to modern readers, the family saga, as it is called in English, or the sagas of Icelanders (*Íslendingasögur*), as they are known in Icelandic. These family sagas, together with the *þættir*, or short tales about Icelanders of the settlement age, chronicle the social lives and adventures of leading families in Iceland during the first hundred and fifty or so years of the new colony and purport to give a realistic account of what it was like to live in the new social space of Iceland. However, as the family sagas were written more than 200 years after the event, they are a medium for what Glauser calls cultural memory, and his chapter indicates how these works of the High Middle Ages can be understood to deconstruct the past through a particular textual genre. Guðrún Nordal follows with a reading of the so-called contemporary sagas and their interpretation of the events of the recent past in Iceland, showing the various figurative strategies the writers adopt to shape recent history as propaganda for their intended upper-class audience.

The two chapters that follow, by Torfi Tulinius and Geraldine Barnes, move us from a predominantly realistic literary mode to the mode of the legendary, the fantastic and the romance. Tulinius investigates the central question of how literary fiction first appeared in Icelandic writings, and how the development of complex fictional narrative in Iceland relates to trends in other parts of contemporary medieval Europe. His chapter also attempts to show the relationship between the evolution of fiction and social change in Iceland during the thirteenth and fourteenth centuries, arguing the suitability of fictional modes to the exploration of the 'uncertain identities' of many Icelanders faced with the social changes of the late Middle Ages. The subject of the relationship between the forms that romance took in Iceland and the audience that is likely to have appreciated it, is one that Geraldine Barnes also tackles in her chapter on the translated and independent Icelandic romances (*riddarasögur*). She argues for a closeness of theme and approach between the independent romances and the *fornaldar-sögur* that are the subject of Tulinius's chapter.

The final two chapters, by Ian Kirby and Margaret Cormack, offer a perspective on a new set of social functions that Christianity brought with it to medieval Iceland. In the case of Kirby's chapter on the Bible and biblical interpretation, we see how the Christian Church in Iceland rose to the occasion of producing vernacular, rather than Latin, translations of the book of the new faith and how translators used some of the techniques that were also applied in secular narrative to get their message across. Incidentally, the accuracy of the translations indicates that those clerics who learned Latin did so thoroughly, and it supports the deduction that we may make from other kinds of evidence that the standard of Latin learning among the educated class was relatively high.

Margaret Cormack's treatment of vernacular Icelandic hagiography gives an account of the Icelandic version of one of the major medieval Christian genres, the saint's life. As in most parts of Christendom, Icelandic hagiography shows a combination of the desire to be part of the Church as a whole and a pressure to promote a national and local image through the veneration of indigenous saints. In Iceland's case, it took some time to develop a local cult and original hagiography, and it is probably significant in the context of local society and politics that all three medieval Icelandic saints were bishops. Cormack concludes her chapter by examining the considerable textual space given to ordinary people and to women in Icelandic saints' lives, in contrast to other saga genres.

This book is an indicative rather than a comprehensive account of the relationship between Old Icelandic literature and society. As its editor, I am only too aware that important areas of the subject have been omitted, though some have been included in part in the course of the treatment of other subjects. Such is the case with the law and sagas of bishops. Other areas, including the learned literature of Iceland, excluding treatises of poetics and mythology and biblical translation, are barely mentioned. There is a rich literature of works inspired by the Christian–classical tradition, some translations, others independent of specific sources. It includes such texts as *Veraldar saga* ('The saga of the world'), Icelandic versions of the popular theological *summa Elucidarius*, and *Leiðarvísir*, an Icelandic pilgrim's guide to the Holy Land. All these and many other works bear witness to the inventiveness and learning of Icelandic scholars in the Middle Ages. In spite of these areas of omission, however, the volume offers an integrated and holistic view of the great variety of Old Icelandic literary production and the social context out of which it grew.

I

Social institutions and belief systems of medieval Iceland (*c.* 870–1400) and their relations to literary production

PREBEN MEULENGRACHT SØRENSEN

translated by Margaret Clunies Ross

OLD NORSE AND OLD ICELANDIC

In the Middle Ages the language spoken in Iceland and the other Norwegian colonies in the West was Norse, most closely related to the southwest Norwegian dialects of Hordaland and Rogaland, where the majority of the settlers in these new lands had their origin. During the settlement of Iceland, and before Norway was united into a single kingdom, the Norse language was also spoken for two or three generations in those parts of the British Isles where people from the western parts of the Scandinavian peninsula had settled. The conventional term for this common language is *Old Norse*. After the introduction of Christianity it developed as a written language, more or less simultaneously in Iceland and Norway and in all probability also in the Orkneys, even though an original literature from the latter has not been preserved. It is common in a national context to speak of *Old Norwegian* and *Old Icelandic*, but the differences between the two written languages are small and without any literary significance. From a linguistic perspective it is therefore natural to speak of *Old Norse literature* as an entity that encompasses both Icelandic and Norwegian literature from before about 1400, and this can be set alongside other linguistically demarcated literatures, for example, Old English. From a literary point of view, however, a quite different picture reveals itself. Here Icelandic literature in comparison to Norwegian is so extensive, both in scope and original-ity, that in some connections, and not least the connection of 'literature and society', it is most practical to speak of *Old Icelandic literature*.

We must keep in mind the fact that *Old Icelandic* is not identical with *Old Norse*, and that Icelandic literature cannot be clearly differentiated from the common West Norse literature in some areas. This is true of poetry from the Viking Age, which on the whole has been transmitted in Icelandic manuscripts, but which, in its origin, is older than the settlement of Iceland. The skalds from the oldest period were Norwegian, and at all events a portion of the eddic poetry that has been preserved must be presumed to have its roots in Norway or Denmark. Later, in the thirteenth century, Icelandic authors probably gained literary inspiration from the European literature which had been introduced into Norway and the Orkney Islands. Courtly culture was known in Norway in the time of Hákon Hákonarson (1217–63) through translations of French literature, including Thomas of Britain's *Tristan* and some of Chrétien de Troyes' Arthurian romances. This literature exerted an influence on sagas of Icelanders (*Íslendinga sögur*). A corresponding role as a meeting place for European and Norse culture was certainly played by the Orkneys. Here we find the earliest example of the renaissance of skaldic poetry in the poem *Háttalykill* (*Clavis rhythmica*), which was composed by the Norwegian-born Earl Rǫgnvaldr kali and the Icelandic skald Hallr Þórarinsson, inspired by the European interest in language and metrics. Finally we must take into account a common connection between the parts of Old Norse literature. That is obviously true of religious texts, which were written both in Norway and Iceland. A second kind of official literature, the histories of Norwegian kings, were partly written as a Norwegian initiative, even though, for the most part, they had Icelandic authors, and they were certainly intended for a Norwegian public.

In what follows both the terms *Old Icelandic* and *Old Norse* will be used.

WHAT IS UNIQUELY ICELANDIC

Norse literature from the High Middle Ages occupies a special place in the European context for several reasons. It is extensive, varied and original and, from a modern perspective, of great artistic value. Important parts of it lack parallels in other places. That is the case with the poetry that Norway and Iceland had in common: skaldic poetry, which is the oldest elite poetry in Europe, and the mythological poems of the Elder Edda, that contain pre-Christian myths, which have not been transmitted to us outside Scandinavia. It is also the case with the uniquely Icelandic sagas of Icelanders, which exist in a highly developed narrative form that both continues traditional historical narrative and anticipates the novel. Almost the whole of this literature was written or at all events preserved in writing in Iceland, and it may appear paradoxical that it was created by a small farming population on the outskirts of Europe, far from the continent's towns and spiritual centres. Iceland itself had no towns. The size of the population scarcely exceeded 50,000 individuals at any time. The island lay many days' journey by ship from the nearest neighbouring countries, Norway, Denmark and the British Isles. The land was virginal and uninhabited, when the first settlers arrived, and the natural environment and the circumstances of life were in many respects quite different from what they were in the lands on the other side of the ocean, as its remarkable name, *Ísland* (lit. 'land of ice'), showed early on. Iceland was settled at the beginning of the tenth century, at a time when the neighbouring countries were being united into kingdoms with increasingly centralized powers. For reasons which are not entirely clear the Icelandic settlers had left these countries, and the society that they then built up was different from the old ones.

There have been two ways in which researchers have tried to explain this apparent paradox, of a copious and highly developed literature in a remote country, which was rather backward from an economic and technological point of view. The first way uses a comparative approach, the second a literary and sociological one. Using the comparative method, scholars have tried to discover the conditions that favoured the development of Icelandic literature in the literature of contemporary Europe. From a broad perspective it is clear that there is a connection, seeing that the precondition for Icelandic literature was writing in Latin and the literature and learning to which the Church's education had opened the door. We may assume that a part of the Icelandic population that gained such an education was also able to read other European literary languages, and we may therefore presume that both Latin literature and literature in the vernaculars were part of the background of learned Icelanders. There is special reason to consider medieval

Icelandic literature in the light of the humanistic interest in language, poetry and philosophy which has come to be called the twelfth-century Renaissance (Haskins 1927). We can can see there a source of inspiration for the preoccupation of Norse written culture with the oral poetry and stories of prehistory. On the other hand we can only be successful to a limited extent in finding concrete European exemplars for the secular Icelandic sagas, and not at all for the sagas of Icelanders.

Using the second, literary and sociological, approach, researchers try to account for Icelandic literature against the background of Iceland's historical and social circumstances. The argument is that an exceptional society, formed in exceptional circumstances, produced an exceptional literature. This view plays an essential part in the present chapter, but it must be emphasised that it does not offer a sufficient explanation on its own. The relationship between society and literature is not so simple, and it operates in both directions. We can probably see the Icelanders' historical experience and special social circumstances as a basis for their literature, but the literature was not only a consequence of that history. The literature also contributed to the shaping of history in a self-affirming process whereby a people with a special historical recollection and mode of thought made narratives about the past a meaningful part of their present.

LITERARY RENOWN

We may see that the present-day appreciation of the Icelanders' literary stature in the Middle Ages was corroborated by the testimony of their contemporaries. Early on it seems to have been an acknowledged fact that the Icelanders were a people with great historical knowledge and particular talents for the art of narrative and poetry. They wrote about their own history in the past and the present, and equally readily about Norwegian kings, the heroes of prehistory and the history of foreign countries. From the Viking Age they had become known in the Scandinavian countries as a people who composed poetry and told stories, and they probably considered themselves in this way too. How this view came about is not entirely clear. The oldest skaldic poetry we know is, as has been stated earlier, Norwegian, but as early as around the year 1000, at the time of the introduction of Christianity to

Norway, the Icelanders had established a solid monopoly on court poetry both in Norway and Denmark. Numerous accounts in sagas of Icelanders and kings' sagas talk of Icelandic court poets and, considered as a whole, give a detailed picture of an institution which may have contributed to the creation of a notion of Icelanders as a nation of poets with an exceptional knowledge of language and history.

After the introduction of writing and the book in the course of the twelfth century that reputation conferred upon the skalds the status of oral *auctoritates* in matters concerning the history of the Scandinavian countries. The Norwegian Theodoricus monachus wrote the short history of Norway, *Historia de Antiquitate regum Norwagiensium*, about 1180, and he begins his prologue by laying stress on Icelanders and their poetry as the source of his narrative. He writes that the remembrance of kings is particularly lively among them, and that they have preserved these events in their old poems, 'qui hæc in suis antiquis carminibus percelebrata recolunt' (Storm 1880: 3). In the same way, in Denmark at the beginning of the thirteenth century, Saxo Grammaticus gave a place of honour among his sources to Icelandic narrators in the prologue to his history of Denmark, *Gesta Danorum*. He writes that the Icelanders compensate for external poverty with the gifts of the intellect by collecting and then disseminating knowledge about other nations' histories, and continues:

> Cunctarum quippe nationum res gestas cognosse memoriæque mandare voluptatis loco reputant, non minoris gloriæ iudicantes alienas virtutes disserere quam proprias exhibere. Quorum thesauros historicarum rerum pignoribus refertos curiosius consulens, haud parvam præsentis operis partem ex eorum relationis imitatione contexui, nec arbitros habere contempsi, quos tanta vetustatis peritia callere cognovi. (Olrik and Ræder 1931: 5)

> (They regard it as a real pleasure to discover and commemorate the achievements of every nation; in their judgment it is as elevating to discourse on the prowess of others as to display their own. Thus I have scrutinised their store of historical treasures and composed a considerable part of this present work by copying their narratives, not scorning, where I recognized such skill in ancient lore, to take these men as witnesses; Fisher and Ellis Davidson 1979: 5)

It is most probably oral narrators that Saxo is referring to here, and when he emphasizes that they are Icelandic, and thus neither Danish nor Norwegian, this may be because, in his day, Icelanders had the status of authorities when it came to historical knowledge. It might appear that the distinguished and learned Latin scholar places the vernacular narrators at a distance with his remark that he has not considered it beneath his dignity to use them as sources, yet we should not understand it as arrogance but rather as an expression of the respect which is revealed by the whole of his reference to Icelandic narrators. Saxo does not refer to skaldic poems, and it is doubtful whether he made use of them. In Icelandic historical writing, however, citations of skaldic stanzas had become a firm convention from the end of the twelfth century. In the prologues to *Óláfs saga helga* and *Heimskringla* Snorri Sturluson stresses the poetry of the skalds as the best source for the ancient kings' journeys and achievements and at the same time casts doubt on the reliability of oral narrative. Skaldic stanzas had now become like a part of the sagas' *prosimetrum*, used as authentic witnesses from prehistory, rather than as sources in the modern sense.

Icelanders were not only renowned for their historical knowledge, however. They were also recognized as especially good story-tellers and authors. When, at the end of the twelfth century, King Sverrir of Norway wanted his own biography to be written, he chose the Icelandic abbot Karl Jónsson from the monastery of Þingeyrar to write the first part of the work. On a par with this, Sverrir's great-grandson King Magnus Lawmender engaged the Icelander Sturla Þórðarson to write sagas about himself and his father, Hákon Hákonarson. We have no evidence to show whether Snorri Sturluson's conversations with Hákon Hákonarson and Earl Skúli in Norway during the years 1219–20 contributed to his writing of *Heimskringla*, but, in any case, most of the sagas about Norwegian kings were composed by Icelanders, and in Norway in the thirteenth century the writing of history can be considered almost completely an Icelandic speciality, just as, earlier, skaldic poetry had been. Icelanders were professionals, a kind of literary Swiss Guard, which was called upon when it became necessary to relate history in poetry or in writing. This position certainly contributed to the fact that, after 1200, Norwegians contributed so astonishingly little to Old Norse literature and preserved an independent tradition neither of skaldic poetry nor of saga writing. Even the literature that was written in the Orkneys was reshaped and taken over by Icelanders. We are indebted to them not only for the original authorship of the major part of Old Norse literature, but also for the fact that it was written down and preserved in its entirety in a manuscript tradition from the thirteenth to the seventeenth centuries.

TEXTUALIZATION

With Ole Bruhn 1999[1] we may use the term *textualization* for the double process which consists in a society's adopting writing as a social usage, and, as a consequence of that, understanding and construing social life, and society considered as a whole, as a text. This process was initiated in Iceland about 1100, and it initially embraced the common institutions of the country, the law, history and language. Over the winter of 1117–18, following a resolution of the Althing, work was begun on the editing and writing down of the country's laws. In the 1120s Ari Þorgilsson wrote the history of Iceland in *Íslendingabók* with guidance from the bishops, and about the same time information about the land's first settlers was gathered together and written down in *Landnámabók*. At some time in the course of the century a now unknown linguist wrote a treatise on the Icelandic language. This little book, which goes by the modern title of *The First Grammatical Treatise*, is a phonological analysis whose objective was to create an alphabet suitable for the Icelandic language. These secular works are, together with some religious writings of the Church, the oldest literature in Icelandic. They possess an ordering, authoritative aim, one in which the country is viewed as an independent entity, a kingdom without a king.

ORIGINS

Consciousness of one's surroundings and one's history, which written culture promoted, satisfied the Icelandic emigrant people's demand to define themselves as a nation with a place in the world and in Christian world history. The conditions necessary for dealing with this task may have already been in place in the collective memory of the land-taking. That made it possible for the Icelanders to write themselves into mainstream history from the perspective of their own traditions and with an emphasis upon their own assumptions and ideals, just as we see in *Íslendingabók* and *Landnámabók*.

Íslendingabók is a pioneering work in which Ari marks out the main lines of a history that were never subsequently altered, selects the most important events, and establishes a chronology. His plan is evident from the chapter summary with which the book begins: I. Concerning the settlement of Iceland; II. Concerning the first settlers and the establishment of law; III. Concerning the foundation of the Althing; IV. On the devising of the calendar; V. On the division of the land into Quarters; VI. Concerning the settlement of Greenland; VII. On the coming of Christianity to Iceland; VIII. On the foreign bishops; IX. Concerning Bishop Ísleifr; X. Concerning Bishop Gizurr. The first five chapters deal with origins and the common institutions. The chapter about Greenland is included because the Scandinavian colonies in Greenland were Icelandic. The central chapter, which is also the fullest, is about the introduction of Christianity, and the last three chapters deal with the earliest history of the Church.

With the help of this common history Ari gives the Icelanders an identity as a people, and his exposition is carefully controlled by a strategy, which on the one hand is designed to show that the society is a whole, but on the other avoids giving it a hierarchical structure. Like a modern historian Ari had to begin his work with the beginning, that is, the question of when Iceland was first settled. For this reason he refers in chapter I to a certain Ingólfr Arnarson as the first land-taker; but immediately afterwards there follows a chapter which enumerates four settlers (one of them a woman) as representatives of the four Quarters. In this way Ari underlines the society's decentralized structure, in which no single person has the highest status.

Íslendingabók's exemplary coordination of the first settlers is carried through on a large scale in *Landnámabók*, of which book Ari was a joint author, according to a remark in *Hauksbók*, one of its later redactions. *Landnámabók* is a catalogue of the men and women who were the leaders of groups of settlers that sailed to Iceland and took new land there. In all approximately 430 colonists are enumerated in topographical order round the island. Information is given about the dimension of each separate piece of territory and the name of the first land-taker's farm. In the majority of cases it is also stated where the immigrants came from and often some of their ancestors and descendants are named. *Landnámabók* no longer exists in its original form. In the course of the Middle Ages it was rewritten several times and enlarged, especially with genealogical information and with concise narratives of the kind that we find expanded in a more detailed fashion in the sagas of Icelanders. *Landnámabók* had no counterpart in contemporary European literature, and there is no agreement on what its original purpose was. However, the work is an exemplary expression of the Icelanders' self-perception at that time in history when they were able, with the aid of writing, to gain an overview of themselves as a people with an origin. In the text the original plurality of families and farms was able to be thought of and represented as a whole. The book's consistently topographical arrangement with a systematic review of places and their names inserts the land itself as well as its inhabitants into history.

There is reason to believe that not all the information in *Landnámabók* is based upon reliable knowledge. The source was oral tradition from all regions of Iceland, and it may have been an impossible task to gather information about all original acts of land-taking more than two centuries after they had taken place. On the other hand, *Landnámabók*'s systematic conception required all the land that was owned when the book was compiled to be described as part of the original land-taking. We may reasonably assume that some of the information in the book is invented with that goal in mind, for example, that a number of the names of the first land-takers are constructed on the basis of false place-name etymologies. However, this phenomenon only emphasises the work's achievement as a text. Just as *Íslendingabók* established the basis of the Icelandic people's oldest history once and for all, so *Landnámabók* gave written form to the very act of taking over empty and nameless territories. We find this textualization of the landscape again in the sagas, and it achieved a permanent meaning in the Icelanders' perception of their land.

Accounts of the land-taking were also an emigration history and, through that, a link with world history. The Icelanders took up the emigration narratives of world history with a special interest. *Íslendingabók* shows that Icelanders early on had knowledge of learned theories on the subject of the origins of royal dynasties in Troy. The book concludes with a genealogy, which traces Ari Þorgilsson's own Icelandic kindred back to the Swedish kings, the Ynglings, and, further, from them to Yngvi, king of the Turks, that is, to the heathen gods, that, in euhemeristic interpretation, were understood to have been kings in Asia. In his *Edda* and *Heimskringla*, Snorri Sturluson supplements this idea with an etymology, which links the term *áss* for the Scandinavian gods with the word *Ásia*, 'Asia'. According to this hypothesis, Óðinn led his people from Troy to Scandinavia, where their dynasties and their language became dispersed. Icelanders' interest in other peoples' history and in foreign historiography must be seen in this light. In one way they made the sum of world history their own by regarding themselves as descendants of the Trojans. From the perspective of literary consciousness, the idea that the Norse language could be considered as directly transferred from Troy took on special meaning. According to Snorri, Óðinn spoke the skaldic language, and he saw in skaldic poetry a genuine expression of the ancestral world picture and way of thinking, not only before the land-taking, but before the emigration from Troy (Clunies Ross 1987).

THE OUTSIDE WORLD

One of the objectives of *Íslendingabók* had been to show that Iceland was an independent land, at the same time as making it very clear that the people had an origin in the Christian world. This comes about through the book's emphasis on Norway as the country of origin, but in a manner that also demonstrates Iceland's independence. The connection is established in the book's first sentence, 'Ísland byggðisk fyrst ýr Norvegi á dǫgum Haralds ens hárfagra, Halfdanarsonar ens svarta', 'Iceland was first settled from Norway in the days of Harald the Finehaired, son of Halfdan the Black' (Benediktsson 1968: 4). This happened in the years between 870 and 930. Thereafter we are informed that Ingólfr, the first land-taker, was a Norwegian, but we are given no information about his home base or his family. Thus no single dominating lineage leads back to the country of origin. The change in religion is explained along similar lines. The conversion to Christianity happens under pressure from Óláfr Tryggvason, but the decision is taken at the Althing by the Icelanders themselves and is represented as a purely political act.

Íslendingabók mentions Irish monks, meaning hermits, who lived in Iceland before the Norse settlers, but did not wish to remain there because they did not want to be members of the same community as heathens. By this means Ari emphasises again that the Icelandic population was Norse, but he obviously found it necessary to come to a decision about the question of an originally Celtic settlement. It is probable that, in the course of the settlement itself, a not inconsiderable number of the immigrants came from the northern parts of the British Isles. *Landnámabók* gives information of a geographic or ethnic kind about approximately 270 land-takers, and 90 per cent of them are ethnic Scandinavians, the rest Irish or other Celts. However, it also appears that scarcely a quarter of the ethnic Scandinavians came from the Norse colonies in the British Isles, in the main from Celtic areas. At the same time, these numbers comprise only a very small, even if a significant, part of the total immigrant population, which was perhaps between 10,000 and 20,000 individuals. Add to this the fact that the small group of settlement leaders was predominantly male and all were farmers of high social status. Thus they cannot by any means be considered a representative sample of the population. It is reasonable to presume that there were more Celts among the women and the lower social groups than the above-given percentage suggests, because the young Norse men, who had earlier settled in Ireland and on the Scottish islands, had married indigenous women and had taken local people as servants and slaves. It was these families and households, settled on both sides of the North Sea, who colonized Iceland, and we may understand the new Icelandic people, not as comprising exclusively Norwegian emigrants, but as part of a people that had been settled on both sides of the North Sea for several generations. The settlement of Iceland may be seen most naturally as a link in a westward expansion which began early in the Viking Age and which also embraced the Orkneys, the Shetlands, the Faroes, the Hebrides, the Isle of Man and Greenland. Later these territories entered the Norwegian sphere of interest and finally became parts of the Norwegian kingdom, and Norwegian influence became dominant.

From a literary perspective the Celtic element in the origin of the Icelanders has given occasion for many considerations. One hypothesis considers skaldic poetry as inspired by Irish elite poetry (Bugge 1894), another sees the Scandinavian myths of the gods and legends of heroes as influenced by Irish poetry and legend (Bugge 1881–89). Icelandic saga narrative has also been connected with Irish traditions (Bugge 1908). None of these hypotheses have convinced everyone, and, apart from some few loanwords and place-names there is no trace of the Irish language in Iceland.

RELIGION

Christianity was officially introduced into Iceland in the year 1000 (or according to an alternative computation in the year 999), less than a century after the establishment of the new society. It happened, according to *Íslendingabók*, by means of a majority decision at the Althing, and thus as a peaceable political act. Two bishoprics were established, one in 1056 at Skálholt in the south, and another in 1106 at Hólar in the north. In the earliest period the Icelandic church was subject to the archbishop of Hamburg–Bremen. From 1104 it belonged to the Danish archbishopric of Lund and after 1154 to the Norwegian archiepiscopal see in Trondheim. Both internally and in relation to foreign countries the Church contributed to political centralization. The law of tithes and the system of individual church ownership, which gave the secular chieftains a substantial portion of the Church's revenue, strengthened the domestic concentration of land and power. After 1154 the Church was laid open to Norwegian influence, and the Christian conception of the state was able to act in opposition to the structure of Icelandic society, because it presupposed that a people had a king, who could exercise secular power on God's behalf. In this way the Church contributed in the long run to the disintegration of the free state; but, characteristically enough, it was from the first subordinated to the Icelandic constitution insofar as the two bishops took their seats in the Althing's legislative assembly side by side with the chieftains, and it was not until after 1230 that the bishops succeeded in freeing themselves from the dominance of the secular chieftains.

We know very little with any certainty about the Icelanders' religion before Christianity. Grave finds show us that a majority of the population were heathen, but *Landnámabók* also mentions Christian immigrants, and it reports that their descendants lost their faith. In the literary sources the change in religion is not represented as a radical breach. Ari Þorgilsson, for instance, tells in *Íslendingabók* that for a transitional period it was permitted to sacrifice to the heathen gods, to expose newborn babies and to eat horse meat. In consideration of the fact that this book was approved by the bishops, this information bears witness to a considerable tolerance, not only in the period after the change in religion, but also in the Icelandic scholarly environment in Ari's own time. It was accepted and even found profitable for such recollections of heathendom to be set down as a part of Iceland's history. In this tolerant attitude we may find part of the explanation for the phenomenon whereby traditions from the time before Christianity, not least skaldic poetry and poems about the heathen gods, could survive the change in religion and continue to be remembered until they were recorded in the literature of the thirteenth century.

Our knowledge of narrative and poetry in Iceland before the change in religion depends exclusively on indirect evidence. We may assume with a high degree of probability that skaldic poetry and eddic poetry lived on in oral tradition until they were written down in manuscript in the thirteenth century. At all events, Scandinavian runic inscriptions show that the verse forms were in use from the ninth century and probably earlier. The circumstances which led to the poetry's written preservation in any form can be attributed both to the Church's liberal attitude and to the interest in the history, language and poetry of the past, which shaped the High Middle Ages in Iceland. The poems gained meaning as part of the memory of the past, and, as has been mentioned above, skaldic poetry in particular experienced a renaissance as a genuine expression of the language, religion and conception of the world of the Icelanders' heathen forefathers. It is from this point of view that Snorri Sturluson wrote a poetics of skaldic verse and reproduced the myths of the gods in his *Edda*.

CONSTITUTION AND ETHICS

A key to the understanding of the Icelanders' exceptional circumstances is to be found in the form of society they chose for themselves. The constitution is briefly described in *Íslendingabók*. We find more detailed information in the legal code *Grágás*, which is preserved in fragments from the end of the twelfth century and as a whole in two manuscripts from the second half of the thirteenth century.

The political and social structure of Icelandic society resembled Norwegian farmer society before Norway became a state (to the extent that we have knowledge of it), but the Icelanders did not organize their community as an imitation of the one they had left behind. Rather, it was a re-formation, which took a different direction from the evolution of society in Scandinavian and British lands. The constitution that the new settlers resolved upon was both innovative and more archaic than those of the old countries. What was new was the absence of a king or any other single leader, and thus there was no collective exercise of power. The most important principle was a decentralized distribution of power and a corresponding emphasis on the integrity of the individual human being.

Business of common concern was transacted at the things or open air assemblies, where the farmers could meet. There were twelve (later sixteen) local things around the country, in addition to a thing for each of the four Quarters the land was divided into. The Althing was a common assembly for the whole country and took place over two weeks during the summer. Here the legislative assembly, the *lǫgrétta*, met together. Before the foundation of the bishoprics, the only official position was that of the law-speaker. He was chosen for three years at a time and his duty was restricted to the oral recitation of the law at the Althing and for other ceremonial functions.

Debates at the things were conducted by chieftains with the title of *goði* (pl. *goðar*). In the beginning there were thirty-six *goðar*, while the number was later increased to forty-eight. Their power was not defined in the law on a territorial basis, apart from the fact that three *goðar* belonged to each local thing. Their strength lay in a client relationship between the chieftain and a number of farmers, who had entered into an obligation to support him. They were called thing-farmers, because one of their duties was to accompany their *goði* to the thing. All farmers were obliged to be associated with a *goði*, but every farmer had the right to choose his *goði* himself and to make it known once a year at the thing if he had attached himself to a new one. At the Althing the *goðar* met in the legislative assembly and they appointed farmers to sit as judges in the juridical courts. Thus the chieftains held legislative power in common and indirectly had influence over the judiciary. The title *goði*, which is derived from the heathen word for a god, *goð*, suggests that the chieftains also had a religious function as cult leaders before the introduction of Christianity.

Just as all farmers had to be attached to a *goði*, so all other free men and women, that is, those who did not own land, were obliged to be members of a farm community as a farmer's servants, but they had the right to change their situation on the moving days twice a year. In this way the whole population, apart from the slaves, was organized into a common social structure, but they also possessed a comparatively large measure of freedom of choice, at least in accordance with the law. The chieftains and thing-farmers were bound together in a relationship of loyalty, as were the farmer and his wife with their servants. The chieftain and the farmer were responsible for their people, and the latter in their turn had to support the former in conflicts.

The strongest and most important relationships of loyalty were between family members. These were not able to be cancelled and substituted with new ones, though family relationships could be extended through marriage and new alliances could be established. For those who were servants and other landless people the community based on the farmstead was certainly more important than kinship with individuals who lived elsewhere, because it gave better protection; but for the farmers kinship was the fundamental social relationship. Society's principal juridical and economic institutions, marriage, maintenance, inheritance and settlements and the receipt of penalties, were all vested in the family, and the same was true of the blood feud. In day-to-day business thing groups and the farmstead society were also most important for the farmers, but in critical situations in life, at betrothal and marriage, in conflicts and death, the kin group and its inescapable obligations came into force.

The Icelandic laws gave the individual great formal independence in decision-making and, in contrast to the Norwegian laws, the Icelandic codes placed all free men and all free women on the same level, when it came to the right to revenge or penalties for infringements or killings, irrespective of the individual's social or economic status. The key concept was *mannhelgi*, that is, an inviolability or integrity, which distinguished the free from slaves. It was not a matter of freedom in the modern sense, as defined, for example, in terms of human rights. It was above all a freedom from being violated.

Along with the legally based right to inviolability went the duty to take vengeance, if a violation had actually taken place. In the society of the Icelandic free state, the blood feud was a principle of law of considerably wider scope than in the Scandinavian countries at that time, and, in accordance with that principle, the form of Icelandic society is imbued with an extremely archaic characteristic. The ethical basis of the blood feud can be summed up in the Norse words *virðing* and *sómi*. The first means literally 'valuation', but, when used of humans, it can be translated by 'esteem, reputation'. The second word means literally 'that which is befitting'. *Sómi* is the good behaviour and conduct which confers esteem on a person. Nowadays we generally use the word 'honour' to refer to this ethical standard. Honour implies that individuals make decisions about themselves and their affairs and take responsibility for them; but, since the individual is also acting under the appraising eye of other people, the action is dependent on the common social norms that the individual strives to comply with. Where there is no strong responsible power to enforce social norms, the peace of society depends on free men and women behaving in accordance with them, under pressure from the collectivity's esteem and the desire of the individual to gain the collectivity's recognition to the highest degree possible. From an ideal perspective, this is how a society functions in which honour is the dominant ethical principle. The risk involved with this form of social order is that it depends absolutely on the individual human being, and that order therefore breaks down and turns into conflict if the members of society ignore the social contract based on honour, or if the individual is involved in a collision of duty between conflicting bonds of loyalty. Such conflicts and crises are the principal themes of the sagas that the Icelanders wrote about themselves.

THE HISTORY OF THE FREE STATE

Both possibilities, peace and conflict, lay within the Icelandic constitution, and both were realized in the course of the commonwealth period from 930 to 1264. In the first period, up to the beginning of the twelfth century, judging by the general picture presented in sagas of Icelanders, the land was marked by numerous local disputes and feuds between individuals and families, but the society as a whole functioned in accordance with the way it had been established in the law, and as is represented in idealized fashion in *Íslendingabók*. In its overall view, this book is itself an expression of the fact that there were secular and spiritual forces at work at the beginning of the twelfth century that desired peace and regulated affairs on the basis of the original constitution. Indirectly, *Íslendingabók* perhaps also demonstrates the necessity to emphasize that original order. The germ of the breakdown of the free state was already present in the increasing concentration of power that characterized the age of Ari Þorgilsson. Gradually, the disputes came to involve whole districts and eventually the whole country, and the constitution ended up working against the ideals that were embodied in it, because it could not prevent specific individuals amassing large landed properties and having many thing-farmers under their control. Peace could not be maintained without a strong central authority, and, in the first half of the thirteenth century, civil war broke out between the most powerful men and families, without any one of them being able to gain a definitive victory over the others. Of necessity the war of attrition for control of the country had to come to an end when the Icelanders submitted to the royal authority that the Icelandic constitution had shut out, and in the years 1262–64 the thing assemblies recognized the Norwegian king as Iceland's overlord in a series of peaceable decisions.

It is difficult to appraise the immediate cultural meaning of this change of political system. The most important consequence for the majority of the population was that there was peace in the land, and that supplies of timber, grain, iron and other vital commodities from Norway were secured. For the time being the common people's way of life and outlook did not change. In the highest echelons of society, however, among the hitherto autonomous chieftains, the change in political system immediately forced a new self-perception. For them the loss of independence had been an historic rupture, which was to be compared in the future with the great epochs of the past, the land-taking and the change of religion. It was this stratum of the population that undertook the writing of literature, and there is thus good reason to see the crisis in and dissolution of the free state as part of the literary context.

The attitude of national romanticism, which has shaped our view of Iceland's history and literature in the Middle Ages throughout the major part of the twentieth century, has considered the period after the dissolution of the free state as a time of cultural and literary decadence. That was not at all the way in which contemporary Icelanders saw it. It is more accurate to speak of new directions. In the course of the fourteenth century a new literature came to be written in Iceland, sagas of ancient times (*fornaldarsögur*) about the legendary and heroic age in Scandinavia before the settlement of Iceland, and foreign stories with comparable themes now got the chance to be written in manuscript. There was a trend towards the fantastic and the fictive. Literature was freed from the requirement that it be anchored in the historical and the realistic. It must be emphasized, however, that the whole of the old saga literature from the preceding century lived on and was used. This demonstrates the comprehensive nature of manuscript production in the fourteenth century, and for us this is the most important source of the corpus of Old Norse literature. All in all the fourteenth century signified both an expansion of literature and a new orientation.

Even though there is no simple connection between the political change in 1264 and the literature that was written in the century before and the century after, it is natural to think that the spirit of the age, and with it the literature, was stamped by the development that led to the dissolution of the free state; but memories of the original, independent Iceland seem to have made a still stronger impression on the generations who copied and edited the sagas in later times.

THE LITERARY MILIEU

The organization of Icelandic society influenced both literary production and the way in which literature was used. Iceland had no single dominant cultural centre, and education and the work of authorship and copying were carried on in many places in the country, at chieftains' farms, in monasteries and at episcopal seats. The first bishop of Skálholt, Ísleifr Gizurarson, who had studied at Herford in Westphalia, established training centre for priests, and training of a similar kind took place at the bishopric of Hólar. Benedictine monasteries were established at Þingeyrar in 1133 and at Munkaþverá in 1155, and in the succeeding decades many monasteries followed them. There were also private schools. Ísleifr's son Teitr ran a school at the chieftainly farm of Haukadalr. It was here that Ari Þorgilsson got his education. At the neighbouring farm of Oddi, the learned Sæmundr, who, according to tradition, had studied in Paris, founded a school at the end of the eleventh century. Later Snorri Sturluson grew up on this farm. In the thirteenth century, education was carried on at Snorri Sturluson's farm at Reykholt and at other chieftains' farms. Books were undoubtedly written at all these places, and the heterogeneous seats of learning, with both ecclesiastical and secular aims and interests, promoted the varied nature of the literature. No single ruler or institution was able to monopolize or dominate the writing process, and we can assume that, in the thirteenth and fourteenth centuries, having books written and owning them came to be part of an Icelandic magnate's prestige.

Variety was also a feature of the use of literature. A large proportion of manuscript codices were written at the initiative of private individuals and were the product of the large farms, where they were read aloud to the members of the household, which included men, women and children, the head of the household and his wife, servants and guests, the learned and the laity. This mixed group of listeners had an influence on the subject matter and point of view of the literature and contributed to the formation of its style. There would have been little purpose in reading Latin before such an audience, and the character of the sagas' public is the most important reason why the literature was composed in the Norse language. What Latin texts there were, were either translated into Old Norse, like Oddr Snorrason's history of Óláfr Tryggvason from about 1190, or have been lost. The practice of reading aloud on the farms also contributed to the formation of the sagas' oral rhetoric and objective style. Last, but not least, the oral narrative situation, of which the written sagas formed part, gave them their stamp of seeming to be true stories. The reader was the narrator and he would have to have answered for his narrative's credibility and ethical value.

LITERATURE AND SOCIETY: A SUMMARY

The history of the Icelanders during their first four hundred years passed through changes which, in the retrospective literary gaze of the succeeding period, were understood as rupture, loss and new beginning. The first rupture was the departure. The voyage out and the land-taking were the first generations' most significant experiences. The life they knew up to that point was cut off and a new existence had to be built up, not only in a material sense, but in a cultural and religious sense too. The land-taking laid the foundation for the Icelanders as a nation, and already in the construction and organization of the new society they had developed a consciousness of themselves as a distinct people. They must have felt the need to remember the time before the departure, including family lines, histories, the law, myths and the old poems, and that remembrance was carried forward into the age of writing, when it turned into literature.

The introduction of Christianity created a new historical conscious-ness and the country's most important common institutions were inscribed in texts by means of the written word. At the same time it was a decisive factor in the development of Icelandic literature that this early unified social vision was not sustained. In the following centuries it had to give way to a literature that went in the opposite direction and gave textual expression to the decentralized ideology which underlay Icelandic society from the very beginning. Writing was privatized and the result was the sagas of Icelanders and the contem-porary sagas, which are characterized by their local and private settings. The forces that combined to shape the oldest literature were not continued. The work that went into editing the law was not carried further into the making of an officially authorized lawbook. That did not happen until the country had become a part of the Norwegian kingdom.[2] *Íslendingabók* seems not to have had any influence worth mentioning upon the thirteenth-century sagas about Iceland's past. We know it only from two seventeenth-century copies of a now lost manuscript from about 1200. The alphabetical reform advocated in *The First Grammatical Treatise* did not bring about any systematic consequences for written Icelandic (Benediktsson 1972: 25–8). Only *Landnámabók*, which approximated most closely in its organization to the sparsely distributed, non-hierarchical structure of Icelandic society, enjoyed a renaissance in the following centuries, but in new, up-to-date redactions, and in an almost intertextual relationship with the sagas of Icelanders.

During the period of political disintegration in the first half of the thirteenth century and probably especially after the political changes of 1262–64, the past assumed a special lustre in the literature. The period between the land-taking and the change in religion was imbued with the quality of an Icelandic Golden Age, separated from and ethically distinct from the actualities of contemporary life. In the sagas of Icelanders that space was filled out with stories that developed the themes of the original society's ideals and problems, as the following ages saw them.

It was in the project of literature that the rupture of the past gained its historical meaning. The three major genres that comprise the Icelanders' stories about themselves and their forefathers, the sagas of ancient times or heroic sagas (*fornaldarsögur*), sagas of Icelanders (*Íslendingasögur*) and the contemporary sagas (*samtíðarsögur*), each created its own epoch by means of the era in which the action took place, in broad outline the time before the land-taking, the time between the land-taking and the change in religion, and the authorial present, from the beginning of the twelfth century until 1264. Icelandic literature was written in many phases and in changing ideological contexts. Seen as a whole, it is a textual recreation of times past. A self-conscious and well-educated class of farmers wrote narratives, which they considered to be true, about themelves, their ancestors and their achievements, and about the history of other countries, because they regarded it as part of their own. In this project all recollections of the past – narratives, skaldic poetry, eddic poetry, pre-Christian myths and foreign stories – were able to be absorbed.

NOTES

1 See especially ch. 6, 'Tekstualisering: Det islandske eksempel' ('Textualization: the example of Iceland').
2 The question is disputed, but see Foote 1977a: 201–5 and 1977b: 52–3.

REFERENCES

Benediktsson, Hreinn (ed.) 1972, *The First Grammatical Treatise*. University of Iceland Publications in Linguistics, 1. Reykjavík: Institute of Nordic Linguistics.

Benediktsson, Jakob (ed.) 1968, *Íslendingabók. Landnámabók*. I. Reykjavík: Hið íslenzka fornritafélag.

Bruhn, Ole 1999, *Historien og skriften. Bidrag til en litterær antropologi*. Aarhus: Aarhus University Press.

Bugge, Sophus 1881–89, *Studier over de nordiske Gude- og Heltesagns oprindelse*. Første Række. Kristiania (Oslo): Alb. Cammermeyer.

1894, *Bidrag til den ældste Skaldedigtnings Historie*. Kristiania (Oslo): H. Aschehoug and Co.s Forlag.

1908, *Norsk sagafortælling og sagaskrivning i Irland*. Kristiania (Oslo).

Clunies Ross, Margaret 1987, *Skáldskaparmál. Snorri Sturluson's* ars poetica *and Medieval Theories of Language*. The Viking Collection, 7. Odense: Odense University Press.

Fisher, Peter (trans.) and Ellis Davidson, Hilda (ed.) 1979, *Saxo Grammaticus. The History of the Danes*. I: *English Text*. Woodbridge and Totowa: D. S. Brewer and Rowman and Littlefield.

Foote, Peter 1977a, 'Some lines in *Lǫgréttuþáttr*', in Pétursson, Einar G. and Kristjánsson, Jónas (eds.), *Sjötíu ritgerðir helgaðar Jakobi Benediktssyni 20. júli 1977*. 2 vols. Reykjavík: Stofnun Árna Magnússonar, I, pp. 198–207.

1977b, 'Oral and literary tradition in early Scandinavian law: aspects of a problem', in Bekker-Nielsen, Hans *et al.* (eds.), *Oral Tradition. Literary Tradition. A Symposium*. Odense: Odense University Press, pp. 47–55.

Haskins, C. H. 1927, *The Renaissance of the Twelfth Century*. Cambridge, Mass.: Harvard University Press.

Olrik, J. and Ræder, H. (eds.) 1931, *Saxonis Gesta Danorum*. I: *Textum Continens*. Copenhagen: Levin and Munksgaard.

Storm, Gustav (ed.) 1880, *Monumenta Historica Norvegiæ*. Kristiania (Oslo): Brøgger, rpt. Oslo: Norsk Historisk Kjeldeskrift Institutt, 1973.

From orality to literacy in medieval Iceland

JUDY QUINN

When the technology of alphabetic literacy was introduced into Scandinavia by the Christian Church, it changed the nature of communication practices in some discourses, such as law, dramatically; in others which were less implicated in the institutional practices of the Church, its effect was probably minimal, or at least gradual. During the first millennium there is evidence that the inscription of runes on stone, wood or bone had been widely, though perhaps not generally, practised throughout Scandinavia. The effect of Christian ideology on all aspects of Scandinavian culture was profound and in relation to writing practices the conversion effected more than a simple change-over of scripts: each technology had been adapted to particular kinds of communication and each preserved particular kinds of texts. Runic texts, necessarily restricted in length, gave voice to a limited number of discourses. Leaving aside transcriptions that are clearly adaptations of alphabetic text types – such as Latin prayers – communication in runes was primarily concerned with the discourses of memorializing, ownership and magic (Elliott 1989; Knirk 1993).

The Christian textual tradition too had its favoured discourses, and religious texts were the first to be produced in the new manuscript culture of medieval Scandinavia. But at an apparently early stage of the new alphabetic industry – extant manuscripts do not allow us to fix precisely when – vernacular texts that were not translations of Latin works came to be written down. The aim of this chapter is to survey what we know of the translation of oral traditions into written texts and to speculate on some of the effects literacy had not only on the nature of literary works which drew from oral traditions but more importantly on cultural change, on the re-evaluation of social roles and modes of expression which Latin manuscript culture stimulated among Scandinavians.

Many literary genres of the Scandinavian Middle Ages point to the existence of rich vernacular oral traditions preceding and accompanying them – traditions of skaldic praise poetry, eddic mythological and heroic poetry, mnemonic lists and genealogies, narrative *prosimetra* and oral sagas. In many cases we know that writers mined oral traditions for their material, yet within their work elements suspected of deriving from oral tradition have been transformed beyond straightforward detection during the process of textualization. An incidental mention or an anecdote may offer more tangible evidence of oral traditions than the whole of a saga set in pre-Christian (and therefore pre-literate) times, despite the deep seams of orally transmitted material its author would almost certainly have exploited. The process of textualization, or literarization as Kurt Schier (1975) termed it, is therefore at the heart of any consideration of a culture's move from oral to literate modes of transmission.

LAWS

The oral transmission of laws and their subsequent textualization is of particular interest in this regard because we possess not only records of the written codes themselves – known collectively, and rather quirkily, as *Grágás* ('grey goose') (Fix 1993) – but also descriptions of the responsibilities of the lawspeaker in the pre-literate period, and commentaries on the process of textualization preserved in historical accounts and in the written law code. In the following section I will focus on how the change from the oral recitation of laws to manuscript recording of the law was not simply a change in the technology of transmission, but entailed a significant shift in power from the office of lawspeaker, an individual custodian of an oral tradition, to the institution of the Church and its technological infrastructure.

The responsibilities of the lawspeaker, originally the only holder of public office in medieval Iceland, are specified by the extant records of the law code and offer a valuable model of a formalized system of oral transmission. Traditionally the Icelandic code of law was preserved in memory and recited each summer at the Althing. The position of the lawspeaker existed expressly to advise people of the law (*Grágás* Ia: 216); he was required to recite the entire body of laws during his term of three summers, and moreover, he was to recite each section (*þáttr*, pl. *þættir*) of the law as extensively as it was known (*Grágás* Ia: 209). If the lawspeaker felt his knowledge to be inadequate on any point, provision was made for him to arrange a meeting the day before the recitation with five or more experts in law (*lǫgmenn*). The audience in this exchange was legally bound to listen to the recitation, whether it was held out of doors or in the church if the weather was inclement (*Grágás* Ia: 216). All fifty members of the law council (*lǫgrétta*) were required to be present whenever the lawspeaker recited the laws, or, if necessary, to appoint two people to listen to the laws for them (*Grágás* Ia: 216) – a measure aimed at ensuring the preservation of the laws in a sizeable number of memories. The recalling of all the *þættir* of the law in detail was a collective effort by a small number of experts. The recitation itself appears to have been the sole responsibility of the lawspeaker. The structure of the laws as written down preserves little sign of intrinsic mnemotechnic devices – such as alliteration or formulaic repetition – even in passages that retain the 'I' of direct dictation. The few instances of rhythmical language are formal speeches to be uttered by parties in law suits, such as oaths, peace speeches and truces (Foote 1977b: 51).

The means by which lawmen retained the law *þættir* in their memories must therefore have depended on memory aids outside the text, or structures within the text not recognized by us as mnemonic. The famous act by the lawspeaker at the 999 Althing of retiring to his booth and lying under a cloak for twenty-four hours is a captivating historical detail, but one which offers no particulars of the intellectual processes involved (see Aðalsteinsson 1999: 103–9, 200). The annual recitation was the only formal means we know of by which members of Icelandic society could learn the laws of the land, and more particularly, the points of law relevant to cases being brought for settlement at the Althing. The lawspeaker's delivery itself constituted the nexus between the stored heritage of laws ratified by successive generations of lawmen, and its effective application in society (Sigurðsson 1994). The position of the lawspeaker was crucial to the successful workings of the legal process, and made great demands on the office-holder – both physically and intellectually. Early in the eleventh century the lawspeaker Grímr Svertingsson had to pass the position on to his nephew because he himself had grown hoarse (Benediktsson 1968: 19). The lawspeaker's declaration of the law must often have amounted to his own interpretation of standing laws, and in a number of cases he appears to have initiated legislation (Dennis, Foote and Perkins 1980: 12). Innovations in law usually originated from the *lǫgrétta* but only became enforceable law if they were included in the lawspeaker's recitation (*Grágás* Ia: 37).

The writing down of the laws in Iceland represents a significant extension of the technology of writing and the concept of fixed and permanent records into an area of secular culture which had hitherto been transmitted orally. Until the first decades of the twelfth century, the written vernacular was probably only employed by priests for writing sermons, a practice known in England and probably adopted by Icelanders who received their clerical training there (Knudsen 1961). The use of the written word in transmitting other kinds of information posed new challenges. The authority of the written word in literate Christian culture is self-evident: Christianity is a religion of the book, not only in the sense of the authority vested in its sacred text, the Bible, but also in the centralized means of control available to the Pope through the medium of written doctrine and directives that could be transmitted authoritatively to the far reaches of Christendom. It is not known what arguments were put forward for the fixing in writing of the lawspeaker's repertoire, but in the second decade of the twelfth century an undertaking was made at the Althing to write down the secular laws of the country. Some sections of the laws may in fact have been written down earlier (Benediktsson 1968: 24 n. 8 and Dennis, Foote and Perkins 1980: 10). According to the historian Ari Þorgilsson, the laws were to be written down during the winter of 1117–18 at the farm of Hafliði Másson (Benediktsson 1968: 23). The lawspeaker, Bergþórr Hrafnsson, was to be assisted by other experts, and these men were also entrusted with the task of improving any section of the law they saw fit, indicating that the transcription process was viewed as an opportunity for the renovation, as well as the preservation, of oral tradition.

The section of the law on homicide and some other parts of the law were apparently completed that winter, but it is not known how long it took to write down the entire code of law, or the relative status of written and unwritten sections during the process of codification. The first known written text of the laws, Hafliði's law text, appears not to have been updated, and this seems to have been the case with the texts commissioned by many law experts. Amending texts written on vellum would have been difficult, time-consuming and costly, especially if earlier texts were as sumptuously produced as the thirteenth-century codices *Konungsbók* and *Staðarhólsbók*. As valid law depended traditionally on its inclusion in the lawspeaker's recitation, the text on which he based his recital would have been crucial. At the Althing in 1118, the year after Hafliði's text was begun, the laws were read out not by the lawspeaker, but by clerics, presumably because the lawspeaker was unable to read (Benediktsson 1968: 24). We might infer from this that the manuscript was also written by clerics, following the dictation of the law experts. Two sources, *Hungrvaka* (Helgason 1938: I 95) and *Grágás* (Ia: 36), mention the fact that the code of Church law, written in the following decade, was dictated under the supervision of the bishops. Since the recitation of the laws functioned traditionally as the current interpretation of them, the recital by clerics amounted to the temporary loss of the mechanism of authoritative interpretation, and opened the way for an accumulation of possibly conflicting written laws.

With the writing down of the laws the arbitration of what was law shifted from a single authoritative declaration (over three summers) to permanent documents, which proliferated. The authority which had been vested in the lawspeaker's recitation was dissipated over space and time, and posed new and fundamental problems for a society moving from oral to written modes of transmission of law and other branches of knowledge. Provisions had to be made in the law code ranking the authority of different written texts in order for the law to be enforceable: the law of the land was defined as that written in the law texts; if the texts differed, then the law was what was written in the texts the bishops owned. If those texts differed, then the one that related the relevant point of law at greater length prevailed. If the two texts were of equal length, then the Bishop of Skálholt's text would prevail (*Grágás* Ia: 213).

It is significant that the lawspeaker was not given jurisdiction in determining which version of the law was valid. Authority in matters of textual exegesis still rested with the Church: as well as his close association with authoritative written texts, the bishop also probably had the best resources for making copies of texts, and updating the code of law he owned. Resort to the opinions of other lawmen also appears to refer to their dictated texts, demonstrating the extent to which written authority had supplanted oral testimony in the legal world (Foote 1977a). It is only in the last resort that the item of contention was to be taken to the law council for resolution. Despite the radical shift in the source of authority, some traditional notions about the nature of authoritative utterance are still perceptible in these procedures. The version of greater length is given greater credence, presumably following the same principle that required the lawspeaker to recite each section of the law as extensively as it was known (*Grágás* Ia: 209). Judging by the attitudes expressed in the text, the idea of a single comprehensive written code of law was not perceived as the goal in the early stages of recording. During this time, written texts functioned within a complex system of reference that included a hierarchy of texts (valued according to owner rather than content) and consultation between owners of texts and legal experts (Dennis, Foote and Perkins 1980: 10–11). Even in the massive law texts produced in the middle of the thirteenth century, particular sections are truncated, or the beginning and end of a section given only briefly, suggesting that whoever used these texts had access to other sources of reference on the full body of laws (Byock 1988: 25).

On top of the lack of authority inherent in the uncontrolled proliferation of law codes, twelfth-century Icelanders faced another problem. The adaptation of the Latin alphabet to their native tongue was still in process, with the result that not all texts were unambiguous representations of the spoken word on which they were based. The First Grammarian, writing sometime between 1125 and 1175, in fact specifies legal texts as the site of significant misunderstandings due to ambiguous transcription practices (Benediktsson 1972: 214). For written texts to provide a useful source of authority they must be subject to some form of centralized control, such as the Church exercised with the production of theological and devotional texts. The need to stipulate procedures relating to the authority of legal texts in twelfth-century Iceland suggests that the multiplication of texts did little to improve the administration of law, at least in the short term. No doubt part of the attraction of possessing a law text was the prestige conferred on the owner due to the rarity and expense of manuscripts, even though expertise in legal matters probably still derived largely from oral training and first-hand experience of legal debate. As time went on, however, it might be expected that the written law code would become an operative factor in all legal discourse, affecting memory recall, the recollection of legal precedent and social hierarchies.

SUPPRESSED TRADITIONS

At the other end of the spectrum of oral discourses are ethnic traditions that were deliberately suppressed by the Church. Needless to say, the textualization of these traditions is unlikely to have taken place, but we do know a little about some of them from the wording of their explicit suppression. Bishop Jón Ǫgmundarson (d. 1121) forbade the reciting of love poems (*mannsǫngskvæði, mannsǫngsvísur*), an apparently popular tradition in which a man and a woman exchanged improvised verses (Jónsson 1953: II 97). The more detailed description of the tradition in *Jóns saga*, that the verses were disgraceful, contemptible and unbecoming, is a reflection of clerical distaste in support of the prohibition and adds little to our knowledge of the tradition itself. Bishop Jón's vigilance was directed against heathen practices (Jónsson 1953: II 96–7) – he had the Icelandic names for days of the week changed to omit reference to the heathen gods – yet his prohibitions extended beyond specific religious acts such as sacrifice to incantations (*galdrar*) and ancient beliefs in general (on the range of meanings of the word *forneskja*, from 'old times' to 'old lore, heathenism', see Fritzner (1883–96 I: 459)). The interpretation of the latter term and the implementation of the injunction may arguably have netted in a wide range of oral traditions. The zeal with which Bishop Jón is said to have campaigned against such practices suggests that they were flourishing in the early twelfth century.

The section of the law code which stipulates penalties for heathen practices makes explicit mention of the worship of heathen deities and the casting of spells (*Grágás* Ia: 22), two activities almost certainly involving formalized utterance preserved and transmitted from generation to generation. The need for laws against such practices also points to the survival of ancient oral traditions into the twelfth century, but whether these traditions continued into the period after the laws had been fixed in writing is another matter, the written code quite possibly preserving a frozen image of former socio-legal practice into the thirteenth century. Nonetheless it is interesting that the article of law also identifies the teaching of spells as a crime, demonstrating that part of the strategy employed in eliminating un-Christian practices was breaking the line of oral transmission.

Poetic recitation in connection with religious ritual is mentioned by Adam of Bremen (d. *c.*1080) in the account of pagan activities at Uppsala in the eleventh century. These texts were unfortunately too shocking to transmit, but Adam does attest to their existence. Ari Þorgilsson also mentions that immediately after the adoption of the Christian faith heathen sacrifices were not illegal as long as they were carried out discreetly (Benediktsson 1968: 17). Whatever verbal accompaniment there was to the rites of sacrifice would presumably also have been driven indoors, and not transmitted – at least not openly. The precise nature of the oral traditions that were integral to heathen religious practices is therefore unknown, but the wording of a report in *Kristni saga* confirms that sacrifices were accompanied by the recitation of ritual formulae. While the missionary Þorvaldr preached the Christian faith, a woman named Friðgerðr carried out a sacrifice in the temple and, according to the saga, each heard the other's words (Kahle 1905: 9).

In addition to references in law codes and Christian histories to sanctions against heathen practices, attitudes to certain oral traditions are also expressed in literary texts. There are two occasions on which manuscript compilers associate the guardianship of knowledge and beliefs from the heathen past with old women. In both cases the comment made is aimed at discrediting the version related, or particular details in it, because it is at odds with the compiler's Christian point of view. Both cases provide evidence that some of the kinds of oral traditions Bishop Jón was hoping to stamp out survived, traditions which drew on ancient cultural beliefs and which circulated outside the control of the scriptorium.

In the prose epilogue to *Helgaqviða Hundingsbana II* in the Codex Regius collection of eddic poems, thought to have been written *c.* 1270, the compiler explicitly dissociates himself from the heathen belief in reincarnation which he understands is inscribed in his source text: 'Þat var trúa í fornescio, at menn væri endrbornir, enn þat er nú kǫlluð kerlingavilla' ('That was the belief in ancient times, that people were reincarnated, but nowadays that is called old wives' tales') (Neckel and Kuhn 1983: 161). The term *forneskja* – used here to refer to the period before Christianity – is the same term used to describe the kinds of practices Bishop Jón wanted to suppress. The comment at the end of *Helgaqviða Hundingsbana II* appears to refer to beliefs associated with, but not explicit in, the written form of the text itself, since the poem which actually tells of the reincarnation of Helgi and Sigrún, *Kárólióð*, is cited by the compiler but not included in the collection. The naming of the unrecorded poem is nonetheless evidence of its existence and suggests that sensitivity to the transmission of *forneskja* was more acute for a scribe on the point of committing a text to vellum than it was for those who were familiar with it from oral recitation. In Iceland in the twelfth and thirteenth centuries, anyone engaged in the transcription and transmission of material on vellum would inevitably have received his education from clerics.

By taking the opportunity to denounce what amounts to heresy in the traditional interpretation of events of the past, in a codex with relatively few scribal interventions and apparently without a prologue, this compiler indicates that the very act of recording a narrative or verse which represented the reincarnation of two legendary figures was tantamount to belief in reincarnation. Whether or not those engaged in the transmission of eddic poems in the thirteenth century did in fact 'believe' in all the ideas expressed by them is a matter of speculation (Lindow 1985: 32), but this compiler's disavowal might be taken as an implied rebuke to anyone reciting the poem orally. Arguably some degree of suppression of ancient poetic traditions must have gone on, since none of the extant eddic verse relates to heathen ritual or hymnody (Foote 1974: 98–9). Nonetheless, it can be presumed that poems and tales instantiating heathen beliefs and values continued to be transmitted in Christian Iceland because they formed a critical part of their audience's broad understanding of the world. And it is possible that belief in some kinds of traditional lore did not seem at variance with the values of Christian culture, at least for those whose training in Christian theology was slight.

In his preface to *Óláfs saga Tryggvasonar* written in Latin in the late twelfth century (but extant only in Icelandic translation), the monk Oddr Snorrason urges the telling of sagas about Christian kings to praise their works and glorify God. He contrasts such didactic Christian narratives with what presumably were popular traditional versions of stories based on the same events: 'Ok betra er slict með gamni at heyra en stivp meðra saugvr, er hiarðar sveinar segia, er enge veit hvart satt er. er iafnan lata konungin minztan isinvm frasognum' ('It is better to listen to such tales for entertainment than step-mothers' sagas, which shepherds tell even though no one knows whether they are true or not, and which always place the king in a diminished position in the story') (Jónsson 1932: 2). The authority of Oddr's account is based not only on the credibility of his own sources – wise men – but on its alignment with a Christian view of history. Oddr's purpose is to recount the works of the evangelical king and saint who was responsible for the conversion of Norway and Iceland to Christianity. By the same token, the disparaging remarks made about the other kind of narrative, which clearly still held currency at the time, attack not simply its lack of credibility but also its questionable priorities in belittling the role of the king. The focussing of Oddr's criticism on the relative importance accorded the king in the two types of narrative suggests that they were probably based on the same stories, but that Oddr was heir to a version which had been passed down within a different ideological context.[1]

The two groups of people associated with transmitting this kind of narrative and perpetuating this view of history, shepherds and step-mothers, are representatives of those sections of Icelandic society which would have had least contact with literate Christian culture. We know from a number of sources that it was only the sons of powerful and wealthy families who received a clerical education (*Íslendingabók* ch. IX and *Jóns saga* ch. 12), and it is precisely to this audience that Oddr addresses his prologue: 'Heyri þær breðr enir kristnv ok feðr' ('Listen, Christian brothers and fathers') (Jónsson 1932: 1). Christian doctrine and history would have been known to most Icelanders at several removes from books. The dissemination of Christian documents and teaching to the Icelandic population must have been difficult, as it must have depended on oral recitations of various kinds. In the year 1200 the *Miracle Book of Saint Þorlákr* was read aloud at the Althing (Helgason

1978: 151), not only to celebrate Þorlákr's recent canonization among those present, but also presumably in the expectation that it would be reported by listeners throughout the land in the following months. While this must have been the method of broadcasting traditionally practised in Iceland, it was probably one which did not lend itself well to the privileging of one authoritative version of a story, or by extension, of official histories.

Under these circumstances it is conceivable that the shepherds and the women on farms responsible for looking after children continued telling traditional stories without realigning them to reflect Christian values and without elevating the figure of the Christian king as upholder of these values. The actual wording of Oddr's comment suggests that the tales were transmitted by farm-workers but identified with step-mothers (either as their composers, or possibly – following the analogy with *skáldasögur* ('sagas of poets') and similar compounds – as their protagonists). Probably neither of the terms 'step-mothers' or 'shepherds' is a literal designation of a social group, but a mechanism of literary reflex, disparaging the transmitters of these kinds of tales as marginal members of society, less likely to have been empowered by literacy, and more likely to have adhered to traditional oral discourses. In this connection it is interesting to note the description Ari gives to one of his female informants, Þuríðr Snorradóttir. Her nickname *in spaka* ('the wise') indicates that she was renowned for her knowledge. In *Flateyjaranáll* she is called Þuríðr *spákona* ('prophetess'), an epithet designating magical powers (Steffensen 1966–69: 188). Ari and later Snorri Sturluson describe Þuríðr as *spaka*, although Ari includes the important qualification that she was *óljúgfróð* ('wise in an unmendacious way'). This rider presumably distinguished his informant, and her material, from other 'wise' women, whose discursive orientation was not necessarily consonant with Christian ideology.

While the Church made some attempts to suppress ethnic oral traditions, it also utilized oral modes for its own purposes. The Christian law section of the Icelandic law code (*Grágás* Ia: 7) outlines those Christian Latin texts that every Icelander was required to know by heart, after the edict of Bishop Jón (Jónsson 1953: II 96): the *paternoster* and Creed. Men were also obliged to know the correct wording for the rite of baptism in case the services of a priest were unavailable. Only a man might perform the rite of baptism, but recourse could be had to women to teach the correct wording, or in dire circumstances to execute the ritual (*Grágás* II: 5). To know a text by heart is usually a product of literate methods of teaching, and presupposes a fixed version of the text which any memorized recitation can be checked against. The disjunction between this kind of 'oral' tradition and that familiar to illiterate Scandinavians is made clear in a story from *Færeyinga saga* (Vigfússon and Unger 1860–68: II 400–1), where the once-heathen Þrándr í Götu is rebuked for teaching his foster-son an idiosyncratic version of the Creed. The boy's mother finds fault with Þrándr's *kredda*, saying his creed does not seem to have a proper form (*mynd*). In finding the *kredda* without *mynd*, she is comparing it to her own picture of the orthodox *credo*, a picture based on a written text, probably not read by her, but taught to her as a fixed form. This kind of visual memory (what is today termed 'photographic memory') is as foreign to Þrándr as the notion of a single authoritative text, at least according to the character-ization of him created by the saga author (Foote 1969). It is significant that in this saga incident, despite his unsatisfactory grasp of Christian learning, Þrándr is said to have taught his foster-son a thorough knowledge of the law – how to prosecute all cases and the full extent of his and others' rights.

POETRY

Our knowledge of poetic traditions in Scandinavia before the introduc-tion of alphabetic literacy comes from a number of sources: verses carved in runes on memorial stones and on wooden sticks, references to poetic activity in sagas and other works, and documentation of poetic forms in works such as Snorri Sturlusons's *Edda* and the *Third Grammatical Treatise* (Fidjestøl 1997). Medieval Icelandic verse has traditionally been divided into two types: anonymous eddic poetry and skaldic poetry – the work of named poets, usually cast in a sophisticated metrical form known as *dróttkvætt* or court metre.[2] The earliest extant *dróttkvætt* stanzas are attributed to Bragi the Old, a Norwegian who lived in the ninth century. The names of a few earlier poets are known, though their works have not survived. As the name suggests, *dróttkvætt* poetry has its milieu at court, where poets composed impressive eulogies for their royal patrons. Over two hundred *dróttkvætt* poets are known by name, many from another thirteenth-century work, *Skáldatal*, which catalogues poets under the names of the princes for whom they composed (Holtsmark 1970: 386). The most celebrated poets belong to the period from the mid-ninth to the mid-eleventh century, although greater quantities of verse are preserved from later periods (Frank 1985: 161). Some fourteen hundred stanzas are thought to survive from the Viking Age. The ornate metrical pattern of skaldic verse makes it unlikely that these early stanzas, antedating the conversion, were significantly revised during the course of oral transmission. For this reason, they may provide some insights into the nature of praise poetry in heathen times. It is also possible that some compositions, such as *Þórsdrápa*, were composed in response to missionary activity in Iceland, as a counter-force to Christian hymns (Lindow 1988: 134), and the picture they present of pre-Christian religious and poetic activity might therefore be questionable (Frank 1986).

The range and extent of the poetic traditions from this early period are probably not fully represented by the collection of verses that have been preserved as quotations in prose works, by authors of kings' sagas and by Snorri, whose selections are obviously biassed towards material appropriate to the subjects of their works (Frank 1985: 162). Compositions by women, for example, are not well documented in these sources: in the early period, seven women poets are known by name but only a few of their stanzas have been preserved. Poetic composition by women apparently waned in the Christian era (Straubhaar 1982), although women may well have continued to compose verse that did not suit the purposes of literary *prosimetrum* and which therefore has left no textual trace. An incident in *Gísla saga* (Þórólfsson and Jónsson 1943: 59) where Þórdís discovers the identity of her husband's murderer by unravelling the poetic knot of a skaldic stanza suggests that women were well versed in the skaldic art, even if they did not habitually use their knowledge in composition. References to women poets in earlier times has them taking on formidable opponents, such as the missionary Þangbrandr. According to *Njáls saga* Steinunn the poetess informs him in two stanzas that it was Þórr who wrecked his ship and rendered Christ's protection of him useless (Sveinsson 1954: 265–7).

Slanderous *níð* verses were a potent weapon in the campaign by heathens to expel Christian missionaries from their shores in the late tenth century (Almqvist 1965, 1974; Meulengracht Sørensen 1980). *Kristni saga* tells of verses commissioned by heathens directed at the missionary Þorvaldr (Kahle 1905: 11) as well as those directed at the beleaguered Þangbrandr, who had more than Steinunn to contend with. Þorvaldr was accused of the ignominious act of having sired children, nine in fact, on his colleague, Bishop Friðrik. But the *níð* weapon could cut both ways, and at a meeting of the Althing Hjalti Skeggjason declared the goddess Freyja to be a bitch (Benediktsson 1968: 15).

The oldest record of a skaldic stanza is in runes on the Karlevi stone in Öland, dated to *c.* 1000 (Jónsson 1912–15: AI, 187; Frank 1978: 121–2, 128–9). The poetic text eulogizes the dead chieftain buried beneath the stone, while the prose text introducing it identifies the chieftain and declares his comrades' intention of making a memorial (*minni*) in his honour. Runes are also used to transcribe skaldic lines on another Swedish artefact, a copper box from Sigtuna, dated to the early eleventh century, and skaldic verse is found carved into rune-sticks from the thirteenth and fourteenth centuries, attesting to the continued tradition of skaldic composition in Norway (Liestøl 1964: 35). The first skaldic poetry to be recorded in the late twelfth century was Christian verse, and as far as we know, no collection of whole skaldic poems was ever preserved in writing in the Middle Ages.

Verse in eddic measure surfaces in written texts of various genres and ages: in runes on a Danish bracteate dating from the period 450–550 (Nielsen 1970: 138–9), in a runic inscription on a fifth-century Norwegian memorial stone (Antonsen 1975: 44–5), on a late twelfth-century rune stick excavated in Bergen (Liestøl 1964: 37), as source material in thirteenth-century scholarly treatises, as quotations in prose accounts of contemporary events written in the thirteenth century, and as the words of legendary heroes in *fornaldarsögur*. The extent of the records suggests that eddic genres were current across a wide expanse of time and lands, and that the tradition continued well into the literate period. The Rök stone inscription shows that heroic legends in versified form were known in Sweden in the early ninth century, and verses are found on other Swedish runestones. The Danish historian Saxo Grammaticus draws on heroic lays in his work that are clearly related to the poems later preserved in eddic collections in Iceland (Lönnroth 1971: 3 and

Friis-Jensen 1987: 58–60). The Roman historian Tacitus, writing in the first century AD, also makes reference to the poems of the ancient Germanic tribes which served as their only record of the past (Much and Jankuhn 1967: 44).

The dating of eddic poems has excited a great deal of speculation (Lindblad 1978: 9–10; Harris 1983: 93–4; and Kristjánsson 1990). Much of it has been fuelled by a hankering after a moment of authorship that is a basic assumption of literary traditions but one that is at odds with what we know to be the protean nature of most oral traditions (Clunies Ross 1994: 20–7). Certainly Snorri viewed some of these poems as very old, referring to poems such as *Vǫluspá* as ancient (*forn*) and their metre as an ancient rhythm (*fornyrðislag*) – indeed if the fiction of *Gylfaginning* is to be believed, eddic poems were understood to represent the words of the gods themselves (Faulkes 1987: 21 and 34). In addition, the compiler of the Regius collection of poems uses the tag *inn forni* ('the ancient') to describe the poem *Hamðismál*. A detailed examination of *Vǫluspá*, an eddic poem that is preserved in more than one version, indicates that despite the relative fixity memorization of alliterative verse provided, significant variations in narrative structure and mythological interpretation could still be generated within such a tradition (Quinn 1990).[3]

There is also reason to believe eddic composition was not simply a relic preserved from the distant past, but a living poetic tradition in the thirteenth century. In the contemporary sagas, set and written in the middle of the thirteenth century, a significant number of eddic verses are preserved, usually within accounts of dreams (Quinn 1987). In their framing and diction they echo both the poetic conventions and the cultural beliefs represented in eddic heroic and mythological poetry preserved in manuscript collections. This suggests that the eddic mode was productive of new verses at this time, verses that expressed warnings and forebodings about political events in terms of traditional motifs and diction that date back to pre-Christian times. While the provenance of some of the verses may be dubious, overall they bear witness to a robust tradition of eddic composition continuing in the latter half of the thirteenth century, with verses representing the words of supernatural figures widely, if not commonly, produced and transmitted (Meulengracht Sørensen 1988). The verses assume their audience's familiarity with heroic figures like Guðrún Gjúkadóttir and mythological phenomena such as valkyries. Most probably this indicates that the sagas' audiences knew a range of the conventions instantiated in the Regius texts, and they knew these from a living oral tradition.

Snorri Sturluson comments in his prologue to *Heimskringla* that people still knew and recited poems about all the kings of Norway since Haraldr Finehair, composed by the skalds who attended them (Aðalbjarnarson 1979: I 5). Debate about the context in which this poetry was transmitted has been long and lively. (Roberta Frank's bibliographic essay (1985: 175–8) summarizes the central arguments.) While most of the verse preserved in family sagas is quoted piece-meal, it has been argued that the saga writers took individual stanzas out of longer poems known to them orally, a thesis that is premised on the oral transmission of whole poems down through the centuries (Poole 1993). It is also possible that from a very early stage in the transmission of the poetry, interpretive or narrative prose became attached to each stanza, forming an oral *prosimetrum* which served as a discursive model for later literary sagas (Harris 1997). Oral transmission of skaldic verse preserved the title and author of each verse, details which presumably contributed to the understanding of each stanza, although these contextualizing details were also subject to reinterpretation over the centuries: at least one *dróttkvætt* stanza is assigned to three different poets, and several share two composers (Frank 1978: 10).

Whatever the actual relation of verse to prose in oral tradition, historical accounts preserved in sagas depict verse accompanying oral narratives in storytelling entertainments. In *Þorgils saga ok Hafliða*, a description is given of the entertainment at a wedding feast at Reykjahólar in the year 1119, though the saga is written in the following century (Brown 1952: xxix). As it is described, the storytelling consists of two compositions: a saga by Hrólfr of Skálmarnes (about Hrǫngviðr the viking, Óláfr the warriors' king and the break-in at the funeral mound of Þráinn the berserk as well as about Hrómundr Gripsson) which contained many verses (*margar vísur*); and a saga told by Ingimundr the priest about Ormr, skald of Barrey, including many verses and with a good *flokkr* (short poem without a refrain) at the end of the saga, which Ingimundr had composed himself (Brown 1952: 17–18).

There is also an account of storytelling in *Norna-Gests þáttr* – a *þáttr* included in the history of King Óláfr Tryggvason. There, the visiting guest tells stories about legendary heroes such as Sigurðr the Vǫlsung, including in his rendition quotations of eddic poems presented as the speech of the characters themselves. In *Sturlu þáttr* it is told how Sturla Þórðarson entertained King Magnús's entourage in 1263 with an oral recitation of a certain *Huldar saga*. When the queen requests a repeat performance of the storytelling, she summons Sturla and directs him 'koma til sín ok hafa með sér trollkonusǫguna' ('to come and bring with him the saga about the trollwoman') (Jóhannesson, Finnbogason and Eldjárn 1946: II 233), a formulation which certainly suggests a material text, though it may simply be a reflection of the queen's assumption that a text existed (Jóhannesson, Finnbogason and Eldjárn 1946: II 310). At what point oral storytelling gave way to text-dependent recitations in Iceland is not clear (Pálsson 1962; Clover 1985: 270; Foote 1974).

GENEALOGIES

Genealogical material appears to have been fundamental to the formulation of the earliest vernacular writing produced in Iceland, and there are clear indications that oral genealogical traditions were the source for much of this material. In oral cultures generally genealogical knowledge plays an important role in justifying the distribution of power among members of society (Duby 1980: 9), and a number of sources point to the importance of a knowledge of lines of descent in pre- and post-literate Icelandic culture. The establishment of kinship bonds to the fifth degree was necessary to ratify legal entitlement to inheritance (*Grágás* Ia: 218ff., II 63ff.), as well as for the enforcement of legal responsibilities, including guardianship (*Grágás* Ia: 225–30; II 69–70), care of dependants and compensation (*Grágás* Ia: 193–207). The proper enumeration of kinship was required in certain procedures in the Norse legal system, and provision was made to ensure its veracity (*Grágás* Ia: 48). The importance of genealogical knowledge in Norse society is also evidenced in genealogical discourse preserved in poetry: in the eddic poem *Hyndluljóð* the goddess Freyja's favourite, Óttarr, needs to learn and memorize his genealogy after he has wagered his inheritance on his pedigree.

46

The earliest vernacular prose text still extant (Benediktsson 1968: xvii–xviii) is *Íslendingabók*, written by Ari Þorgilsson around the third decade of the twelfth century. In his prologue, Ari refers to an earlier version of his work – now lost – which included genealogical material (*ættartala*, 'kinship tally') (Benediktsson 1968: 3). Appended to Ari's extant book is a short genealogy of the bishops of Iceland, and another that details Ari's own line of descent. The impress of genealogies on new literary genres can be seen not only in the provision of the raw material of history, but in other forms as well: in Ari's extant book the genealogy is manifest as organizing principle, as source material and as appendices, situating both the author and his patrons in relation to the matter of the book. This latter interest in the glory reflected by the subject matter of a text on those who have commissioned its production becomes a very important dynamic in the literary history of medieval Iceland (Clunies Ross 1998: 97–121). Whether the genealogical material Ari drew on was in the form of numbered lists, dynastic poems, prose accounts, or some other genre, we cannot know, but since Ari is generally credited with having been the first to put this kind of learning into writing, the genealogies he transcribed were almost certainly derived from oral tradition.

The First Grammarian lists the genres of Icelandic letters as laws, genealogies (*áttvísi*), interpretation of religious texts and the learned works of Ari (Benediktsson 1972: 208). *Áttvísi* probably constituted a genre of narrative prose, a kind of family history, incorporating the brief *ættartǫlur* known from earlier sources (Turville-Petre 1953: 166–7). A subsequent list of written genres of vernacular prose is found in *Hungrvaka* ('Appetizer'), a short history of the bishops of Iceland written just after the turn of the thirteenth century. The genres then current are described as laws, sagas and historical lore (*mannfrœði*) (Helgason 1938: I 72). Whereas literary traditions tend towards a defined set of genres and sub-genres that form models for future compositions, in an oral milieu the range of discursive forms appears to have been broader (Lönnroth 1996) and their descriptive terms tend to encode more of the social situation of verbal exchange. Something of this shift in descriptive practices is probably evident in the plethora of terms for genealogical material encountered in these sources, reflecting the emergence of new written genres out of a variety of oral genealogical traditions. The meaning of *mannfræði* is uncertain, but literally it denotes a knowledge of men, or more broadly, a knowledge of people who are identified with important events and values upon which the society's ideological system depends. Another native tradition which bears witness to this conceptualization of history through periodization is the *lǫgsǫgumannatal* ('the list of lawspeakers'), which frequently formed the basis of historical accounts (Turville-Petre 1978–9: 7–79).

Snorri Sturluson's thirteenth-century preface to *Heimskringla* is the most explicit appraisal of oral traditions as sources for written works, and although his purpose is to justify their use and establish their reliability, he also divulges the range of oral traditions available to him and provides a telling assessment of their relative stability during transmission. Snorri states that his history of the kings of Norway, stretching back into legendary time, is based on genealogical material – *kynslóðir* ('kin-lines'), *langfeðgatal* ('ancestral lists') – and poetry (Aðalbjarnarson 1979: I 3–4). Although the precise textual significations of *áttvísi, mannfræði, kynslóð* and *langfeðgatal* are open to speculation, it is clear that they all enunciate genealogical information of some kind. In certain cases at least, the kinds of texts Snorri is thinking of can be identified or inferred. Some of the works in his second category he goes on to name – the dynastic poems *Ynglingatal* by Þjóðólfr of Hvinir and *Háleygjatal* by Eyvindr Finnsson skáldaspillir, are usually dated to *c.* 900 and the second half of the tenth century respectively (Halvorsen 1964: 91), though their antiquity has been doubted (see Krag 1985). The tradition of genealogical poems continues into the literate period, with, for example, the composition in the late twelfth century of *Nóregs konunga tal* for the Icelandic chieftain Jón Loptsson. In this tradition, the subject of the praise poem is honoured by the listing of his illustrious forebears, who are usually traced back through kings to gods, such as Óðinn and Freyr.

While the habit of tracing one's ancestors back to mighty figures of the past was in all likelihood an ethnic tradition, in texts from the twelfth century and later it appears to have been combined with the learned European fashion for tracing lineage back to Christian and classical forebears, such as Adam, Noah or the Trojan King Priam (Halvorsen 1965). An example of this type of genealogical text, or *langfeðgatal*, is found in the second appendix to *Íslendingabók*, which lists Ari's own pedigree, naming thirty-six forebears back to Njǫrðr, King of the Swedes and Yngvi, King of the Trojans. It is possible that oral genealogical traditions may have spanned shorter periods than the written dynastic works they were subsumed into, and in this sense they would only have been rough precursors to the literary genealogies so popular in the twelfth and thirteenth centuries (Faulkes 1978–79: 97). However there is considerable evidence for belief in divine descent in heathen Scandinavia, including the epithets *reginkunnigr* ('descended from gods') and *goðborinn* ('born of gods') used in eddic poems, whether or not this belief was expressed in the structure of genealogies. It has been argued that the move from oral to written genealogies in medieval France between the tenth and eleventh centuries not only represented changed traditions but resulted in a profound mutation in the representation of kinship itself (Stock 1984: 25–6). While the same effect may have been true to some extent in Iceland, at least some of the impetus for such a widespread and intense interest in genealogical writings might have come from oral habits of memorizing kinship lines (Strömbäck 1975: 3). The attention paid to genealogical knowledge in the early literature of Iceland may well have been bound up with the emigrants' heightened awareness of new social formations and the need to establish claims to power and to land (Hastrup 1985: 192).

In the Prologue to *Heimskringla* Snorri declares he has based his written narrative on what he has heard learned people say as well as what is found in dynastic lists (Aðalbjarnarson 1979: I 3–4), suggesting that well into the thirteenth century there was a robust oral genealogical tradition which he could learn from, as well as a growing archive of written documents. The cast of a sentence such as this may imply a distinction operating in the perception of the writer, even if details of generic forms and their respective media are left unstated. The primary written source Snorri cites in his prologue is Ari's book (Aðalbjarnarson 1979: I 5), the elder *Íslendingabók*, now lost. Using a similar distinction, Snorri claims Ari's work combined old and new traditions of learning (*fræði* both old and new), a characterization which refers directly to native and Latin models, and implicitly to oral and written traditions (Aðalbjarnarson 1979: I 5). The ancient learning Ari had committed to writing almost certainly included genealogies, given his own account of the history of his writings. Another source attests to the continuing oral transmission of genealogical material in the decades following Ari's work, this time in a household well supplied with books. According to the author of *Þorláks saga*, the bishop-to-be was taught genealogical and historical knowledge (*ættvísi* and *mannfrœði*) at his mother's knee (Helgason 1978: II 181).

Oral traditions clearly ran parallel to written traditions in the teaching of the young, and would have been essential for the perpetuation of indigenous traditions of learning and the preservation of the Icelandic cultural heritage. Later in life, Bishop Þorlákr is said to have learnt from a range of other orally transmitted discourses, which we can assume were widespread and common forms of communication. Here too the categories *sǫgur* ('sagas') and *kvæði* ('poems') are listed, along with the discussion of dreams and debate between wise people (Helgason 1978: II 221). While some of the amusements included in this list, such as instrumental music, are probably of Continental origin, the traditions of storytelling and verse recitation are most probably the continuation of ethnic traditions. Without going over the already well-tilled ground of the prehistory of saga genres (see Clover 1985: 241–53) it is important to note here that storytelling traditions are frequently attested in sources and were considered important and authoritative enough to be drawn on by writers such as Snorri and the composers of bishops' sagas.

Writing in a literate tradition in which authority generally derived from books, Snorri was at pains to elevate his oral sources above the level of hearsay. Of the different types of discourse he canvasses, Snorri concludes that the praise-poetry of kings is the most reliable because it was recited before the kings themselves, who would have viewed fabrication as mockery rather than praise (Aðalbjarnarson 1979: I 5). The very nature of the skaldic stanza was also regarded by Snorri as a guarantor of its trustworthiness as a source (*ibid.* 7), as was the high reputation of those who kept alive these oral traditions (*ibid.* 4). The provision of credentials for sources or informants is central to the methodology of early writers in Iceland, and to medieval historiography generally. Informants are usually praised for their good memories, and the exercise of integrity. The reliability of individuals in the line of transmission usually derives from either first-hand experience of events or domestic connections (through birth or fosterage) with those involved in past events, such as Ari's informants Teitr Ísleifsson and Þuríðr Snorradóttir. Þuríðr, whose wisdom was mentioned earlier, was the daughter of Snorri goði who was thirty-five when Christianity was adopted in Iceland, a year before the death of King Olaf the Holy (Aðalbjarnarson 1979: I 7). The value of Þuríðr's testimony is the direct link she provides between twelfth-century scholars and the momentous events marking the beginning of Icelandic Christianity which had occurred in her father's lifetime.

<h1 style="text-align:center">LISTS</h1>

The use of listing as a means of structuring information in pre-literate and early literate practice in Scandinavia is attested to by a variety of extant genres (Clunies Ross 1987: 80–7). While many of the extant texts are informed by learned literate traditions, the structural principle of listing, and, as we have seen, the compilation of genealogical lists, pre-date the advent of alphabetic writing in Iceland. Lists of kings were used to structure praise poems such as *Ynglingatal, Háleygjatal, Nóregs konunga tal* and *Háttalykill*, as well as two prose works on the early history of Norway preserved in *Flateyjarbók* (*Hversu Nóregr byggðisk* and *Fundinn Nóregr*) (Halvorsen 1964), and the institution of the lawspeaker was apparently used by medieval Icelanders as a form of historical accounting, with lawspeakers remembered in sequential order, and in association with significant legal and historical events. The list of lawspeakers (*lǫgsǫgumannatal*) is basic to the structure of Ari's *Íslendingabók*, although he also uses the Christian chronological system in his history (Hastrup 1985: 47–8). Ari also describes his dependence on the accounts of lawspeakers themselves (Benediktsson 1968: 22).

Metrical lists or *þulur* constitute an important genre of Norse verse, appearing in extant texts either independently or subsumed within other generic forms (for example the list of dwarves' names in *Vǫluspá* or the lists of names for Óðinn and for rivers in *Grímnismál*). The structure of another eddic poem, *Rígsþula*, depends on a list of three mothers on whom Rígr begets a son, and includes three lists of names for boy children. The word *þula* is incorporated into the title of a list of horse names preserved in Snorri's *Edda* (Jónsson 1931: 169) and the same name, *Þórgrímsþula*, is cited as the source for a shorter list of ox names in the same chapter of *Skáldskaparmál*. Horse names are the subject of yet another list cited by Snorri (entitled *Kálfsvísa* in one manuscript but *Alsvinnzmál* in most). Recondite knowledge of lists of names constitutes the subject of a longer eddic poem with a similar title, *Alvíssmál*. Whatever the textual history of these particular verses, list poems appear to have been a traditional poetic genre in Iceland. *Þulur* which comprise lists of poetic names or *heiti* probably served the purpose of *aides-mémoire* to skaldic poets (Turville-Petre 1976: xli), and the oral composition of these lists is thought to have been practised before literacy became widespread, and may go back as far as the tenth century (Clunies Ross 1987: 81).

The production of exhaustive lists has been noted as a product of newly adopted writing systems in other cultures (Goody 1987: 116), and this impulse is evident in the antiquarian *þulur* composed from the twelfth century onwards, which supplemented traditional material with learned names, some Latin and Greek. Snorri censures the use of these lists as resources for poets, because some of the words listed are not attested in the poetry itself (Jónsson 1931: 166). The traditional formulation of poetic lists involved intermittent announcements contextualizing the material of the list. Lists of poetic *heiti* often begin with a formula such as 'I shall now enumerate the *heiti* for . . .' which inscribes the authoritative speaking subject in a mode similar to that found in *Vǫluspá* (stanza 12: 'nú hefi ec dverga . . . rétt um talða' ('now I have correctly enumerated the names of dwarves')). This construction of the 'telling' voice belongs to the poem as a whole (stanzas 1 and 28, for example), suggesting that the mythological material encoded in eddic poems and *þulur* (within them and independent of them) was closely related in the minds of their composers. Although *þulur* must have been primarily intended for use by poets, especially in the thirteenth century, they may also have been more widely transmitted as mnemonic catalogues of important information about mythological beings, sites and events.

The fact that Snorri only records *þulur* that are germane to the study of poetic diction does not preclude the possibility that other kinds of culturally valued material was cast in the form of a *þula*. The word *þula* is related to the verb *þylja* ('to recite') and the noun *þulr* ('sage'), a semantic nexus that discloses another movement in social values brought about by the introduction of the alphabet and the textual transformations and literary predilections that attended it. The eddic poem in which the discourse of traditional wisdom is most copiously demonstrated is *Hávamál*. Relating this text to an oral tradition requires some subtlety since so little of the context of the High One's recitation is provided by the poem and so much about the poem challenges modern, literate notions of unity and coherence. Nonetheless, the role of the *þulr* in the discourse of wisdom seems clear (Evans 1986: 123–4). The runes which symbolize the knowledge the master imparts to the initiand are described as having been created by the mighty gods and coloured by *fimbulþulr* ('the mighty *þulr*') – usually taken to be Óðinn himself (*Hávamál* 80 and 142; Evans 1986: 135–6) . At the beginning of a long sequence of counsel Óðinn announces: 'Mál er at þylia, þular stóli á, Urðar brunni at' ('It is time to recite on the *þulr*'s seat, at the well-spring of Fate') (st. 111). One aphorism he proclaims is that a person eager for knowledge ought never to laugh at the grey-haired *þulr* (st. 134). The respect an aged seer deserved is underlined in another encounter narrated in the poem *Vafþrúðnismál*, where Óðinn challenges the giant Vafþrúðnir to a wisdom contest. Very much on his home turf, Vafþrúðnir tries to intimidate the visitor by describing the contest as between the guest and the old *þulr* (*Vafþrúðnismál* 9), a formulation that turns the odds in the giant's favour.

This literary evidence is corroborated by an archeological text. The Snoldelev runestone (Jacobsen and Moltke 1941–42, *Danmarks rune-indskrifter* no. 248), dated to around the turn of the eighth century, commemorates Gunvaldr, the son of Hroald, the *þulr* of Salhaugar. The combination of the words *þulr* and *haugr* ('burial mound') occurs in a number of place-names, and may suggest some kind of traditional recitation practice from a raised location (Moltke 1976: 131). Whether the title *þulr* designated public acclaim or public office is uncertain: there can be little doubt, however, that a *þulr* traditionally commanded respect. There are a number of occasions in the poetic corpus on which a poet describes himself as a *þulr*, suggesting that the word continued to denote a venerable orator. In the eddic poem *Víkarsbálkr*, quoted in *Gautreks saga*, the poet Starkaðr bemoans the humiliation he has had to endure in Uppsala after he participated in the sacrifice of his former king to Óðinn. In particular, he describes the cold reception the people gave to him, the taciturn *þulr*, an old man cruelly ridiculed by berserks (Jónsson 1954: IV 33). The antiquity of the poem is not certain, and as so much of the story is burlesque its relation to social reality is unstable. Nonetheless there does appear to be a semantic relation between the word *þulr* and the figure of a wise old man who holds his own counsel in the face of ignorant ruffians. Þorleifr jarlaskáld ('earls' poet'), a tenth-century poet who gained some fame from killing berserks, is also described as a *þulr* by the later poet Haukr Valdísarson in *Íslendinga-drápa*, a twelfth-century celebration of famous Icelanders. Another poet, the Orcadian Earl Rǫgnvaldr kali, who is attributed with co-authorship of the accomplished twelfth-century composition *Hátta-lykill*, likewise describes himself as a *þulr*. The context of his identification is thoroughly Christian – the *þulr* carries a cross and palm-frond on a pilgrimage to Jerusalem – suggesting that the attraction of the term to this poet may simply have been the alliterative potential of its initial consonant, þ, 'thorn', rather than connotations of antique sagacity.

Whatever grandeur a *þulr* might once have commanded, it is brought decisively to ground in the thirteenth-century poem known as *Málsháttakvæði*, thought to have been composed by Bjarni Kol-beinsson, Bishop of Orkney (Fidjestøl 1993). In a lively parody of traditional gnomic verse, the poet sports with poetic form to highlight his accomplishment as a *skáld*. In stanza 11 he introduces a *stef* (refrain), lest his composition be judged a *þula*, as though he were just 'gathering crumbs' (Jónsson 1912–15: B II 140). The verse-form he chooses is a sophisticated combination of metres (Holtsmark 1966), a showcase of the metrical dexterity necessary to a Norse poet of the new literate tradition (Quinn 1995). His attitude to the ancient oral tradition of proverbial wisdom is patently ironic, the once prestigious mode of encoding knowledge a casualty of alphabetic literacy's superior tech-nology for preserving, analysing and categorizing knowledge. The days had passed when knowledge could be equated with listing, yet one of the antiquarian *þulur* recorded in manuscripts of *Snorra Edda* (Jónsson 1931, 192) preserves the identification for posterity: 'Vit heitir . . . minni' ('Wisdom . . . is called memory').

NOTES

1 An explicit statement to the effect that old stories should be understood as glorifying the Christian values of missionary kings and casting doubt on the worth of heathen ideals is made by one of the compilers of *Flateyjarbók*, in the coda to *Eiriks þáttr viðfǫrla* (Vigfússon and Unger 1860–68: I 35–6).
2 See further Gade 1995 and her chapter in this volume, and the bibliographic essays of Harris 1985 and Frank 1985.
3 A detailed account of eddic poetry as oral poetry is given by Harris 1985, and of the implications of oral-formulaic studies for Norse poetry by Acker 1998.

REFERENCES

Acker, Paul 1998, *Revising Oral Theory: Formulaic Composition in Old English and Old Icelandic Verse*, New York and London: Garland.

Almqvist, Bo 1965, *Norrön niddiktning: Traditionshistoriska studier i versmagi*. I: *Nid mot furstar*, Nordiska texter och undersökningar XXI, Stockholm: Almqvist & Wiksell.

1974, *Norrön niddiktning: Traditionshistoriska studier i versmagi*. II: 1–2: *Nid mot missionärer: Senmedeltida nidtraditioner*, Nordiska texter och undersökningar XXIII, Stockholm: Almqvist & Wiksell.

Antonsen, Elmer H. 1975, *A Concise Grammar of the Older Runic Inscriptions*, Tübingen: Niemeyer.

Aðalbjarnarson, Bjarni (ed.) 1979, *Heimskringla* I–III, Íslenzk fornrit XXVI–XXVIII, 3rd edn., Reykjavík: Hið íslenzka fornritafélag.

Aðalsteinsson, Jón Hnefill 1999, *Under the Cloak: a Pagan Ritual Turning Point in the Conversion of Iceland*. 2nd. extended edn., ed. Jakob S. Jónsson. Reykjavík: Háskólaútgáfan Félags-vísindastofnun.

Benediktsson, Hreinn (ed.) 1972, *The First Grammatical Treatise*, University of Iceland Publications in Linguistics 1, Reykjavík: Hið íslenzka fornritafélag.

Benediktsson, Jakob (ed.) 1968, *Íslendingabók, Landnámabók*, Íslenzk fornrit I, Reykjavík: Hið íslenzka fornritafélag.

Brown, Ursula (ed.) 1952, *Þorgils saga ok Hafliða*, Oxford: Oxford University Press.

Byock, Jesse L. 1988, *Medieval Iceland: Society, Sagas and Power*, Berkeley, Los Angeles and London: University of California Press.

Clover, Carol J. 1985, 'Icelandic Family Sagas,' in Clover and Lindow (eds.) pp. 239–315.

Clover, Carol and Lindow, John (eds.) 1985, *Old Norse–Icelandic Literature: A Critical Guide*, Islandica XLV, Ithaca and London: Cornell University Press.

Clunies Ross, Margaret 1987, *Skáldskaparmál, Snorri Sturluson's ars poetica and*

Medieval Theories of Language, The Viking Collection 4, Odense: Odense University Press.

1994, *Prolonged Echoes: Old Norse Myths in Medieval Northern Society*, I: *The Myths*, The Viking Collection 7, Odense: Odense University Press.

1998, *Prolonged Echoes: Old Norse Myths in Medieval Northern Society*, II: *The Reception of Norse Myths in Medieval Iceland*, The Viking Collection 10, Odense: Odense University Press.

Dennis, Andrew, Foote, Peter and Perkins, Richard (trans.) 1980, *Laws of Early Iceland: Grágás*, University of Manitoba Icelandic Studies 3, Winnipeg: University of Manitoba Press.

Duby, Georges 1980, 'Memories with No Historian', *Yale French Studies* 59: 7–16.

Elliott, Ralph W. V. 1989, *Runes: an Introduction*, 2nd edn., Manchester and New York: Manchester University Press and St Martin's Press.

Evans, David A. H. (ed.) 1986, *Hávamál*, Viking Society for Northern Research Text Series VII, University College London: Viking Society for Northern Research.

Faulkes, Anthony 1978–79, 'Descent from the Gods', *Mediaeval Scandinavia* 11: 92–125.

(trans.) 1987, *Snorri Sturluson: Edda*, London and Melbourne: Everyman Classics.

Fidjestøl, Bjarne 1993, 'Bjarni Kolbeinsson', in Pulsiano *et al.* (eds.), p. 48.

1997, 'Norse-Icelandic composition in the oral period', in Haugen, Odd Einar and Mundal, Else (eds.) *Bjarne Fidjestøl. Selected Papers*, The Viking Collection 9, Odense: Odense University Press, pp. 303–32.

Fix, Hans 1993, 'Grágás', in Pulsiano *et al.*, pp. 234–5.

Foote, Peter 1969, 'Þrándr and the Apostles', in *Medieval Literature and Civilization: Studies in memory of G. N. Garmonsway*, pp. 129–40, repr. in Barnes, Michael, Bekker-Nielsen, Hans and Weber, Gerd W. (eds.) 1984, *Aurvandilstá: Norse Studies*, The Viking Collection 2, Odense: Odense University Press, pp. 188–98. All page references to articles by Peter Foote reprinted in *Aurvandilstá* are to the reprint.

1974, 'Observations on "Syncretism" in Early Icelandic Christianity', in *Árbók Vísindafélags Íslendinga*, pp. 69–86, repr. *Aurvandilstá*, pp. 84–100.

1977a, 'Some Lines in Lǫgréttuþáttr' in Pétursson, Einar G. and Kristjánsson, Jónas (eds.) *Sjötíu ritgerðir helgaðar Jakobi Benediktssyni*, 2 vols. Reykjavík: Stofnun Árna Magnússonar, I pp. 198–207, repr. *Aurvandilstá*, pp. 155–83.

1977b, 'Oral and Literary Tradition in Early Scandinavian Law: Aspects of a Problem', in Bekker-Nielsen, Hans *et al.* (eds.) *Oral Tradition: Literary Tradition: a Symposium*, Odense: Odense University Press, pp. 47–55.

Frank, Roberta 1978, *Old Norse Court Poetry: the Dróttkvætt Stanza*, Islandica XLII, Ithaca and London: Cornell University Press.

1985, 'Skaldic Poetry', in Clover and Lindow, pp. 157–96.

1986, 'Hand Tools and Power Tools in Eilífr's *Þórsdrápa*', in Lindow, John *et al.* (eds.) *Structure and Meaning in Old Norse Literature: New Approaches to Textual Analysis and Literary Criticism*, The Viking Collection 3, Odense: Odense University Press, pp. 94–109.

Friis-Jensen, Karsten 1987, *Saxo Grammaticus as Latin Poet: Studies in the Verse Passages of the Gesta Danorum*, Analecta Romana, Instituti Danici, Supplementum 14, Rome: Bretschneider.

Fritzner, Johann 1883–96, repr. 1973, *Ordbog over det gamle norske sprog* I–III, with a supplementary volume Hødnebø, Finn (ed.) 1972, Oslo, Bergen and Tromsø: Universitetsforlaget.

Gade, Kari Ellen 1995, *The Structure of Old Norse* Dróttkvætt *Poetry*, Islandica XLIX, Ithaca and London: Cornell University Press.

Goody, Jack 1987, *The Interface Between the Written and the Oral*, Studies in Literacy, Family, Culture and the State, Cambridge: Cambridge University Press.

Grágás References to the medieval Icelandic law code are to the edition of Vilhjalmur Finsen (1852–83, repr. 1974), volumes I–III, Copenhagen: Gyldendal.

Halvorsen, Eyvindr Fjeld 1964, 'Konungatal', *Kulturhistorisk leksikon for nordisk middelalder* 9, cols. 91–2.

1965, 'Langfeðgatal', *Kulturhistorisk leksikon for nordisk middelalder* 10, cols. 311–13.

Harris, Joseph 1983, 'Eddic Poetry as Oral Poetry: the Evidence of Parallel Passages in the Helgi Poems for Questions of Composition and Performance', in Glendinning, R. J. and Bessasson, Haraldur (eds.) *Edda: a Collection of Essays*, University of Manitoba Icelandic Studies 4, Winnipeg: University of Manitoba Press, pp. 210–42.

1985, 'Eddic Poetry', in Clover and Lindow, pp. 68–156.

1997, 'The Prosimetrum of Icelandic Saga and Some Relatives', in Harris, Joseph and Reichel, Karl (eds.) *Prosimetrum: Crosscultural Perspectives on Narrative in Prose and Verse*, Cambridge: D. S. Brewer, pp. 131–63.

Hastrup, Kirsten 1985, *Culture and History in Medieval Iceland: an Anthropological Analysis of Structure and Change*, Oxford: Clarendon.

Helgason, Jón (ed.) 1938, *Byskupa Sǫgur* I, Copenhagen: Munksgaard.

(ed.) 1978, *Byskupa Sǫgur* II, Editiones Arnamagnæanae, Series A, XIII 2, Copenhagen: Reitzel.

Holtsmark, Anne 1966, 'Heroic Poetry and Legendary Sagas', *Bibliography of Old Norse–Icelandic Studies* 1965: 9–21.

1970, 'Skáldatal', *Kulturhistorisk leksikon for nordisk middelalder* 15, col. 386.

Jacobsen, Lis and Moltke, Erik 1941–42, *Danmarks runeindskrifter*, Copenhagen: Munksgaard.

Jóhannesson, Jón, Finnbogason, Magnús and Eldjárn, Kristján (eds.) 1946, *Sturlunga saga* I–II, Reykjavík: Sturlunguútgáfan.

Jónsson, Finnur (ed.) 1912–15, *Den norske-islandske Skjaldedigtning*, AI–II (Tekst efter håndskrifterne) BI–II (Rettet tekst), Copenhagen: Gyldendal.

(ed.) 1931, *Edda Snorra Sturlusonar udgivet efter håndskrifterne*, Copenhagen: Gyldendal.

(ed.) 1932, *Saga Óláfs Tryggvasonar af Oddr Snorrason munk*, Copenhagen: Gad.

Jónsson, Guðni (ed.) 1953, *Byskupa Sögur* I–II, Reykjavík: Íslendingasagnaútgáfan.

(ed.) 1954, *Fornaldar Sögur Norðurlanda* II, Reykjavík: Íslendingasagnaútgáfan.

Kahle, B. (ed.) 1905, *Kristnisaga . . . Hungrvaka*, Altnordische Saga-Bibliothek Heft 11, Halle: Niemeyer.

Knirk, James 1993, 'Runes and Runic Inscriptions', in Pulsiano *et al.*, pp. 545–52.

Knudsen, Tryggve 1961, 'Homiliebøker', *Kulturhistorisk leksikon for nordisk middelalder* 6, cols. 657–66.

Krag, Claus 1985, 'Element-Guddommene – Mytologi eller Skolelærdom?' in *Workshop Papers of the Sixth International Saga Conference, 28.7. – 2.8. 1985*, Copenhagen: Det arnamagnæanske Institut, pp. 613–27.

Kristjánsson, Jónas 1990, 'Stages in the Composition of Eddic Poetry', *Atti del 120 Congresso internazionale di studi sull'alto medioevo. The Seventh International Saga Conference, Spoleto 4–10 settembre 1988*, Spoleto: Presso la sede del centro studi, pp. 201–18.

Liestøl, Aslak 1964, 'Runer frå Bryggen', *Viking* 27: 5–53.

Lindblad, Gustaf 1978, 'Centrala eddaproblem i 1970–talets forskningsläge', *Scripta Islandica* 28: 3–26.

Lindow, John 1985, 'Mythology and Mythography', in Clover and Lindow, pp. 21–67.

Lönnroth, Lars 1971, 'Hjálmar's Death-Song and the Delivery of Eddic Poetry', *Speculum* 46: 1–20.

1996, 'Den muntliga kulturens genrer. Diskursformer i Snorre Sturlassons Edda', in Hedman, Dag and Svedjedal, Johan (eds.) *Fiktionens förvandlingar: En vänbok til Bo Bennich-Björkman den 6 oktober 1996*, Uppsala: Avdelingen för litteratursociologi vid Litteraturvetenskapliga institutionen i Uppsala, pp. 182–93.

Meulengracht Sørensen, Preben 1980, *Norrønt nid: Forestillingen om den umandige mand i de islandske sagaer*, Odense University Press. trans. Turville-Petre, Joan (1983), *The Unmanly Man: Concepts of Sexual Defamation in Early Northern Society*, The Viking Collection 1, Odense: Odense University Press.

1988, 'Guðrún Gjúkadóttir in Miðjumdalr. Zur Aktualität nordischer Heldensage im Island des 13 Jahrhunderts', in Beck, Heinrich (ed.) *Heldensage und Heldendichtung im Germanischen*, Ergänzungsbände zum Reallexikon der Germanischen Altertumskunde 2, Berlin and New York: W. de Gruyter.

Moltke, Erik 1976, *Runerne i Danmark og deres oprindelse*, Copenhagen: Forum.

Much, Rudolf and Jankuhn, Herbert (eds.) 1967, *Die Germania des Tacitus*, 3rd edn., Heidelberg: Carl Winter.

Neckel, Gustav and Kuhn, Hans (eds.) 1983, *Edda: Die Lieder des Codex Regius nebst verwandten Denkmälern*, 5th edn., Heidelberg: Carl Winter.

Nielsen, Niels Åge 1970, 'Notes on Early Runic Poetry', *Mediaeval Scandinavia*, 3: 138–41.

Pálsson, Hermann 1962, *Sagnaskemmtun Íslendinga*, Reykjavík: Mál og menning.

Poole, Russell 1993, *Viking Poems on War and Peace: a Study in Skaldic Narrative*, Toronto Medieval Texts and Translations 8, Toronto, Buffalo and London: University of Toronto Press.

Pulsiano, Philip, Wolf, Kirsten, Acker, Paul and Fry, Donald K. (eds.) 1993, *Medieval Scandinavia: an Encyclopedia*, New York and London: Garland.

Quinn, Judy 1987, 'The Use of Eddic Poetry in Contemporary Sagas', *Frá Suðlægri Strönd* 3: 54–72.

1990, '*Vǫluspá* and the Composition of Eddic Poetry', *Atti del 12o Congresso internazionale di studi sull'alto medioevo. The Seventh International Saga Conference, Spoleto 4–10 settembre 1988*. Spoleto: Presso la sede del centro studi, pp. 303–20.

1995, '*Eddu list:* the Emergence of Skaldic Pedagogy in Medieval Iceland', *Alvíssmál* 4: 69–92.

Schier, Kurt 1975, 'Iceland and the Rise of Literature in "terra nova": Some Comparative Reflections', *Gripla* 1: 168–81.

Sigurðsson, Gísli 1994, 'Bók í stað lögsögumanns: Valdabarátta kirkju og veraldlegra höfðingja', in Sigurðsson, Gísli, Kvaran, Guðrun and Steingrímsson, Sigurgeir (eds.) *Sagnaðing helgað Jónasi Kristjánssyni sjötugum 10 april 1994*. Reykjavík: Hið íslenska bókmenntafélag, pp. 207–32.

Steffensen, Jón 1966–69, 'Aspects of Life in Iceland in the Heathen Period', *Saga-Book of the Viking Society* 17: 177–205.

Stock, Brian 1984, 'Medieval Literacy, Linguistic Theory, and Social Organization', *New Literary History* 16, 1: 13–29.

Straubhaar, Sandra Ballif 1982, *Critical Notes on the Old Icelandic Skáldkonur*. Dissertation, Stanford University.

Strömbäck, Dag, trans. Foote, Peter 1975, *The Conversion of Iceland: a Survey*, Viking Society for Northern Research Text Series VI, University College London: Viking Society for Northern Research.

Sveinsson, Einar Ól. (ed.) 1954, *Brennu-Njáls saga*, Íslenzk fornrit 12, Reykjavík: Hið íslenzka fornritafélag.

Turville-Petre, Gabriel 1953, *Origins of Icelandic Literature*, Oxford: Clarendon.

1976, *Scaldic Poetry*, Oxford: Clarendon.

Turville-Petre, Joan 1978–9, 'The Genealogist and History: Ari to Snorri', *Saga-Book of the Viking Society* 20: 7–23.

Vigfússon, Guðbrandur and Unger, C. R. (eds.) 1860–68, *Flateyjarbók: En samling af norske konge-sagaer med indskudte mindre fortællinger om begivenheder i og udenfor Norge samt annaler* I–III, Nordisk historisk kildeskriftfonds skriften 4, Kristiania: Malling.

Þórólfsson, Björn K. and Jónsson, Guðni (eds.) 1943, *Vestfirðinga Sǫgur: Gísla saga Súrssonar, Fóstbrœðra saga* . . . Íslenzk fornrit 6, Reykjavík: Hið íslenzka fornritafélag.

3

Poetry and its changing importance in medieval Icelandic culture

KARI ELLEN GADE

The purpose of this chapter is to examine the function of poetry in Icelandic culture from the tenth to the end of the thirteenth century. It will show not only how the societal changes that took place during this period had a profound impact on the different genres of Old Norse poetry, but also how the image of poetry and the social status of poets projected in the narratives passed down in oral tradition and recorded in the thirteenth century in turn came to play a crucial role in shaping the cultural and political developments of late medieval Iceland. The first part of the chapter outlines the formal and functional features that characterize eddic and skaldic poetry. The second part discusses the transmission of these two types of poetry, with special attention to the narrative *prosimetrum* of the thirteenth-century kings' sagas, sagas of Icelanders and contemporary sagas. Part three is devoted to the skaldic panegyric and its subgenres. It illustrates how the conversion to Christianity affected a poetic tradition steeped in pagan imagery; how new poetic genres emerged in the service of the Christian faith; and how certain types of poetry ceased to be productive while others adapted themselves to the new cultural climate and continued to be extremely important in maintaining Icelandic national identity and setting the members of the Icelandic free state apart from their Scandinavian neighbours. The fourth section discusses the role of the Icelandic court poet from the tenth to the twelfth century, focussing in particular on the status of the poets and their relations to the kings of Norway as portrayed in thirteenth-century Icelandic kings' sagas and family sagas. The final part of the chapter deals with the renaissance of skaldic poetry in thirteenth-century Iceland. It shows how the codification of the kings' sagas and the family sagas not only reinforced the importance of poetry in a literary context, but also provided a social model that prominent members of thirteenth-century Icelandic society put to good use in their attempts to solicit support from Norwegian dignitaries in the ongoing power struggle that would eventually culminate in the collapse of the Icelandic free state.

EDDIC AND SKALDIC POETRY: FORMAL AND FUNCTIONAL FEATURES

Old Norse poetry is traditionally divided into two categories, eddic and skaldic poetry, that differ in terms of form (metre, diction), function (subject matter, genre, social status), and transmission.[1] The most common eddic metre, *fornyrðislag* ('metre of old lore'), represents a tightening of the Germanic alliterative long line. Each line consists of two half-lines divided by a metrical caesura and joined by alliterating staves (one or two syllables in the a-line alliterating with the first stressed syllable in the b-line). Consider the following stanza from *Vǫluspá* (st. 46; Neckel–Kuhn 1962: 11):

> Leika **M**íms synir,   enn **m**jǫtuðr kyndisk
> at enu **g**amla   **G**jallarhorni;
> **h**átt blæss **H**eimdallr,   **h**orn er á lopti,
> **m**ælir Óðinn   við **M**íms hǫfuð.

> (Mímr's sons play, and fate is ignited by the old Gjallarhorn; Heimdallr blows loudly, the horn is in the air, Óðinn speaks with Mímr's head.)

In contrast to eddic *fornyrðislag*, which is firmly rooted in the tradition of Germanic alliterative poetry, skaldic poetry is a unique Scandinavian creation that emerged in more or less fully fledged form in the ninth century and remained in vogue for five centuries until its demise in the fourteenth century. The earliest attested skaldic metre, *dróttkvætt* ('metre to be recited before royal retainers'), stylizes the alliterating and metrical patterns of *fornyrðislag*, but it is also syllable-counting (six syllables in a line, ending in a cadence of a long syllable followed by a short) and mora-counting, and each line contains two internal rhymes involving rhymes on the vocalic onset and the postvocalic environment of stressed syllables. In a-lines, such internal rhymes (*skothendingar* 'inserted rhymes'; von See 1968) consist of different vowels with similar postvocalic environments (v*i*nar : m*í*na; g*ó*ma- : gl*ym*ja, below), whereas the rhymes in b-lines (*aðalhendingar* 'noble rhymes') are required to have identical vowels as well as identical postvocalic environments (f*und*r : Þ*und*ar; gl*aum*– : str*aum*a, below). In both a- and b-lines the second internal rhyme falls on the fifth, long syllable.

Unlike Germanic alliterative poetry, which was stichic, both eddic and skaldic poetry are stanzaic. A *dróttkvætt* stanza consisted of eight lines which were divided into two syntactically independent units called *helmingar* (half-stanzas). The following *helmingr* by the Icelandic skald Vǫlusteinn illustrates the formal features of *dróttkvætt* (*Skj* IA: 98):

> Heyr **M**íms v*i*nar **m**ína
> (**m**érs f*und*r gefinn Þ*und*ar)
> við **g**ó*m*asker **g**l*ym*ja
> **g**l*aum*bergs Egill str*aum*a.

> (Egill, listen to my streams of Mímr's friend's [ÓÐINN's] pleasure mountain [CHEST>POETRY] roaring against the gums' skerry [TONGUE]: I have been given the gift of Þundr [ÓDINN, POETRY].)

Eddic and skaldic poetry differ not only on the structural level but also in terms of content and function. Eddic poetry is concerned with mythological, heroic, and didactic lore.[2] The mythological corpus in the Poetic Edda (Codex Regius; see below) comprises eleven mythological poems,[3] whose subject matter ranges from such sombre events as the beginning and end of the pagan world (*Vǫluspá*) to the entertaining accounts of Freyr's wooing of the giantess Gerðr (*Skírnismál*); the flyting of Loki (*Lokasenna*); Þórr's fishing expedition and fight with the Miðgarðsormr, 'World Serpent' (*Hymiskviða*); the theft and subsequent retrieval of Þórr's hammer (*Þrymskviða*); and the burlesque battle of words between Óðinn and Þórr contained in *Hárbarðsljóð*. The heroic matter in the Poetic Edda (eighteen poems) can be divided into three cycles: 1. the lays of Helgi Hundingsbani ('the slayer of Hundingr') and Helgi Hjǫrvarðsson;[4] 2. the poems of Sigurðr the Dragonslayer;[5] and 3. the poems leading up to and detailing the fall of the Burgundians and deaths of Hamðir and Sǫrli.[6] The corpus of mythological eddic poetry

also contains whole poems of a didactic nature, such as *Hávamál,*
Vafþrúðnismál, Grímnismál, and *Alvíssmál,* presented either in mono-
logue or dialogue form, and stanzas of a similar didactic nature are
incorporated into some of the heroic poems (e. g., *Reginsmál* 4, 19–22;
Fáfnismál 12–15; *Sigrdrífumál* 5–37). Whereas eddic poetry with a
mythological content appears to be a unique Scandinavian creation and
has no counterpart in Germanic poetic tradition, much of the heroic
matter can be tied to heroic legends dating back to the time of the Great
Migration as far as characters and events are concerned.[7]

Unlike eddic poetry, whose subject matter was clouded in a dim
heroic and mythological past, skaldic poetry commemorated contemporary persons and events. A skald could eulogise a ruler, praise a gift,
lament a dead son, ridicule his enemies, or extol his own prowess as a
poet, lover, and warrior. In this respect, then, skaldic poetry was a very
powerful tool that functioned as an instrument of both praise and
punishment.

Whereas the eddic poets availed themselves of a traditional poetic
vocabulary, skaldic poetry is characterized by a complex system of
nominal circumlocutions, the *kenningar* (for a summary of the research
in this area see Frank 1985: 163–4). A *kenning* consists of a baseword and
one or more qualifiers. Hence 'sword' could be circumscribed as *Mistar*
laukr ('the leek of Mist [A VALKYRIE]'), 'shield' as *Mistar lauka grund*
('the land of the leeks of Mist [LAND OF SWORDS]'), and 'warrior' as
skerðendr Mistar lauka grundar ('the cleaver of the land of the leeks of
Mist'). More often than not the *kenningar* were rooted in the mythological realm, that is, the same myths that were often the subject matter of
eddic poetry were used to provide a framework for the skaldic
circumlocutions. The two stanzas quoted above illustrate that point. In
the stanza from *Vǫluspá,* which describes the onset of the events that
will culminate in the destruction of the world and the pagan gods,
Óðinn converses with the head of Mímr, the head of wisdom in Old
Norse mythology. In his skaldic stanza Vǫlusteinn uses that imagery to
circumscribe Óðinn as *Míms vinr* ('Mímr's friend'), and at the same
time he draws on the myth (*SnE* I: 216–18; Frank 1981) about how
Óðinn obtained the mead of poetry from the giants by imbibing it and,
in the shape of an eagle, transporting it back to the gods' residence:

'listen to my streams of Mímr's friend's [ÓÐINN'S] pleasure mountain [CHEST>POETRY] roaring against the gums' skerry [TONGUE]: I have been given the gift of Þundr [ÓÐINN, POETRY]'.

Because of the strict formal requirements the word order of *dróttkvætt* poetry could be very convoluted, and, given the highly complex and often obscure system of *kenningar*, scholars have debated whether such stanzas could have been fully understood by the audience during the first recitation (for a summary of the debate see Gade 1995: 21–7). However, it is also clear that the formal features that made *dróttkvætt* poetry difficult to understand not only facilitated the memorization of such stanzas, but also to some extent prevented subsequent distortion of the poems: words bound by internal rhyme and alliteration occurring within a set metrical framework based on syllable and mora counting could not easily be replaced without causing the stanza to collapse structurally. Whereas eddic poetry was narratively and metrically flexible, that is, episodes could be added and deleted, and words and lines could be changed each time the poem was recited, the skaldic stanzas remained relatively fixed in their wording (but see Frank 1985: 174–5). Although the order of stanzas and half-stanzas within a longer skaldic poem could be shifted around, the wording and structure of a half-stanza remained a fairly stable unit that was committed to memory and passed down in oral tradition.

Like West Germanic alliterative poetry, eddic poetry is anonymous, and, like the anonymous authors of the Icelandic family sagas, the eddic poets must have considered themselves perpetuators of commonly known lore. Just as the saga writers committed events of the past to parchment, the eddic poets retold stories of pagan gods and legendary heroes in poetic diction, and they evidently did not regard the creative process involved in composing eddic poetry as a conscious individual artistic endeavour. The skaldic poets, however, were aware of the uniqueness of their craft, and like artisans and rune carvers they often provided their artistic signatures by incorporating their own names into the poetry (Steblin-Kamenskij 1973, esp. 54–5, 62–4). No name of an eddic poet has been preserved, but Finnur Jónsson's edition of skaldic poetry from the ninth to the fourteenth century contains the names of 256 skalds (*Skj* IIA: 543–52), and that number can be augmented by skalds whose poetry is no longer extant but whose names are listed in *Skáldatal*, a catalogue of poets who eulogized Scandinavian and foreign dignitaries (*SnE* III: 251–69).

THE TRANSMISSION AND DATING OF EDDIC AND SKALDIC POETRY

The major corpus of eddic poetry (twenty-nine poems connected by prose sections) is recorded in a manuscript from around 1270, the Codex Regius (GkS 2365 quarto), while additional poems and fragments are contained in the manuscripts of *Snorra Edda* (see chs. 5 and 6), in the *Flateyjarbók* compendium, and in mythic–heroic sagas (*fornaldarsǫgur*, see ch. 10) (Harris 1985: 68). The dating of the eddic poems is notoriously difficult and has sparked considerable debate among scholars (Kristjánsson 1990). The date of Codex Regius (1270) ensures a *terminus ante quem* for the composition of the poems contained in that collection, and the eddic poems in *Snorra Edda* cannot be later than from around 1230, but there are echoes of eddic lines in datable skaldic poetry that suggest a familiarity with such poems as *Hávamál*, *Vǫluspá*, and *Fáfnismál* going back as far as the tenth and eleventh centuries.[8] Furthermore the skaldic poetic language from the earliest attested period on presupposes a thorough familiarity with the heroic and mythological lore related in the eddic poems, and it also appears likely that the skaldic metres developed from the eddic metre *fornyrðislag* (Gade 1995: 226–38). It is safe to assume, then, that eddic poetry was in place in Scandinavia by the ninth century, but the content and form of these poems cannot be ascertained. Nor do we know anything about the history of the eddic poems before they were recorded in the thirteenth century. The Icelandic sagas, which abound with information about individual skalds and skaldic poetry, contain few episodes that shed light on the composition, recitation, and transmission of the eddic poems.

The earliest skaldic poems have been dated to the ninth century. None of these early dates has remained unchallenged, but the occurrence of a stanza in a skaldic metre (*kviðuháttr*) in the Swedish Rök inscription testifies to the existence of skaldic poetry in Scandinavian territory as early as 850 (Gade 1995: 235–7). Although the bulk of the skaldic corpus can be tied to historical persons and events, and although linguistic and metrical criteria can be employed in the dating of such poetry (Gade forthcoming), there can be no doubt that many of the stanzas in the family sagas, for instance, are spurious and must have originated at a considerably later stage than their purported dates of composition (Frank 1985: 172–5).

Like eddic poetry, the extant skaldic poetry is transmitted in manuscripts dating from the thirteenth century onwards. Skaldic stanzas occur interspersed with prose in the kings' sagas, in the family sagas, and in the contemporary sagas (see Frank 1985: 175–8, and Meulengracht Sørensen forthcoming). Longer poems and separate stanzas are found in *Snorra Edda* and in the grammatical treatises, and other longer poems and fragments of such poems are recorded separately in a variety of manuscripts and manuscript compilations.

In the kings' sagas skaldic stanzas are incorporated into the prose to serve as historical verification and as integral parts of the narrative. As has emerged from the discussion above, skaldic poetry must have been fairly easy to memorize. It was passed down in oral tradition throughout the centuries, and the authors of the royal compendia regarded skaldic verses as extremely valuable sources of historical information. Consider the following programmatic statement from Snorri's *Separate Saga of St Óláfr* (*ÍF* 27: 422; *ÓSH* 4; see also Meulengracht Sørensen forthcoming):

> En þó þykki mér þat merkiligast til sannenda, er berum orðum er sagt í kvæðum eða ǫðrum kveðskap, þeim er svá var ort um konunga eða aðra hǫfðingja, at þeir sjálfir heyrðu, eða í erfikvæðum þeim, er skáldin fœrðu sonum þeira. Þau orð, er í kveðskap standa, eru in sǫmu sem í fyrstu váru, ef rétt er kveðit, þótt at hverr maðr hafi síðan numit af ǫðrum, ok má því ekki breyta.

> (And yet I find that most important for veracity, which is said straightforwardly in poems or other poetry that was composed about kings or other chieftains so that they themselves heard it, or in those commemorative poems which the skalds brought to their sons. Those words which stand in poetry are the same as they were in the beginning, if the recitation is correct, although each person has since learned it from another; and for that reason nothing can be distorted.)

The thirteenth-century Icelandic compendia of kings' sagas, such as *Morkinskinna* (*Msk*), *Fagrskinna* (*ÍF* 29), and *Heimskringla* (*ÍF* 26–8), therefore contain a wealth of skaldic stanzas from longer panegyrics that are cited separately to confirm the events described in the prose (Einarsson 1974; Hofmann, 1978–79; Fidjestøl 1982; Poole 1991). Other *lausavísur* ('loose stanzas') are introduced as part of the narrative, for instance, as a person's comment on a situation or in the form of a poetic dialogue. Clusters of *lausavísur* occur in the smaller episodes (*þættir*) about Icelandic skalds at the Norwegian royal courts, and they figure prominently in *Morkinskinna*, the sagas of St Óláfr, and in the four-teenth-century *Flateyjarbók*.

The Icelandic family sagas, in particular the earliest sagas, are filled with skaldic stanzas that serve the same function as the *lausavísur* in the kings' sagas. The protagonists of such sagas as *Egils saga* (*ÍF* 2), *Hallfreðar saga* (*ÍF* 8), *Kormáks saga* (*ÍF* 8), *Gunnlaugs saga ormstungu* (*ÍF* 3), *Bjarnar saga Hítdœlakappa* (*ÍF* 3), and *Fóstbrœðra saga* (*ÍF* 6) were all court poets in the service of foreign dignitaries, and, although these sagas contain astonishingly little evidence of their courtly produc-tion (Whaley forthcoming), their *lausavísur* give ample evidence of the skalds' poetic abilities. Longer poems of non-courtly contents are referred to in some of the sagas (*ÍF* 3, 169–70, 174; *ÍF* 6, 171; *ÍF* 8, 193; *Msk* 239) but such poems are exceptionally rare, and scholars have argued that, just as single stanzas from longer panegyric poems were cited separately for historical verification in the kings' sagas, many of the *lausavísur* in the Icelandic family sagas originally belonged to longer poems that were distributed throughout the prose to lend verisimilitude to and serve as the basis for the narrative (von See 1977; Poole 1975, 1985, 1991; Meulengracht Sørensen forthcoming).

The contemporary sagas in the Sturlung compilation also contain skaldic stanzas interspersed with the prose. Stanzas from longer poems composed to commemorate persons and events, especially battles, are cited individually (*Sturl* II, 55, 59, 67, 70, 71, 73–5, 215), and *lausavísur* are distributed throughout the narrative as part of individual comments on events that took place. From the evidence that can be gleaned from the family sagas, the kings' sagas, and the contemporary sagas, then, *lausavísur* seem to have fulfilled the same important function in late twelfth- and early thirteenth-century Icelandic society as they did during the pre-Christian era and the period immediately following the conversion to Christianity in the year 1000.

The origin of the Old Norse *prosimetrum* is obscure. The earliest historical work, Ari Þorgilsson's *Íslendingabók* (*c.* 1133), only contains one couplet, which is an integral part of the narrative (*ÍF* 1: 15). As far as the vernacular kings' sagas are concerned, the earliest saga, Eiríkr Oddsson's *Hryggjarstykki (*c.* 1150?; Guðnason 1978: 158) appears to have contained little or no poetry (*ibid.*, 44–8). In the preface to his Latin history of the kings of Norway (*c.* 1180) Theodoricus lists Icelandic poetry as one of his sources of information (*MHN* 3), but the rest of his work is devoid of references to skaldic poetry. The Norwegian *Ágrip* (*c.* 1190) contains seven stanzas or fragments that are used as part of the narrative (*ÍF* 29, 33, 44), as historical verification (*ÍF* 29, 4, 31), or as illustrations of personal characteristics (*ÍF* 29, 12, 41, 50). Karl Jónsson's *Sverris saga* (before 1212), which was based on contemporary information, contains very few stanzas (pp. 47, 50–1, 72, 75, 90–1, 112–13, 122), and *Bǫglunga sǫgur* (*c.* 1220) have no poetry at all.[9]

The first historical works to make extensive use of skaldic stanzas, both as a source of historical information and as part of *þættir* about Icelanders at the Norwegian court, are the *Oldest Saga of St Óláfr* (Storm 1893; Louis-Jensen 1970) and *Morkinskinna*, a royal compendium that chronicles the lives of the kings of Norway from 1035 to 1157 (Fidjestøl 1982: 21–2, 26–7). The sagas of St Óláfr and *Morkinskinna* are preoccupied with skalds and skaldic poetry, and much of the information about Icelandic court poets, their poetry, and their social status in Iceland and abroad in the eleventh and twelfth centuries must be gleaned from these sources.

The date of the *Oldest Saga of St Óláfr* is disputed, but it was probably written no earlier than the beginning of the thirteenth century (Kristjánsson 1972: 223; 1976). The oldest, no longer extant version of *Morkinskinna* has been dated to around 1220 (Aðalbjarnarson 1937: 136). Thus the time of composition of these two works coincides with that of the earliest family sagas and with the antiquarian and scholarly interest in skaldic and eddic poetry that culminated in such works as Snorri's *Edda*. As was pointed out above, on the face of the evidence provided by the family sagas, the kings' sagas, and the contemporary sagas, the function and the importance of skaldic poetry in Icelandic culture and literature do not appear to have changed very much from the tenth to the thirteenth century. We may ask, however, whether we are indeed dealing with an unbroken, four-hundred-year tradition, or whether the renewed interest in skaldic poetry and skaldic biographies in early thirteenth-century Iceland could have projected back on the images of the poets presented in the family sagas and in the *þættir* of the kings' sagas. Or could it be that the poetry and the stories about skalds that had been passed down in oral tradition rekindled an awareness of skaldic poetry as a tool of power; that is, not only as a means of commemorating a person and his or her deeds, as had been the core function of skaldic poetry in oral culture, but as a conscious device to establish national identity and to forge political alliances, especially in terms of soliciting support from Norwegian dignitaries eulogized in thirteenth-century panegyrics?

In an attempt to shed light on these questions, the remaining sections of this chapter will focus on one particular genre of Icelandic poetry, namely, the skaldic panegyric, and on the poets associated with the composition of such encomia. The reason for doing so is threefold. First of all, the panegyric poems are more reliable in terms of dating than the *lausavísur* in the family sagas and the kings' sagas. Secondly, whereas we have no sagas of Icelanders to fill the gap between the period immediately following the conversion (and the death of Óláfr Har- aldsson in 1030) and the onset of the contemporary sagas that chronicle events in Iceland from around 1120, the kings' sagas, in particular *Morkinskinna*, contain an abundance of information about Icelanders and their relations to Norwegian royalty. And thirdly, because the composition of royal panegyrics was closely connected with social status, we should expect changes in the importance of skaldic composi- tion to be reflected in the status of the poets and in their cultural environment.

SKALDIC PANEGYRIC POETRY AND ITS SUBGENRES

Panegyric poetry fulfilled an important function in Old Norse society. Just as rune stones immortalized people in an earlier period, praise poems preserved the memory of a person's name and deeds for posterity. Because skaldic poetry must have been fairly easy to memorize and not readily distorted in oral transmission, it was eminently suited for commemorative purposes. Like the rune carvers, the skaldic poets promised their benefactors that their memory would live on in 'a not easily broken praise pile' (*óbrotgjarn lofkǫst*; *Skj* IA: 48), or in the words of Eyvindr Finnsson: 'And the feast of the gods [POETRY] I have provided, praise of the ruler, [strong] as a stone bridge' (*Jólna sumbl / en vér gátum / stillis lof / sem steina brú*; *Skj* IA: 71).[10] It is clear that the skalds, from the earliest period on, were very much aware of the durability of their words, and it is not difficult to understand why Snorri and other thirteenth-century authors of kings' sagas placed such a high value on the historical information contained in skaldic panegyric poetry.

The custom of composing praise poetry in Old Norse society entailed an exchange of favours. The person eulogized would receive undying fame, and, in return, the skald was rewarded with gifts, high social status, and royal protection. The Icelandic family sagas and kings' sagas are very detailed in their accounts of the rewards Icelandic skalds received from the recipients of their panegyrics, which could range from gold rings, silver-inlaid axes, swords, precious clothing, to cash. According to *Gunnlaugs saga*, a praise poem ought to be rewarded with swords or gold rings; anything exceeding that, such as the gift of two merchant ships, was considered inappropriate (*ÍF* 3: 76). There are also examples throughout the centuries of Icelandic skalds gaining a king's favour and advancing to high positions in the royal household (see Whaley forthcoming; Clunies Ross forthcoming). From the earliest period on, then, the episodes in Icelandic literature describing the composition and recitation of skaldic praise poetry focussed very much on the financial and social advantages a poet could receive from his benefactors. The author of the thirteenth-century *Knýtlinga saga* even felt compelled to report that, around 1150, the Icelandic skald Einarr Skúlason presented a praise poem to King Sveinn Eiríksson of Denmark and received no reward for his efforts (*ÍF* 35: 275).

Skaldic eulogies were produced for a variety of purposes and can be divided into a number of subgenres. Whereas some were adapted to accommodate the social and religious changes that occurred in Scandinavia from the ninth to the thirteenth century, others became extinct, and new types of panegyrics emerged and took on important functions

in society. The alleged earliest skaldic *dróttkvætt* poems, Bragi Boddason's *Ragnarsdrápa* (*Skj* IA: 1–4) and Þjóðólfr of Hvinir's *Haustlǫng* (*Skj*
IA: 16–20), are so-called shield poems, that is, narrative poems in which
the poets praise a shield they received as a gift from their benefactors by
detailing the mythological and heroic legends painted on the shields
(see Frank 1985: 179 and the literature cited there). Both Bragi and
Þjóðólfr were Norwegian skalds, but the genre survived in tenth-
century Iceland (*ÍF* 2: 271–3, 275–6). Úlfr Uggason's *Húsdrápa* ('House
Poem', *c.* 983; *Skj* IA: 136–8), which describes the pagan myths painted
on the walls and the roof of the sleeping hall of the Icelandic chieftain
Óláfr pái ('peacock'), belongs to the same narrative poetic genre as the
shield poems. Úlfr recited that poem at a feast at Óláfr's estate and was
handsomely rewarded (*ÍF* 5: 80). All these poems are rooted in pagan
myth and have been transmitted in the context of Snorri's *Edda* (see ch.
5). That is also the case with Eilífr Goðrúnarson's *Þórsdrápa* ('Poem to
Þórr'; *Skj* IA: 148–52), a long narrative poem describing Þórr's
encounter with the giant Geirrøðr and his daughters (Clunies Ross
1981).

Among the earliest recorded panegyrics are two Norwegian genealogical poems, *Ynglingatal* ('Enumeration of the Ynglingar'; *Skj* IA: 7–15)
by Þjóðólfr of Hvinir and *Háleygjatal* ('Enumeration of the Háleygjar';
Skj IA: 68–71) by Eyvindr Finnsson skáldaspillir ('poetaster'), which
commemorate the ancestry of Haraldr hárfagri ('fair-hair') and Hákon
Earl of Hlaðir respectively.[11] *Ynglingatal* traces the lineage of the
Vestfold dynasty to Yngvi-Freyr of Uppsala and provides the consolidator of Norway not only with a divine ancestry but also with ties to the
famous Swedish dynasty of Uppsala. *Háleygjatal*, which was an imitation of *Ynglingatal* with regard to both metre and content, outlines the
genealogy of the Earls of Hlaðir from Óðinn to Hákon jarl Sigurðarson.
Both of these poems are highly propagandist in nature and were clearly
parts of Haraldr's and Hákon's political agenda (Ström 1981: 446–8).

The most common type of panegyric during this early period
consisted of poems composed in praise of living or dead dignitaries.
Poems recited before a living recipient praised his luck, generosity, and
power, focussing especially on his warlike prowess by enumerating his
victories and detailing events that took place in the heat of battle. That
was also the case with commemorative poems, which gave an account

of the deceased person's life and deeds. Stanzas from such poems constitute the bulk of the poetic corpus dispersed throughout the thirteenth-century royal compendia, and they were the target of Snorri's comment on the veracity of skaldic poetry cited above (*ÍF* 27: 422).

The earliest skaldic panegyrics were all steeped in pagan myth and pagan imagery. The shield poems and mythological narrative poems rendered vivid descriptions of pagan myth, and the genealogical poems presented to Norwegian dignitaries traced their ancestry to the pagan gods and established them as the earthly descendants of the powerful Freyr and Óðinn. The wealth of mythological *kenningar* used in skaldic praise poems reinforced the connection between the persons eulogized and the world of the pagan gods, a feature which is particularly striking in the encomia presented to Hákon Earl of Hlaðir (Frank 1978: 63–5; Ström 1981). The conversion to Christianity in Norway under the two missionary kings Óláfr Tryggvason (995–1000) and Óláfr Haraldsson (1015–28) and the conversion of Iceland by legal proclamation in the year 1000 caused the demise of several of the genres of panegyric poetry outlined above. The mythological narrative poems ceased to be productive as a genre, and genealogical poems like *Ynglingatal* and *Háleygjatal* disappeared, only to be resurrected in the late twelfth century in the service of the Icelandic aristocracy. Although such poems were no longer composed, like mythological and heroic eddic poetry they must have continued to be recited in Iceland throughout the centuries for the purpose of entertainment. Snorri comments on this oral tradition in the preface to *Heimskringla* when he states that 'some things [in *Heimskringla*] are written according to ancient poems or historical lays which people have had for their entertainment' (*sumt er ritat eptir fornum kvæðum eða sǫguljóðum, er menn hafa haft til skemmtanar sér*; *ÍF* 26: 4).

The conversion to Christianity also had a profound impact on skaldic language. The system of skaldic *kenningar* was structured around a framework of pagan myth, and the earliest Christian rulers did not take kindly to the pagan imagery that saturated skaldic poetry. Whereas Hákon Earl of Hlaðir undoubtedly felt much honoured by being referred to as *kneyfir Þundar hyrjar* ('the crusher of Þundr's [ÓÐINN's] fire [SWORD>WARRIOR]'; *Skj* IA: 126) or *Yggs niðr* ('Yggr's [ÓÐINN's] descendant'; *Skj* IA: 127), such circumlocutions did not sit well with the two Óláfrs, whose initial reluctance to listen to skaldic praise poetry is documented in several sources (*ÍF* 8: 155–6; *ÍF* 27: 54). The upshot of this upheaval was, however, that the skalds, rather than abandoning their craft, adapted their poetic language to accommodate the demands of the new faith (Frank 1978: 65–7; Lange 1958).

The poetry of Hallfreðr Óttarsson vandræðaskáld, who eulogized both the pagan Hákon Earl of Hlaðir and the Christian Óláfr Tryggvason, offers a good illustration of this change. Hallfreðr's *Hákonardrápa* ('Poem to Hákon'; *Skj* IA: 155–6) is placed within a pagan mythological framework in which Hákon's subjugation of Norway is depicted in terms of the marriage between the goddess Jǫrð ('earth') and Óðinn, Hákon's ancestor (see Frank 1978: 63–5; Ström 1981: 452–6). In this poem Norway is paraphrased by the following *kenningar*: *barrhǫdduð biðkván Þriðja* ('the pineneedle-haired woman desired by Þriði [Óðinn]'; st. 3); *ítr systir Auðs* ('the splendid sister of Auðr [mythological brother of Jǫrð]'; st. 4); *viði gróin eingadóttir Ónars* ('the wood-grown only daughter of Ónarr [mythological brother of Jǫrð]'; st. 5); *breiðleit brúðr Báleygs* ('the broad-featured bride of Báleygr [Óðinn]'; st. 6). In Hallfreðr's commemorative poem to the dead Óláfr (*Skj* IA: 159–66), however, Óláfr is referred to in such neutral terms as *flugþverrir* ('flight-diminisher'; st. 1); *hertryggðar hnekkir* ('destroyer of the army's peace'; st. 2); *þjóðar sessi* ('bench-mate of the people'; st. 2), and Hallfreðr ends the panegyric with the following pious invocation: 'may the pure Christ keep the wise king's spirit above the lands [in heaven]' (*kœns hafi Kristr enn hreini / konungs ǫnd ofar lǫndum*; st. 29).

The change that took place in skaldic language did not occur overnight. Nor did pagan imagery disappear entirely from the poetry, and the skalds and their audience certainly retained knowledge of the old myths and the pagan kenning system. When called upon, Þjóðólfr Arnórsson, one of the Icelandic court poets of King Haraldr Sigurðarson (d. 1066), produced two *lausavísur* in which he described the fight between a tanner and a blacksmith as the fights between Sigurðr the Dragonslayer and Fáfnir and between Þórr and the giant Geirrøðr, respectively (*Msk* 235–6; *Skj* IA: 380). In the twelfth century Einarr Skúlason, the poet who composed a praise poem of seventy-one stanzas to St Óláfr, also composed a poem packed with mythological *kenningar* about an axe he had received (*Skj* IA: 477–9). With the renewed antiquarian interest in pagan mythology and poetry in the thirteenth century, mythological *kenningar* were resurrected and became productive once more, although they never reached the complexity of the *kenningar* found in the poetry of the pre-Christian period.

In the wake of Christianity new types of panegyric emerged, and skaldic praise poetry became a vehicle of the Church. In the twelfth century longer poems eulogising St Óláfr, foreign saints, the apostles, and the Virgin Mary became part and parcel of skaldic production. In 1152 the Norwegian King Eysteinn Haraldsson commissioned a panegyric in honour of St Óláfr from the Icelandic skald and priest Einarr Skúlason, which Einarr proceeded to recite in Kristkirken ('Christ Church') in Niðaróss (the city of Trondheim) (*Msk* 446; *Skj* IA: 459–73), and ecclesiastical panegyrics constitute the bulk of the extant skaldic poetry from the thirteenth and fourteenth centuries. Unlike secular praise poetry, however, much of the extant religious panegyric is anonymous, and the composition of such poetry appears to have been the domain of Icelandic clerics rather than of secular poets.

The panegyric genre that remained most stable throughout the centuries and was the least affected by the new religion was the secular encomium that commemorated the deeds of dignitaries living and dead. As discussed above, the skaldic language underwent a fairly radical change shortly after the conversion to Christianity, and this change also affected the word order of the poetry with a move towards a simpler sentence structure with fewer nominal elements, and it also facilitated the introduction of new and simpler metres that were used in praise poetry.[12] Hence the postconversion poetry must have been more readily accessible to the listeners, and in turn must have been appreciated by foreign nobility of later centuries who may not have been schooled in the intricacies of *dróttkvætt* metre.

According to the traditional view, by the end of the tenth century the art of composing skaldic poetry was entirely in the hands of Icelanders (see Jónsson 1894–1901 I: 416–74; II: 27–50; Frank 1985: 181). That view is reinforced by the many *þættir* in *Morkinskinna* which detail the relationship between the Icelandic court poets and their Norwegian benefactors, and also by the curious fact that, with the exception of a Norwegian fisherman (*Msk* 247–9), the only known persons to compose skaldic poetry after the tenth century are the Norwegian kings and Icelandic skalds.[13] According to the picture presented in thirteenth-century Icelandic literature, then, the ability to compose skaldic poetry was a gift that had been bestowed on Scandinavian (especially Norwegian) royalty and on the Icelanders, a gift that certainly set Icelanders apart from their mainland Scandinavian neighbours and emphasized the relations between the Norwegian royal dynasty and the people of the Icelandic free state. We may feel justified in asking, however, whether this is an accurate depiction of the conditions in eleventh- to thirteenth-century Scandinavia, or whether skaldic poetry had become one of the vehicles by which late twelfth- and early thirteenth-century Icelanders sought to assert their national uniqueness.

ICELANDIC COURT POETS IN NORWAY FROM THE TENTH TO THE TWELFTH CENTURY

The tradition of composing panegyric poetry was firmly established in Norway prior to the time of the Icelandic settlement *c.* 870–930. The consolidator of Norway, Haraldr hárfagri, was eulogized by a number of Norwegian skalds, and according to *Haraldskvæði* ('Poem to Haraldr') he was very generous to his poets, who were easily recognizable by their red cloaks, gold rings, and weapons (adorned shields, swords inlaid with silver, iron-woven coats of mail, and green helmets) (st. 19; *Skj* IA: 28). *Egils saga* reports that Haraldr valued the skalds more highly than his other retainers and placed them on the seat directly opposite himself (*ÍF* 2: 19).

The first Icelandic skalds to eulogize foreign dignitaries were Egill Skalla-Grímsson, Glúmr Geirason, and Kormákr Ǫgmundarson.[14] Egill appeared at the court of King Aðalsteinn (Athelstan) of England in 926, fought alongside him in a battle presumed to be Brunanburh, and presented a praise poem in his honour after the battle. As a reward Egill received two gold rings and a cloak which the king had worn himself (*ÍF* 2: 146–7). On a later occasion Egill found himself yet again in York in the hands of his deadly enemy, the exiled King Eiríkr blóðøx ('bloodaxe') of Norway, and was forced to redeem his life by reciting a praise poem to Eiríkr (*Hǫfuðlausn*, 'Head Ransom') (*ÍF* 2: 180–93).

Glúmr Geirason composed about Eiríkr blóðøx and his son, Haraldr gráfeldr ('greycloak') (*Skj* IA: 75–8). We do not know anything about his status at court, but in his commemorative poem to Haraldr gráfeldr, composed after Haraldr was killed in the battle in the Limfjord in 975, Glúmr explicitly addressed the precarious position of a court poet whose benefactor is dead: 'Half of my hope of wealth disappeared when the sword shower [BATTLE] deprived the king of his life: Haraldr's death did not lead me to wealth' (*Fellumk holf, pás hilmis / hjǫrdrífa brá lífi / réðat oss til auðar / auðván Haralds dauði*; st. 11; *Skj* IA: 77–8). We do not know if Glúmr's hopes of reward from Haraldr's brothers, expressed in the same stanza, were fulfilled, but he does not appear to have gained much profit from his poetic profession since he is described as a poor man upon his return to Iceland (Jónsson 1894–1901, I: 535).

Kormákr Ǫgmundarson is the protagonist of *Kormáks saga* (*ÍF* 8), but although that saga details his life and contains an abundance of skaldic stanzas attributed to him (*Skj* IA: 80–91), there is no mention of Kormákr as a court poet (see Clunies Ross forthcoming). *Skáldatal*, however, lists him among the court poets of Haraldr gráfeldr and Sigurðr Earl of Hlaðir (*SnE* III: 253, 256, 261, 265), and Snorri's *Edda* records six stanzas of a panegyric by Kormákr, steeped in pagan imagery and dedicated to Sigurðr, Earl of Hlaðir (d. 963) (*Skj* IA: 79–80; Marold 1990). Snorri also cites another stanza from the same poem in his *Heimskringla* as evidence of the splendid pagan sacrifices conducted by Sigurðr (*ÍF* 26: 168). Although we know nothing about Kormákr's relations with the persons he eulogized, one of the stanzas from *Sigurðardrápa* mentions that he received a headband from the earl as reward for his poetry (st. 3; *Skj* IA: 79).

The court of Hákon Earl of Hlaðir, Sigurðr's son and the last pagan ruler of Norway (970–95), became a centre for skaldic composition, and numerous Icelanders, among them Einarr Helgason skálaglamm ('tinkle-scales'), Þorleifr Rauðfeldarson jarlsskáld ('the earl's poet'), Tindr Halkellsson, Hallfreðr Óttarsson vandræðaskáld, Skapti Þoroddsson, Þorfinnr munnr ('the mouth'), and Vígfúss Víga-Glúmsson, are said to have sung his praise (*SnE* III: 256, 266; *ÍF* 8: 151). After his defeats of the sons of Eiríkr blóðøx and the crushing victory over the Danish invaders in the battle of Hjǫrungavágr, Earl Hákon was the supreme ruler of Norway until his death in 995. By the beginning of Hákon's reign (970) Iceland had been settled for forty years, and, with no new land to acquire, young Icelanders must have regarded Hákon's political agenda as a golden opportunity to gain fame and fortune abroad.

Hákon is hailed as a strong supporter of paganism, and he entered a profitable relationship with the skalds, whose poetic craft was steeped in pagan myth (Ström 1981). By employing their services as a tool of political propaganda he consolidated his power and justified his divine claim to the Norwegian crown. We know little about what the poets received as their part of that bargain, but according to *Hallfreðar saga*, he rewarded Hallfreðr Óttarsson with a great silver-inlaid axe and good clothing and invited him to stay with him during the winter (*ÍF* 8: 151). *Egils saga* mentions that Hákon made Einarr skálaglamm his retainer and gave him a shield adorned with gold and precious stones and painted with tales of old (*ÍF* 2: 269, 271–2). The earl's generosity does not seem to have made a lasting impact on Einarr's economy, however. He gave the shield as a gift to Egill Skalla-Grímsson, and *Egils saga* describes Einarr as 'a valiant man, most often poor, but a very capable and brave man' (*ǫrr maðr ok optast félítill, en skǫrungr mikill ok drengr góðr*; *ÍF* 2: 269). The title of Einarr's encomiastic poem to Earl Hákon, *Vellekla* ('shortage of gold'), also indicates Hákon might have needed some prodding to fulfil his part of the contract.

The two missionary kings of Norway, Óláfr Tryggvason (d. 1000) and Óláfr Haraldsson (d. 1030), and the interim rulers Earls Eiríkr and Sveinn of Hlaðir (1000–14) were surrounded by court poets. Altogether seventeen skalds, fifteen of whom we know for certain to be Icelanders, reportedly gathered at their courts and at one point or another joined their service (*SnE* III: 253, 257, 261, 266). Óláfr Haraldsson was eulogized by ten poets, all Icelanders (*SnE* III: 253), and, according to Styrmir Kárason's additions to *Óláfs saga helga*, 'King Óláfr had many Icelandic men with him and held them in good esteem and made them his retainers' (*Óláfr konungr hafði með sér marga íslenzka menn ok hafði þá í góðu yfirlæti ok gerði þá sína hirðmenn*; *Flat* III: 243). Among the skalds who joined the royal courts of Norway during the period 1000–30 were the protagonists of many of the Icelandic family sagas, such as Hallfreðr Óttarsson vandræðaskáld (*Hallfreðar saga*), Bjǫrn Arngeirsson Hítdœlakappi ('champion of the people of Hítardalr') and Þórðr Kolbeinsson (*Bjarnar saga Hítdœlakappa*), Gunnlaugr Illugason ormstunga ('serpent tongue'; *Gunnlaugs saga ormstungu*), and Þormóðr

Bersason kolbrúnarskáld ('Kolbrún's poet'; *Fóstbrœðra saga*). Their lives are commemorated in verse and prose in those sagas, and the encomiastic poetry that earned them fame abroad was passed down in Iceland in oral tradition. It is noticeable that all these skalds returned to Iceland, and that most of the poetry transmitted in the family sagas addresses events that took place in Iceland – in most instances the sojourns abroad only served to establish the poets' credentials and enhance their social status and financial situtation (see Whaley forthcoming).

Some of the poets who entered royal service during this period belonged to powerful Icelandic families with strong poetic traditions. Skúli Þorsteinsson, for instance, skald and retainer of Earl Eiríkr Hákonarson, was the grandson of Egill Skalla-Grímsson, and Gunnlaugr Illugason was the nephew of Tindr Hallkelsson, who had been the court poet of Hákon Earl of Hlaðir. However, some of the skalds belonged to professional families of poets about whose social background we know very little. That is the case with Sigvatr Þórðarson, whose father, Þórðr Sigvaldaskáld was the poet of Earl Sigvaldi of Denmark, and whose nephew, Óttarr svarti ('the black') eulogized the Norwegian Óláfr Haraldsson, the Swedish kings Óláfr sœnski ('the Swede') and Ǫnundr, as well as Knútr enn ríki ('the great') of Denmark and England (Jónsson 1894–1901: I, 588–90).

We catch fragmentary glimpses of the lives and personal poetry of these professional skalds in the *þættir* and smaller episodes incorporated in the kings' sagas, but there are no separate sagas, for instance, that chronicle the lives of Sigvatr and his nephew, Óttarr svarti (cf. Clunies Ross forthcoming). Sigvatr certainly gained fame, fortune, and social status outside Iceland, but, although his poetry constitutes the main source of poetic documentation about the life of St Óláfr, what we know about his life must gleaned from the sagas about Óláfr Haraldsson. Common to most of the professional poets is that they never returned to Iceland but spent the remainder of their lives abroad. The kings' sagas testify to the fact that the longer, panegyric poems of these poets were known in Iceland, and separate anecdotes, mainly dealing with the Icelandic skalds' ability to compose poetry, must have circulated and been preserved in oral tradition in Iceland (Fidjestøl 1982: 22–3; Sigurður Nordal 1914: 106). However, because these poets had more or less severed their ties with their home countries, many of the details of their lives abroad must have been unknown and, furthermore, of little interest to an Icelandic audience.

As in the pre-Christian period, the relationship between the kings and their poets was clearly one of mutual benefit. King Óláfr Haraldsson appointed Sigvatr Þórðarson his retainer and later his marshal (*ÍF* 27: 55, 293), and on several occasions he used him as his emissary abroad. Among the duties of the poets were certainly those of entertainment (*ÍF* 6: 281, 288; *Flat* III: 241–4), but it emerges from the kings' sagas that the most important aspect of their profession was to preserve the king's deeds for posterity (cf. *ÍF* 27: 358, and Meulengracht Sørensen forthcoming). There can be no doubt that, like his predecessors Haraldr hárfagri and Hákon Earl of Hlaðir, Óláfr Haraldsson was highly conscious of the political power of praise poetry. Óláfr's claim to the Norwegian crown was certainly not undisputed, and his reign was constantly threatened by the powerful alliance of Knútr enn ríki and the Earls of Hlaðir. The many panegyrics that detail Óláfr's victories over his Danish and Norwegian enemies show that he certainly put poetry to good use in the attempt to enhance his own image and to establish a firm grasp on the Norwegian crown.

The next great exodus of Icelandic poets to Norway came during the reign of Haraldr Sigurðarson (1046–66), Óláfr's half-brother. Haraldr was himself an accomplished poet (*Skj* IA: 356–61) who not only knew the value of praise poetry, but was also able to appreciate the finer nuances of skaldic rhetoric and metre (*Msk* 116–17, 235–44, 247–50, 252–4, 276). *Morkinskinna* goes to great length to emphasize that Haraldr was a great friend and supporter of the Icelanders on account of their poetic talent, a statement which is repeated in both *Fagrskinna* and *Heimskringla*: 'Er mikil saga frá Haraldi konungi í kvæði sett, þau er honum samtíða váru um hann kveðin ok fœrðu honum sjǫlfum, þeir er ortu. Var Haraldr konungr því mikill vinr þeira, at honum þótti gótt lofit' (*Msk* 170; cf. *ÍF* 29: 261; *ÍF* 28: 119) (A great saga of King Haraldr is contained in the poems that were composed during his lifetime and brought to him by those who composed them. King Haraldr was their greatest friend because he appreciated the praise).

The turbulent life of Haraldr Sigurðarson harðráði ('hardruler') was commemorated by thirteen skalds, eight of whom can be identified as

Icelanders (*SnE* III: 254, 262). Many of them were professional poets of insignificant social background, such as Þjóðólfr Arnórsson, his brother Bǫlverkr, and Sneglu-Halli (*Msk* 239–41), but some belonged to prominent families with strong skaldic traditions. Arnórr Þórðarson jarlaskáld ('earls' skald') was the son of Þórðr Kolbeinsson, court poet and retainer of Jarl Eiríkr of Hlaðir, and Stúfr Þórðarson blindi ('the blind') was the grandson of Guðrún Ósvífrsdóttir, the heroine of *Laxdælasaga* (*ÍF* 5), and could trace his family back to Glúmr Geirason, court poet of Eiríkr blóðøx and Haraldr gráfeldr. Steinn Herdísarson was the great-grandson of Einarr Helgason, poet and retainer of Hákon Earl of Hlaðir and related to Stúfr Þórðarson (Einarr's brother, Ósvífr, was the father of Guðrún). Steinn's uncle, Úlfr Óspaksson, was the esteemed marshal ('stallari') of Haraldr harðráði, and Úlfr's family later became extremely powerful in Norway, counting among its members the Machiavellian Archbishop Eysteinn Erlendsson of Niðaróss (d. 1188). With the consent of the court, Haraldr made Stúfr Þórðarson his retainer (*Msk* 254), but none of his other poets appear to have enhanced their social status significantly.

Because Haraldr took such a pleasure in skaldic poetry, his saga provides important information on the lives of his poets, especially of the ones whose panegyrics are used as historical sources in the saga (Arnórr Þórðarson, Þjóðólfr Arnórsson, Stúfr Þórðarson). Again the focus is on the Icelanders' poetic talent, often portraying them as intimate friends of the king who distinguished themselves in verbal duels and poetic competitions. Such episodes must have been highly appreciated by an Icelandic audience, and undoubtedly served to forge a link between the unique capabilities of the members of the Icelandic free state and Norwegian royalty.

With the death of Haraldr at the battle of Stamford Bridge in 1066 the heyday of the Icelandic court poets came to a temporary close. The rule of Haraldr's son, Óláfr kyrri ('the quiet'; 1066–93) was commemorated by five poets, two of whom are known to have been Icelanders (*SnE* III: 254, 262), but only the poetry of Steinn Herdísarson survives (*Skj* IA: 409–13). Óláfr's son, Magnús berfœttr (1093–1103) is said to have been surrounded by six poets (*SnE* III: 254, 262), but only three, Gísl Illugason, Ívarr Ingimundarson and Bárðr svarti ('the black'), can be identified as Icelanders, and only Gísl's commemorative poem composed after Magnús's death in Ulster in 1103 is extant (*Skj* IIA: 440–4).

The information about Icelandic skalds in royal Norwegian service during the twelfth century is surprisingly scarce. According to *Skáldatal*, Norwegian kings and dignitaries continued to be eulogized by poets, but, although their names are given, we know the identity of very few. The following list speaks for itself (*SnE* III: 254–5, 263–4): Óláfr (1103–15); Eysteinn (1103–23); and Sigurðr jórsalafari (1103–30) Magnússynir (6 poets, 3 of unknown identity); Magnús Sigurðarson (1130–35; 1 poet); Haraldr Magnússon (1135–36; 3 poets, 2 of unknown identity); Sigurðr slembir Magnússon (1136–39; 1 poet); Sigurðr (1136–55), Eysteinn (1142–57), and Ingi (1136–61) Haraldssynir (7 poets, 5 of unknown identity); Hákon Sigurðarson (1157–62; 2 poets of unknown identity); Magnús Erlingsson (1131–84; 6 poets, 5 of unknown identity); Sverrir Sigurðarson (1177–1202; 13 poets, 11 of unknown identity). Some of the poets of known identity composed about more than one ruler: Einarr Skúlason, for instance, sang the praise of Eysteinn and Sigurðr Magnússynir, Magnús Sigurðarson and Haraldr Magnússon, as well as the sons of Haraldr Magnússon (Sigurðr, Eysteinn, and Ingi); Ívarr Ingimundarson is said to have composed about Magnús berfœttr, Eysteinn Magnússon, Sigurðr jórsalafari, and Sigurðr slembir, but only his commemorative poem to Sigurðr slembir is extant (*Skj* IA: 495–502).

We see, then, that of the thirty skalds known to have eulogized Norwegian kings during the period 1103–1202, twenty-two are poets whose names are not recorded elsewhere. Of the remaining eight Árni fjǫruskeifr ('shore-slanting'?) appears to have been Norwegian (Jónsson 1894–1901: II, 28–9), and about the families of three others, Máni, Ívarr Ingimundarson, and Þórarinn stuttfeldr ('short-cloak'), we know very little. According to *Sverris saga* (p. 91) Máni entertained the court of Magnús Erlingsson in 1184 by reciting Halldórr skvaldri's ('the prattler') poem about Sigurðr jórsalafari's journey to Jerusalem, and in 1214 he composed a stanza about gifts sent to the Icelandic chieftain Snorri Sturluson from Earl Hákon galinn ('the mad') of Norway (*Sturl* I: 235–6), but we know nothing about his family. Ívarr Ingimundarson is said to have come from a distinguished Icelandic family (*Msk* 354), but his genealogy is given nowhere, and that is also the case with Þórarinn stuttfeldr, the Icelander who shows up at the court of Sigurðr jórsalafari and presents a poem in his honour (*Msk* 385–7). Two Icelandic chieftains, Þorvarðr Þorgeirsson and Snorri Sturluson, allegedly commemorated Ingi Haraldsson and Sverrir Sigurðarson respectively, but none of these poems survives (*SnE* III: 255, 263).

The most famous Icelandic skald of the twelfth century was Einarr Skúlason, a descendant of Egill Skalla-Grímsson. Einarr was a professional poet who, in addition to eulogizing two generations of Norwegian kings, also plied his trade in both Sweden and Denmark, albeit with mixed success (*ÍF* 35: 275 and above). He is said to have been a dear friend of King Eysteinn Haraldsson, who held Einarr in such high esteem that he appointed him his marshal (*Msk* 446). Episodes from Einarr's life at the Norwegian courts are detailed in *Morkinskinna* (pp. 375, 390–2, 446–8, 458–9) and his poetry is quoted extensively throughout the kings' sagas to verify events that took place during the years 1108–59.

The lack of information about most of the skalds who allegedly composed panegyrics about Norwegian dignitaries throughout the twelfth century is conspicuous indeed, and the explanation is not immediately apparent. It is very likely, however, that this circumstance is closely connected with the transmission of the Norwegian kings' sagas. As was pointed out above, the earliest recorded kings' sagas in the vernacular were based on eye-witness accounts and contain very little poetry. King Sverrir Sigurðarson, for example, is said to have been eulogized by a total of thirteen poets (*SnE* III: 253, 264), but not one stanza of their poetry is preserved in his saga. Similarly, Sverrir's mortal enemy and predecessor Magnús Erlingsson allegedly kept six court poets (*ibid.*), and nothing remains of their panegyrics. Furthermore, we only know the identity of three of these nineteen poets, and, except for one instance recounted in *Sverris saga* (p. 91), there are no anecdotes about their lives or about their relations with Norwegian dignitaries. The only poets from the twelfth century who are mentioned in shorter episodes are Ívarr Ingimundarson, whose poem about Sigurðr slembir is represented by forty-six stanzas in the *Morkinskinna* version of **Hryggjarstykki* (*Skj* IA: 495–502); Þórarinn stuttfeldr, whose *Stuttfeldardrápa* (*Skj* I: 489–91) is quoted extensively in *Morkinskinna's Sigurðar saga jórsalfara*; and Einarr Skúlason, marshal of King Eysteinn

Haraldsson and the poet whose stanzas are quoted in all the kings' sagas as documentation for the years 1108–59.

Based on this information, it is tempting to draw the following conclusions: (1) from the beginning of the twelfth century the composition of royal panegyrics was mostly in the hands of professional poets who spent their lives in Norway and had scant ties to Iceland; (2) as far as the earliest part of this period is concerned, some of the panegyrics composed by Icelanders and detailing the battles and journeys of such kings as Sigurðr jórsalafari, Haraldr gilli, Sigurðr slembir, Ingi and Eysteinn Haraldssynir, were known in Iceland and stories about these poets, in particular anecdotes containing *lausavísur* and centring around skaldic composition, served to establish the credentials of these poets and were closely connected with the preservation and recitation of the panegyrics; (3) the earliest vernacular kings' sagas were based on eye-witness reports and did not require poetic documentation, hence there was no need to record panegyrics composed by skalds at the Norwegian court, and the absence of such poems, along with the great number of skalds whose identities are unknown, suggests that most of these poems never reached Iceland.[15]

THE RENAISSANCE OF SKALDIC PRAISE POETRY IN THIRTEENTH-CENTURY ICELAND

The end of the twelfth and the beginning of the thirteenth century saw a renewed interest in skaldic poetry from an antiquarian, learned point of view. At the same time the earliest Icelandic family sagas (1200–20), which frequently chronicled the lives of Icelandic skalds and their relations to foreign, especially Norwegian, dignitaries were recorded, and we see the emergence of full-blown kings' sagas in the vernacular, such as the earliest versions of *Óláfs saga helga* and *Morkinskinna*, in which skaldic poetry was used extensively to corroborate historical events, and which contained a wealth of information about the dealings between the skalds and their royal benefactors. In the family sagas, the Icelandic poets returned home to Iceland with royal gifts and honour. The professional poets of later centuries acquired wealth and sometimes important positions in the royal household, and, according to the kings' sagas, even people of low social standing in Iceland could, by means of their poetic abilities, become close friends and confidants of the kings. The kings' sagas also reinforce the notion that Icelandic poets were endowed with a gift that they shared with the kings of Norway, namely, the gift of composing poetry, which emphasizes the special status of the members of the Icelandic free state in medieval Scandinavian society.

It is precisely at this point in time that we see a remarkable change in the status and function of skaldic poetry in Iceland. First of all, as Guðrún Nordal has pointed out, chieftains belonging to the Icelandic aristocracy began to surround themselves with professional poets who sang their praises and recorded their deeds.[16] Around 1190, for example, Jón Loptsson of Oddi was presented with a eulogy of eighty-three stanzas in the metre *kviðuháttr* which, in a blatant attempt to imitate *Ynglingatal* and *Háleygjatal*, traced his family back to Haraldr hárfagri (*Skj* IA: 579–89). Secondly, the contemporary sagas record an increase in *lausavísur* and poetic exchanges spoken by most of the members of the ruling Icelandic families (Nordal forthcoming), and, even in cases where no poetry is known to exist, a prominent member of a family is still hailed for his poetic abilities (*Sturl* II: 276). Thirdly, and most importantly, members of the families contending for power in Iceland suddenly begin to encroach on the territory of the professional poets in Norway. In 1212 Snorri Sturluson, whose family had produced such illustrious poets as Egill Skalla-Grímsson, Skúli Þorsteinsson, Bjǫrn Hítdœlakappi, and Einarr Skúlason, sent a praise poem to Earl Hákon galinn of Norway, and in return, the earl sent him a sword, a shield, and a coat of mail, and invited him to join him in Norway (*Sturl* I: 235–6). In 1219 Snorri presented a praise poem to Hákon's widow, Kristín, in Sweden and received as a reward a banner which had belonged to King Eiríkr Knútsson of Sweden (*Sturl* I: 238). During the years 1218–20 Snorri eulogized Earl Skúli Bárðarson, the guardian of the young King Hákon Hákonarson of Norway, who rewarded him with 'fifteen great gifts' and a merchant ship (*Sturl* I: 244), and King Hákon made him his retainer (*lendr maðr*). In return Snorri promised to support their efforts to force Iceland to submit to Norwegian sovereignty (*Flat* III: 38).

Snorri's attempt to ingratiate himself with the Norwegian dignitaries in the style of the Icelandic court poets of old was not well received in Iceland, where members of the opposing factions ridiculed his poetry with derogatory *lausavísur* imitating some rather clumsy lines in his panegyric to Jarl Skúli (*Sturl* I: 244, 249). It seems, however, that members of other powerful families took note of Snorri's success, and among the persons who eulogized King Hákon Hákonarson was Gizurr Þorvaldsson (*Skj* II A: 98), the arch-enemy of the Sturlungar who was appointed Earl of Iceland by Hákon upon the collapse of the Icelandic free state.

Not only Snorri Sturluson, but also the later generations of the Sturlungar, notably Snorri's nephews, Óláfr and Sturla Þórðarsynir, continued along the path paved by their uncle. Óláfr, the author of the *Third Grammatical Treatise* (see ch. 6), eulogized Hákon Hákonarson, Skúli Bárðarson, Earl Knútr Hákonarson, and King Valdimarr enn gamli ('the old') of Denmark (Jónsson 1894–1901: II, 95–8), and Sturla, who by 1263 had fallen out of favour with Norwegian royalty, redeemed himself by appearing at the court of Magnús lagabœtir ('lawmender') with panegyrics to Magnús and his deceased father, Hákon (*Sturl* II: 271–2).

Sturla was also commissioned to chronicle the sagas of Magnús's father, Hákon, and of Hákon himself. Only fragments of the saga of Magnús remain, but *Hákonar saga Hákonarsonar* shows that Sturla carried out the work in the spirit of his uncle Snorri. Like Eiríkr Oddsson's **Hryggjarstykki* and Karl Jónsson's *Sverris saga*, the content of *Hákonar saga* is based more or less on contemporary information, but, unlike the earlier sagas which contained little poetry, Sturla's *Hákonar saga* is full of stanzas from longer panegyrics, most of which were composed by himself or by members of his family. These stanzas were certainly not needed for historical verification; rather, Sturla, as well as his intended audience, must have felt that the accepted form of a king's saga was *prosimetrum*, and he therefore proudly inserted his own poetic works to be preserved for posterity.

SUMMARY AND CONCLUSION

Both eddic and skaldic poetry must have been well established in Scandinavian territory during the ninth century. The anonymous narrative eddic poetry, which related mythological and heroic lore, survived throughout the centuries in oral tradition, most likely for the purposes of entertainment, and was recorded in the thirteenth century as the result of a renewed interest in the pagan subject matter. That was also the case with the narrative skaldic poems with mythological content, which ceased to be productive as the result of the conversion to Christianity around the turn of the millennium. Although the conversion had a significant impact on skaldic diction in that mythological *kenningar* tended to be replaced by circumlocutions devoid of pagan imagery, skaldic poetry continued to be an integral part of Old Norse culture. Of particular importance were the tradition of royal encomia and the new genres of religious panegyrics, but there can be no doubt that, in Iceland, poetry of a personal character, such as commemorative poems and occasional poetry, continued to be composed throughout the centuries and fulfilled an important function in society.

Royal encomia and situational *lausavísur* which originally could have belonged to longer poems are transmitted in the *prosimetrum* of the kings' sagas and the Icelandic family sagas, and the contemporary sagas also contain *lausavísur* that function as comments on situations and as supplements to the narrative. Although the origin of *prosimetrum* is obscure, it would appear that prose narratives evolving around single stanzas or groups of stanzas were passed down in oral tradition (cf. the *þættir* in the kings' sagas). The royal panegyrics that chronicled the events in the lives of the kings of Norway were certainly known and recited in Iceland, and, from the recording of the *Oldest saga of St Óláfr* onwards, single stanzas from these panegyrics were incorporated into the prose and served as historical verification of the narrative. By the time Snorri compiled his *Heimskringla*, the *prosimetrum* that characterizes the kings' sagas was firmly established and this literary form not only emphasized the importance of the royal panegyrics, but also provided a model for such later, contemporary sagas as *Hákonar saga Hákonarsonar*. It could well be that the renewed importance that the royal panegyric acquired within the context of the *prosimetrum* in the kings' sagas breathed new life into this genre in the early thirteenth century.

The composition of royal panegyrics was closely connected with the social and financial status of the poets. Norwegian rulers, such as Haraldr hárfagri, Earl Hákon of Hlaðir, and Óláfr Haraldsson used poetry to further their own political ends, and they appear to have held their court poets in high esteem and rewarded them handsomely.

During the time of the Icelandic settlement the court poets were all Norwegian, but from the reign of Hákon of Hlaðir on there was a steady influx of Icelandic poets into the royal courts of Norway. These early Icelandic court poets clearly sought to gain fame and fortune abroad. Most of them returned to Iceland, and the lives of a number of them are recorded in the Icelandic family sagas. There can be no doubt that the stories of these skalds, which must have been passed down in oral tradition, served to reinforce and to maintain the importance of skaldic poetry in Icelandic society, and that the family sagas and the *þættir* of later Icelandic skalds who sought employment abroad ultimately became a vehicle for Icelandic nationalism.

The reality must have been a little different from the rosy picture painted by the Icelandic family sagas and the *þættir*. By the end of the eleventh century the trade of the court poet appears to have been in the hands of professional poets. The names recorded in *Skáldatal* show that foreign and Norwegian dignitaries continued to be eulogized in skaldic poetry, and, as *Sverris saga* shows (p. 91), poems detailing the lives of earlier kings were certainly recited at court as part of royal entertainment. But the fact remains that the identities of the majority of the poets are unknown, and furthermore, with the exception of the poetry by such prominent poets as Einarr Skúlason, very little of their poetic production survives. All indications are that by the middle of the twelfth century the composition of royal panegyrics was no longer an occupation that could or did enhance a poet's financial and social status very much, and it does not appear to have been an occupation that members of prominent Icelandic families found it profitable to engage in. Given this background the change that took place in the early thirteenth century is all the more remarkable.

There can be no doubt that there was a close connection between literary activity in late twelfth- and early thirteenth-century Iceland and the political developments that took place in society at this point, and that, at least for one faction in the political struggle for power, namely the Sturlung family, skaldic poetry became a very important tool indeed. The sagas of the Norwegian kings had established skaldic poetry as a valuable historical source, and Snorri's programmatic statement in the preface to the *Separate Saga of St Óláfr* shows that he was acutely aware of that circumstance. It is tempting see this statement as a conscious attempt on Snorri's part to draw the attention of his audience to the historical value of skaldic poetry and, indirectly, to himself as one of the main perpetuators of this literary tradition in medieval Iceland. As we have seen, the image of the court poet and the function of skaldic poetry presented in the kings' sagas and the family sagas furnished a social model for the budding Icelandic aristocracy. Members of the powerful families, the Sturlungar included, styled themselves in the manner of foreign royalty by having their deeds immortalized in skaldic panegyrics, and, like their countrymen of earlier centuries, they brought their own panegyrics to Norwegian dignitaries to obtain political advantages. This was especially the case as far as the members of the Sturlung family were concerned, and there can be no coincidence that the importance of skaldic poetry is brought to the forefront in the literary works attributed to the members of this family. In this respect, the circle is complete when Sturla Þórðarson shows up with a panegyric at Magnús lagabœtir's court in 1263 and, like his ancestor Egill Skalla-Grímsson in York three hundred years earlier, uses his poetry to restore himself to the king's good graces.

NOTES

1 For a good introduction to skaldic poetry, see Frank 1978. Frank 1985 and Harris 1985 give overviews of the state of the art of research on skaldic and eddic poetry. For the most recent discussion of the structure and metre of skaldic poetry, see Gade 1995. In the following, all quotations from Old Norse non-standardised texts have been normalised, and all translations from the Old Norse to English are my own.

2 For a complete edition of the poems in Codex Regius, see Neckel–Kuhn. An edition of the poems in eddic metres in legendary and mythic-heroic sagas is found in Heusler and Ranisch 1903.

3 *Vǫluspá* ('the Prophecy of the Seeress'), *Hávamál* ('the Sayings of the High One'), *Vafþrúðnismál* ('the Sayings of Vafþrúðnir'), *Grímnismál* ('the Sayings of Grímnir'), *Skírnismál* ('the Story of Skírnir'), *Hárbarðsljóð* ('the Lay of Hárbarðr'), *Hymiskviða* ('the Poem about Hymir'), *Lokasenna* ('the Flyting of Loki'), *Þrymskviða* ('the Poem about Þrymr'), and *Alvíssmál* ('the Sayings of Alvíss'). The status of *Vǫlundarkviða* ('the Poem about Vǫlundr') is problematic, but has been included here among the mythological poems. For the most recent editions, translations, and commentaries on the mythological eddic poems, see von See *et al.* 1997–, II (*Skírnismál, Hárbarðsljóð,*

Hymiskviða, Lokasenna, Þrymskviða), and Dronke 1969–97, II (*Vǫluspá, Rígsþula, Vǫlundarkviða, Lokasenna, Skírnismál*).

4 *Helgakviða Hundingsbana* I–II, *Helgakviða Hjǫrvarðssonar*.

5 *Grípisspá* ('Grípir's Prophecy'), *Reginsmál* ('the Story of Reginn'), *Fáfnismál* ('the Story of Fáfnir'), *Sigrdrífumál* ('the Sayings of Sigdrífa'), *Brot af Sigurðarkviðu* ('Fragment of the Poem about Sigurðr'), *Guðrúnarkviða* I–III ('the Poem about Guðrún I–III'), *Sigurðarkviða in skamma* ('the Short Poem about Sigurðr'), *Helreið Brynhildar* ('Brynhildr's Journey to Hel'), *Oddrúnargrátr* ('Oddrún's Lament').

6 *Atlakviða* ('the Poem about Atli'), *Atlamál* ('the Story of Atli'), *Guðrúnarhvǫt* ('Guðrún's Incitement'), *Hamðismál* ('the Story of Hamðir'). For an English edition, translation, and commentary on some of the heroic poems, see Dronke 1969–97, vol. I (*Atlakviða, Atlamál, Guðrúnarhvǫt, Hamðismál*).

7 For a brief overview of the heroic eddic poems and their Germanic antecedents, see Hallberg 1975: 60–103. For further readings on eddic poetry, see Glendinning and Bessason 1983.

8 See the verbal echoes in *Hákonarmál* 21:1–2 and *Hávamál* 76:1–2, 77:1–2 (*Skj* IA: 68; Neckel–Kuhn 1962: 29); *Þorfinnsdrápa* 24:1–2 and *Vǫluspá* 57:1–2 (*Skj* IA: 348; Neckel–Kuhn 1962: 13); *Haraldsdrápa* 2:2–3 and *Fáfnismál* 27:4 (*Skj* IA: 384; Neckel–Kuhn 1962: 185).

9 For an overview of the number of stanzas contained in these sagas and compilations, see Fidjestøl 1982: 19–31. See also Meulengracht Sørensen forthcoming. A detailed introduction to the kings' sagas and scholarship on the kings' sagas is given in Andersson 1985.

10 Comparable poetic statements to the effect that a deceased person's memory would last as long as the stone and the runes endure are found in Swedish runic inscriptions (see Musset 1965: 414, 426).

11 According to Snorri, *Ynglingatal* was originally composed in honour of Haraldr's uncle, Rǫgnvaldr heiðumhárr ('High in Glory') of Vestfold (*ÍF* 26: 4, 83).

12 An overview of eddic and skaldic metres and their structural peculiarities is given in Snorri's *Háttatal* (Faulkes 1991).

13 Poetry has survived from the following kings after 1000: Óláfr Haraldsson (d. 1030), Magnús Óláfsson (d. 1047), Haraldr Sigurðarson (d. 1066), Magnús berfœttr (d. 1103), Sigurðr jórsalafari (d. 1130), Sigurðr slembir (d. 1139) (*Skj* IA: 220–3, 330, 356–61, 432–3, 454–5, 495). In addition stanzas are attributed to two Norwegian dignitaries, Steigar-Þórir and Ingimarr af Aski (*Skj* IA: 434, 494). Earl Rǫgnvaldr kali of Orkney (d. 1159) was also an accomplished poet (*Skj* IA: 505–28), and poetry has been attributed to Bjarni Kolbeinsson (d. 1222), bishop of Orkney (*Skj* IIA: 1–10).

14 *Landnámabók* also mentions that Þorgils orraskáld, son of Þorbjǫrn svarti, stayed with Óláfr kvaran (938–80) in Dublin (*ÍF* 1: 71). Þorgils's identity is unknown.

15 In the light of the Norwegian skaldic poetry from the twelfth and thirteenth centuries that has surfaced in the runic inscriptions from the Bryggen excavations in Bergen, it is tempting to speculate that some of the unidentified poets from the eleventh, twelfth, and thirteenth centuries could have been Norwegian. For the most recent discussion of these inscriptions, see Marold 1998.

16 See Guðrún Nordal forthcoming, especially ch. 5, 'The Profession of the Skald,' which offers the the most detailed discussion to date of Icelandic skalds of the thirteenth century, focussing on their social status, educational background, family relations, and occupation. I am grateful to the author for making the MS available to me and for giving me permission to quote her work.

REFERENCES

Abbreviations

BGDSL (T) *Beiträge zur Geschichte der deutschen Sprache und Literatur* [Tübingen]

Flat III Vigfússon and Unger 1860–6a

ÍF 1 Benediktsson 1968a
   Benediktsson 1968b

ÍF 2 Nordal 1933

ÍF 3 Nordal and Jónsson 1938a
   Nordal, Sigurður and Jónsson, Guðni (eds.) 1938b

ÍF 5 Sveinsson 1934

ÍF 6 Þórólfsson and Jónsson 1958a
   Þórólfsson and Jónsson 1958b

ÍF 8 Sveinsson 1939a
   Sveinsson 1939b

ÍF 26–28 Aðalbjarnason 1941–51

ÍF 29 Einarsson 1984a
   Einarsson (ed.) 1984b

ÍF 35 Guðnason 1982

MHN Storm 1880

MScan Mediaeval Scandinavia

Msk Jónsson 1928–32

Neckel–Kuhn Neckel 1962

ÓSH Johnsen and Helgason 1941

Skj I–IIA Jónsson 1912–15

SnE I–III Sigurðsson *et al.* 1848

SS Scandinavian Studies

Sturl I–II Vigfusson 1878

Primary literature

Aðalbjarnarson, Bjarni (ed.) 1941–51, *Heimskringla*. 3 vols. Íslenzk fornrit, 26–8. Reykjavík: Hið íslenzka fornritafélag.

Benediktsson, Jakob (ed.) 1968a, *Íslendingabók*. In: *Íslendingabók. Landnámabók*. Íslenzk fornrit, I1. Reykjavík: Hið íslenzka fornritafélag, pp. 1–28.

(ed.) 1968b, *Landnámabók*. In: *Íslendingabók. Landnámabók*. Íslenzk fornrit, I1 & 2. Reykjavík: Hið íslenzka fornritafélag, pp. 29–397.

Dronke, Ursula (ed.) 1969–97, *The Poetic Edda*, I: *Heroic Poems*; II: *Mythological Poems*. Oxford: Clarendon.

Einarsson, Bjarni (ed.) 1984a, *Ágrip af Nóregskonunga sǫgum*. Íslenzk fornrit, 29. Reykjavík: Hið íslenzka fornritafélag, pp. 1–54.

(ed.) 1984b, *Fagrskinna – Nóregs konunga tal*. Íslenzk fornrit, 29. Reykjavík: Hið íslenzka fornritafélag, pp. 55–373.

Faulkes, Anthony (ed.) 1991, *Snorri Sturluson. Edda. Háttatal*. Oxford: Clarendon.

Guðnason, Bjarni (ed.) 1982, *Knýtlinga saga*. In: *Danakonunga sǫgur*. Íslenzk fornrit, 35. Reykjavík: Hið íslenzka fornritafélag, pp. 91–321.

Indrebø, Gustav (ed.) 1920, *Sverris saga etter Cod. AM 327 4o*. [Rpt. Oslo: Norsk historisk kjeldeskrift-institutt, 1981.]

Johnsen, Oscar Albert and Helgason, Jón (eds.) 1941, *Saga Óláfs konungs hins helga: Den store saga om Olav den Hellige efter pergamenthåndskrift i Kungliga Biblioteket i Stockhom nr. 2 4to med varianter fra andre håndskrifter*. 2 vols. Oslo: Kjeldeskriftfondet.

Jónsson, Finnur (ed.) 1912–15, *Den norsk–islandske skjaldedigtning*. IA–IIA: *Tekst efter håndskrifterne*. [Rpt. Copenhagen: Rosenkilde and Bagger, 1967–73.]

(ed.) 1928–32, *Morkinskinna*. Samfund til udgivelse af gammel nordisk litteratur, 53. Copenhagen: J. Jørgensen.

Magerøy, Hallvard (ed.) 1988, *Bǫglunga sǫgur*. 2 vols. Oslo: Solum forlag og Kjeldeskriftfondet.

Neckel, Gustav (ed.) 1962 (4th rev. ed. by Kuhn, Hans), *Edda: Die Lieder des Codex Regius nebst verwandten Denkmälern*, I: *Text*. Heidelberg: Carl Winter Universitätsverlag.

Nordal, Sigurður (ed.) 1933, *Egils saga Skalla-Grímssonar*. Íslenzk fornrit, 2. Reykjavík: Hið íslenzka fornritafélag.

Nordal, Sigurður and Jónsson, Guðni (eds.) 1938a, *Bjarnar saga Hítdœlakappa*. In: *Borgfirðinga sǫgur*. Íslenzk fornrit, 3. Reykjavík: Hið íslenzka fornritafélag, pp. 109–212.

(eds.) 1938b, *Gunnlaugs saga ormstungu*. In: *Borgfirðinga sǫgur*. Íslenzk fornit, 3. Reykjavík: Hið íslenzka fornritafélag, pp. 49–108.

Sigurðsson, Jón *et al.* (eds.) 1848, *Edda Snorra Sturlusonar. Edda Snorronis Sturlæi*. 3 vols. [Rpt. Osnabrück: Zeller, 1966.]

Storm, Gustav (ed.) 1880, *Theodrici Monachi Historia de Antiquitate Regum*

Norwagiensium. In: *Monumenta Historica Norvegiae: Latinske kildeskrifter til Norges historie i middelalderen.* [Rpt. Oslo: Aas and Wahl boktrykkeri a.s, 1973, pp. 1–68.]

Sveinsson, Einar Ólafur (ed.) 1934, *Laxdœla saga.* Íslenzk fornrit, 5. Reykjavík: Hið íslenzka fornritafélag.

(ed.) 1939a, *Hallfreðar saga.* In: *Vatnsdœla saga.* Íslenzk fornrit, 8. Reykjavík: Hið íslenzka fornritafélag, pp. 133–200.

(ed.) 1939b, *Kormáks saga.* In: *Vatnsdœla saga.* Íslenzk fornrit, 8. Reykjavík: Hið íslenzka fornritafélag, pp. 201–302.

Vigfússon, Gudbrand (ed.) 1878, *Sturlunga saga, Including the Islendinga Saga of Lawman Sturla Thordsson and Other Works.* 2 vols. Oxford: Clarendon.

Vigfússon, Guðbrandur and Unger, C. R. (eds.) 1860–68a, *Flateyjarbók: En samling af norske konge-sagaer med indskudte mindre fortællinger om begiven-heder i og udenfor Norge samt annaler.* 3 vols. Oslo: Malling.

(eds.) 1860–68b, *Hákonar saga Hákonarsonar.* In: *Flateyjarbók: En samling af norske konge-sagaer med indskudte mindre fortællinger om begivenheder i og udenfor Norge samt annaler.* 3 vols. Oslo: Malling, III, pp. 1–233.

Þórólfsson, Björn K. and Jónsson, Guðni (eds.) 1958a, *Fóstbrœðrasaga.* In: *Vestfirðingasǫgur.* Íslenzk fornrit, 6. Reykjavík: Hið íslenzka fornritafélag, pp. 119–276.

(eds.) 1958b, *Þáttr Þormóðar,* In: *Vestfirðingasǫgur.* Íslenzk fornrit, 6. Reykjavík: Hið íslenzka fornritafélag, pp. 277–88.

Secondary literature

Aðalbjarnarson, Bjarni 1937, *Om de norske kongesagaer.* Skrifter utgitt av det norske videnskaps-akademi i Oslo II. Hist.-filos. klasse, 1936, no. 4. Oslo: Jacob Dybwad.

Andersson, Theodore M. 1985, 'Kings' Sagas (*Konungasögur*)', in Clover, Carol J. and Lindow, John (eds.), *Old Norse–Icelandic Studies: an Introduction.* Islandica, 45. Ithaca and London: Cornell University Press, pp. 197–238.

Clunies Ross, Margaret 1981, 'An Interpretation of the Myth of Þórr's Encounter with Geirrøðr and his Daughters', in Dronke, Ursula, Helgadóttir, Guðrun, Weber, Gerd Wolfgang and Bekker-Nielsen, Hans (eds.), *Speculum norrœnum: Norse Studies in Memory of Gabriel Turville-Petre.* Odense: Odense University Press, pp. 370–91.

forthcoming, 'Defining the Genre of the *Skáld* Saga', in Poole, Russell (ed.), *The Skald Sagas: Poetry and Poetic Identity in Medieval Scandinavian Society.*

Einarsson, Bjarni 1974, 'On the Rôle of Verse in Saga-Literature', *MScan* 7: 118–25.

Fidjestøl, Bjarne 1982, *Det norrøne fyrstediktet.* Universitetet i Bergen Nordisk institutts skriftserie, 11. Øvre Ervik: Alvheim and Eide akademisk forlag.

Frank, Roberta 1978, *Old Norse Court Poetry: the Dróttkvætt Stanza*. Islandica, 42. Ithaca and London: Cornell University Press.

1981, 'Snorri and the Mead of Poetry', in Dronke, Ursula, Helgadóttir, Guðrun, Weber, Gerd Wolfgang and Bekker-Nielsen, Hans (eds.), *Speculum norrænum: Norse Studies in Memory of Gabriel Turville-Petre*. Odense, Odense University Press, pp. 155–70.

1985, 'Skaldic Poetry', in Clover, Carol J. and Lindow, John (eds.), *Old Norse–Icelandic Studies: an Introduction*. Islandica, 45. Ithaca and London: Cornell University Press, pp. 157–96.

Gade, Kari Ellen 1995, *The Structure of Old Norse* dróttkvætt *Poetry*. Islandica, 49. Ithaca and London: Cornell University Press.

forthcoming, 'Age and Authenticity of the *lausavísur* in the Skald Sagas', in Poole, Russell (ed.), *The Skald Sagas: Poetry and Poetic Identity in Medieval Scandinavian Society*.

Glendinning, Robert J. and Haraldur Bessason (eds.) 1983, *Edda: a Collection of Essays*. University of Manitoba Icelandic Studies. Winnipeg: University of Manitoba Press.

Guðnason, Bjarni 1978, *Fyrsta sagan*. Studia Islandica, 37. Reykjavík: Bókaútgáfa menningarsjóðs.

Hallberg, Peter 1975, *Old Icelandic Poetry: Eddic Lay and Skaldic Verse* (trans. Paul Schach and Sonja Lindgrenson). Lincoln and London: University of Nebraska Press.

Harris, Joseph 1985, 'Eddic Poetry', in Clover, Carol J. and Lindow, John (eds.), *Old Norse–Icelandic Studies: an Introduction*. Islandica, 45. Ithaca and London: Cornell University Press, pp. 68–156.

Heusler, Andreas and Ranisch, Wilhelm 1903, *Eddica Minora: Dichtung eddischer Art aus den Fornaldarsögur und anderen Prosawerken*. Dortmund: Ruhfus.

Hofmann, Dietrich 1978–79, 'Sagaprosa als Partner von Skaldenstrophen', *MScan* 11: 68–81.

Jónsson, Finnur 1894–1901, *Den oldnorske og oldislandske litteraturs historie*. 2 vols. Copenhagen: Gad.

Kristjánsson, Jónas 1972, *Um Fóstbræðrasögu*. Reykjavík: Stofnun Árna Magnússonar.

1976, 'The Legendary Saga', in Kolbeinsson, Guðni *et al.* (eds.), *Minjar ok menntir: Afmælisrit helgað Kristjáni Eldjárn: 6 desember 1976*. Reykjavík: Bókaútgáfa menningarsjóðs, pp. 281–93.

1990, 'Stages in the Compositions of Eddic Poetry', in Pàroli, Teresa (ed.), *Atti del 12. Congresso Internationale di Studi sull' Alto Medioevo: Poetry in the Scandianvian Middle Ages*. The Seventh International Saga Conference. Spoleto: Centro Italiano di Studi sull' Alto Medioevo, pp. 201–18.

Lange, Wolfgang 1958, *Studien zur christlichen Dichtung der Nordgermanen 1000–1200*. Palaestra, 222. Göttingen: Vandenhoeck and Ruprecht.

Louis-Jensen, Jonna 1970, ' "Syvende og ottende brudstykke": Fragmentet AM 325 IV a 4to.', *Opuscula* 4. Bibliotheca Arnamagnæana, 30. Copenhagen: Munksgaard, pp. 31–60.

Marold, Edith 1990, 'Skaldendichtung und Mythologie', in Paroli, Teresa (ed.), *Atti del 12. Congresso Internationale di Studi sull' Alto Medioevo*: *Poetry in the Scandianvian Middle Ages*. The Seventh International Saga Conference. Spoleto: Centro Italiano di Studi sull' Alto Medioevo, pp. 107–30.

1998, 'Runeninschriften als Quelle zur Geschichte der Skaldendichtung', in Düwel, Klaus (ed.), *Runeninschriften als Quellen interdisziplinärer Forschung*. Reallexikon der germanischen Altertumskunde, Ergänzungsband, 15. Berlin and New York: de Gruyter, pp. 667–93.

Meulengracht Sørensen, Preben forthcoming, 'Archaeology of Verses', in Poole, Russell (ed.), *The Skald Sagas*: *Poetry and Poetic Identity in Medieval Scandinavian Society*.

Musset, Lucien 1965, *Introduction à la runologie*. Paris: Aubier-Montaigne.

Nordal, Guðrún forthcoming, *Tools of Literacy: the Role of Skaldic Verse in Icelandic Textual Culture of the Twelfth and Thirteenth Centuries*.

Nordal, Sigurður 1914, *Om Olaf den helliges saga*: *En kritisk undersøgelse*. Copenhagen: Gad.

Poole, Russell G. 1975, *Skaldic Poetry in the Sagas: The Origins, Authorship, Genre, and Style of Some Saga Lausavísur*. Dissertation, University of Toronto.

1985, 'The Origins of the *Máhlíðingavísur*'. *SS* 57: 244–85.

1991, *Viking Poems on War and Peace: a Study in Skaldic Narrative*. Toronto Medieval Texts and Translations, 8. Toronto and Buffalo: University of Toronto Press.

See, Klaus von 1968, 'Skothending: Bemerkungen zur Frühgeschichte des skaldischen Binnenreims', *BGDSL* (T) 90: 217–22.

1977, 'Skaldenstrophe und Sagaprosa: Ein Beitrag zum Problem der mündlichen Überlieferung in der altnordischen Prosa', *MScan* 10: 461–85.

See, Klaus von, La Farge, Beatrice, Picard, Eve, Prieba, Ilona and Schulz, Katja 1997–, *Kommentar zu den Liedern der Edda*. 6 projected vols. II: *Götterlieder* (only vol. in print) Heidelberg: Universitätsverlag Carl Winter.

Steblin-Kamenskij, M. I. 1973, *The Saga Mind* (trans. Kenneth Ober). Odense: Odense University Press.

Storm, Gustav 1893, *Otte brudstykker af Den Ældste Saga om Olav den hellige*. Christiania [Oslo]: Grøndahl and søns bogtrykkeri.

Ström, Folke 1981, 'Poetry as an Instrument of Propaganda: Jarl Hákon and his Poets', in Dronke, Ursula, Helgadóttir, Guðrun and Weber, Gerd Wolfgang (eds.), *Speculum norrænum*: *Norse Studies in Memory of Gabriel Turville-Petre*. Odense: Odense University Press, pp. 44–58.

Whaley, Diana forthcoming, 'Troublesome Poets at the Courts of Scandinavia', in Poole, Russell (ed.), *The Skald Sagas*: *Poetry and Poetic Identity in Medieval Scandinavian Society*.

4

Óláfr Þórðarson hvítaskáld and oral poetry in the west of Iceland *c.* 1250: the evidence of references to poetry in *The Third Grammatical Treatise*[1]

GÍSLI SIGURÐSSON

How much did a literary enthusiast in Iceland know of skaldic poetry around the middle of the thirteenth century? Who were his favourite authors? Where did they come from? How wide was his literary horizon? The problem with these questions, as with so many others, is that we have no straightforward answers to them. We all know that direct references and field reports about the oral literary tradition of thirteenth-century Iceland have been severely lacking for quite some time now.

In order to make up for this loss I have tried to squeeze indirect evidence out of *The Third Grammatical Treatise* in Codex Wormianus (AM 242 folio, a compilation from the second half of the fourteenth century), sometimes known as *Málskrúðsfræði*, by Óláfr Þórðarson hvítaskáld (1210/12–59)[2], the older brother of Sturla Þórðarson (1214–84) and nephew of Snorri Sturluson (1178/9–1241), both of whom were law speakers, poets and prominent writers of historical and mythological material. All three belonged to the so-called Sturlung family, one of the two most powerful families in thirteenth-century Iceland, alternating the post of law speaker with the so-called Hauk-dælir who were less literary but had closer links with the bishops than the Sturlungs did (Sigurðsson 1994). The Sturlungs originated in the west of Iceland but were expanding their power in the early thirteenth century when one member of the family established himself in the north around the Eyjafjörður region.

Óláfr's treatise is divided into two sections, on grammar and rhetoric, drawing mostly on Priscian and Donatus but also demonstrating sound knowledge of the Norse runes, which Óláfr shows to be inferior to Latin letters for the purpose of expressing the various sounds in Icelandic. He also reveals a considerable familiarity with skaldic poetry, examples of which are used in order to explain the terminology of classical rhetoric about the principal figures of speech.

Óláfr appears in the major contemporary source about his lifetime, *Sturlunga saga*, as well as *Hákonar saga* and *Knýtlinga saga*. He was born around 1210–12 and was present at many of the most dramatic moments of his age. In 1237 he travelled abroad with his uncle Snorri and performed as a poet at the royal courts of Norway, Sweden and Denmark. Back in Iceland in the early 1240s he settled down as a writer and sub-deacon in Stafaholt, Borgarfjörður in the west of the country, where he is believed to have taught priests. He was also held in such high esteem that he was elected as a law speaker for a few years around 1250, shortly before he died in 1259.

Óláfr is often thought to have written *Knýtlinga saga* about the kings of Denmark based on the model of *Heimskringla*, which Snorri Sturluson wrote about the Norwegian kings (Guðnason 1982: clxxix–clxxxiv), and even *Laxdæla saga* (Hallberg 1963), a family saga from his own family region – even though others have expressed their doubts (Allén 1971; Thorsson 1994). Apart from these written works some of his poetry is preserved about King Hákon the Old in Norway and his rival Skúli, an Icelandic friend Aron Hjǫrleifsson and Thomas à Becket, whereas all is lost of what the sources tell us that he composed about Earl Knútr Hákonarson, Eiríkr king of the Swedes, Valdimar the old king of the Danes and the Icelandic saint Þorlákr, bishop of Skálholt. Because of Óláfr's family background and his prolific literary activities he can thus serve as a prime example of a learned man and a trained oral poet in the traditional art of the skalds. Table 4.1 summarizes the main known events of Óláfr's life.

It is believed that Óláfr wrote his *Málskrúðsfræði* shortly after his return to Iceland from abroad. This work has not been at the centre of attention in the continuing debate on the contribution of the oral versus the written to medieval literature in Iceland. Rather it has been used as a prime example of the high status of Latin learning, in which a member of the Sturlung family shows his full command of Donatus's teachings. The focus of attention has thus been on finding out which Latin sources

Table 4.1. *Chronology of events in the life of Óláfr Þórðarson hvítaskáld, based on* Sturlunga saga, Hákonar saga *and* Knýtlinga saga

1226	present at Yule-feast held by his uncle Snorri in Reykholt in the west
1227	(summer) promoter of peace by his father Þórðr in Hvammur in the west, when Þórðr's nephew Sturla Sighvatsson arrives in a militant mood
1234	Óláfr (and his brother Sturla) struggle with Órækja, son of Snorri Sturluson
1236	moves his farm at Snorri's advice from his father's estate in Hvammur to Borg on Mýrar, further south in the west and closer to Snorri
1237	(spring) inherits from his father and composes a *drápa* about Saint Þorlákr. Is present at the battle at Bær (*Bæjarbardagi*) and during the summer he flees to Norway with his uncle Snorri, in order to escape the fury of Sturla Sighvatsson. They are accompanied by Þórðr kakali
1239	Óláfr is with Skúli when Snorri leaves for Iceland, and composes a verse about his ship
1240	after the battle at Láka, Óláfr is with King Hákon and has by then probably spent some time in Sweden and composed poetry about King Eiríkr
1240–41?	was with King Valdimar I, king of the Danes, and was greatly honoured by him
1248	Þórðr kakali has Óláfr elected law speaker. From indirect evidence it may be deduced that he returned to Iceland somewhere between 1242 and 1245 as he is not present when Sturla and Órækja are arrested by the bridge on Hvítá in 1242 but in 1245 he has told his relatives about his stay in Denmark (Ólsen 1884)
1250	Sturla Þórðarson becomes law speaker after Óláfr
1253	Óláfr becomes law speaker again but steps down the same year *fyrir vanheilsu sakir* ('because of his bad health')

Óláfr may have used and how he interpreted them (Ólsen 1884; Collings 1967; Raschellà 1983; Albano Leoni 1985–86; Tómasson *et al.* 1992: 529–32). His section on grammar has been scrutinized (Micillo 1993), Árnason (1993) has discussed pitch in Old Icelandic in view of Óláfr's evidence, Ólsen (1884) and Raschellà (1994) have looked into the origins of the chapter on runes and Tómasson (1993) has analysed the prefaces to the grammatical treatises in the Codex Wormianus.

What concerns us here, however, is that Óláfr uses references to secular native skaldic poetry as examples to explain the concepts he is introducing to his readers. The possible source value of these skaldic examples has not received much attention from scholars.[3] It is not implausible to assume that Óláfr's selection of examples might reveal his knowledge of and taste in the poetry that was known to him and his contemporaries, and which he also expected of his readers, the students. It has been observed by Finnur Jónsson (1923: 924), without any further commentary, that Óláfr cites poetry from all ages of Icelandic history, by both Norwegian and Icelandic poets. His examples may serve as evidence for systematic thinking about the art of poetry at an oral stage before the advancement of Latin learning (Raschellà 1983: 293, 298) but their source value has nevertheless escaped scholars, as can be seen from this reference in a recent literary history: *Einstaka vísur eru og hvergi til annars staðar* ('A few of the verses are not found elsewhere') (Tómasson 1992: 531). A simple counting of the lines cited by Óláfr reveals that about two thirds of them are not to be found in other sources.[4]

In spite of scholars' lack of interest in the indigenous verses cited by Óláfr, this poetry deserves a specific study. It is to be expected that, when Óláfr cites stanzas and poetic fragments by named poets without any further identification, he expects his readers or audience to be familiar with them – assuming of course that Óláfr's work was written for students who were reasonably well informed and knowledgeable about poetry up to the point that can be expected from beginners in advanced formal education (the whole treatise is written in such a way that it assumes prior knowledge among its readers or audience of both runes and skaldic poetry). Óláfr's examples may therefore be used to draw up a map of the poetic environment of a learned and travelled poet in the west of Iceland in the midst of what we believe to have been the golden age of saga writing. Who were the poets that are so close to his heart that he cites them as examples to explain his learned Latin terminology? Where did they come from and how did Óláfr learn this poetry? Did he take it from written works or was he familiar with it from his oral training? By scrutinizing the actual examples we can perhaps approach some answers to the questions introduced at the beginning of this chapter.

Óláfr names 34 poets and refers to 123 examples of poetry in his treatise, 354 lines in all. Most of these contain a fragment of a stanza, but seven

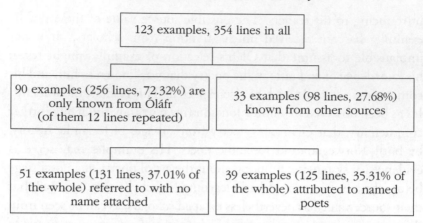

Figure 4.1 Classification of examples from *The Third Grammatical Treatise*

stanzas are quoted in full, one of which is repeated once. If we try to classify these examples according to what we know about them from other sources the following picture emerges (figure 4.1).

Our next question is: Where did Óláfr get his examples from? There are at least four possible channels:

1 From written sources;
2 From oral tradition;
3 Óláfr composed them himself;
4 They were translated or adapted from Latin.

If Óláfr composed some of his examples himself, these are most likely to be found amongst the fifty-one examples that are both unknown from other sources and referred to without a name attached to them. About this group very little can therefore be said.

Next we may look at the thirty-three examples which are known from other sources. These are cited by Óláfr in the manner set out in table 4.2. If we make a list of the works in which these stanzas and fragments can be found it becomes clear that most of the works were either written before Óláfr wrote his treatise or else they are of such a nature that they could have existed as separate works at an oral stage (that is *Gátur Gestumblinda*, *Grímnismál* and *Arinbjarnarkviða*). It is of particular interest that the stanzas which also appear in *Bjarnar saga*

Table 4.2. *References in* The Third Grammatical Treatise *to stanzas that are also known from other sources*

'sem Snorri kvað' ('as Snorri composed')
2 lines (from *Háttatal* 83)

'sem hér' ('as here'): 1 line (from a stanza by Þormóðr Kolbrúnarskáld, *in Fóstbrœðra saga* but not in *Heimskringla*)

'sem Egill kvað' ('as Egill composed'):
8 lines (*Arinbjarnarkviða* 16)

'sem kvað Hárekr í Þjóttu' ('as Hárekr in Þjótta composed')
2 lines (*Óláfs saga helga* refers to him as Hárekr Eyvindarson)

'sem Glúmr kvað' ('as Glúmr composed')
4 lines (Geirason, *Gráfeldardrápa* in *Heimskringla*)

'sem hér' ('as here'): 2 lines (said to be by Bjǫrn hítdœlakappi in his saga)

'sem hér' ('as here'): 2 lines (by Einarr, from *Vellekla* in *Heimskringla*)

'sem Eyvindr kvað' ('as Eyvindr composed')
2 lines (that is *skáldaspillir*, in *Heimskringla*)

'sem Arnórr kvað' ('as Arnórr composed')
2 lines (from *Hrynhenda* about King Magnús in *Morkinskinna*)

'sem kvað Halldór skvaldri' ('as Halldór skvaldri composed')
4 lines (from *Útfarardrápa* ?)

'sem Sighvatr kvað' ('as Sighvatr composed')
1 line (from *Nesjavísur*, in *Fagrskinna*)

'sem Snorri kvað' ('as Snorri composed')
2 lines (from *Háttatal* 28)

'sem Bjǫrn kvað' ('as Bjǫrn composed')
2 lines (by Hólmgǫngu-Bersi in *Kormaks saga*)

'sem Sighvatr kvað' ('as Sighvatr composed')
1 line (Þórðarson, in *Heimskringla*)

'sem Snorri kvað' ('as Snorri composed')
3 lines (from *Háttatal* 15–16)

'sem hér' ('as here')
4 lines (from *Háttatal* 40)

'sem Snorri kvað' ('as Snorri composed')
4 lines (from *Háttatal* 73)

'sem Hallfreðr kvað' ('as Hallfreðr composed')
2 lines (in *Heimskringla*, not in *Hallfreðar saga*)

'sem kveðið er í Grímnismálum' ('as is recited in *Grímnismál*')
2 lines (from *Grímnismál* 47)

'sem Máni kvað' ('as Máni composed')
4 lines (in *Skáldskaparmál*)

'sem Eyvindr kvað' ('as Eyvindr composed')
4 lines (from *Háleygjatal*, in *Heimskringla*)

'sem Markús kvað' ('as Markús composed')
2 lines (Skeggjason, in *Snorra Edda*)

'sem Ormr Steinþórsson kvað' ('as Ormr Steinþórsson composed')
2 lines (in *Snorra Edda*)

'sem Snorri kvað' ('as Snorri composed)
2 lines (from *Háttatal* 5, not in W)

'enn sem Snorri kvað' ('again as Snorri composed')
2 lines (from *Háttatal* 5, not in W) 'sem hér' ('as here')
4 lines (by Þórðr Kolbeinsson, in *Heimskringla*)

'sem hér er kveðið' ('as is composed here')
4 lines (in *Snorra Edda*)

sem hér' ('as here')
1 line (by Earl Gilli in *Njáls saga* about the Battle of Clontarf in 1014)

'sem Sighvatr kvað' ('as Sighvatr composed')
4 lines (from *Bersǫglisvísur* in *Heimskringla*)

'sem Einarr kvað' ('as Einarr composed')
4 lines (Skúlason, from *Geisli* 1)

'sem hér' ('as here')
3 lines (from *Gátur Gestumblinda*)

'sem Egill kvað' ('as Egill composed')
4 lines (in *Egils saga*)

'sem Snorri kvað' ('as Snorri composed')
8 lines (in the saga of King Hákon)

Table 4.3. *Works containing stanzas which are referred to in* The Third Grammatical Treatise

WRITTEN WORKS	ORAL WORKS?	UNCERTAIN SOURCES?
Snorra Edda	*Arinbjarnarkviða*	*Bjarnar saga hítdælakappa*
Heimskringla	*Grímnismál*	(referred to by Óláfr
*Older Morkinskinna	*Geisli*	without a named author
Fagrskinna	*Gátur Gestumblinda*	but attributed to Bjǫrn in
Egils saga		the saga)
Snorri Sturluson's poetry		*Fóstbrœðra saga*
in *Hákonar saga*		(referred to by Óláfr
*Brjáns saga		without a named author
		but attributed to Þormóðr
		in the saga)
		Kormaks saga
		(attributed to Bjǫrn by
		Óláfr but to Hólmgǫngu-
		Bersi in the saga)

hítdælakappa and *Kormaks saga* are not attributed to the same authors there as by Óláfr. This inconsistency might suggest that Óláfr learned these verses orally rather than from a written book. The works known to Óláfr are thus classifiable into three kinds, written, oral and uncertain, as table 4.3 demonstrates.

Table 4.3 confirms our ideas that the kings' sagas in *Fagrskinna*, *Morkinskinna* and *Heimskringla*, along with *Egils saga* and *Snorra Edda*, all existed in written form in the first half of the thirteenth century. *Hákonar saga*, by Óláfr's brother Sturla, was not written until later but it is only natural that Óláfr knew Snorri's poetry, which was to be included in the work later. On the whole the list in table 4.3 is an indication of the written works and poems that were known to a learned Icelander in Borgarfjörður in the west of Iceland around the middle of the thirteenth century. We have here the works of Snorri Sturluson as well as the sources which Snorri had access to when writing *Heimskringla*. Óláfr had therefore read all the most recent literature in Borgarfjörður, but he does not seem to have known much from other parts of the country – except for *Morkinskinna* which may have been written in Eyjafjörður where Snorri's brother, Sighvatr, moved in 1215 (Andersson 1993).

The only known poet from the *Íslendingasögur* referred to by name in Óláfr's treatise is Egill – which might be an indication that he did not know more poets from the sagas by name. That again might be of significance to the recent discussion about *Egils saga* possibly being one of the first of the written *Íslendinga sögur*, compiled by Snorri during the last years of his life (see Kristjánsson 1990; Hafstað 1990 and Ólason 1991).

The examples from *Fóstbrœðra saga* and *Bjarnar saga* are curious however: either Óláfr did not know the authors (because he learned the stanzas from oral tradition), or else he thought the verse-samples were too well known to need an attribution (like the examples which are also known from *Vellekla*, *Háttatal*, *Heimskringla*, *Brjáns saga and *Gátur Gestumblinda*, but which Óláfr does not attribute to a named author). If they were so well known, that would indicate that Óláfr knew more poets from the *Íslendinga sögur* than just Egill, either from books or from oral tradition. But as so many of the works on this list already existed in writing or as separate oral works, it seems likely that the examples from *Fóstbrœðra saga* and *Bjarnar saga* could be used to question the arguments put forward by Kristjánsson 1972: 292–310 and Guðnason 1994 that these two sagas are much younger than an earlier generation of scholars thought. Or we could use the opportunity to reconsider the commonly held idea that a saga did not exist unless it was written.

Turning now to the 90 examples with 256 lines which are *not known* to us from other sources, these are introduced by Óláfr with the formulae that are set out in table 4.4.

In these references Óláfr mentions three poems which are otherwise unknown:

*Hafliðamál (could be about Hafliða Másson, according to Jónsson 1912–15);
*Bjúgar vísur;
*Kúgadrápa (Kúgi is a character in *Orkneyinga saga*).

Óláfr mentions a number of the lines or stanzas, listed in table 4.4 as unknown elswehere, as the work of named poets. Table 4.5 lists the

Table 4.4 *References in* The Third Grammatical Treatise *to stanzas that are* not known *from other sources*

'sem kvað Auðunn illskælda' ('as Auðunn illskælda composed'): four lines, one other stanza preserved in a *þáttr* about the poets of King Haraldr hárfagri in the saga of Óláfr Tryggvason. Jónsson (1912–15) says he is a Norwegian poet from the ninth century.

'sem Arnórr kvað' ('as Arnórr composed'): one line (*jarlaskáld*). Much is preserved by this skald (Whaley 1998), composing in the latter half of the eleventh century about earls and kings, Magnús the Good and Haraldr harðráði. Arnórr was from Hítarnes in Hnappadalssýsla in the west. There is a *þáttr* about him in *Morkinskinna*.

'sem hér' ('as here'): two lines with mythological content (that is the kenning *Brynhildar bróðir*).

'sem kvað Eilífr Guðrúnarson' ('as Eilífr Guðrúnarson composed'): four lines. Jónsson (1912–15) attributes them to Eilífr *kúlnasveinn*, a twelfth-century Icelander and author of *Kristsdrápa*). Eilífr Goðrúnarson is also said to be of Icelandic origin and composing in the tenth and eleventh centuries, for example *Þórsdrápa* and Christian verse, known from *Snorra Edda*.

'sem hér' ('as here'): two lines.

'sem Einarr kvað' ('as Einarr composed'): two lines (Skúlason?), about the middle of the twelfth century. If these two Einars are the same person, he was from Borg on Mýrar and there is a *þáttr* about him in *Morkinskinna*. He was a prolific poet and Óláfr refers elsewhere to his well-known poem, *Geisli*.

'sem Skraut-Oddr kvað' ('as Skraut-Oddr composed'): four lines. Skraut-Oddr is only mentioned here (another stanza later) and Jónsson (1912–15) says he is an Icelandic poet from the eleventh century.

'sem Starkaðr gamli kvað' ('as Starkaðr the old composed'): four lines. A well-known prehistoric character from the legendary sagas.

'sem hér' ('as here'): two lines.

'sem hér' ('as here'): one line.

'sem Óláfr Leggsson kvað' ('as Óláfr Leggsson composed'): one line (mythological). An Icelandic poet from the thirteenth century, nicknamed *svartaskáld* ('the black poet'); composed verse about King Hákon, Earl Skúli and Christ. Belonged to the family of Lundamenn in Borgarfjörður in the west; was guilty of the death of Jón murti, son of Snorri Sturluson, in 1231.

'sem hér' ('as here'): one line (mythological).

'sem Einarr kvað' ('as Einarr composed'): two lines (Skúlason, see above).

'sem hér er kveðið' ('as is composed here'): two lines.

'og sem þetta' ('and like this'): two lines.

'sem hér er kveðið' ('as is composed here'): two lines.

'sem Þorleifr jarlsskáld kvað' ('as Þorleifr earl's poet composed'): four lines (Rauðfeldarson), in the tenth century, from Brekka in Svarfaðardalur in the north. A *þáttr* about him is preserved in *Flateyjarbók*. This particular verse is about Hákon (?Earl of Hlaðir), but *Heimskringla* has another verse about him by Þorleifr. Þorleifr spent his last years in Mýrdalur in the south.

'sem Snorri kvað' ('as Snorri composed'): two lines; looks like the only piece of religious poetry by Snorri.

'sem hér' ('as here'): two lines.

'sem í Haflíðamálum' ('as in *Haflíðamál*'): 3 lines; Jónsson (1912–15) claims this to be from the twelfth century (1121), referring to Haflíði Másson, known from *Þorgils saga ok Haflíða* in *Sturlunga*.

'sem hér er kveðið' ('as is composed here'): two lines.

'sem Þjóðólfr kvað' ('as Þjóðólfr composed'): four lines, Arnórsson, from Svarfaðardalur. Left Iceland as a young man, spent time with Magnús the Good and Haraldr the Hardruler and died in 1066 at Stamford Bridge, three days before the battle of Hastings. He could have composed this on the occasion of Magnús's death in 1047. Much of Þjóðólfr's poetry is referred to in *Heimskringla, Sneglu-Halla þáttr* and *Brands þáttr ǫrva*.

'sem hér er kveðið' ('as is composed here'): two lines.

'sem hér' ('as here'): five lines.

'sem Kolbeinn kvað' ('as Kolbeinn composed'): four lines (Tumason?), from the family of the Ásbirningar in the north; died in 1208.

'sem hér er kveðið' ('as is composed here'): four lines.

'sem Arnórr kvað í Magnúsdrápu' ('as Arnórr composed in *Magnúsdrápa*'): two lines (this particular stanza only here, possibly from an introduction to the *drápa*); on Arnórr, see above.

'sem Guðbrandr kvað í Svǫlu' ('as Guðbrandr in Svala composed'): two lines. Jónsson (1912–15) identifies this man with the Guðbrandr in *Hrafns saga* (c. 1200) who is said to have composed a verse there which confirms that Hrafn accepted a certain Loftr Markússon who said he had been sent to Hrafn from Mýrar in the west by Sighvatr Sturluson.

'sem Sneglu-Halli kvað' ('as Sneglu-Halli composed'): four lines; he was with King Haraldr the Hardruler about the middle of the eleventh century. A *þáttr* about him is preserved in *Morkinskinna, Hulda* and *Hrokkinskinna*.

'sem hér er kveðið' ('as is composed here'): four lines.

'ok sem hér er kveðið' ('and as is composed here'): two lines.

'sem Þjóðólfr kvað' ('as Þjóðólfr composed'): two lines, Arnórsson. This fragment has been linked with Haraldr the Hardruler in *Heimskringla*; see above.

'sem Guðlaugr kvað' ('as Guðlaugr composed'): four lines. Nothing else is preserved by anyone of that name but Jónsson (1912–15) nevertheless claims he is a twelfth-century Icelander! Several Guðlaugrs appear in *Sturlunga saga*.

'sem hér er kveðið' ('as is composed here'): two lines.

'sem hér er kveðið' ('as is composed here'): two lines.

'sem Óláfr kvað' ('as Óláfr composed'): four lines (Óláfr hvítaskáld himself?).

'sem Hallar-Steinn kvað' ('as Hallar-Steinn composed'): two lines (Herdísarson), c. 1200; his name may be derived from the farm-name Höll in Þverárhlíð in Borgarfjörður in the west. Composed *Rekstefja*, thirty-five stanzas about King Óláfr Tryggvason.

'sem Egill kvað' ('as Egill composed'): two lines. The only fragment of this kind by Egill, meaning obscure.

'sem hér' ('as here'): two lines (from *Íslendingadrápa*?).

'sem Bragi hinn gamli kvað' ('as Bragi the old composed'): two lines.

'sem Kormakr kvað' ('as Kormakr composed'): two lines (not in *Kormaks saga*!). Kormakr was from Melur in Miðfjǫrður. Fragments of his *Sigurðardrápa* are preserved in *Snorra Edda* and *Heimskringla*.

'sem Arnórr kvað' ('as Arnórr composed'): two lines (from an introduction to *Magnúsdrápa*?). On Arnórr, see above.

'sem hér' ('as here'): one line (previously quoted here).

'sem fyrr er ritað' ('as written previously'): one line (previously quoted here).

'sem fyrr er ritað' ('as written previously'): one line (previously quoted here).

'sem í Bjúgum vísum' ('as in *Bjúgar vísur*): one line. Jónsson (1912–15) claims this to be from the twelfth century.

'sem Sighvatr kvað' ('as Sighvatr composed'): two lines (from a memorial poem about King Óláfr?). Sighvatr was from Apavatn in Grímsnes and there is a *þáttr* about him in Snorri Sturluson's saga of St Óláfr.

'í þessum orðum' ('in these words'): one line (previously quoted here).

'sem hér er kveðið' ('as is composed here'): four lines (similar to Latin, possibly by Óláfr himself?).

'sem hér er kveðið' ('as is composed here'): four lines (probably the *pater noster*).

'sem hér' ('as here'): four lines (from a praise poem by Óláfr?).

'sem hér er kveðið' ('as is composed here'): one line.

'sem Glúmr kvað' ('as Glúmr composed'): two lines (Geirason, a fragment about Eiríkr). An Icelandic poet of the tenth century, lived by Mývatn and in Króksfjörður, composed a poem on the death of king Eiríkr Blood-axe and the *Gráfeldardrápa* about King Haraldr gráfeldr, recorded in *Heimskringla*.

'sem hér' ('as here'): four lines (from a praise poem by Óláfr?).

'sem hér' ('as here'): four lines.

'sem hér' ('as here'): two lines (in K, not W).

'sem hér er kveðið' ('as is composed here'): two lines.

'sem hér' ('as here'): two lines.

'sem hér' ('as here'): four lines.

'sem hér er kveðið' ('as is composed here'): four lines.

'sem hér er kveðið' ('as is composed here'): two lines.

'sem Egill kvað' ('as Egill composed'): eight lines (from *Arinbjarnarkviða*?). The two stanzas here (this one and another below), normally thought to be the final stanzas of *Arinbjarnarkviða*, could have been written in *Möðruvallabók* after *Egils saga* where the text of the poem is now illegible.

'sem hér' ('as here'): eight lines.

'sem hér' ('as here'): four lines (resembles the poem *Haustlǫng*).

'sem hér' ('as here'): four lines.

'sem Skraut-Oddr kvað' ('as Skraut-Oddr composed'): two lines, on him, see above.

'sem hér' ('as here'): one line.

'sem Þjóðólfr kvað' ('as Þjóðólfr composed'): four lines. Jónsson (1912–15) identifies him with Þjóðólfr of Hvinir and feels that the verse resembles *Ynglingatal*. Óláfr, however, does not distinguish this Þjóðólfr from Þjóðólfr Arnórsson, to whom he has already referred. It therefore seems reasonable to assume that this man is the Þjóðólfr who has already been mentioned.

'sem Markús kvað' ('as Markús composed'): two lines, probably Skeggjason, who died in 1107 and was law speaker 1084–1107. Lived in the south and composed a *drápa* about Eiríkr Sveinsson the Good, King of the Danes, and sent it abroad. Fragments from it are preserved in *Knýtlinga saga*.

'sem hér' ('as here'): a lacuna in the manuscript.

'sem Þjóðólfr kvað' ('as Þjóðólfr composed'): four lines.

'sem hér' ('as here'): two lines.

'sem hér' ('as here'): two lines.

'sem hér' ('as here'): two lines.

'sem hér' ('as here'): four lines.

'sem hér' ('as here'): two lines.

'sem hér' ('as here'): two lines (reminiscent of *Arinbjarnarkviða*).

'sem Leiðólfr kvað' ('as Leiðólfr composed'): two lines. A certain Leiðólfr appears in *Njáls saga* but this is the only piece of poetry attributed to a person of that name. Nothing else is known about him.

'sem hér er kveðið' ('as is composed here'): two lines.

'sem hér er kveðið' ('as is composed here'): four lines.

'sem Egill kvað' ('as Egill composed'): eight lines (possibly the final stanza of *Arinbjarnarkviða*?).

'sem hér' ('as here'): two lines.

'sem hér' ('as here'): two lines.

'sem Sveinn kvað' ('as Sveinn composed'): four lines (similar to a stanza by Úlfr). Jónsson (1912–15) indentifies this Sveinn with the Sveinn who composed the *Norðrsetudrápa*, which is quoted in *Snorra Edda*. Jónsson assigns him to the eleventh century.

'sem í Kúgadrápu' ('as in *Kúgadrápa*'): two lines. Kúgi appears in *Orkneyinga saga*.

'sem Sveinn kvað' ('as Sveinn composed'): one line. On Sveinn, see above.

'sem hér er kveðið' ('as is composed here'): four lines.

'sem Egill kvað' ('as Egill composed'): eight lines. This is the same stanza as the one quoted above that was assigned to *Arinbjarnarkviða*.

'sem Nikulás ábóti kvað' ('as Abbot Nikulás composed'): eight lines. Possibly the same Nikulás (now generally identified as Nikulás Bergsson d. 1159) who wrote *Leiðarvísir*, an itinerary for pilgrims to Rome and the Holy Land, and composed a *drápa* about the Apostle John. The stanza here is thought to be about Christ.

'sem hér er kveðið' ('as is composed here'): four lines.

Table 4.5. *Named authors of stanzas referred to in* The Third Grammatical Treatise, *which are unknown from other sources, listed in the order in which they appear in the* Treatise

Auðun illskælda	Arnórr jarlaskáld (2nd time)	Glúmr
Arnórr jarlaskáld	Guðbrandr í Svölu	Egill (2nd time)
Eilífr Goðrúnarson	Sneglu-Halli	Skraut-Oddr (2nd time)
Einarr (Skúlason)	Þjóðólfr (2nd time)	Þjóðólfr (3rd time)
Skraut-Oddr	Guðlaugr	Markús (Skeggjason)
Starkaðr gamli	Óláfr (hvítaskáld?)	Þjóðólfr (4th time)
Ólafr Leggsson	Hallar-Steinn (Herdísarson)	Leiðólfr
Einarr (Skúlason)	Egill (Skallagrímsson)	Egill (3rd time)
Þorleifr jarlsskáld	Bragi inn gamli	Sveinn
Snorri	Kormakr	Sveinn (2nd time)
Þjóðólfr (Arnórsson)	Arnórr jarlaskáld (3rd time)	Egill (4th time)
Kolbeinn (Tumason)	Sighvatr	Nikulás ábóti

poets that Óláfr refers to by name as the composers of these otherwise unknown stanzas.

The thirty-nine examples of the work of named poets are attributed to twenty-six authors who can be put into two main categories: those of uncertain origins and those whom we know more about. Those of uncertain origins are divisible into three groups, well-known characters from prehistory, poets known from Snorri's scriptorium, and poets who are unknown except for Óláfr's testimony. These three groups are set out in table 4.6.

The remaining poets are mentioned in other sources and may be identified as shown in table 4.7.

Now we may ask: How did Óláfr get to know the poets whose verses he quoted? Most of the well-known ones were court poets whose works appear in works like *Heimskringla*, *Snorra Edda* and *Morkinskinna*, even though these particular examples of their compositions do not appear there. Some were poets who lived geographically close to Óláfr, while a smaller group were well-known public figures. The poets Óláfr quotes may thus be divided into four distinct categories, as table 4.8 demonstrates.

In spite of the fact that the poets listed in table 4.8 are known to us

Table 4.6. *Three groups of authors (of poetry otherwise unknown) of uncertain origin mentioned in* The Third Grammatical Treatise

well-known prehistoric characters	poets known from Snorri's scriptorium	poets unknown except from Óláfr's *Treatise*
Starkaðr gamli *Bragi gamli*	*Auðun illskælda*, whose name appears *in Óláfs saga Tryggvasonar* as a poet of Haraldr hárfagri *Eilífr Goðrúnarson*, whose name appears in *Snorra Edda* and who might have lived in the tenth or eleventh century *Sveinn*, who could have composed *Norðrsetudrápa* in *Snorra Edda*, and perhaps lived in the eleventh century	*Guðbrandr í Svölu*, who could be the same as the man who is mentioned with Sighvatr Sturluson and Hrafn in *Hrafns saga* *c.* 1200 *Skraut-Oddr*, who is only mentioned here and credited with two fragments of poetry *Guðlaugr*, who is most likely an Icelander from the twelfth century *Leiðólfur*, about whom nothing more than his name is known

from written works, it is impossible for Óláfr to have learned his examples of their poetry from the texts we know. It is therefore interesting to note that most of the identifiable poets (apart from the generally known public figures of the thirteenth century) are court poets whom we know from written works like *Heimskringla*, *Snorra Edda* and *Morkinskinna*. Those who do not appear in these written works all come from the west of Iceland. We can thus differentiate between them all according to their origin. It may be that Óláfr's knowledge of poets from the north could be explained if *Morkinskinna* was written in Eyjafjörður, as has been suggested (Andersson 1994), and also by the fact that the Sturlung family had close ties with the north after Sighvatr Sturluson moved to Grund in Eyjafjörður in 1215.

What is even more interesting is to note the absentees on Óláfr's list, such as major poets from the *Íslendinga sögur* who never became court poets, like Gísli Súrsson. This might be an indication that the common poetic tradition in the country had its centre at royal courts in other

Table 4.7. *Well-known and otherwise identifiable poets referred to in* The Third Grammatical Treatise, *whose verses quoted in the* Treatise *are not known from other sources*

Arnórr jarlaskáld from Hítarnes in Hnappadalssýsla in the west (eleventh century)
Einarr Skúlason from Borg on Mýrar in the west (twelfth century)
Óláfr Leggsson of Lundamannaætt in Borgarfjörður in the west (thirteenth century)
Þorleifr jarlsskáld from Svarfaðardalur near Eyjafjörður in the north (tenth century)
Snorri Sturluson in Borgarfjörður in the west (thirteenth century)
Þjóðólfr Arnórsson from Svarfaðardalur near Eyjafjörður in the north (eleventh century)
Kolbeinn Tumason, of the Ásbirning family in Skagafjörður in the north (thirteenth century)
Sneglu-Halli from the north (around 1050)
Óláfr hvítaskáld himself
Hallar-Steinn ?from Höll in Þverárhlíð, Borgarfjörður in the west (*c.* 1200)
Egill Skallagrímsson from Borg on Mýrar in the west (tenth century)
Kormakr from Melur in Miðfjörður in the northwest (tenth century)
Sighvatr Þórðarson from Apavatn in Árnessýsla in the south (eleventh century)
Glúmr Geirason lived at Mývatn and in Króksfjörður in the north and the west (tenth century)
Markús Skeggjason law speaker in 1084–1107, and lived in the south
Nikulás abbot at Munkaþverá in Eyjafjörður in the north, died in 1159

Table 4.8. *Four discernible groups of identifiable authors referred to in* The Third Grammatical Treatise, *whose verses in the* Treatise *are not known from other sources*

Well-known poets from Óláfr's immediate surroundings	Poets well-known from Snorri's works (*Heimskringla* and *Snorra Edda*)	Poets known from the *þættir* in *Morkinskinna*	Generally known public figures in thirteenth-century Iceland
Óláfr Leggsson	*Þorleifr jarlsskáld*	*Arnórr jarlaskáld*	*Kolbeinn Tumason*
Snorri Sturluson	*Þjóðólfr Arnórsson*	*Einarr Skúlason*	*Markús Skeggjason*
Óláfr hvítaskáld	*Hallar-Steinn*	*Sneglu-Halli*	*Nikulás*
Egill Skallagrímsson	*Kormakr*		
	Sighvatr Þórðarson		
	Glúmr Geirason		

Table 4.9. *Two main groups of identifiable authors referred to in* The Third Grammatical Treatise, *whose verses in the* Treatise *are not known from other sources*

Poets from the West of Iceland, including well-known court poets	Court poets and travellers, mainly from the north
Egill Skallagrímsson from Borg á Mýrum	Kormakr from Melur in Miðfjörður
Arnórr jarlaskáld from Hítarnes in Hnappadalssýsla	Glúmr Geirason who lived at Mývatn and in Króksfjörður
Einarr Skúlason from Borg á Mýrum	Þorleifr jarlsskáld from Svarfaðardalur
Hallar-Steinn from Höll in Þverárhlíð, Borgarfjörður ?	Þjóðólfr Arnórsson from Svarfaðardalur
	Sighvatr Þórðarson from Apavatn in Grímsnes, Árnessýsla
Óláfr Leggsson of Lundamannaætt in Borgarfjörður	Sneglu-Halli from the north
Snorri Sturluson in Borgarfjörður	
Óláfr hvítaskáld himself	

countries rather than at the Althing, the annual general assembly held at Þingvellir, in the south of Iceland. It is also peculiar that Óláfr does not refer to Gunnlaugr ormstunga from Borgarfjörður as Snorri did in his *Edda*. The feud between Gunnlaugr and Skáld-Hrafn was well known in the first half of the thirteenth century as it is referred to in *Egils saga*. According to *Gunnlaugs saga*, Gunnlaugr was a well-known poet but his absence from Óláfr's work might suggest that his poetic talent increased somewhat in the tradition before his saga was written late in the thirteenth century.

In conclusion it may be said that Óláfr used the written works which were known in his day, the works of his uncle Snorri in particular. He refers to unknown stanzas by poets who are known from these works, which might suggest that Snorri and his nephew knew more poetry than was used in Snorri's books, and that in turn points to a more lively poetic tradition than the written works show. This surplus of poetry would also speak against all the speculation about Snorri composing the verses himself and attributing them to different saga-characters.

Finally we may draw up a picture, as shown in figure 4.2, of the apparently clear categories of the poetry which Óláfr is likely to have

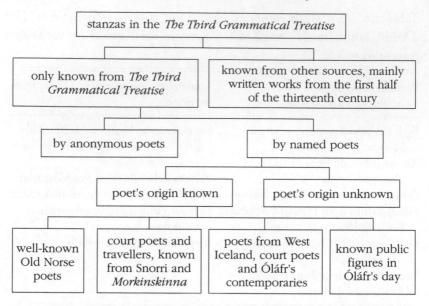

Figure 4.2 Categories of stanzas and known poets, referred to in *The Third Grammatical Treatise*

learned from the oral tradition of skaldic poetry in thirteenth-century west Iceland. First, there were well-known Old Norse skalds; second, Icelandic skalds and travellers who had made a name for themselves at royal courts during the previous centuries, and are known from Snorri and *Morkinskinna*; third, poets from the west of Iceland, both court poets and Óláfr's contemporaries; and fourth, public figures and well-known characters in Iceland.

In view of these well-defined categories it is unlikely that the absence of poets from other parts of the country should be explained by the suggestion that their poetry did not contain suitable examples for Óláfr's purpose. It is more likely that these conclusions suggest that the continuity in the skaldic tradition was kept alive by Icelanders at the Scandinavian courts rather than in Iceland, where the evidence shows a limited knowledge of stories and poetry from remote areas; stories and poetry which people had never heard and could also not read before the later, fourteenth-century compilations appeared, such as *Möðruvallabók* and *Vatnshyrna*. And even then it is difficult for us to assume a general familiarity with written sagas which only existed in a few expensive vellum books, in a culture where most people must have received the major part of their 'literary' entertainment from oral performers rather than from book readers or book reading. Óláfr's court-and-region-bound literary horizon therefore gives us reason to believe that knowledge of narratives about events and families in Iceland was limited to the neighbourhood where the audience, the poets and tellers of tales knew the landscape as well as the characters and events which they staged on the familiar scene in front of them.

NOTES

1 An earlier version of this chapter was delivered at the Ninth International Saga Conference in Akureyri in August 1994, and published in Icelandic in the conference preprints (*Samtíðarsögur* vol. I, pp. 220–32), as 'Ólafur Þórðarson hvítaskáld og munnleg kvæðahefð á Vesturlandi um miðja 13. öld. Vitnisburður vísnadæmanna í 3. málfræðiritgerðinni'.

2 Strictly speaking, it is only that part of the treatise that deals with rhetorical figures that goes by the name *Málskrúðsfræði* (see further chapter 6 of the present volume). Óláfr's treatise is not only preserved in Codex Wormianus (W) but also in AM 748 I, quarto, and in fragments in AM 757a quarto and AM 757b quarto. The text has been edited in *Edda Snorra Sturlusonar* 1848–87, II, pp. 397–427 (with a Latin translation), Ólsen 1884 and Jónsson 1924. Translations into English are available in Collings 1967 (part only) and Wills 2000, and into German by Krömmelbein 1998. See also the discussion of Tranter in chapter 6 of this volume.

3 Here I exclude Óláfr's example of *ofljóst*, discussed by Snædal 1993: 216–17, one verse of which Óláfr attributes to the skald Kormakr (which is not in *Kormaks saga*) and one which is anonymous according to Óláfr but which is attributed to Bjǫrn Hítdælakappi in his saga (Einarsson 1961: 57–9). The two famous verses which are usually placed at the end of Egill Skallagrímsson's intimate praise poem about his friend Arinbjǫrn are also not preserved except as quotations in Óláfr's treatise.

4 This counting is based on the information supplied in the standard editions of Jónsson 1912–15: 590–602 and 1927.

REFERENCES

Albano Leoni, Federico 1985–86, 'Donato in Thule. *Kenningar* e *tropi* nel terzo trattato grammaticale islandese', *AION-Filologia Germanica* 28–9: 1–15.

Allén, Sture 1971, 'Om text attribution: Kring en avhandling af Marina Mundt', *Arkiv för nordisk filologi* 86: 82–113.

Andersson, Theodore M. 1993, 'Snorri Sturluson and the Saga School at Munkaþverá', in Wolf, Alois (ed.), *Snorri Sturluson. Kolloquium anläßlich der 750. Wiederkehr seines Todestages*. Tübingen: Gunter Narr Verlag, pp. 9–25.

1994, 'The Literary Prehistory of Eyjafjọrðr', in *Samtíðarsögur. Forprent. Níunda alþjóðlega fornsagnaþingið*. 2 vols. Reykjavík, I, pp. 16–30.

Árnason, Kristján 1993, 'Málfræðihugmyndir Sturlunga', *Íslenskt mál* 15: 173–206.

Collings, Lucy G. 1967, 'The Málskrúðsfræði and the Latin Tradition in Iceland'. Unpublished MA thesis, Cornell University.

Edda Snorra Sturlusonar, editio Arnamagnæana 1848–87, 3 vols. Copenhagen: Sumptibus Legati Arnamagnæani.

Einarsson, Bjarni 1961, *Skáldasögur: Um uppruna og eðli ástaskáldasagnanna fornu*. Reykjavík: Bókaútgáfa Menningarsjóðs.

Guðnason, Bjarni 1982, 'Formáli', in Guðnason, Bjarni (ed.), *Danakonunga sögur*, Íslenzk fornrit, 35. Reykjavík: Hið íslenzka fornritafélag, pp. v–cxciv.

1994, 'Aldur og einkenni Bjarnarsögu Hítdælakappa', in Sigurðsson, Gísli, Kvaran, Guðrun and Steingrimsson, Sigurgeir (eds.), *Sagnaþing helgað Jónasi Kristjánssyni sjötugum 10. apríl 1994*. Reykjavík: Hið íslenska bókmenntafélag, pp. 69–85.

Hafstað, Baldur 1990, 'Konungsmenn í kreppu og vinátta í Egils sögu', *Skáldskaparmál* 1: 89–99.

Hallberg, Peter 1963, 'Ólafr Þórðarson hvítaskáld, *Knýtlinga saga* och *Laxdæla saga*: Ett försök till språklig författarbestämning', *Studia Islandica* 22. Reykjavík: Heimspekideild Háskóla Íslands og Bókaútgáfa Menningarsjóðs.

Jónsson, Finnur (ed.) 1912–15, *Den Norsk-Islandske Skjaldedigtning*. 4 vols. Copenhagen and Kristiania: Gyldendalske boghandel and Nordisk forlag.

Jónsson, Finnur 1923, *Den oldnorske og oldislandske litteraturs historie*. 3 vols. 2nd. edn. II. Copenhagen: Gad.

(ed.) 1927, *Ólafr Þórðarson. Málhljóða- og málskrúðsrit. Grammatisk–retorisk afhandling*. Copenhagen: Det Kgl. Danske Videnskabernes Selskab. Historisk–filologiske Meddelelser XIII, 2.

Kristjánsson, Jónas 1971, *Um Fóstbræðrasögu*. Rit 1. Reykjavík: Stofnun Árna Magnússonar á Íslandi.

1990, 'Var Snorri Sturluson upphafsmaður Íslendingasagna?', *Andvari* NS32: 85–105.

Krömmelbein, Thomas (ed.), *Ólafr Þórðarson Hvítaskáld. Die Dritte Grammatische Abhandlung*. Studia Nordica, 3. Oslo: Novus forlag.

Micillo, Valeria 1993, 'Classical Tradition and Norse Tradition in the *Third Grammatical Treatise*', *Arkiv för nordisk filologi* 108: 68–79.

Mundt, Marina (ed.) 1977, *Hákonar saga Hákonarsonar etter Sth. 8 fol., AM 325 VIII, 4o, og AM 304, 4o*. Norrøne skrifter, 2. Oslo: Norsk historisk kjeldeskrift-institutt.

Ólason, Vésteinn 1991, 'Jórvíkurför í Egils sögu: Búandkarl gegn konungi', *Andvari* NS 33: 46–59.

Ólsen, Björn Magnússon 1884, 'Indledning', in Ólsen, Björn Magnússon (ed.), *Den Tredje og Fjærde Grammatiske Afhandling i Snorres Edda*. Copenhagen: Samfund for udgivelse af gammel nordisk literatur, pp. i–lxxxii.

Pálsson, Hermann 1992, 'Hirðskáld í spéspegli', *Skáldskaparmál* 2: 148–69.

Raschellà, Fabrizio D. 1983, 'Die altisländische grammatische Literatur', *Göttingische Gelehrte Anzeigen* 235: 271–315.

1994, 'Rune e alfabeto latino nel *Trattato grammaticale* di Óláfr Þórðarson', in Sigurðsson, Gísli *et al.* (eds.), *Sagnaþing helgað Jónasi Kristjánssyni sjötugum 10. apríl 1994*. Reykjavík: Hið íslenska bókmenntafélag, pp. 679–90.

Sigurðsson, Gísli 1994, 'Bók í stað lögsögumanns: Valdabarátta kirkju og veraldlegra höfðingja', in Sigurðsson, Gísli *et al.* (eds.), *Sagnaþing helgað Jónasi Kristjánssyni sjötugum 10. apríl 1994*, 2 vols. Reykjavík: Hið íslenska bókmenntafélag, 1, pp. 207–32.

Snædal, Magnús 1993, 'Yfirlit yfir forníslenskar málfræðiritgerðir', *Íslenskt mál* 15: 207–20.

Thorsson, Örnólfur (ed.) 1988, *Sturlunga saga amd sskýringar og fræði*. 3 vols. Reykjavík: Svart á hvítu.

1994, 'Grettir sterki og Sturla lögmaður', in *Samtíðarsögur. Forprent. Níunda alþjóðlega fornsagnaþingið*. 2 vols. Reykjavík, Ii, pp. 907–33.

Tómasson, Sverrir 1993, 'Formáli málfræðiritgerðanna fjögurra í Wormsbók', *Íslenskt mál* 15: 221–40.

Tómasson, Sverrir *et al.* (eds.) 1992, *Íslensk bókmenntasaga*. I. Reykjavík: Mál og menning.

Whaley, Diana 1998, *The Poetry of Arnórr jarlaskáld. An Edition and Study*. Westfield Publications in Medieval Studies, 8. Turnhout: Brepols.

Wills, Tarrin (ed.) 2000, *The Third Grammatical Treatise in the Codex Wormianus: Óláfr Þórðarson hvítaskáld*. Edition, commentary and annotated translation (in progress) [http://sctis.library.usyd.edu.au/nordic].

5

The conservation and reinterpretation of myth in medieval Icelandic writings

MARGARET CLUNIES ROSS

Before the Icelanders adopted the Christian religion by a decision of the Althing in AD 1000, they were attached to other gods and viewed the world in ways that were often different from the perspective of medieval European Christendom. Yet the year 1000 was barely one hundred years after the settlement of the island by people of predominantly Norwegian descent, and a proportion of the early settlers, according to Ari Þorgilsson's *Íslendingabók* as well as to *Landnámabók* and many a saga, had already been converted to Christianity in Ireland, Northern Scotland, the Hebrides and the other Norwegian Viking colonies, and were Christians when they came to Iceland. From one vantage point, and it is arguably one adopted by Ari Þorgilsson (Lindow 1997; Clunies Ross 1998a: 145), the hundred years or so of paganism at the beginning of Iceland's history as a nation was an aberration of faith in a land that had already been sanctified by Christian hermits (the *papar* of *Íslendingabók*) and potential saints (Clunies Ross 1999) and was, as Ari pictured it, paradisal, with its surface covered with trees between the mountains and the shore.

From another perspective, however, the Icelandic community was one in closer touch with its pre-Christian roots in 1000 than almost any other contemporary society of medieval Europe. For many reasons, Icelanders did not wish to deny their pagan past (von See 1993). Iceland was a society that had received Christianity late by Western European standards, and, according to its own historiography, by a rational decision of its chief legislative body, the Althing. Christianity was the religious change Iceland had to have in order to maintain political and legal stability at home and to become a full member of medieval European society. Christianity was imposed from outside (and generally Icelanders resented external impositions, particularly if they were supported, as this one was, by the Norwegian king), but it was also desirable for what it brought with it – access to the wider world of trade, travel, communication, ideas and education. Christian education brought many advantages to Icelanders, not the least of them literacy and books, and they were quick to take these up. The establishment of the Christian Church in Iceland was also swiftly turned to the advantage of the traditional sponsors of the old religion, the chieftains, who instituted new, Christian structures of power on top of the old ones. Moreover, the traditional bases of intellectual authority that resided in the law, in poetry, and in the maintenance of historical records in oral form, were turned to the task of preserving the old customs of the Icelanders in writing as well as to the creation of new textual genres that contact with the Christian-Latin world had made possible.

Three things combined in medieval Icelandic society to produce an astonishing wealth of vernacular written texts across a range of genres over a period of about two centuries. These were the settlement itself in a new land, requiring the invention of new social, legal and political structures; the introduction of the new religion of Christianity; and the Icelanders' self-identification as the custodians of their own and all Scandinavia's traditional history and culture. In Kurt Schier's memorable phrase (1975), a new literature arose in *terra nova*. It was a literature that developed innovative forms, like the saga, while conserving and still developing older genres, like skaldic poetry. It was also a literature that sought to preserve traditional customs and beliefs, while at the same time offering to its principal audience, Icelanders of the twelfth, thirteenth and fourteenth centuries, a reinterpretation of the old beliefs and customs from a Christian point of view. In any study of the extant texts, which were composed in many cases well after the events and customs they purport to describe, we must not forget that the pre-Christian world is mediated by the interpretative stance of Icelandic Christians. In respect of pre-Christian myth and religion, the subject of the present chapter, this observation is particularly important. Indeed, it is part of the modern interest generated by Icelandic mythological texts that they offer medieval interpretations of the old, pre-medieval beliefs.

The challenge to Christian Icelanders intent on rehabilitating pagan traditions or representations of pagan society within overtly Christian writings was not to throw the baby out with the bathwater, as had often happened in most other early medieval Western European societies, for whom it had been virtually impossible to preserve more than a few vestiges of non-Christian traditions. The control of the Church over manuscript production, coupled with generally negative attitudes towards paganism as an evil delusion produced by the work of Satan, combined to inhibit the recording of pre-Christian myth and custom in early medieval writings over most of the continent of Europe and in Anglo-Saxon England. It was only on the Western European peripheries, like parts of the Celtic world and Scandinavia, that those who controlled textual production were interested in preserving knowedge and traditions of the time before their communities accepted Christianity.

It has often been observed (Lönnroth 1969; Dronke and Dronke 1977; Faulkes 1983; Weber 1981) that a good deal of Old Icelandic writing offers a more tolerant attitude towards paganism than we find in other medieval writings, while at the same time indicating, often in subtle ways, how the society of the time before Christian enlightenment had an imperfect understanding of the basic dogmas in which Christians believed and through whose operation they considered the world was controlled. These writings often stress the continuities of belief and social structures through Icelandic history from before the conversion period and into Christian history, in order to draw attention to the various ways in which Icelanders, especially those of superior intellectual gifts, had had an intuitive awareness of Christian beliefs and mores even before they had been converted. These narratives also reveal that Icelanders had developed social institutions which could be viewed as precursors to those of a fully Christian society.

Landnámabók's account of Ingólfr Arnarson, the first permanent settler in Iceland, and his immediate descendants, provides a paradigm of this kind of approach and at the same time articulates a common Icelandic conceptual schema, that of the inheritance of special talents, appropriately modified to suit specific religious and historical contexts

(Clunies Ross 1998a: 158–64). Such a schema, which can be found in many other Old Icelandic writings, constitutes a myth that serves to rationalize Icelandic history as the dynastic record of a small group of powerful families, whose influence can be traced without a break from pagan through to Christian times.

> Þenna vetr fekk Ingólfr at blóti miklu ok leitaði sér heilla um forlǫg sín . . . Fréttin vísaði Ingólfr til Íslands . . . Ingólfr var frægastr allra landnámsmanna, því at hann kom hér at óbyggðu landi ok byggði fyrstr landit; gerðu ðat aðrir landnámsmenn eptir hans dœmum. Ingólfr átti Hallveigu Fróðadóttir, systur Lopts ens gamla; þeira son var Þorsteinn . . . son Þorsteins var Þorkell máni lǫgsǫgumaðr, er einn heiðinna manna hefir bezt verit siðaðr, at því er menn vitu dœmi til. Hann lét sik bera í sólargeisla í banasótt sinni ok fal sik á hendi þeim guði, er sólina hafði skapat; hafði hann ok lifat svá hreinliga sem þeir kristnir menn, er bezt eru siðaðir. Son hans var Þormóðr, er þá var allsherjargoði, er kristni kom á Ísland. (Jakob Benediktsson SH7, S9, H10 1968 I: 42, 46–7)
>
> (That winter Ingólfr held a great sacrifice in order to discover the omens about his destiny . . . The intelligence directed Ingólfr to Iceland . . . Ingólfr was the most famous of all the first settlers, because he arrived here when the land was still uninhabited and he was the first to settle in the country; other settlers followed suit, according to his example. Ingólfr married Hallveig, daughter of Fróði and sister of Loptr the old; their son was Þorsteinn . . . Þorsteinn's son was Þorkell moon the lawspeaker, who was the most civilized of heathen men, from the examples that people know. In his last illness, he had himself carried out into a ray of sunshine and commended himself to the god who created the sun. He had also lived as purely as the best-lived of Christians. His son was Þormóðr, who was the supreme chieftain when Christianity came to Iceland.)

Not only does Ingólfr's story carefully avoid revealing the identity of the spiritual power that directed his voyage to Iceland, thus allowing one to infer that it was the Christian God, but his son's son, Þorkell moon the lawspeaker, is said to have been the noblest heathen who ever lived, a man who, on his deathbed, had himself carried out into the sunlight so he could give himself to the god who had created the sun. The *Landnámabók* narrative goes out of its way to state that Þorkell had lived as purely (*hreinliga*) as the best of Christians. Appropriately, then, in view of his father's holy life, it was Þorkell moon's son þormóðr who held the principal chieftaincy (*allsherjargoði*) in Iceland at the time when Christianity was officially adopted by the Althing. The *allsherjargoði* is likely to have held the supreme priestly authority in the pre-Christian Althing, which involved him in consecrating the gathering at the opening of the assembly. Hence he was the official celebrant of the old religion in its most important social dimension, the rule of law, and the story of his family reveals a continuity of religious and legal authority from paganism into the Christian era.

The above example shows how specific Old Norse texts with a mythic dimension need to be considered in the context of the whole complex of myths that a society gives expression to at any particular time, if the richness of their meanings is to be perceived. Individual myths cannot be considered on their own or out of the more general context of early Norse society's view of itself. Myths function as both cognitive and communicative systems and need to be understood within a contemporary social context. Until quite recently approaches to Norse myths tended to privilege the quest for 'original' forms and meanings of myths over the study of the texts we actually know, in order to push behind them to supposed earliest forms which have been considered to reveal the structural and conceptual similarities between Scandinavian and other mythological systems. Although such approaches are interesting, they are usually highly speculative. More important for a study of the relationship between literature and society is a recognition that 'the mythic process, concerned with explaining the origin and form of the world, did not stop with the conversion to Christianity. Rather, Christianity became one of the impulses combining in such thought' (Lindow 1985: 53).

Old Norse mythic texts may be divided into two groups. The first group represents Old Norse myths and the Norse mythic world as its central focus of interest and main subject (Clunies Ross 1994). Texts in this group are mostly in the Old Icelandic language and extant in manuscripts of Icelandic provenance, though we know from a significant body of poetic texts on runic staves from Bergen that Norwegian versions of some of the poetry also existed. The chief sources of this first group of mythic texts are the anonymous poetry of the Elder Edda; a large corpus of skaldic mythological verse, mostly attributed to named poets, both Norwegian and Icelandic; the *Edda* and *Heimskringla* of the Icelander Snorri Sturluson (1179–1241); and the roughly contemporary Latin *Gesta Danorum* of the Dane Saxo Grammaticus, completed some time after 1216 (Christiansen 1993).

The second group comprises works that do not foreground myth though they utilize myths and mythic references in their larger discourse, just as the example cited above from *Landnámabók* does. A significant proportion of the literature of medieval Iceland comes under this heading, excepting only texts and genres that are exclusively Christian devotional or learned works or reasonably close translations of foreign language texts such as romances. We find mythic frames of reference in skaldic poems of most kinds, for skaldic diction is predicated upon a knowledge of Norse mythology, and many subclasses of the saga employ mythic references systematically in their creation of fictional worlds. Clunies Ross 1998a offers a study of Icelandic texts in this group and suggests that Icelandic writers' recourse to mythological frames of reference in their creation of saga narrative is much greater and more diverse than has previously been suspected. Recent studies by other scholars (Tulinius 1995; Nordal 1999) have supported this contention.

There were many purposes for which writers of Old Icelandic literature employed conceptual schemas that involved myth. Lindow (1995) has shown how representations of the bloodfeud partake of mythic paradigms, while he (1994) and Hastrup (1985: 145–54) have revealed the importance of the geographical configuration of the Norse mythic world in the designation of social space in medieval Iceland and the wider Scandinavian world. Guðrún Nordal (1999 and chapter 9 of this volume) shows how Sturla Þórðarson uses mythological references to the Norse gods or to figures of the settlement age to guide his audience's opinion of the near-contemporary protagonists of his *Íslendinga saga*. My own recent work (Clunies Ross 1998a) demonstrates the importance of mythic schemas in the presentation of such topics as the settlement of Iceland, the inheritance of family talents, the conceptualization of Icelandic history, and the development of a range of subclasses of the dominant medieval Icelandic literary form, the saga.

The texts whose primary focus is myth also, in their collectivity, express a number of social concerns that can be mapped with little effort onto the fabric of what we know of medieval Icelandic social life. The extant corpus of Old Norse myths about the pre-Christian gods, the Æsir, and their principal opponents, the giants (*jǫtnar*), reveals early Scandinavian society's interests in ontology and ontogeny, both on the level of the mythic world's own developmental history and from the point of view of individual supernatural beings. To the extent that these beings and their life experiences reflect the desires and frustrations of humankind, myths about their adventures and relationships explore a number of basic ontological questions of fundamental interest to humans. These include the subjects of the world's creation and the creation of classes of living beings, including humans; the operation of time in the mythic world; the existence and operation of fate as it affects the individual lifespan, and the concomitant inevitability of death, which, the myths show, might be delayed but could not eventually be avoided.

Old Norse myths also had meanings which relate to human social organization as we understand it to have operated in the medieval period in Scandinavia. There are similarities between the social hierarchy of the classes of supernatural beings in the Norse mythic world and that of Icelandic society in the commonwealth period. The marriage system postulated for Norse myth can also be understood in terms of what we know of such practices in the real world of medieval Scandinavia, though the mythic system is one in which reciprocity in the exchange of women had evidently broken down (Vestergaard 1991). There is comparability between the often-repeated stand-offs between gods and giants and the behaviour of feuding factions of chieftains and their supporters in thirteenth-century Iceland. Again, the condition of negative reciprocity (Sahlins 1965; Clunies Ross 1994: 103–43) in which the gods and giants conduct their relationships, and the strategies of treachery, theft and deception they characteristically adopt to maintain their positions, or seek to improve them, are reminiscent of many of the behaviour patterns represented in saga literature as characterizing Icelanders from the age of settlement and the commonwealth period. The 'reality' of the world of the gods thus partakes of the same basic metaphysical reality as that of the humans represented in predominantly non-mythic textual genres. However, the gods behave in ways that are more extreme and more flamboyant than are usual for humans

– they test the metaphysical system to its utmost and thereby reveal the sources both of human fears and anxieties and of human desires and pleasures. Conversely, those humans whose behaviour is most extreme in saga literature are often tagged as god-like by a variety of myth-based signifiers.

The foregoing summary of some of the major social concerns of Old Norse myths are the conclusions of a modern analytical method that is able to bring together all the extant texts and examine them as a whole to detect repeated themes. It is unlikely that medieval Icelanders were fully aware of the meanings of these structures. The modern reader also needs to realize that the forms in which mythological texts were available to medieval people were significant in their influence on their perception and understanding of myths. The actual forms in which Icelanders and other medieval Scandinavians knew their myths in the age before writing are not fully recoverable, and the written texts of medieval provenance that we know today as the output of the thirteenth and fourteenth centuries were almost certainly different in a number of ways from their oral antecedents.

The society in which the myths we know were formed and took literary expression was one in which the whole community would have had a basic knowledge of the Norse mythological system and world view. Some people, like poets and experts in runic lore, in all probability knew the system in greater detail and complexity than others did. However, archaeology and place-name studies from the whole of Scandinavia confirm that in the Viking Age (*c.* 800–1100) the names and cults of the Scandinavian gods we recognize from mythic texts were widespread, suggesting that they formed the subjects of rituals and were thought to influence everyday life. In all probability, then, it was not necessary for every telling of a myth to set out its details fully and in chronological sequence. As with much early medieval narrative (the Old English poem *Beowulf* comes to mind here as a good example), story-telling is allusive, selective, repetitive and accretive, often involving such devices as the flash-back and flash-forward. All these practices are possible, and indeed aesthetically satisfying, for those who already know the basic narrative but enjoy hearing it again and again told from a new or striking point of view.

In the Viking Age, and probably earlier, the normal vehicle for the literary realization of Old Norse myth would have been poetry. As chapter 3 of this volume explains, there were two basic kinds of Old Norse poetry, eddic and skaldic, the first of which probably had a longer prehistory than the second, though precise chronology is notoriously difficult. Even though most eddic poetry is almost certainly old, the manuscripts in which it has been preserved are quite young. The most important of them, the Codex Regius of the Elder Edda (GkS 2365, quarto), is generally considered on palaeographic grounds to date from about 1270, though there are signs within the text that it is probably a copy of an older manuscript or manuscripts (Lindblad 1954 and 1980). Other poems in eddic measures are quoted by Snorri Sturluson in his *Edda* and appear in manuscripts of this work, none of which is older than the beginning of the fourteenth century, while an additional collection of eddic poems is found in the manuscript AM 748 I quarto of the early fourteenth century along with parts of Snorri's *Edda*.

There has been considerable speculation about when poems in eddic measures first came to be written down in Iceland.[1] Snorri Sturluson evidently knew a number of these poems, but whether, in the 1220s, he had access to written texts of the poetry he quotes is still an open question (Einar G. Pétursson 1993). What is important to note here is that the eddic poetry that has been written down is mostly part of larger compilations and bears marks of having been edited by Icelanders of the thirteenth century (Meulengracht Sørensen 1991). The Codex Regius collection is particularly noteworthy for a number of signs of editorial activity. First, the twenty-nine poems it contains are arranged in a certain order, with the first eleven poems being about supernatural beings (gods, giants, dwarves, elves) and the mythological world. The remaining poems are about the heroes of the Germanic world. Some of these heroic poems, like those dealing with the life of Helgi Hundings-bani, are of Norse provenance, others, like the complex myths associated with Sigurðr and the Niflungar, are the common stock of Germanic heroic tradition. Not only does the compiler (or compilers) provide his texts in a certain order, implying a hierarchy of importance of the divine over the heroic material, possibly based on his view of the age and high seriousness of the material, but he also inserts prose prefaces, internal prose bridges and colophons to many of the poems in order to make the narrative details underlying the myths explicit or, in some cases, to offer a comment from a contemporary, Christian perspective on pagan customs (Harris 1983).

The editorial activity apparent in the Codex Regius manuscript suggests that some aspects of the narrative art of eddic poetry may have become difficult for thirteenth-century Icelanders to comprehend or else that different ideas of what constituted a satisfying poem had begun to apply. It is certainly true that one needs special knowledge to understand the narrative sequence of many of the poems, both heroic and mythological, for much is left unsaid and much background narrative is sketched allusively in such a way as to make it difficult for anyone to follow who does not know the underlying stories upon which the extant poems depend. Indeed, only about half of the known mythological poems in eddic measures are primarily narrative in kind, in the sense that they tell a narrative or narratives from beginning to end.[2] Many of the others are agonistic dialogues between two mythological beings, usually a male god and a giant or dwarf, which take the form of what has come to be called a wisdom contest, in which the two supernatural beings vie with one another to prove one of them the wiser in esoteric, mythological lore. In the course of these contests numerous myths and fragments of mythic knowledge are alluded to. A variant on the agonistic encounter is the type of poem, like *Vǫluspá* or *Baldrs Draumar*, in which the god Óðinn rouses a dead or comatose seeress and forces her to tell him mythological secrets relating to the past and the future which he does not know himself (Quinn forthcoming).[3]

The beginning of the eddic poem *Skírnismál* in the two medieval manuscripts in which it was recorded (the Codex Regius and AM 748 I quarto) demonstrates how thirteenth-century compilers set the scene for a poetic narrative carried by a high proportion of dialogue. It is prefaced by an explanatory prose introduction that provides background information for what follows. The poem begins thus in the Codex Regius text:

> For Scírnis
> Freyr, sonr Niarðar, hafði sezc í Hliðsciálf oc sá um
> heima alla. Hann sá í Iotunheima, oc sá þar mey fagra,
> þá er hon gecc frá scála fǫður síns til scemmo. Þar af fecc
> hann hugsóttir miclar.

Scírnir hét scósveinn Freys.   Niorðr bað hann qveðia
Frey máls. Þá mælti Scaði:
'Rístu nú, Scírnir,   oc gacc at beiða
    occarn mála mǫg,
oc þess at fregna,   hveim inn fróði sé
    ofreiði afi.'
(Neckel–Kuhn 1983: 69)

The journey of Skírnir

Freyr, son of Njǫrðr, had seated himself in Hliðskjálf and looked
over all worlds. He looked into Giantland and saw there a beautiful
    girl,
walking from her father's hall to the store-room. From that he derived
great affliction of mind.
Skírnir was the name of Freyr's servant. Njǫrðr ordered him
to engage Freyr in conversation. Then Skaði said:
'Rise up now, Skírnir, and go and ask
    our kinsman for speech,
and question him on this, with whom the wise one
    is so angry.'

In fact, if one knows Norse mythology and the relationships of the
supernatural beings to one another, the only information that is
introduced in the prose and is not eventually available in the poetry is
the revelation that Freyr had stationed himself in Óðinn's watchtower
Hliðskjálf, which gave him vantage over all worlds, and it was from
there that he caught sight of the giantess Gerðr and immediately desired
her. In his prose account of this same myth in his *Edda*, Snorri
Sturluson represents this action as transgressive – Freyr should not have
presumed to sit in the high-seat of the chief of the gods, and for that
reason he was afflicted with great grief (Faulkes 1982: 31; Faulkes 1987:
31; Bibire 1986). This may also be the implicit message of the prose
introduction to the poem here. It performs another favourite function
of the Codex Regius compiler, to present the action of the myths, as
told in poetry, within the framework of family relations. Here Skírnir's
conversation with Freyr, which leads to the god's importuning his
servant to woo Gerðr on his behalf while he stays at home, appears to be
provoked by the anxious solicitude of Freyr's father Njǫrðr and his step-
mother Skaði.[4]

    Skaldic poetry, even more than eddic verse, generally required of its audience a good knowledge of Norse myths and of the conceptual world that underlay them in order to be understood. For a period after the conversion to Christianity, skaldic poets avoided using poetic figures that made reference to paganism or the pagan gods, but they later returned to the use of references to the old mythology as an ornament to their poetry even when they composed poems with Christian subjects. One skald of the conversion period, Hallfreðr Óttarsson, is credited in his saga with the remark that Christian lore was not as suitable to poetry (*eru þau fræði ekki skáldlegri*) as the old religion was, for poetry was particularly associated with the god Óðinn (Sveinsson 1939: 155). Its characteristic diction, its kennings and *heiti* (synonyms), were formed on the basis of pagan myths. This connection between mythology and skaldic poetry provides one of the dynamic links between the four parts of Snorri Sturluson's *Edda*, where Snorri first gives an overview of the old mythology and then proceeds to explain the diction and metrics of skaldic verse.

A couple of kennings from the mythological poem *Haustlǫng* ('Autumn Long') by the Norwegian skald Þjóðólfr of Hvinir, composed about 900, will illustrate the necessity of mythological knowledge to the understanding of skaldic diction. This poem, and a great deal of the mythological lore required for its comprehension, are available only in Snorri Sturluson's *Edda*, where the poem is quoted in two separate sections to illustrate its two mythological subjects, the giant Þjazi's abduction of the goddess Iðunn and her apples of immortality that kept the gods young, and the myth of the god Þórr's duel with another giant, Hrungnir.[5] Two kennings in the section of the poem on Iðunn's abduction contain references to the giantess Skaði, who had a role in the prose introduction to *Skírnismál* as the wife of the god Njǫrðr, father of Freyr. The kennings in question are 'the bow-string-Vár's [Skaði's] whale [ox]', which refers to an ox that a party of three gods are trying to cook in an earth-oven, and 'the ski-deity's [Skaði's] fosterer [her father, Þjazi]'.[6]

To someone well-versed in Norse myth, there are several reasons why kennings for Skaði convey significant meaning in a poem about Iðunn's abduction. First, as the gloss to the second kenning makes clear, the giant abductor Þjazi is Skaði's father, and there is an important sequel to the abduction myth. As Snorri and Þjóðólfr tell it, the gods recover

Iðunn and kill the giant, but his daughter, apparently his sole heir, is keen to seek revenge from the gods for her father's death, and she bargains with them for recompense. One of her rewards is to be married to one of their number, Njǫrðr, god of the sea, though they tricked her out of Baldr, the husband she really wanted. This marriage, made in inauspicious circumstances, is unstable and, according to Snorri, the partners dislike each other's favourite haunts, Njǫrðr by the sea listening to the sea birds, and Skaði up in the mountains where the wolves howl and she is able to travel around on skis. There she carries a bow and shoots game, hence the reference in the two kennings quoted here to ski and bow-string (Snorri Sturluson, *Edda, Gylfaginning*, Faulkes 1982: 24 and 1987: 23–4).[7] Hence, for those in the know, the references to Skaði in *Haustlǫng* increase that poem's density of meaning and underline the theme of tension and instability in heterosexual relations between the gods and the giants which the group of myths involving father and daughter all explore (Clunies Ross 1994: 115–27).

Virtually none of the mythological information mentioned above nor its poetic expression would now be known to us if Snorri Sturluson had not composed the treatise known as *Edda* in the early thirteenth century. Norse mythology as we know it is largely the product of his mythographic activity. It is a salutary exercise to imagine what the medieval Icelandic mythological record would be like without Snorri and to assess just how much of our knowledge we owe to him and to those who compiled the manuscripts in which his treatise has come down to us. We do not have the *Edda* quite as Snorri conceptualized it (assuming that he was its mastermind); rather, it is mediated by those whom Krömmelbein (1992) has called 'creative compilers' (cf. Seelow 1998). The three main medieval manuscripts of the *Edda*, Codex Regius, Codex Wormianus and Codex Upsaliensis, all present Snorri's *oeuvre* with different emphases (see further chapter 6). Regius stresses the mythological dimensions of the work, and is probably more concerned than the other manuscripts to emphasize the compatibility of the mythology presented by Snorri with Christian belief. Wormianus, which includes the four grammatical treatises, is heavily interested in the rhetorical aspects of Norse poetic diction, while Upsaliensis focusses on Snorri himself as a figure of authority, both in person and as an authority on poetry. Whatever the contributions of the creative compilers of the chief manuscripts of the *Edda*, however, we are, I think, entitled to assume that their work would not have been possible without Snorri's own fundamental creativity.

It has often been assumed that Snorri wrote in part to revive what he may have perceived as a flagging or ill-informed interest in skaldic verse among young Icelanders of his day. This may well have been one of his motivations, but his vision went far beyond that particular pedagogical aim. He was apparently concerned to legitimate Icelandic vernacular poetry and poetics, and its underpinning ideology, in the face of antique classical models as medieval Christian learning presented them. He may also have had personal motives, in the political climate of his day, for promoting his own abilities as a skald and a scholar, as Gade suggests in Chapter 3. Snorri's intellectual talents lay in the areas of analysis and synthesis of a wealth of knowledge and traditional culture. His star has been in the ascendant ever since his works began to be made available both within and outside Iceland after the revival of learning about the Icelandic Middle Ages began in the late sixteenth and seventeenth centuries (Tómasson 1996). His *Edda* speaks to the modern desire to know about the time before Christianity overlaid older forms of European thought.

Snorri had mastered the art of narrative, and the information he has to impart comes packaged in that dominant modern literary mode (Clunies Ross 1998b). Yet at the same time, because his *Edda* was also a work that drew on the conventions of the medieval school textbook at a number of points, he cleverly fulfilled the twin objectives of medieval as well as modern discursive writing, namely, to instruct and to entertain. We can point to his use of question and answer format, the medieval encyclopedic tradition (Clunies Ross 1987: 151–73), the *clavis metrica*, handbooks of grammar, such as those of Donatus and Priscian, where figures and tropes are classified and listed, as standard medieval modes of instruction. By combining these common instructional methodologies of the medieval Christian classroom with narrative techniques he created a new and very effective medium. His writings have had a lasting appeal, partly because both the narrative mode and the pedagogical techniques have endured into our own day and are still very much part of modern rhetorical and instructional conventions.

Another of the characteristics of Snorri's *Edda* that appeals to modern readers is that he is, or appears to be, thorough and exhaustive in his treatment of his subject. If we think of the organization of his *Heimskringla* for a moment, it is done in such a way as to persuade the reader or audience that it is systematic and exhaustive, even though it is in fact selective of the considerable range of inherited written and oral sources that Snorri had at his disposal. The format he adopted, of a series of royal biographies arranged in chronological order, suggests both systematic research and organizational inclusiveness. The format of the quadripartite *Edda* is more complex from a narratological point of view, because Snorri needed to qualify the truth value of the pagan myths recounted there. For this reason, the work has a Prologue in which the rationale of the whole work and its interpretative parameters are set out (Tómasson 1988). For this reason also the second and third parts, *Gylfaginning* and *Skáldskaparmál*, employ frame narratives to qualify the subordinate narrative material encapsulated within them. The fourth part, *Háttatal*, following a partially similar model, uses a dialogue technique initially and then an apparently exhaustive enumeration of all the possible variations of poetic measures in a dazzling display of Norse poetic technique.

It is possible to surmise what Snorri's purpose was in bringing together a body of mythological information that had probably previously existed only in the fragmentary, allusive, often contradictory form that we have seen characterized Old Norse traditional poetry. His work shows that he recognized the advantages of literacy and the system of Christian-classical written literature in giving status and legitimacy to Norse poetic traditions. He is likely to have known how Christian grammarians from Bede onwards used quotations from the works of Christian Latin poets as well as from the pre-Christian poets of classical antiquity to exemplify figures and tropes in Latin verse. Without apparently drawing closely on any one model, in contrast to his nephew Óláfr Þórðarson in his *Third Grammatical Treatise*, Snorri seems to have set out to provide for Icelandic poetry a vernacular version of Latin handbooks of grammar and metrics and to place the native Icelandic poetic tradition, indebted as it was to its oral inheritance and pagan in origin, on a par with the inherited pagan literature of Greece and Rome and its *interpretatio christiana*.

We see the objective of legitimating vernacular poetics in the face of antique models and the categorization of indigenous verse forms to answer the categories of Latin metrics most clearly in the case of *Háttatal*. The first three parts of the *Edda*, on the other hand, are concerned with the mythological infrastructure of Norse poetics and, within *Skáldskaparmál*, with a systematic exposition of the kenning system. Snorri prepares the ground for his *interpretatio christiana* of Norse mythology very carefully (Clunies Ross 1987). The mythological world view he presents in the *Prologue* and *Gylfaginning* is one in which echoes of Christianity, albeit distorted ones, are almost always present and would have been perceived as such by the Icelandic reader or audience. It is, I think, arguable that from time to time, particularly within the extended mythological narratives that occur in both *Gylfaginning* and *Skáldskaparmál*, Snorri gets carried away with the sheer delight of telling the myth, and gives the story a more extensive treatment than one would expect in a handbook of poetics. That is all part of his very medieval desire to instruct and to entertain. Even, however, in the longest mythic narratives the presentation does not lose sight of the reasons why the myth has been narrated in the first place. Almost always those reasons are twofold: first, to expound the pre-Christian world view of a particular phenomenon and to show that, even in its crude and sometimes laughable imperfections, it was not too dissimilar to Christian ideas about the same thing (Holtsmark 1964); and, second, to lay the groundwork for the prescriptions to come within *Skáldskaparmál* on how to interpret and use the major categories of skaldic diction.

As a mythography compiled by a Christian writer, we cannot accept Snorri's *Edda* uncritically as a faithful reflection of pagan ideology, as many have been inclined to do. Nevertheless, there is a vast range of information about Norse myths, to use a neutral phrase that bypasses the interpretative process for the moment, that we know only or largely from Snorri. No less significantly, the form in which he has transmitted Norse myths has been very influential. Like the Icelandic saga form, which was in active development at the time he was writing the *Edda*, the Norse myths preserved in Snorri's *Edda* are told in prose with embedded verse quotation from the older poetry.

A large number of Snorri's mythic narratives have no counterpart elsewhere as coherent stories (though a few can be found, in often almost unrecognizable form, in the *Gesta Danorum* of Saxo Grammaticus). Examples are legion and include: the myth of the death of Baldr; Þórr's journey to the overwhelmingly powerful Útgarða-Loki, for which we know no poetic exemplar; the binding of the wolf Fenrir; the origin of Óðinn's eight-legged horse Sleipnir; the events surrounding the end of the mythological world at Ragnarǫk (though these could be made out from *Vǫluspá* which Snorri quotes extensively); the myth of the gods' dealings with the giant Þjazi and his daughter Skaði; the myth of the nature and origin of the mead of poetry (narrated again and differently in *Heimskringla's Ynglinga saga*); Þórr's duel with the giant Hrungnir and its aftermath; Þórr's visit to the giant Geirrøðr; Ægir's feast for the gods (referred to in the prose preface to *Lokasenna* and taken for granted there); how and why some dwarves made several precious things for the gods (e.g. Sif's gold wig, Óðinn's spear); Loki and the myth of the 'otter-gold', which leads into the complex narrative of the Niflungar (told also in *Vǫlsunga saga* and *Þiðreks saga*). This leads on to the story of Jǫrmunrekkr, Hamðir and Sǫrli, also narrated in the heroic eddic poem *Hamðismál*, though that poem is not quoted by Snorri. The narrative behind *Grottasǫngr*, an eddic poem quoted in full in two manuscripts of the *Edda*, is then told. This is the only poem in an eddic measure to be quoted in *Skáldskaparmál*. It leads on in turn to legends surrounding Hrólfr kraki, then to the story of the everlasting battle (*Hjaðningavíg*) and the life and descendants of Halfdan the Old. Faulkes has suggested (1982: xxiii) with some plausibility, that the movement from myth through prehistoric legend to stories surrounding Danish and other Scandinavian rulers on the cusp of historical times might owe its genesis to the structure of the now lost *Skjǫldunga saga*, a legendary history of the Kings of Denmark.

It is noteworthy that where some of the myths Snorri tells are partially narrated or alluded to in poetic sources, we often owe our knowledge of these very poems to his *Edda*. Virtually the whole extant corpus of skaldic mythological poems comes to us from *Edda* manuscripts, including Bragi Boddason's *Ragnarsdrápa*, Þjóðólfr of Hvinir's *Haustlǫng*, Eilífr Goðrúnarson's *Þórsdrápa* and Úlfr Uggason's *Húsdrápa*. These long poems are given specially privileged status in several manuscripts of the *Edda* by being quoted in runs of numerous stanzas rather than piecemeal in separate verses (*lausavísur*), as is more often Snorri's habit. The first three of these *drápur* are cited to back up the prose narrative of myths and not to give examples (*dœmi*) of particular kinds of skaldic diction, as is the normal practice in *Skáldskaparmál*.

We know from his Preface to *Heimskringla* that Snorri considered ancient poems (*fornkvæði*) as a pre-eminent source for his own (and presumably others') historical writing. In *Heimskringla* are embedded some of the major compositions of the chief court skalds, both Norwegian and Icelandic, of the tenth through the twelfth centuries. The *Edda*, too, shows a preference for the work of the early masters of the skaldic art, those who are called *hǫfuðskáld* ('chief poets') in the *Edda* text. These are Snorri's vernacular *auctoritates*, the Scandinavian equivalents to classical authors such as Virgil and Horace and early Christian poets like Fortunatus in the Latinate tradition whose poetry was quoted in Latin grammars to illustrate rhetorical figures and tropes. By establishing that his chief skalds set the standards for those who came after them, and by quoting a good deal of their work as *dœmi* of the correct figures and tropes of the skaldic art, Snorri established a canon of poetics which privileges certain kinds of poetry (poems rich in mythological allusion, for example) as the standard against which other and later skalds had to operate. One may say that, as a rule of thumb, poems or verses which were rich in kennings for the topics that Snorri treated as central to the skaldic art, or contained allusions to the pagan deities, were the most likely to be preserved in his prose text. For example, a series of *lausavísur* attributed to Eyvindr Finnsson which contain many gold kennings are found in *Skáldskaparmál* (these are *lausavísur* 8–14 in Finnur Jónsson 1912: 64–5). On the other hand, there are poets who are working clearly and unequivocally within the Christian framework, whose practice Snorri also saw as exemplary, like Árnórr jarlaskáld (d. *c.* 1075), for example. These later, Christian poets can be equated with the Christian Latin poets of the medieval tradition who rendered the classical rhetorical inheritance acceptable (Clunies Ross 1987: 135–7).

Our debt to Snorri for the preservation of a large amount of eddic poetry is also substantial. In *Gylfaginning*, he quotes a good deal of the poetry of the Elder Edda, either in a discursive context, or as part of an extensive narrative. It is arguable that, without Snorri's explanatory narratives (whether or not they represent the consensus of Icelandic traditional belief) it would be very difficult for us to make much sense of the allusive narrative forms of some of the poetic texts. An example is Snorri's narrative of how three gods find a pair of logs upon the seashore and from them create the first human pair, Askr and Embla (Faulkes 1982: 13; 1987: 13). This myth is alluded to in *Vǫluspá* stanzas 17 and 18 and, though he does not quote these verses, Snorri almost certainly had them in mind as he wrote his prose narrative. The verses themselves are cryptic and without Snorri's explanatory prose we could not be sure of our understanding that the beings created were the first humans, nor that they were made from logs of wood.

Of the known corpus of eddic mythological poetry, Snorri makes extensive use of *Vǫluspá* as quotation and as the schematic background plan for *Gylfaginning*. This poem occupies a privileged position and is the only eddic poem almost consistently identified by name in the text. *Grímnismál* and *Vafþrúðnismál* are frequently quoted and, as wisdom contest poems, they exert a paradigmatic influence upon *Gylfaginning*'s frame narrative of the Swedish king Gylfi's quest to discover the myths and religion of the Æsir from Troy. Information from a large number of other eddic poems, known and unknown, has helped to shape Snorri's Old Norse mythology.[8]

The mere existence of Snorri's *Edda* is at once our greatest source of knowledge of Old Norse myth and the greatest stumbling block to our understanding of how myths were normally expressed and transmitted in the early Middle Ages. In some respects Snorri's influence as a mythographer upon those who came after him was almost bound to be greater than it could have been upon his contemporaries, for the intellectual bases of the major works of synthesis that he undertook would largely have been known to his fellow Icelanders, albeit in a form that was probably unsynthesized and unreflected upon in their minds. Snorri was a man with an outstanding knowledge of Norse myth, of Norse poetry and poetics (he was himself an accomplished poet) and of Norse history, as well as of Latin grammar and rhetoric. Never before, in all probability, nor since has anyone had the idea to do what he did: to legitimate Old Icelandic poetry against the background of Christian-Latin culture in terms of its subject-matter and in terms of its diction and verse-forms. His achievement is truly remarkable, measured in both medieval and modern terms, and its power comes from his enormous synthetic abilities. He took information that was partial and allusive, and quite possibly often pointing in disparate directions, and he pulled it all together in a way that gave Old Norse mythological and poetic traditions written and authorized status and allowed those of us who have come after him to gain entry into an otherwise lost intellectual world.

NOTES

1 We now know a number of runic inscriptions on wooden staves from the Bryggen merchants' quarter of the Norwegian town of Bergen (Knirk 1993). There are over thirty examples of poetic texts, some in eddic measures, others in skaldic ones, mostly dating from the period 1150–1350. A number of these refer to the pagan Norse gods. Although these inscriptions are fragmentary, they show that Iceland did not have a monopoly on Old Norse poetry, though unfortunately little Norwegian material has survived in the written record.

2 Among eddic mythological poems that are primarily narrative in kind are *Skírnismál*, *Hymiskviða*, *Þrymskviða*, *Vǫlundarkviða*, *Rígspula* and *Grotta-sǫngr*, though the last two are not in the Codex Regius collection. Among those that are dialogic, we find *Vǫluspá*, *Vafþrúðnismál*, *Grímnismál*, *Hárbarðsljóð*, *Lokasenna* and *Alvíssmál*. *Hávamál*, 'The Words of the High One', that is, Óðinn, is monologic for the most part and, through various subtle or not-so-subtle extratextual identifiers, indicates that the speaking voice of the poem is either this god or a being who has assumed some of the god's characteristics (Clunies Ross 1990). Klingenberg 1983 offers an excellent analysis of the different kinds of eddic mythological poetry.

3 A further variation on this last pattern is provided by the eddic poem *Hyndluljóð*, extant only in the manuscript *Flateyjarbók* from the late four-teenth century. Here it is the goddess Freyja who awakens the giantess Hyndla in order to find out about the ancestors of her male protégé Óttarr, who needs to know his pedigree in order to contest a lawsuit (Gurevich 1973).

4 The trend to make myths into family affairs can be seen in a number of the prose introductions to the Codex Regius of the Elder Edda, and applies to the heroic as well as to the mythological poetry. The giantess Skaði was almost certainly Freyr's step-mother rather than his natural mother for, according to Snorri Sturluson (*Heimskringla*, *Ynglingasaga* 4), Njǫrðr's two children Freyr and Freyja were his offspring from an incestuous liaison with his sister.

5 The two parts of *Haustlǫng* and its accompanying prose retellings of the myths are to be found in the *Skáldskaparmál* ('Poetic Diction') section of

Snorri's *Edda*. For the Icelandic text, see Finnur Jónsson 1931: 78–81, 100–5 and 110–13 and Faulkes 1998, 1: 1–2, 20–4, 30–3; and for an English translation Faulkes 1987: 59–61, 77–81 and 86–8. The poem's name is generally thought to be a rueful reflection on the length of time it took the skald to compose it.

6 The kennings come in verses 5 and 7 of the poem: *hvalr Várar þrymseilar* (5/ 2–4) and *fóstri ǫndurgoðs* (7/1–4).

7 The stanzas, otherwise unrecorded, that Snorri quotes here as the complaints of the marriage partners forced to share each other's homes, have a counterpart in Saxo Grammaticus's *Gesta Danorum*. Though Saxo converts them into Latin verse, he is almost certainly dependent on an Old Norse poetic original (Friis-Jensen 1987: 158–61).

8 There are short quotations only from the following eddic poems in the *Edda*: *Hávamál*; *Vǫluspá in skamma* (named); *Fáfnismál*; *Lokasenna*; the Njǫrðr–Skaði incompatibility complaint (the rest has not survived); *Heimdallargaldr* (only two lines); an exchange between some Vanir and Frigg's emissary Gná (only nine lines, not recorded elsewhere); *Skírnismál*; an unnamed poem about Baldr, in which the giantess Þǫkk refuses to weep for him; a single stanza of an unnamed poem in which the god Þórr addresses the river Vimur and orders her not to rise (in *Skáldskaparmál*); a pair of lines on Glasir, a tree with golden leaves that stands in front of the doors of Valhalla; stanzas in eddic measures from the *þulur* (lists of poetic synonyms) called *Alsvinnsmál* and *Þorgrimsþula* plus other *þulur*, though these are unlikely to be Snorri's work. Quite a high proportion of these eddic poems Snorri quotes in fragmentary form are otherwise unknown to us, suggesting that we have, with his help, just scraped the tip of the iceberg.

REFERENCES

Benediktsson, Jakob (ed.) 1968, *Íslendingabók. Landnámabók*. Íslenzk fornrit 11 and 12. Reykjavík: Hið íslenzka fornritafélag. [S and H refer to the *Sturlubók* and *Hauksbók* versions of the text, both given by Benediktsson.]

Bibire, Paul 1986, 'Freyr and Gerðr: the Story and its Myths', in Simek, Rudolf, Kristjánsson, Jónas and Bekker-Nielsen, Hans (eds.), *Sagnaskemmtun: Studies in Honour of Hermann Pálsson on his 65th Birthday, 26th May 1986*. Vienna, Cologne and Graz: Hermann Böhlaus Nachf, pp. 19–40.

Christiansen, Eric 1993, 'Saxo Grammaticus', in Pulsiano, P. and Wolf, K. (eds.), *Medieval Scandinavia: An Encyclopedia*. New York and London: Garland, pp. 566–9.

Clunies Ross, Margaret 1987, *Skáldskaparmál: Snorri Sturluson's Ars Poetica and Medieval Theories of Language*. The Viking Collection, 4. Odense: Odense University Press.

1989, 'The Art of Poetry and the Figure of the Poet in *Egil's saga*', in Tucker, John (ed.), *Saga of the Icelanders*. New York: Garland, pp. 115–30; first published in *Parergon* 22 (1978): 3–12.

1990, 'Voice and Voices in Eddic Poetry', in Pàroli, Teresa (ed.), *Poetry in the Scandinavian Middle Ages, Atti del 12° Congresso Internazionale di Studi sull'Alto Medioevo*, Spoleto: Centro Italiano di Studi sull'Alto Medioevo, pp. 219–30.

1994, *Prolonged Echoes: Old Norse Myths in Medieval Northern Society*, I: *The Myths*. The Viking Collection, 7. Odense: Odense University Press.

1998a, *Prolonged Echoes: Old Norse myths in medieval Northern society*, II: *The Reception of Norse Myths in Medieval Iceland*. The Viking Collection, 10. Odense: Odense University Press.

1998b, 'Snorri's *Edda* as Narrative', in Fix, Hans (ed.), *Snorri Sturluson: Beiträge zu Werk und Rezeption*. Reallexikon der germanischen Altertums-kunde: Ergänzungsbände 18. Berlin and New York: Walter de Gruyter, pp. 9–21.

1999, ' "Saint" Ásólfr', in Brogyanyi, Bela and Krömmelbein, Thomas (eds.), *Germanisches Altertum und Christliches Mittelalter. Festschrift für Heinz Klingenberg zum 65 Geburtstag*. Freiburg: HochschulVerlag, pp. 1–21.

Dronke, Ursula and Dronke, Peter 1977, 'The Prologue of the Prose Edda: Explorations of a Latin Background', in Pétursson, Einar G. and Krist-jánsson, Jónas (eds.), *Sjötíu Ritgerðir helgaðar Jakobi Benediktssyni*. 2 vols. Reykjavík: Stofnun Árna Magnússonar, I, pp. 153–76.

Faulkes, Anthony (ed.) 1982, *Snorri Sturluson Edda: Prologue and Gylfaginning*. Oxford: Clarendon.

1983, 'Pagan Sympathy: Attitudes to Heathendom in the Prologue to *Snorra Edda*', in Glendinning, R. J. and Bessason, H. (eds.), *Edda: A Collection of Essays*. University of Manitoba Icelandic Studies, 4. Winnipeg: University of Manitoba Press, pp. 283–314.

(trans.) 1987, *Snorri Sturluson Edda*. London: (Everyman Paperback) Dent. Reissued 1992.

(ed.) 1998, *Snorri Sturluson Edda: Skáldskaparmál*. 2 vols. London: University College, Viking Society for Northern Research.

Friis-Jensen, Karsten 1987, *Saxo Grammaticus as Latin Poet: Studies in the Verse Passages of the Gesta Danorum*. Analecta Romana; Instituti Danici, Supple-mentum 14. Rome: Bretschneider.

Gurevich, Aron Ya. 1973, 'Edda and Law: Commentary upon *Hyndlolióð*', *Arkiv för nordisk filologi* 88: 72–84.

Harris, Joseph 1983, 'Eddic Poetry as Oral Poetry: the Evidence of Parallel Passages in the Helgi Poems for Questions of Composition and Perfor-mance', in Glendinning, R. J. and Bessason, H. (eds.), *Edda: a Collection of Essays*. University of Manitoba Icelandic Studies, 4. Winnipeg: University of Manitoba Press, pp. 210–42.

Hastrup, Kirsten 1985, *Culture and History in Medieval Iceland: an Anthropological Analysis of Structure and Change*. Oxford: Clarendon.

Holtsmark, Anne 1964, *Studier i Snorres mytologi*. Skrifter utg. av Det Norske Videnskaps-Akademi i Oslo. II. Hist.-filos. kl. Ny serie 4. Oslo: Universitetsforlaget.

Jónsson, Finnur (ed.) 1912, *Den Norsk-islandske Skjaldedigtning*. B. Rettet tekst, 1. Copenhagen and Christiania (Oslo): Gyldendal; reprinted Copenhagen: Rosenkilde og Bagger, 1973.

  1931, *Edda Snorra Sturlusonar udgivet efter håndskrifterne*. Copenhagen: Gyldendaske Boghandel.

Klingenberg, Heinz 1983, 'Types of Eddic Mythological Poetry', in Glendinning, R. J. and Bessason, H. (eds.), *Edda: A Collection of Essays*. University of Manitoba Icelandic Studies, 4. Winnipeg: University of Manitoba Press, pp. 134–64.

Knirk, James E. 1993, 'Runes and Runic Inscriptions. 3. Norway', in Pulsiano, P. and Wolf, K. (eds.), *Medieval Scandinavia: An Encyclopedia*. New York and London: Garland, pp. 553–4.

Krömmelbein, Thomas 1992, 'Creative Compilers: Observations on the Manuscript Tradition of *Snorra Edda*', in Bragason, Úlfar (ed.), *Snorrastefna*. Rit Stofnunar Sigurðar Nordals 1. Reykjavík: Stofnun Sigurðar Nordals, pp. 113–29.

Kuhn, Hans and Neckel, Gustav (eds.) 1983, *Edda: Die Lieder des Codex Regius nebst verwandten Denkmälern*, I: Text. 5th. edn. Heidelberg: Carl Winter Universitätsverlag.

Lindblad, Gustaf 1954, *Studier i Codex Regius av äldre Eddan*. Lundastudier i nordisk språkvetenskap, 10. Lund: Gleerup.

  1980, 'Poetiska Eddans förhistoria och skrivskicket i Codex regius', *Arkiv för nordisk filologi* 95: 142–67.

Lindow, John 1985, 'Mythology and Mythography', in Lindow, John and Clover, Carol J. (eds.), *Old Norse–Icelandic Literature: A Critical Guide*. Islandica 45. Ithaca and London: Cornell University Press, pp. 21–67.

  1994, 'The Social Semantics of Cardinal Directions in Medieval Scandinavia', *Mankind Quarterly* 34: 209–24.

  1995, 'Bloodfeud and Scandinavian Mythology', *Alvíssmál* 4: 51–68.

  1997, '*Íslendingabók* and Myth', *Scandinavian Studies* 69 (4): 454–64.

Lönnroth, Lars 1969, 'The Noble Heathen: a Theme in the Sagas', *Scandinavian Studies* 41: 1–29.

Meulengracht Sørensen, Preben 1991, 'Om eddadigtenes alder', in Steinsland, Gro, Drobin, Ulf, Pentikäinen, Juha and Meulengradht Sørensen, Preben (eds.), *Nordisk Hedendom: Et symposium*. Odense: Odense University Press, pp. 217–28.

Nordal, Guðrún 1999, *Ethics and Action in Thirteenth-Century Iceland*. The Viking Collection, 11. Odense: Odense University Press.

Pétursson, Einar G. 1993, 'Codex Regius', in Pulsiano, P. and Wolf, K. (eds.), *Medieval Scandinavia: An Encyclopedia*. New York and London: Garland, pp. 100–1.

Quinn, Judy forthcoming, 'Dialogue with a vǫlva: *Hyndluljóð, Baldrs Draumar* and *Vǫluspá*', in Larrington, Carolyne and Acker, Paul (eds.), *Mythological Poetry of the Edda*. New York and London: Garland.

Sahlins, Marshall 1965, 'On the Sociology of Primitive Exchange', in Banton, M. (ed.), *The Relevance of Models for Social Anthropology*. Association of Social Anthropologists, Monograph 1. London, pp. 139–236.

Schier, Kurt 1975, 'The Rise of Literature in *terra nova*', *Gripla* 1: 168–81.

See, Klaus von 1993, 'Snorris Konzeption einer nordischen Sonderkultur', in Wolf, Alois (ed.), *Snorri Sturluson: Kolloquium anläßlich der 750. Wiederkehr seines Todestages*. Tübingen: Gunter Narr Verlag, pp. 141–77.

Seelow, Hubert 1998, 'Zur handschriftlichen Überlieferung der Werke Snorri Sturlusons', in Fix, Hans (ed.), *Snorri Sturluson: Beiträge zu Werk und Rezeption*, Reallexikon der germanischen Altertumskunde: Ergänzungsbände 18. Berlin and New York: Walter de Gruyter, pp. 246–54.

Sveinsson, Einar Ól. (ed.) 1939, *Vatnsdœla saga, Hallfreðar saga etc.* Íslenzk fornrit 8. Reykjavík: Hið íslenzka fornritafélag.

Tómasson, Sverrir 1988, *Formálar íslenskra sagnaritara á miǫldum*. Rit 33. Reykjavík: Stofnun Árna Magnússonar á Íslandi.

(ed.) 1996, *Guðamjöður og Arnarleir. Safn ritgerða um eddulist*. Reykjavík: Háskólaútgáfan.

Tulinius, Torfi H. 1995, *La 'Matière du Nord': Sagas légendaires et fiction dans la littérature islandaise en prose du XIIIe siècle*. Paris: Presses universitaires de Paris-Sorbonne.

Vestergaard, Torben A. 1991, 'Marriage Exchange and Social Structure in Old Norse Mythology', in Samson, Ross (ed.), *Social Approaches to Viking Studies*. Glasgow, Cruithne, pp. 21–34.

Weber, Gerd Wolfgang 1981, 'Irreligiosität und Heldenzeitalter: Zum Mythencharakter der altisländischen Literatur', in Dronke, Ursula, Helgadóttir, Guðrún, Weber, Gerd Wolfgang and Bekker-Nielsen, Hans (eds.), *Speculum Norrænum: Norse Studies in Memory of Gabriel Turville-Petre*. Odense: Odense University Press, pp. 474–505.

6

Medieval Icelandic *artes poeticae*

STEPHEN TRANTER

PREAMBLE

Þat var eitt sumar á alþingi, at Einarr gekk til búðar Egils Skalla-
Grímssonar, ok tókusk þeir at orðum, ok kóm þar brátt talinu, at þeir
ræddu um skáldskap; þótti hvárumtveggja þær rœður skemmtiliggar.
Síðan vanðisk Einarr optliga at ganga til tals við Egil. (Nordal 1933:
268)

(It was one summer at the general assembly, that Einarr went to the
hut of Egill Skallagrímsson, and they fell to talking, and quickly the
conversation turned to poetry; both of them enjoyed the discussion.
After that Einarr often used to go and talk to Egill.)

Old Icelandic sources are remarkably reticent about the training of
poets. The same is of course true for Old English, where, as far as we
can judge, one basic metrical form predominated. But Icelandic developed a highly sophisticated system, not only of actual metrical composition, but also of metatextual reflection; the available lexicon not only
permits sharp distinctions to be drawn between a wide variety of
different stanzaic forms and between different forms of complete
poems, but also allows the exact denotation of the component parts of
both poem and stanza in terms of metrical theory and practical
realization.

It seems a matter of course that a poetic tradition which practised the
most densely regulated metrical art in Western medieval literature
should have made provision for the dissemination of technique and

terminology to subsequent generations. Yet in comparison to Irish, for example, where tracts survive in which the legal status of poets and poetry, the curriculum of trainee poets and the metrical definition of individual verse-forms are all laid down, where individual problems of composition are discussed in detail, or where the properties of a specific class of metres are delineated,[1] technical literature on poetics in Icelandic is almost entirely lacking.

However, it is questionable whether the motivation for the composition of *artes poeticae* is purely that of instructing the next generation, and whether a complicated metrical system inevitably demands works of analysis or prescription. Metrical tracts in Ireland were closely bound up with reward and payment. The poet's mastery of specific forms determined his rank and legal entitlements, so that the definition of poetic form had concrete legal implications (Breatnach 1987: 81–9). In Norse society the link between poetic form and the extent of the poet's reward appears to have been much less strict. Outside the Celtic world, poetic tracts were basically concerned with Latin versification. Such tracts had become necessary because of the academic nature of verse composition, in particular following the loss of quantity distinctions in vernacular Latin. As a result, the art of composing in quantitative verse could hardly be learned merely by following the example of the ancients; it was a written art requiring writing-based analysis.

Egill Skallagrímsson's fictive conversation with Einarr skálaglamm gives a glimpse of how the art of poetry might have been disseminated in the pre-literate period: behind the few words it is possible to imagine an acknowledged poet passing on the secrets of his art to the gifted youngster. This is admittedly a lot to read into the phrase 'þeir ræddu um skáldskap' ('they spoke about poetry'). Elsewhere, saga sources are remarkably silent; even the *ástaskáldasögur*, the romantic sagas of skalds, say little of how their subjects acquired their art, giving the impression that the skald was born rather than trained.[2] Poetic manuals as exemplified by the bardic tracts and the Latin *artes versificatoriae* would seem, in this context, to be unnecessary. In surveying what material does exist in this field, we are inevitably confronted with the question as to what purpose it fulfilled, if didactic texts were unnecessary.

THE MATERIAL

There is only one text that can be regarded as an equivalent to the bardic type of tract, from which it would be possible to learn how to compose according to a prevailing metrical system and how to distinguish different forms within that system, and that is the *Háttatal* tract (*Ht*).[3] However, poetic techniques of various kinds are also alluded to in tracts on vernacular grammar and rhetoric. The most informative of these for our purposes is the grammar ascribed to the thirteenth-century poet Óláfr Þórðason hvítaskáld, generally known as *The Third Grammatical Treatise* (*3GT*), and in particular that part of it dealing with rhetorical figures, known in Icelandic as *Málskrúðsfræði* (*Mskr*) ('the art of poetic ornament').

The *Háttalykill* (*Hl*) (lit. 'key of forms') of Hallr Þórarinsson and Rǫgnvaldr Earl of Orkney is not in itself a contribution to the *ars poetica*, since it makes no theoretical comment on the composition of the forms displayed, but it allows certain conclusions as to the state of that art at the time of composition to be drawn.

The mythological portions of *Snorra Edda*, i.e. *Gylfaginning* (lit. 'Deluding of Gylfi', the first narrative section of the Prose Edda) and *Skáldskaparmál* (lit. 'Poetic Diction'), can be seen as tracts on poetic diction and therefore as components of the Nordic *ars*, though they have no direct precedents in the tradition of classical antiquity (see section on *Háttatal* below). Scholars up to the middle of the twentieth century tended to focus on the above texts as individual works, disregarding the manuscript context. More recently (the pioneering study in this area is Klingenberg 1974) it has been customary to view the manuscript compilations in which the texts occur as carefully arranged wholes, in accordance with the late medieval practice of distinguishing between *compilatores* and *scriptores* (Minnis 1988). This can be seen in particular in the transmission of Snorri's *Edda*. The complete text or substantial portions of it are found in three fourteenth-century manuscripts, Codices Regius, (R) Wormianus (W) and Uppsaliensis (U) (Faulkes 1991: xxiv–xxv). Of these, only R gives the *Edda* as we conventionally know it, with *Ht* following the Prologue, then *Gylfaginning* and *Skáldskaparmál* as conventional in modern editions. In W, it is separated from the preceding three sections to form part of a grammatico-metrical complex comprising *Ht* and the four Grammatical Treatises. In U, it is incorporated within a section on phonetics and syllable structures. Clearly, therefore, our traditional interpretation of *Snorra Edda* as one integral 'book of instruction on native poetics' (Kristjánsson 1988: 178) need not reflect the uses to which the texts within it were put in the years following their composition (cf. Lönnroth 1992: 147; Krömmelbein 1992: 114–15).

ARTES GRAMMATICAE, ARTES METRICAE

Óláfr hvítaskáld and, to a lesser extent, Snorri Sturluson, as men of letters operating within an Icelandic vernacular poetic tradition, were faced with a problem with no obvious solution. On the one hand, they were educated within a conventional Latin framework, within which grammar meant Latin grammar and metrics meant quantity, or at the least syllable counting. On the other hand, they were working within a scholarly tradition which had already embraced the vernacular as a prime medium for the dissemination of works which in analogous situations elsewhere in Europe would have been written in Latin[4] and which therefore could not be simply discounted as vulgar.

In this context, the work of Óláfr hvítaskáld and the other grammarians can be seen as an attempt to establish a secure footing for the continued use of Icelandic as a *Schriftsprache* with a suitable scholarly apparatus similar to that enjoyed elsewhere by Latin, and for this it was essential that a recognized and codified grammar should be available. In this respect scholarship in thirteenth-century Iceland was in a position analogous to that of seventh-century Ireland and responded in a similar fashion, by producing a Latin-based vernacular grammar far earlier in relation to the introduction of Latinity than was the case in England or on the Continent.[5]

As the *ars poetica* was an integral part of the classical description of grammar, a native grammatical tract with any claim to completeness would have to include it; however, in the surviving Icelandic grammatical material, particularly *3GT*, poetical material is given considerably more prominence than this basic need for inclusion would stipulate. Thus ostensibly, Óláfr hvítaskáld's tracts are prescriptive works laying down, as do his classical authorities, the requirements for acceptable use of language in rhetoric. However, they read much more like an apologia for native poetics, and there seems to be a case for saying that, although they cannot be termed *artes poeticae* in any strict sense of the word, since they do not systematically lay down a basis for the construction of metrical texts, the generic term grammatical treatise generally applied to them is somewhat misleading, and the term poetico-grammatic tract, though unwieldy, would be more appropriate (cf. Marold 1995: 108).

ÓLÁFR HVÍTASKÁLD AND THE GRAMMATICAL TREATISES

The grammatical treatises, in particular *3GT* and its successor, the fourteenth-century *4GT,* closely follow models established in Antiquity and given canonical status by Priscian and Donatus, to whom they continually refer (cf. Clunies Ross 1987: 24–5). In matters of style and elsewhere, where examples longer than the individual word are required, these exemplars use the accepted standard works of Latin literature, the majority of them in verse. This gives the Icelandic tractarians their chance of raising the native poetry to canonical status by employing it in the place of classical examples. However, in doing so they are faced with the following basic problems:

1 The metrical system on which vernacular versification is based has very little in common with Latin versification.
2 Native versification does not accept the aesthetic strictures imposed on classical rhetoric.

The solutions can be seen in the works of Óláfr hvítaskáld, who reacts to these problems in the following ways.

As far as possible, he shows the principles of native versification to be consonant with classical specifications. He accounts for this first in terms of aetiology; since Óðinn and the Æsir (Óláfr hvítaskáld's *Asíemenn*) were believed to have originated from Troy (*SnE* I: 24–30), it was logical to assume that, like the Romans, they had learned rhetoric and associated arts from the Greeks before moving north, thus lending the authority of antiquity to the native art (*SnE* II: 94; Klingenberg 1993: 46–9, Clunies Ross 1987: 27–8). Secondly, as a consequence of this line of argument, the constituent metrical recurrences of native poetry are shown wherever possible to be founded on rhetorical devices recommended by classical authorities, and thus showing that they are at least in principle sanctioned by Antiquity. Thus *aðalhending* (intra-linear tonic-syllable rhyme) is considered a form of paranomasia:

> Paranomasia setr saman líkar raddar, þær er újafnt merkja, sem hér er kveðit:
> > Heldr vill hilmir
> > Herja en erja.

> Þetta köllum vér aðalhendingar í skáldskap, ok taka af þessi figúru upphaf þeir hættir er með hendingum eru saman settir (*SnE* II: 148)

> (Paranomasia juxtaposes similar sounds with different meanings as in:
> > The hero would rather
> > Harry than harrow

> We call this *aðalhending* in poetry, and those metres which are composed in rhyme are all derived from this rhetorical figure)

and alliteration is seen as a form of paromoeon.

> Paromeon er þat, er mörg orð hafa einn upphafsstaf, sem hér:
> > Sterkum stilli
> > styrjar væni (*SnE* II: 148)

> (It is paromoeon when many words have the same initial, as here:
> > For the stern ruler
> > Hope of strife.)

Óláfr hvítaskáld sees the kenning as central to skaldic diction:

> Með þessum figúrum eru saman settar allar kenningar í norrænum skáldskáp, ok hon er mjök svá upphaf til skáldskaparmáls. (*SnE* II: 162)

> (All *kenningar* in Norse versification are composed using these rhetorical figures [Donatus's four categories of metaphor, cf. Keil IV: 399], so that they are more or less the foundation of poetic diction)

and is therefore at pains to tie it into standard classical practice:

> sem Ovidius segir:
> > Tiphis et Automedon dicar amoris ego (*SnE* II: 160)

> (as Ovid says:
> > Let me be called the Tiphis and Automedon of love.)

He is obviously aware that this is a sensitive area; it is the only occasion in *Mskr* in which a Latin author is quoted directly.[6] Somewhat ingenuously, the choice of quotation hints at three aspects in which skaldic diction is only vestigially comparable with the metaphor as categorized by Donatus. First, the kenning as used by skalds, and as implicitly defined both by Óláfr and by Snorri, relies on a complex system of allusion shared by poet and audience. A chapter on classical mythology is not an essential part of a classical grammatical or metrical tract, nor would a classical author of a tract on poetical diction have felt it necessary, as Snorri obviously does, to devote the bulk of his poetic tract to an exposé of native mythology. Second, no genre of classical Latin poetry revolves as fixedly around systematic use of metaphor as skaldic diction does around the kenning. Third, Ovid's example, seen as skaldic diction, is almost laughable in its simplicity.

Óláfr draws attention to the fact that apparent barbarisms can fulfil an aesthetic function in poetry and thus defends their use by the skalds:

> Um stundar afdrátt verðr barbarismus, sem hér:
>> Svanr þyrr beint til benja
>> blóðs vindara róðri
>
> *Vindara* er sett fyrir *vind-ára* róðri, ðat er flugr. Þess samstafa er skömm gjör fyrir fegraðar sakir, þvíat ðá hljóðar betr. (*SnE* 102)

> (Reduction of length results in a barbarism, as here:
>> The swan of blood flies by the rowing of wind-oars straight to wounds
>
> Here *vindara* is used for the rowing of *vindára* [wind-oars], that is flying. This syllable is made short for beauty's sake, because it sounds better like that.)

He maintains a distinction between the Latin versification (*versagjörð*) of the clerics (*Latínuklerkar*) and the native tradition and draws attention to the different aesthetic standards involved.

> Latínu-klerkar hafa ok þessa hending í versum, er þeir kalla *consonancia* . . . þessar hendingar er lítt geymt í norrænum skáldskap (*SnE* II: 84)

> (Latin scholars in their verses also use the rhyme they call*consonantia* . . . but this rhyme is not used much in Norse poetry)

By maintaining a distinction between native and Latinate aesthetics Óláfr hvítaskáld establishes the principle that the native poetic tradition need not be judged as inferior to the models of Antiquity although it does not always comply with Antique principles. By incorporating skaldic verse into his grammatical tracts he maintains the equal right of the native tradition to be treated, like the works of Latin Antiquity, as a canonical corpus. Óláfr hvítaskáld's incorporation of examples of skaldic poetry is thus that of a self-confident believer in the value of his own poetic tradition.

HÁTTATAL

This apparent personal faith of Óláfr hvítaskáld's in his native tradition has a slightly polemical touch, as if he does not expect it to be shared without question. His repeated mention of 'meistari Donatus' reminds us not only of the venerable nature of the authorities he is following; implicitly, it is a reminder that the grammars his tract is modelled on were designed for the analysis of Latin verse. It therefore raises the question of whether native verse is fit to be measured against the giants of Antiquity. Óláfr hvítaskáld may be convinced that it is, but the onus of proof is his, and the concept of the Latin poetic standard pervades the whole of his work.

In the *Ht* tract, on the other hand, this atmosphere of implicit comparison is completely lacking. The influence of classical scholarship is to be felt in the structure and mode of commentary, but these are subservient to the main purpose of displaying native versification. The text is the one single Icelandic work[7] that can lay claim to being, in essence at least, an *ars poetica*.[8]

In form and substance, the poem at the centre of the *Ht* tract can be regarded as a continuation of the traditions set by the Icelandic skalds in the courts of Norway since they began to achieve preeminence over native Norwegians in the tenth century. Its primary note, as we would expect of any skaldic poem, is panegyric; it presents the persona of the poet as a traveller attracted irresistibly by the fame of his patron, whose undying fame the skill of the poet is set to guarantee. The mode of address is direct, the exploits of the patrons being alluded to rather than directly narrated,[9] and the framework of expectations is predominantly martial. In its self-confident acceptance of the poet's competence and value to its patron it is directly in the tradition of the tenth-century heyday of Icelandic *skaldskápr* in Norway.

The cultural ambiguity of Ht^{10} starts with its mode of transmission; in all likelihood the work was presented to its dedicatees in written form, rather than being performed by the poet himself in the traditional manner (Faulkes 1991: ix). Concomitantly, therefore, the poem starts without the traditional plea for silence (in contrast, for example, to *Háttalykill* (*Hl*), and makes no final allusion to the patron's duty to reward. Whether or not the poem was conceived from the start as the basis of a commentary is uncertain, but its status as a demonstration piece can hardly be disputed in view of the author's utterance on completion of the hundredth stanza: 'Gløggva grein/hefi ek gert til bragar' ('I have rendered a clear account of poetic form'). Again, the extent to which it was consciously modelled on existing tracts cannot be established with absolute certainty (for an assessment see Marold 1995: 105–7); the commentary seems to show familiarity with classical models of exposition both in its use of the dialogue form and in its approach to the subject from first principles (Tranter 1997: 94). Parallels have been noted between Snorri's opening and the beginning of Fortunatianus's *Ars Rhetorica* 3 (Faulkes 1991: xv)[11] and with the structure of Donatus's *ars maior* (Marold 1995: 106–7), whilst its use of terminology generally appears to reflect a desire to find appropriate native terms for the distinctions found in classical *artes grammaticae* (Marold 1995: 109–14). Similarly, although the decimal hundred is an obvious choice of number for a prestigious collection of metrical forms, it does not seem unreasonable, given the other echoes of learned Latinity within the text, to postulate the influence, direct or indirect, of the *libri centimetri* whose existence is witnessed by Bede and of which one example survives in the form of Servius's *de centum metris*[12] (Faulkes 1991: xiv; Tranter 1993: 182–5).

Where Óláfr hvítaskáld concerns himself primarily with the rhetorical and aesthetic aspects of metrical composition, *Ht* is more a handbook on the technical construction of verse; characteristically, the acoustic and aesthetic effect of Snorri's variations is rarely considered.

Construction, for *Ht*, must be regulated on two interconnected and equally valued levels, phonology and semantics; compared with both classical and bardic metric tracts, the degree of attention given to semantic organization and the high status accorded it are quite remarkable. This starts with the attention given the use of *kenningar*, and continues with the delineation of syntactic or semantic criteria for the distinction of verse-forms such as *sextanmælt* (which stipulates sixteen subject–verb sentence units within the eight-line stanza) or *refhvörf* (in which the paradoxical juxtaposition of apparent semantic opposites is the distinctive feature of the form). The degree of attention given to semantic organization may reflect the need, in a highly arcane system of poetic diction designed for oral transmission, to ensure that units of meaning are placed predictably enough within a given form to allow their content to be decoded (cf. Gade 1995b: 24–8, 224–6), according to what has been termed the 'co-operative principle' (Poole 1988: 159, 162). In this case, it would be a clear indication of the survival of pre-Latinate standards of analysis into the literate era.

Ht appears to stand at the intersection of a native tradition which we can simplistically refer to as oral, and a Latin, written tradition, and is thus schizophrenic to a degree not evident in *Gylfaginning* and *Skáldskaparmál*, which fall more happily within the oral, semantic and myth-narrating base. This is most apparent in the terminology used in the classification of metres. The majority of names consist of one significant element only (excluding the denominations *henda, háttr, lag* etc.) and are metrically arbitrary, giving at best an impressionistic idea of the type of metre involved.[13]

However, traces can be seen in the tract of an attempt to impose a system of classification akin to that of Servius, in which metres, as well as being given their traditional denominations, *aristophanium, euripidium*, etc., are defined in terms of metrical units and syllables, *anapæstici dimetrum brachycatalecticum* and *iambici dimetrum catalecticum*.[14] However, unlike Servius, *Ht* does not impose a structural terminology on pre-existing metrical designations, but, where existing categories allow, uses additional categories of subdivision e.g. *meiri stúfr, mesti stúfr*, or even double subdivision, eg. *mesti refhvörf hinn þriði*.

In one category the commentator seems to enjoy free rein; the end-rhymed *runhenda* group. The commentary subsumes fifteen different end-rhymed metres under the overall heading of *runhenda*, dividing them into five different sections (*bálkr*), each of these consisting of three different stages, *rétt, minni, minnst.* The parallel to the conventional arrangement of Latin adjectives into three genders and (for the majority of the declensions) five cases is particularly striking.

The treatment of nomenclature suggests the tension within the commentary between the pressure exerted by pre-Latin, presumably preliterate tradition, and the desire to reap the benefits of prestige bestowed by Latin scholarship. In showing that the native poetic tradition can be analysed along Latin lines,[15] *Ht*, like Óláfr hvíta-skáld, is staking a claim for native poetry as equal in rank to imported Latin. Nonetheless, in deference to the existing tradition, there is a limit to the tampering allowed with old-established conventions of nomenclature. The less well established the tradition, the more likely it is to be forced into a Latinate mould; with the *runhenda* metres, marked out clearly by their end-rhyme as being cultural imports, the commentator is free to do more or less what he likes; and in the case of the other metres, the more exotic and less well established the metrical feature being presented, the less care needs to be taken about the treatment given it.

HÁTTATAL AND HÁTTALYKILL

Some indication of the extent to which *Ht* represents an attempt to Latinize the native systems of metrical denomination can be gained from comparison with the fragmentary twelfth-century *Háttalykill* (*Hl*) attributed to Rǫgnvaldr Earl of Orkney and the Icelander Hallr Þórarinsson.[16] As far as we can tell from the problematical manuscript preservation,[17] there is no metapoetical content to this *clavis*. Its stanzas sketch the exploits of mythical and historical heroes and kings in roughly chronological order (from Gunnarr and Atli to Magnús Bareleg as the poem now stands); the order in which the metres are presented appears haphazard (Faulkes 1991: xvi–xvii). The only subclassification present is that of *refrún*, but as *refrún in minni* and *refrún in meiri* are not adjacent in either surviving manuscript, it is arguable that these terms were superimposed on the poem at a later date.[18]

The opinion that *Hl* is a product of learned Latinity (Helagson and Holtsmark 1941: 120–4) must be accepted with reservations. The 'learned and foreign influences' (Faulkes 1991: xvi) are restricted to the use of numerous forms which are previously unattested in skaldic poetry, and the use of such forms and the desire to exemplify them in a poetic demonstration. There may be modelling on foreign forms, but there is no analysis; in this respect the foreign learning had yet to make its mark.

HÁTTATAL IN ITS MANUSCRIPT ENVIRONMENT

Although in the following I confine my remarks to *Hl*, it should be borne in mind that there is only one surviving manuscript in which *SnE* is found independently of non-Snorronian material (Codex Trajectinus, T) and this is late (*c.* 1595; Faulkes 1991: xxv). Indeed, of the three medieval manuscripts of *Snorra Edda* (R, U and W), R is the only one to present all four sections in one uninterrupted sequence, adding *Jómsvíkingadrápa* and *Málsháttakvæði* after *Ht*. Where older research has tended to regard these non-Snorronian items as intrusions, modern scholarship tends to view the compilation strategies of each different manuscript as a meaningful reflection of the concerns of the different compilers (cf. Krömmelbein 1992: 113–16). It is hardly coincidental, for example, that in both U and W, *Ht* is directly preceded by grammatical instruction.

R (Codex Regius: Reykjavík Stofnun Árna Magnússonar GkS 2367 quarto) and T (Codex Trajectinus: Utrecht University Library 1374)

R has tended to form the textual basis for all editions, while T can be regarded as the justification for assuming that *SnE* was originally conceived as a quadripartite work free of extranea. If this is so, we can disregard the question of compilation strategy completely in the case of T and its lost medieval exemplar, and restrict our comment on R to the conclusion that mythological concerns are paramount.[19]

U (Uppsala University Library DG 11)

This composite manuscript contains all four parts of SnE, but *Ht* breaks off after the commentary to stanza 56. Apparently extraneous material ('quatuor Codicis folia, quippe huc non pertinentia'; *SnE* II: 301, fn. 2) is used to form partitions between *Gylfaginning* and *Skáld-*

skaparmál[20] and the latter and *Ht* respectively. The first partition consists of the *Skáldatal*, a list of the court poets from the beginnings of the skaldic tradition to the end of the thirteenth century grouped according to the kings whose praises they sang (fols. 43–7) followed by a genealogy of Snorri Sturluson and a list of lawspeakers up to Snorri Sturluson. The fragment is significant as marking off the purely mythological section of the tract from the portion dealing with actual skaldic practice (Krömmelbein 1992: 122). Since skaldic practice is to be defined as that which is practised by the recognized skalds, the compiler is setting out his authorities in advance: first the corpus of known skalds, then the credentials of his author according to the criteria of descent and public office.[21]

Similarly, the second partition, fols. 88–92, anticipates the concerns of *Ht*. Here, the accent is on phonemic and syllabic structures. The compiler relates the three divisions of sound according to standard practice into inanimate, animate and human (this section closely follows *2GT*, ch. 2; cf. *SnE* II: 46–8), following this with two commentated diagrammatical representations of phonotactic relations and of syllabic combinations, with commentaries (cf. *2GT*, chs. 3–5, *SnE* II: 48–58). Again, this partition marks a logical boundary within the tract as a whole; from this point on, as far as the commentator is concerned, we leave the domain of semantic regulation of verse, and approach that of phonological recurrence. This implies recognition of Snorri's concern in *Ht* with aspects of phonetic regulation within verse-form. The implication is that the nature of the variations demonstrated in *Ht*, in particular the specific deployment of alliteration and the different types of *hending* cannot be understood unless their phonological basis is understood in terms of the written units of Latin grammar.

W (Codex Wormianus: Copenhagen Arnamagnæan Institute AM 242 folio)

This is the nearest approach in medieval Icelandic to a complete *ars grammaticopoetica*. The manuscript contains *Snorra Edda* in the order *Prologus, Gylfaginning, Skáldskaparmál* (abbreviated) then provides us with the four *Grammatical Treatises, Háttatal, Rígspula* and fragments on *ókennd heiti*.

By adopting this order, W represents a distinct change of emphasis compared with U. The specifically phonetic portions of grammatical instruction, represented here by *1GT, 2GT,* and the first nine chapters of *3GT (SnE* II: 62–92) are now separated from *Ht* by two lengthy tracts on poetic diction in its rhetorical aspects, *3GT,* chs. 10–16, 92–188, and *4GT,* 190–248. In addition, the manuscript concludes with two further non-Snorronian texts on poetic diction; both concerned with *ókennd heiti.* (The value of the narrative-mythological poem *Rígsþula* in this context is obviously the fact that it forms a convenient mnemonic framework for a large number of synonyms denoting men and women in different stations.)

THE COMPOSITION OF THE TRACTS AND THE MANUSCRIPT TRADITION

It is not at all certain whether the aims of the tractarians, as far as we can guess them today, and those of the manuscript compilers, were identical. Arguably, though, there was a certain degree of congruence between the aims of the *Grammatical Treatises* and those of the four parts of the *Edda.*[22] The *Grammatical Treatises,* in particular Óláfr hvítaskáld, and *Ht* had the common objective of legitimizing vernacular poetics in the face of Antique models, Óláfr hvítaskáld doing so by pointing out the extent to which native poetic diction conformed to classical patterns, *Ht,* less obviously so, by demonstrating that native poetry could be analysed and categorized in a manner analogous to the metrical tracts of Antiquity.[23] In the first three parts of the *Edda,* on the other hand, the emphasis is shifted somewhat, though there still seems to be a need for legitimization. The situation is here more akin to the use of allusions from classical mythology in the grammarians of Antiquity, and the debate in the early Church as to whether these tracts could be used in Christian education. Snorri's primary concern is to codify the system of poetic diction, by means of which for him, the native poetic code retains its individuality; the same concern infects the first sections of *Ht.* To do this he must present a key, within the Christian context, to the mythological allusions without which this diction cannot be sustained to any length.

ICELANDIC *ARTES* AND THE PRE-LITERATE SYSTEM OF VERSIFICATION

Assuming that the thirteenth-century grammatical and metrical tracts represent an Icelandic *ars poetica*, we are forced to raise the question as to what poetry this *ars* was intended to apply to, and how well it analysed the existing material. One tends to assume that Snorri understood Egill's system of versification, and yet there were as many years separating him from Egill as between Chaucer and Dryden, who manifestly did not understand Chaucer's principles of versification.

At the hub of the argument lies the problem of the syllable and its applicability to non-written versification. The treatment given in U exemplifies this. Above all, it displays a tension inherent in the basic assumption of Latin grammar: 'littera est pars minima vocis',[24] with its inevitable confusion of the written sign with the spoken phoneme. This confusion is evident in the phonetical portions of U, in particular in the first of the two diagrams depicting phonotactic relations. Here the graphemes of the language are portrayed in a series of concentric circles;[25] initial consonants, consonants, vowels, geminates and final consonants.[26] Here, the originally runic grapheme *thorn* <þ>, for example, is given as an initial-only consonant, its counterpart *eth* <ð> as a (syllable-) final-only consonant, although this in no way corresponds to the orthographical convention of the manuscript, in which *thorn* and *eth* are both used interchangeably medially and finally (cf. vitið, fol. 88, l.18; vitiþ, fol. 88, l.20). The discrepancy obviously arises because the tractarian wishes to render the phonetic distinction between an affricative onset and the purely fricative medial, a distinction that the graphematical convention is unable to sustain. Similarly, the third circle contains vowel sounds in three groups; single graphemes, the ligatures æ, a/ (a + upstroke) and ay, and the digraphs ei, ey. Although it seems that a phonetic classification is being attempted, here, too, the tractarian is unable to distinguish between the phonetic and graphematic levels, so that diphthongs and digraphs are confused. We are forced to conclude that the tracts that are being used to provide the necessary grounding in phonetic recurrences are inadequate for the task.

With the notable exception of Árnason (1991, esp. 93), standard authorities on skaldic verse have on the whole been happy to accept Snorri's account that the system is based on strict syllable count,[27] the standard pattern for *dróttkvætt* being an isosyllabic line of six metrical positions = six syllables. However, recent studies in Germanic metrics have been suggesting that the traditional dichotomy between conventional accentual-alliterative Germanic long-line metres and syllabic skaldic metres is overdrawn,[28] and that both depend on a metrical position involving a conglomerate of acoustically perceptible features in which both stress-accent and quantity play a significant part.[29] Arguably, in the commentary to the eighth stanza of *Ht*, which explains how a line can be extended to nine syllables, we can see a Latin-based, written-syllable-driven analysis of a form for which an acoustic-driven analysis is also applicable (Arnason 1991: 91–2). At some stage we have to face the question as to whether the syllable as *Ht* understands it[30] could ever have been the unit of metrical recurrence in a preliterate society; if Egill ever did pass on the elements of *skáldskapr* to Einarr, what exactly did these elements consist of?

CONCLUSION

None of the tracts examined above appears to be primarily concerned with the didactics of poetry. In *Hl*, we can see a demonstration piece, showing the state of the art in terms of formal variability, with a sideways glance at foreign cultures able to boast of high formal sophistication in metrics. *Ht*, on the other hand, seeks equal status with classical Latin metrical analysis. It demonstrates that Iceland, too, can produce its *liber centimeter*, and that a sophisticated metapoetical tradition is available for formal metrical analysis. Finally, Óláfr hvíta-skáld makes the case for Icelandic as a literary language, in which the schemes and tropes of classical rhetoric are as much at home as they are in Latin, and furthermore there is a sophisticated tradition of native poetry to prove it.

By the time these tracts were included in manuscript compilations, the focus of concern had shifted. Native poetics had already been established as equal-ranking with foreign poetical tradition: it now had to be embedded in the overall scholastic framework. R therefore secures the poetic art, in particular its mythological connotations, within the discipline of Christian theology; U establishes Snorri and the native poets as *auctores*; and W locates poetic diction within the framework of classical rhetoric.

NOTES

1 *Uraicecht na Ríar*, the second and first of the *Mittelirische Verslehren* respectively, the short tracts concerning *trefhocul* and *dían* in the Book of Leinster, details in Tranter 1997: 78–9.

2 Cf. Þorólfsson and Jónsson 1943: 170 (about Þormóðr), Sveinsson 1939: 141 (Hallfreðr).

3 That is, the composite text containing the 102 stanzas of Snorri Sturluson's panegyric on Earl Skúli and King Hákon, together with the commentary in conjunction with which it is preserved in Codices Wormianus (W) and Regius (R).

4 The classic examples are doubtless *Elucidarius* and *Physiologus*, and of course the grammatical treatises themselves.

5 Cf. Calder 1917: xxii–xxvii; Ahlqvist 1983: 33–4; the Irish tradition differs from the Icelandic in having also contributed significantly to the tradition of teaching grammar in Latin.

6 A similarly sensitive occasion, in which Norse rhyming practice is shown to be related to Latin, is also supported by a Latin quotation, this time an anonymous couplet in Goliardic measure, in the opening section of *3GT* (*SnE* II: 84).

7 From a vernacular point of view, *Snorra Edda* as a whole is to be seen as an *ars poetica*, the specialist handbooks on mythology and poetic diction *Gylfaginning* and *Skáldskaparmál* serving the purpose of poetical instruction, although these two parts of the work do not obviously resemble metrical or grammatical tracts current in the thirteenth century (Clunies Ross 1987: 22–9).

8 'beim genauen Hinsehen entdeckt man, daß er keimhaft eine vollständige skaldische Poetik enthält' (Marold 1995: 102).

9 The relation of content and cliché in skaldic narrative has been proficiently assessed by Poole 1988.

10 This is another instance of Snorri in the position of a 'medieval author between Norse and Latin culture', cf. Clunies Ross 1987: 175–6.

11 Faulkes qualifies his remark by pointing out that the tracts are different in purpose, the one being rhetorical, the other poetical. However, the use of rhetorical tracts as models for *artes poeticae* only reinforces the idea of the fluid boundary between the poetic discipline and those of the *trivium* which Óláfr hvítaskáld's treatment of poetry within the confines of grammar suggests.

12 Edited in Keil IV: 456–67.

13 For a breakdown of *Ht*'s nomenclature in terms of denominational elements see Tranter 1997: 113–18, the largest class of denominators being those in 'henda/hent'. If Marold's suggestion, that this element is an attempt to render the Graeco-Latin concept of the syllable in native terms, should find acceptance, then my remarks above require reappraisal. See also Tranter 1993: 182 for the inconsistency of the application of *lag* and *háttr* to eddic metres.

14 This method is forced on Servius by the fact that the traditional designations had in many cases, including those of *euripidium* and *aristophanium* been applied to more than one verse-form.

15 Appositely formulated by Marold 1995: 113: 'In ihnen [i.e. the more impressionistic stanza-names] könnte man die alten Strophennamen und metrischen Traditionen sehen, die nun bei Snorri einer wissenschaftlichen Systematik unterworfen werden'.

16 The attribution is made in *Orkneyinga saga* (ch. 81), where it is alleged that the composers wished to give five stanzas in each form but reduced the number to two to avoid an inordinately long poem; none of the manuscripts of *Orkneyinga saga* give us the text of the poem, and it is only extant in later fragments. This means we cannot be sure whether any of the names ascribed to various metres were current at the time of composition; where they coincide with Snorri's usage we cannot rule out contamination from the later work, but even divergence from Snorronian usage cannot be considered absolute proof.

17 Our only surviving records are two paper copies transcribed by Jón Rugmann between 1665 and 1672 (Helgason and Holtsmark 1941: 6, 17).

18 At what stage this might have happened is uncertain, but the discrepancies of terminology between *Hl* and *Ht* suggest that it cannot have been under the direct influence of Snorri's work; cf. Faulkes 1991: xvii.

19 If we follow Krömmelbein 1991: 124–5, we might add that the compiler of R seems concerned to emphasize the compatibility of the mythology summarized by Snorri with Christian belief.

20 There is disagreement among editors as to where *Skáldskaparmál* begins; since Finnur Jónsson, there has been a general consensus that the division be made where the narrative persona of Gylfi is replaced by Ægir; this corresponds to fol. 35 of U. However, there is no manuscript authority for this placing. U assigns the whole of the section in which Ægir questions the gods on the origins of poetry (which is given in abbreviated form in this manuscript) to the mythological section. The new section opens at the top of fol. 51 with the title 'her hefr skalldskapar mal' corresponding to SnE, ch. 2 and Jónsson 1900, ch. 3.

21 Although I agree in essentials with Krömmelbein's interpretation of the compilation strategy here, I see a difference in emphasis; where Krömmelbein interprets the inserted material as reflecting an interest in the person of Snorri

('encomiastic intent' 1992: 123), I would prefer to see it as reflecting a concern with his *auctoritates* in the scholastic sense; with the *hǫfuðskáld* on whose reputations the canonicity of poetic diction relies, and with the dignity of his chief *auctoritas* Snorri in birth (he can trace his descent, like King Alfred, to Adam through Odin) and in civil position.

22 The problems are succinctly outlined in Margaret Clunies Ross's 'Response to Klaus von See'(1990); readers of German may be amused to read the incredible outburst (characteristically entitled *Korrektur*nachtrag [my italics]) this moderate refutation elicited from Klaus von See himself in Wolf 1993: 173–7.

23 Judy Quinn sees this as Óláfr's development of the pedagogical principles first applied by Snorri as the result of 'the rising tide of learned Latin scholarship' (1994: 81); I prefer to see it less as a historical development (can we be sure that Óláfr formed his opinions significantly later than the commentary was being added to *Ht*?) than as the result of a more defensive attitude on the part of a poet less eminently self-confident within his own tradition than Snorri most clearly was.

24 *3GT* in the formulation 'Stafr er hinn minnsti lutr samansettrar raddar, sá sem rita má' (*SnE* II: 66) adopts the identity of spoken and written language, 'því at stafr er rödd, en rödd er lopt' (*SnE* II: 66). Cf. Donatus, *Ars Gramm.* I, 2, 'Littera est pars minima vocis articulatae' (Keil IV: 367), Priscianus *Inst. Gramm.* I, 3, 'Litera [sic] est pars minima vocis conpositae' (Keil II: 6).

25 The same scheme is followed by U, but with some apparent confusions.

26 The first of these is described by the tractarian of the second treatise as follows: 'I fyrsta hríng eru fjórir stafir. þá má til einskis annars nýta, en vera upphaf ok fyrir öðrum stöfum' (*SnE* II: 48), giving the letters þ, v, h, q. The diagram in U gives the letters q (ku), y (ups), þ (thorn) and h (ha) reading clockwise; the text adds runic f and repeats h.

27 '*dróttkvætt* poetry, unlike Germanic alliterative poetry, depends on syllable counting' (Gade 1995b: 7). Turville-Petre (1976: xvii) is probably the most extreme statement of this position: 'To be fully scaldic, as I use the term a poem must be in syllable-counting measure'. Kuhn 1983: 67, refers to a line of six positions ('sechs Glieder') without explicitly equating these with syllables.

28 The position is stated overtly in Árnason 1991: 149–72; see Kendall 1991, e.g. 6 ('delicate interplay'), Russom 1987: 5, Cable 1991, e.g. 11 ('Old English metres founded on two equal principles [stress-count and syllable count] which pull in opposite directions').

29 The problem is most concisely stated in Árnason 1991: 147–8.

30 Presumably, following the standard authorities, as *conprehensio litterarum*, as in Donatus's *Ars Grammatica* I, 3, 'Syllaba est conprehensionis litterarum vel unius vocalis enuntiatio temporum capax' (Keil IV: 368; cf. Marold 1995: 111).

REFERENCES

Ahlqvist, A. 1983, *The Early Irish Linguist*. Commentationes Humanarum Litterarum 73, 1982. Helsinki: Societas Scientiarum Fennica.

Árnason, K. 1991, *The Rhythms of Dróttkvætt and Other Old Icelandic Metres*. Reykjavík: University of Iceland, Institute of Linguistics.

Bragason, Ú. (ed.) 1992, *Snorrastefna*. Rit Stofnunar Sigurðar Nordals, 1. Reykjavík: Stofnun Sigurðar Nordals.

Breatnach, L. 1987, *Uraicecht na Ríar*. Dublin: Dublin Institute for Advanced Studies.

Cable, T. 1991, *The English Alliterative Tradition*. Philadelphia: University of Philadelphia Press.

Calder, G. 1917, *Auraicept na N-Éces: the Scholar's Primer*. Edinburgh: John Grant.

Clunies Ross, M. 1987, *Skáldskaparmál: Snorri Sturluson's* Ars Poetica *and Medieval Theories of Language*. The Viking Collection, 4. Odense: Odense University Press.

1990, 'Response to Klaus von See', *Saga-Book of the Viking Society* 23(2): 73–9.

Edda Snorra Sturlusonar, editio Arnamagnæana 1848–87, 3 vols. Copenhagen: Sumptibus Legati Arnamagnæani.

Faral, E. (ed.) 1958, *Les Arts Poétiques du XIIe et du XIIIe Siècle*. Paris: Champion.

Faulkes, A. 1993, 'The Sources of *Skáldskaparmál*: Snorri's Intellectual Background', in Wolf, pp. 59–76.

(ed.) 1991, *Snorri Sturluson: Edda Háttatal*. Oxford: Clarendon. [Repr. with addenda and corrigenda, Viking Society for Northern Research, University College London, 1999.]

Fix, H. (ed.) 1995, *Quantitätsproblematik und Metrik: Greifswalder Symposium zur germanischen Grammatik*. Amsterdamer Beiträge zur Älteren Germanistik 42. Amsterdam: Rodopi.

Gade, K. E. 1995a, 'Quantitätsverschiebungen in der Dróttkvættdichtung des 13. und 14. Jahrhunderts', in Fix, pp. 31–40.

1995b, *The Structure of Old Norse dróttkvætt Poetry*. Islandica, 49. Ithaca and London: Cornell University Press.

Guðmundsson, F. (ed.) 1965, *Orkneyinga saga*. Íslenzk fornrit, 34. Reykjavík: Hið íslenzka fornritafélag.

Helgason, J. and Holtsmark, A. (eds.) 1941, *Háttalykill enn forni*. Bibliotheca Arnamagnæana, 1. Copenhagen: Munksgaard.

Holtsmark, A. 1961, 'Háttalykill', *Kulturhistorisk leksikon for nordisk middelalder* sub verbo.

Jónsson, F. (ed.) 1931, *Edda Snorra Sturlusonar*. Copenhagen: Gyldendal.

Keil, H. (ed.) 1961 (reprint) *Grammatici Latini*. 8 vols. Hildesheim: G. Olms. [First published Leipzig, 1857–80.]

Kendall, H. 1991, *The Metrical Grammar of Beowulf.* Cambridge: Cambridge University Press.

Klingenberg, H. 1974, *Edda: Sammlung und Dichtung.* Beiträge zur nordischen Philologie, 3. Basel and Stuttgart: Helbing & Lichtenhahn.

1993, 'Odin und die Seinen', *alvíssmál* 2: 31–80.

Kristjánsson, J. 1988, *Eddas and Sagas.* Reykjavík: Hið íslenzka bókmenntafélag.

Krömmelbein, T. 1991, 'Creative Compilers: Observations on the Manuscript Tradition of *Snorra Edda*', in Bragason, pp. 113–29.

Kuhn, H. 1983, *Das Dróttkvætt.* Heidelberg: Carl Winter.

Lönnroth, Lars 1992, 'The Reception of Snorri's Poetics: an International Research Project', in Bragason, pp. 143–54.

Marold, E. 1995, 'Die Poetik von *Háttatal* und *Skáldskaparmál*', in Fix, pp. 103–24.

Minnis, A. 1988, *Medieval Theory of Authorship: Scholastic Literary Attitudes in the Later Middle Ages.* 2nd edn. London: Scolar Press.

Nordal, S. (ed.) 1933, *Egils saga Skalla-Grímssonar.* Íslenzk fornrit, 2. Reykjavík: Hið íslenzka fornritafélag.

Poole, R. 1988, 'The Cooperative Principle in Medieval Interpretations of Skaldic Verse: Snorri Sturluson, Þjóðólfr Arnórsson and Eyvindr skáldas-pillir', *Journal of English and Germanic Philology* 87: 159–78.

Quinn, J. 1994, *Eddu List,* the Emergence of Skaldic Pedagogy in Medieval Iceland', *alvíssmál* 4: 69–92.

Russom, G. 1987, *Old English Metre and Linguistic Theory.* Cambridge: Cambridge University Press.

Sveinsson, E. Ó. (ed.) 1939, *Vatnsdœla saga.* Íselnzk fornrit, 8. Reykjavík: Hið íslenzka fornrafélag.

Tranter, S. N. 1993, 'Das Háttatal von Snorri Sturluson', in Wolf, pp. 179–92.

Tranter, S. N. 1997, *Clavis Metrica: Háttatal, Háttalykill and the Irish Metrical Tracts.* Beiträge zur nordischen Philologie, 25. Basel and Frankfurt am Main: Helbing & Lichtenhahn.

Turville-Petre, E. O. G. (1976), *Scaldic Poetry,* Oxford: Clarendon.

Þórólfsson, B. and Jónsson, G. (eds.) 1943. *Vestfirðinga saga.* Íslenzk fornrit, 6. Reykjavík: Hið íslenzka fornritafélag.

Wolf, A. (ed.) 1993, *Snorri Sturluson, Kolloquium anläßlich der 750. Wiederkehr seines Todestages.* Tübingen: Gunter Narr Verlag.

7

A useful past: historical writing in medieval Iceland

DIANA WHALEY

AN INTRODUCTION TO HISTORICAL WRITING IN MEDIEVAL ICELAND

One could gain the impression from many handbooks on medieval European historiography that there was none in Iceland, and it is perhaps easy to see why authors such as Ari Þorgilsson and Snorri Sturluson are so often left unmentioned. Clearly, writing in a little-known vernacular and on a remote island in the North Atlantic does not favour wide impact. Moreover, a small, generally impoverished nation, deficient in kings and battles, but also lacking roads, towns and the other preconditions for social, economic and political diversity, might seem to have little to offer to serious historians; especially when that nation's records of the past more often take the form of saga rather than of chronicle.

However, the Icelanders, as recent colonists of a near-virgin territory far from the cultural centres of Europe, and as possessors of a constitution unique in the known world, had, and have, more reason than most to reflect both on their origins and on their uniqueness.[1] By the time written history began in the early twelfth century they had abundant oral materials to work with, while the tools of international scholarship had been available at least since the official conversion to Christianity *c.* 1000. Indeed, the Icelanders have cultivated their own history with a vigour out of proportion to their resources and population size. In medieval and post-medieval times the sagas were a vital boost to national morale in the face of natural disasters and foreign domination, and they supplied much of the rhetoric and ideology for the independence struggles of the nineteenth and early twentieth centuries.

Historical themes were among the earliest uses to which the literacy that came with conversion was applied. Ari Þorgilson's *Íslendingabók*, which arguably comes the closest of all early Icelandic writings to modern historical method, is also the earliest written text known from medieval Iceland.[2] It was written down at some time between 1122 and 1133, hence only a few years after the law-book *Hafliðaskrá* (1117–18, now lost). A few decades later, another pioneer applied foreign techniques to vernacular materials, this time to the language itself, especially its phonology and orthography. The anonymous author of the so-called *First Grammatical Treatise* recognized Icelandic as a separate language,[3] and designed a new alphabet to facilitate literary production in the vernacular – law, genealogy, translations or interpretations of religious works (*þýðingar helgar*), and 'the learned lore (*frœði*) which Ari Þorgilsson has set down in books'. The importance of history is, moreover, signalled in the opening sentence, which points out that in most countries people record events in their own land and the most memorable from abroad. Further evidence for interest in history in the mid-twelfth century comes from Eiríkr Oddsson's *Hryggjarstykki*, which appears from its indirect preservation in *Fagrskinna*, *Morkinskinna* and *Heimskringla* to have given a detailed account of Norwegian events of the writer's own times. It has been dubbed 'the first saga' (Guðnason 1978).

The value placed on historical knowledge is also clear from the fact that many of the greatest intellectuals of the Icelandic *þjóðveldi* ('commonwealth') were distinguished by the honorific nickname *inn fróði* 'the wise, learned' or the near-synonymous *inn vitri*, and people referred to as (*sann-*)*fróðir, vitrir* etc. are often mentioned as respected oral sources in the prologues to historical writings (Tómasson 1988: 222–7).[4] Iceland in her early centuries even exported historians in the form of skalds (poets) who from *c.* 1000 became the chief providers of poetic propaganda and commemoration at the royal courts of Scandinavia. Foreign authors – the Norwegian Theodoricus and the Dane Saxo – paid tribute, around AD 1200, to the Icelanders' preservation of historical materials in their ancient poems (*in suis antiquis carminibus*, Theodoricus p. 3), and used them as sources for their own Latin histories. Expertise in vernacular prose was also exported, as when one of the earliest sagas of kings was written in the 1180s by the Icelander Karl Jónsson for the Norwegian king Sverrir Sigurðarson (r. 1177–1202) who 'sat over him and told him what to write' (*Sverris saga*, p. 1).

The Icelanders were unique in Europe in having, in terms of human settlement, a temporally finite history, and there seems in retrospect to have been almost a coordinated, collaborative effort to cover the whole of that history. It appears, for instance, that Sturla Þórðarson (1214–84) planned no less than a complete history of Iceland, comprising his redaction of *Landnámabók*, *Kristni saga* and much of *Sturlunga saga*, while the *Sturlunga* collection itself seems to aim for comprehensiveness, presenting 'contemporary sagas' (*samtíðarsögur*) which between them cover Icelandic events spanning 1117–1264.[5] Sturla is also widely thought to have been involved in the compilation of annals, that most concise but comprehensive form of historical record.[6] The crucial period from just before the settlement to a generation after the conversion (mid-ninth century to c. 1030), is covered, albeit in retrospective narratives of 'realistic historical fiction' (Harris 1986: 189), by sagas of Icelanders (*Íslendinga sögur*) from all four quarters of Iceland. *Færeyinga saga*, a tale of defiant Faeroe-islanders, explores similar issues to the *Íslendinga sögur*, including chieftainly politics, the conversion, and relations with Norwegian kings. *Eiríks saga rauða* and *Grænlendinga saga*, which trace the voyages of discovery west to Greenland and 'Vinland', are also usually counted as generically akin to the *Íslendinga sögur*. The period between c. 1030 and 1117 is something of a gap in the otherwise continuous coverage of secular native history, but it is covered by the sagas of bishops (*Biskupa sögur*). Among these, *Hungrvaka* is a prelude to *Þorláks saga*, which is followed chronologically by *Páls saga*. This sequence, together with a shared, incorrect chronological scheme going back to Gerland de Lorraine c. 1100 (Bekker-Nielsen 1965: 40–1), suggests coordination also in the writing of *Biskupa sögur*. As for the history of the other Nordic-speaking lands, the sagas of kings (*konunga sögur*) cover the whole sweep of Norwegian kings, from their mythical beginnings to the later thirteenth century, while the imperfectly preserved *Skjǫldunga saga* together with *Knýtlinga saga* survey the Danish royal line from prehistoric times down to the late twelfth century, and *Orkneyinga saga* (also known in medieval times as *Jarla saga*) does the same for the earls of Orkney. In all these groups, there is relatively little duplication of coverage, though it is difficult to gauge how far this is due to planning and how far to the partly accidental pattern of preservation or loss of texts.

The early decades of the Icelandic church saw fertile contacts with the rest of Christendom, as foreign clerics participated in the establishment of Christian institutions in Iceland and prominent Icelanders studied abroad: Ísleifr Gizurarson, the first native bishop, in Herford, Saxony, and Sæmundr Sigfússon in France (*Frakkland*), for example. Hallr Teitsson travelled widely and spoke like a native wherever he went (*Biskupa sögur* I: 80), and Þorlákr Þorhallsson studied in Paris and Lincoln.[7] The new learning provided by such contacts could be applied both to recording Nordic history and to translating and adapting foreign histories from Latin sources, especially within clerical schools such as the one at Skálholt, first bishopric of Iceland. Believed to be among the earliest of these are *Veraldar saga*, compiled from works by Bede, Isidore of Seville and others *c.* 1190 in Iceland or Norway, and *Rómverja saga*, mainly from Sallust, also from the end of the twelfth century. *Gyðinga saga* (History of the Jews), based on Josephus and others, is usually placed in the mid-thirteenth century. From approximately the same period come three works which have kinship both with historiography and *riddarasaga* (chivalric saga): *Breta sögur* (Sagas of Britons), based on Geoffrey of Monmouth's *Historia Regum Britanniae*, *Trójumanna saga*, based on the *De excidio Trojae* of 'Dares Phygius', and *Alexanders saga*, from Galterus de Castellione's *Alexandreis*.[8] Although it has been argued that some of these works, notably *Breta sögur* and *Trójumanna saga*, may have been associated with the court of Hákon Hákonarson (r. 1217–63), and hence of Norwegian rather than Icelandic provenance (Halvorsen 1957: 222, and Louis-Jensen 1974: 654, reporting Halvorsen), they are all preserved in Icelandic manuscripts. The range of historical writings available to, and appreciated by, a single Icelandic householder (one who happened to spend some years in Norway) by the beginning of the fourteenth century is demonstrated by the remarkable codex *Hauksbók*, whose contents include Haukr Erlendsson's redaction of *Landnámabók*, as well as texts of *Kristni saga*, *Eiríks saga rauða*, *Breta sögur*, *Trójumanna saga*, and a regnal list of West Saxon kings from Cædwalla to Æðelstan.

The profusion and variety of Icelandic writings about the past make defining the field of 'historical writings' problematic, and the titles of works are of only limited help. No single Icelandic word is semantically coterminous with Latin *historia* or English 'history' (which is anyway multivalent, referring to (a) the phenomena of the past; (b) oral or written accounts of past phenomena,[9] 'historiography' being a usefully unambiguous term for written history; and (c) the study of past phenomena). As will be suggested below, the use of the term *bók* in the two most important treatments of vernacular history may be significant, but *saga* embraces a vast spectrum of writings from relatively sober, if somewhat hagiographical, narratives such as *Kristni saga* or Oddr Snorrason's *Óláfs saga Tryggvasonar* to the self-declaredly fantastic *lygisögur*.[10] Meanwhile, the content of historical writing is expressed by the word *fræði* or *fróðleikr* 'wisdom, learning, especially about the past'.[11]

One category of texts can be excluded from the outset: the 'unconscious' or 'unintentional' documents such as charters, letters and inventories, produced for functional reasons of doing business with one's contemporaries, which have been taken as a form of evidence distinct from, and more reliable than, the more conscious, more literary products of medieval historians who crafted accounts of *their* past with an eye on a contemporary audience and on posterity. Although this distinction has been questioned,[12] the 'unconscious' documents remain more germane to the study of history than to the study of historical writing, and for this reason, as well as because of the paucity of such documents from the earliest centuries in Iceland,[13] we shall pass on to retrospective accounts of the past.

What texts, then, can be counted as historical? Any criteria adopted will be debatable (not least those involving the thorny problem of intentionality), and under each criterion the texts present a spectrum, not discrete categories. However, as a pragmatic starting-point, one might look among other things for evidence of a primary intent to preserve information and ideas about the past, rather than, for instance, merely to entertain. Outer signs of such intent might include the fact that the writing is non-anonymous and accompanied by a first-person authorial prologue or epilogue (Tómasson 1988). One would also expect the matter of the work to have importance beyond the local and immediate, either because it is concerned with persons, groups and happenings which have a significant effect on society, during their lifetime and beyond, or because persons and events insignificant in themselves, by accumulation or representativeness, point to more general phenomena or trends. The work will also, of course, recognize the alterity or differentness of the past, and show some concern for representing or reconstructing the past in a factually accurate way.[14] The author may, for instance, cite his evidence, admit uncertainty where evidence is lacking or where alternative scenarios are possible, and declare his openness to correction if better information should become available. On the basis of criteria such as these, the *Íslendinga sögur, konunga sögur, samtíðar sögur* and *Biskupa sögur* all claim serious attention as windows on the early Nordic world. The *Íslendinga sögur*, to take the most popular and most difficult case, show many signs of a genuinely historical sensibility: they are strongly genealogical and chronological, concerned with central events and issues such as settlement, conversion and the rule of law. They are sensible both of the alterity of the past, and of 'historical–causal entailment'; they also most interestingly intertwine matters of private and public import (Harris 1986, esp. 190). It could, moreover, be argued that, although imaginative reconstruction of dialogue, character and event are deployed with a liberality that frequently amounts to pure invention, the historical deficiency on one side is compensated elsewhere. Scholars have found more and more evidence to confirm the long-held suspicion that the sagas reveal more about the time of composition and about their authors' view of the past than they do about the past which is narrated, and that what can be discovered is less to do with 'facts' and more to do with attitudes, 'mentality' and social structures. The *Íslendinga sögur* are thus being reappraised as ethnographic documents.[15] They also gain credit relative to more sober-seeming histories in the light of recent developments in the theory of language, literature and history. Of especial relevance are the increasing realization of the selectivity and bias in all narrative history, and more broadly of the nature of language as a system of signs which does not directly represent reality (e.g. White 1978), not to mention the constructivist claim that 'facts' are anyway human intellectual constructs rather than objective realities. Nevertheless, some early Icelandic works, and in particular two whose titles, perhaps significantly, end in *bók* rather than *saga*, match the criteria outlined above more closely. For this reason, and since most branches of saga literature are discussed separately within this volume, they will be at the centre of the present chapter. The two works are *Íslendingabók*, 'Book of the Icelanders', by Ari Þorgilsson and *Landnámabók*, 'The Book of Settlements'. Although the main focus will be Icelandic history, reference will also be made to the sagas of kings.

ORAL TRADITION

How and why, then, did the Icelandic historiographical endeavour come about? I will first address the question 'how' before asking 'why'. The starting-point is unquestionably oral tradition, though by definition this is an extremely elusive entity. The only variety that is now believed to have survived more or less intact into the literate era is skaldic verse, preserved by its tight and intricate metre in a way that even legal formulae and genealogies could not match (see ch. 3 in this volume). Most of the earliest preserved skaldic poetry, whether its materials are genealogical, mythical, legendary or historical, was composed in praise of Nordic rulers, and the chief metrical form is called *dróttkvætt* ('court metre'). Where they appear to be genuinely contemporary, skaldic verses take us closer to events than any other source, and since functionary poets often served their masters as warriors as well as propagandists, they are in effect despatches from the front line. Despite their often stereotyped and vague content, they were highly valued, and much quoted by the authors of the prose *konungasögur*. Snorri Sturluson, for instance, singles out ancient poems (*forn kvæði*) as a pre-eminent source for his *Heimskringla*, and includes over six hundred skaldic quotations from over seventy skalds.[16] Respect for the poetic traditions of Icelanders among historians in mainland Scandinavia has already been mentioned.

From the end of the tenth century Iceland was the main, perhaps the only, breeding-ground for functionary skalds, but the earliest ones known are Norwegian, and the extraordinary genius of Egill Skalla-grímsson appears to spring out of rather thin Icelandic soil. When the medium is transplanted to Iceland the subject-matter is scaled down, and the personal conflicts of Icelandic farmers commemorated in free-standing occasional verses (*lausavísur*) seem less momentous than those of Norwegian kings commemorated in extended poems. The *lausavísur* are widely quoted in the *Íslendinga sögur*, especially the sagas about poets such as Kormakr or Gunnlaugr, where they form part of the action rather than being used, as extracts from court poems are, to authenticate narratives. There is no skaldic verse about such great collective moments as the settlement of Iceland, the establishment of the Althing or the conversion to Christianity. The poem *Íslendinga-drápa*, attributed to the obscure Haukr Valdísarson, might sound like a verse analogue to *Íslendingabók*, but it is far from it. It certainly postdates *Íslendingabók*, and is a catalogue of great individuals, not a national history (*Skjaldedigtning* A I: 556–60 and B I: 539–45; and see Einarsson 1993). Overall, then, although skaldic tradition must have helped create the conditions for all historical prose in Iceland by sustaining interest in the past and demonstrating the power of public commemoration, its chief role was in the evolution of writings about Norway, not of those about Iceland.

Other types of oral tradition may have had a more direct impact on Icelandic historical writings, although they took a much more fluid form, fixed in memory not by tight metrical schemes, but perhaps by 'landmarks' in the physical or social environment where the past penetrates the present. Stories were, for instance, prompted by natural features, burial mounds or other visible antiquities – a phenomenon common to many cultures. Richard Perkins speaks of 'kernels' for oral tradition and lists six varieties (1989: 242). The remembered hurts or triumphs of neighbourhood feuds must have provided the cue for many stories, as did place names and personal names, including colourful nicknames (Whaley 1993b) or given names passed down from grandfather to grandson.[17] And names, of course, constitute the most fundamental type of oral tradition: genealogy, whose huge importance is seen in works like *Landnámabók*, and in the mainly thirteenth-century *Íslendingasögur*, which are estimated to show approximately 95 per cent agreement where the same genealogical ground is shared by different sagas.[18]

Around the end of the first millennium, the conversion brought the preconditions for historiography of a recognizably European kind – literacy and quite possibly a heightened awareness of teleology, linear chronology and causal relationship (Harris 1986: 195). Yet, despite the favourable conditions, Icelandic historiography seems to have had a rather nervous start. About a century elapses before any detectable historical endeavour or manuscript production takes place, and it appears that the codification process began with Sæmundr Sigfusson (1056–1133). Sæmundr is frequently cited by later writers as an authority for events in Norway and Iceland, and, in the poem *Nóregs konunga tal*, for a chronology of Norwegian kings (see Whaley 1993c). His work is lost, but if indeed he *wrote* any history at all (and some have doubted this), it was quite likely rather brief, and probably in Latin. This is normally inferred from the fact that Snorri Sturluson (d. 1241) saluted Ari Þorgilsson, in the Prologues to his separate *Óláfs saga helga* and *Heimskringla*, as the first vernacular historian (*Heimskringla* I: 5–7 and II: 419–20). and it would square with the fact that Sæmundr was a priest who studied abroad in 'Frakkland'. In later Icelandic folklore, Sæmundr became a magician who outwitted the Devil with all sorts of tricks. It may be, though, that his greatest trick was to import a new kind of historical self-consciousness to Iceland.

The first historiography: Ari's Libellus Islandorum–Íslendingabók

That the earliest piece of extant historiography from medieval Iceland has both a Latin title and a Norse one is symptomatic of its dual origins in learned and oral tradition. And we may note that the title is *bók*, not *saga*. This is something to be read, not to be heard, whereas *saga*, etymological sister to *segja* 'to say', hints at a narrative which communicates, often by oral performance. At the risk of over-simplification, one could say that the content of *Íslendingabók* is mainly native, while the presentation is strongly influenced by Latin clerical learning. This is not surprising, given that the author is a priest writing with the encouragement of the two bishops Þorlákr and Ketill, and the learned priest Sæmundr. (The work was also rescued for modern times by another bishop – Brynjólfur Sveinsson – in the seventeenth century.) The *Libellus* looks in some respects like a modern scholarly book. The brief preface to Ari's own second edition (the only one to survive) contains what amount to acknowledgements and an admission that improvement might be possible in light of better information;[19] there is a clear list of contents and chapter divisions; and the citation of the best oral informants and of archaeological and ethnographic evidence appears as a pledge of methodological goodwill. In citing his informants, and praising their reliability, Ari the priest is bringing his inherited oral materials into the literate era – just as Bede, similarly positioned close to an interface of oral and literary cultures in eighth-century England, acknowledges his witnesses in the *Life* of St Cuthbert and *Historia Ecclesiastica* (pp. 142–5 and 7 respectively). Further, although written in the vernacular, the fact that *Íslendingabók* is in prose may (as Björn Sigfússon pointed out, 1944: 75) be taken as an 'international' feature, since poetry or more recently Latin had been the normal vehicles for the preservation of historical traditions. Vernacular prose was a courageous choice, for a literary prose style had to be forged, and indeed the style is Latinate in some particulars, such as the handling of subordinate clauses and the use of paired synonyms (such as *at ætlun ok tölu* 'according to the opinion and reckoning'). The text is, moreover, lightly peppered with Latin words and phrases, such as *rex, obiit* and datings such as *Kalend. Junii*.

Ari was intensely interested in chronology – as witness the prominence he gives to the early Icelanders' attempts to improve the correlation between the solar year and the lunar month (ch. 4). The establishment of a chronological framework is one of the great achievements of *Íslendingabók*, and here too, we find a dualism. A list of Icelandic lawspeakers provides the basic framework, within which events are dated both according to the international *anno domini* system and, in what seems to be the native fashion, relatively to one another, although the points of reference are often sought in the wider Nordic world and beyond. The slaying in 870 of the English martyr king Edmund, and the deaths in battle of the two proselytizing Olafs – Tryggvason (1000) and Haraldsson (1030) – are especially favoured as chronological reference-points. Papacies are also often used as points of reference, and when Ari reaches the death of Gizurr Ísleifsson after his thirty-six year episcopacy (1118), a galaxy of obits drawn from unidentified foreign annals is appended, as we are told that it coincided with the deaths of Pope Paschal II, Baldwin, King of Jerusalem, Arnaldus, patriarch in Jerusalem, Philip, King of the Swedes, and Alexius [Comnenus], Emperor of the Greeks (ch. 10).

Despite the international references and the many devices gathered from Latin historiography, the content of *Íslendingabók* is thoroughly

Icelando-centric. It may, indeed, be viewed schematically as a series of concentric circles:

- Genealogy of individual Icelandic families, including the author's own
- Origins of the Icelandic nation:
  Settlement, establishment of law; the four quarters; internal conflict;
  Conversion, establishment of church
- Settlement of Greenland
- Icelandic relations with Norway; Norwegian rulers and events
- Rulers and events in the wider world

Space does not permit a full examination of these themes in *Íslendingabók* (some of them have already been taken up in chapter 1), but their centrality can be briefly demonstrated by the fact that they are all embryonically present even in the two short genealogical lists which are appended to *Íslendingabók* (pp. 26–28), and which go under the editorial heading of *Ættartala*.[20] In the first, headed 'This is the family and genealogy of the bishops of the Icelanders' (*Þetta es kyn byskupa Íslendinga ok ættartala*), one prominent settler from each quarter is identified, and his (or her, in the case of Auðr) family traced down to one of the first or current bishops of Skálholt or Hólar. Thus the essential connection of the first settlers (*landnámsmenn*) with the bishops is asserted, while the treatment of the quarters is balanced and systematic and shows the representativeness of the bishops. In the second genealogical list, headed 'These are the names of the ancestors of the Ynglings and the people of Breiðafjǫrðr' (*Þessi eru nǫfn langfeðga Ynglinga ok Breiðfirðinga*), the author locates himself in a wider world, by tracing a thirty-eight-generation line down from 'Yngvi Tyrkjakonungr' and 'Njǫrðr Svíakonungr' (the famous gods patently euhemerised as kings of the Turks and Swedes), through Freyr, Swedish and Norwegian kings, and then through six generations of Icelanders. The sixth is Þorgils, the author's father, 'and I', he finally adds, 'am called Ari' (*en ek heitik Ari*). The information is purely genealogical, except that the two great landmarks on Ari's conceptual map of the past are signalled, when Óláfr feilan is identified as the one 'who was the first of them to settle in Iceland', and Eyjólfr as the one 'who was baptized in his old age, when Christianity came to Iceland'. The theme of conversion is also very economically alluded to by the placing in the manuscript of a cross above the name of the first Christian in each family covered in the genealogy of bishops (though Gizurr hvíti lacks one; *Íslendingabók* 26, n.1).

The preoccupations reflected here in germinal form are worked out in the main body of *Íslendingabók*, which, despite its brevity, despite uncertainties about its antecedents (including the first edition), despite the fact that it survives in no medieval manuscript, has earned Ari the title of 'father of Icelandic history'. His work was admired and used by many later authors. The subject-matter sweeps, albeit briefly, through the favoured themes of the later *Íslendinga sögur* – settlement, conversion, conflict – as well as touching on matters worked out in the *Biskupa sögur, konunga sögur* and *Sturlunga saga*. One can even see the germs of Snorri Sturluson's euhemerized mythology in the Yngling genealogy, and the beginnings of the *prosimetrum* form so common in the sagas in Ari's inclusion of a verse, even if it is only the two lines of Hjalti Skeggjason's lampoon (*kviðlingr*) against the gods. Dreams, another salient feature of *Landnámabók* and the sagas, also make their first appearance here.

Nevertheless, Ari's first courageous step was not the start of a great twelfth-century march. No other Icelander wrote about national history in quite the same way, and none used the same methodology, especially not Snorri Sturluson, who is most vocal in his praise of Ari's approach. Most of the historiographical effort in the decades after Ari goes on Norwegian, not Icelandic, subjects – for instance *Hryggjarstykki*, 'the first saga', or early works about Óláfr helgi – and when, around the end of the twelfth century, the Icelanders start celebrating their own history again, it is in the dramatized form of saga. Meanwhile some topics, especially lives of saintly kings or of bishops, are dealt with in Latin in the years around 1200.

LANDNÁMABÓK

A more strongly native strand of historiographical tradition can nevertheless be seen in *Landnámabók*, 'The Book of Settlements', also known as *Landnáma*. The work survives in five main redactions, of which three – *Sturlubók, Hauksbók* and *Melabók* – are medieval and, though not

earlier than the later thirteenth century, are widely believed to have
their origins in the time of Ari Þorgilsson in the early twelfth century.
Landnámabók offers a marvellously systematic and often entertaining
account of some four hundred and thirty settlers, taken quarter by
quarter in a clockwise direction, beginning in the south.[21] This book
shows huge tracts of land being claimed, cultivated and shared out by
dynamic pioneers such as Ingólfr Arnarson, Auðr Ketilsdóttir and
Skalla-Grímr. No fewer than thirty-eight chapters of the *Sturlubók* text
(chs. 30–67), for instance, are devoted to Skalla-Grímr's distribution of
land.[22] As an example of the kind of information given about individual
settlements, we could take the case of Hvamm-Þórir:

> Hvamm-Þórir nam land á milli Laxár ok Forsár ok bjó í Hvammi.
> Þórir deildi við Ref enn gamla um kú þa, er Brynja hét; við hana er
> dalrinn kenndr. Hon gekk þar úti með fjóra tigu nauta, ok váru ǫll frá
> henni komin. Þeir Refr ok Þórir bǫrðusk hjá Þórishólum; þar fell
> Þórir ok átta menn hans. (*Landnámabók* S 18 I: 56–8)

> (Hvamm-Thorir took possession of land between Lax and Fors
> Rivers, and made his home at Hvamm. Thorir quarrelled with Ref
> the Old over a cow called Brynja. The valley Brynjudale takes its
> name from her. She used to roam there wild with forty head of cattle,
> all of them her offspring. Ref and Thorir fought at Thorishills and
> Thorir was killed there with eight of his men. (trans. Pálsson and
> Edwards 1972: 25))

The tradition of origins promoted in *Landnámabók* and elsewhere is
that the first Icelanders were well-born and dynamic people of mainly
Norwegian kin, who chose to emigrate rather than bow to the territorial
expansionism of King Haraldr hárfagri. Settlers named in *Landnámabók* include many men of distinction: Geirmundr heljarskin, a
warrior king (*herkonungr*) with a base in Rógaland (S112, H86), Brúni
enn hvíti, son of Hárekr Upplendingajarl (S213, H180), and Hrollaugr,
son of Rǫgnvaldr, Earl of Mœrir (Møre, S309, H270). As the progenitor
of the distinguished southern dynasty of the Síðumenn, Hrollaugr is
also one of the four select settlers who represent the four quarters in
chapter 2 of *Íslendingabók*. Several have connections with Irish kings,
and some are the kin of legendary heroes such as Ragnarr loðbrók.[23]
However, not all the settlers are presented as noble of birth or
behaviour. Þorbjǫrn bitra is a *víkingr ok illmenni* (S165), and Þormóðr

enn rammi flees from Norway after a killing and causes a great deal more trouble in Iceland (S215; cf. Molda-Gnúpr in S329). Nor is independent-minded revolt against the tyranny of Haraldr hárfagri the unvarying reason for emigration. Ingimundr Þorsteinsson fights for the king at the critical battle of Hafrsfjǫrðr and emigrates on his advice (S179), as do others.

To what extent do *Íslendingabók* and *Landnámabók* express pre-existing ideas about Icelandic identity, and to what extent do they create them? Because the oral (and possible written) background can now only be guessed at, and for other reasons, it is impossible to be certain. As far as *Íslendingabók* is concerned, however, it seems reasonable to conclude, with Meulengracht Sørensen (1993: 1), that it is in some sense the official line, not least because it was written under the supervision of the two bishops and the learned priest Sæmundr Sigfússon, himself a historian. It also seems likely, as Rafnsson argues, that the term *land-námsmaðr* used by Ari hints at the influence of some kind of central authority (which he presumes to be the Althing) in the encoding of the *landnám* tradition at some point before 1104 (1974: 229). The formidably complex textual history of *Landnámabók* itself, and the lateness of the extant manuscripts, make it still more problematic, but it seems that this too was organized from above, as it were. In the title, *Landnáma* is plural – the narratives are of settlements, not of *the* settlement: it is an aggregation of local and family histories.[24] But it is also a *bók*, and a highly organized one. There is also reason to see early twelfth-century historical endeavour as working to a programme, in which the *Landnámabók* project covered the genealogy of the Icelanders and the story of the settlement period, while *Íslendingabók* dealt with these summarily in order to continue the story up to the author's present. The two works are also complementary to the extent that *Íslendingabók* is concerned with the Icelanders as a nation, and *Land-námabók* with families and individuals.

THE PURPOSES OF HISTORICAL WRITING

Reflecting on *Íslendingabók*, Jakob Benediktsson asks, 'Was it pure scholarship, or was the book intended to preach a message to the Icelanders?' (*Var það hreinræktuð fræðimennska eða átti bókin að flytja*

Íslendingum boðskap? Íslendingabók: xviii). In one way, historical study is pure scholarship, needing no explanation. It is a natural expression of human curiosity, and it is as vital to the mental health of social groups as memory is to the individual. But, like memory, historiography is a transforming and creative activity, not merely a direct recording of past phenomena. As Sparkes says about classical Greece, 'The past . . . was not what actually happened, it was what was remembered, and what could most practically be brought to bear on the present. It sanctioned the way in which later generations lived and thought' (1989: 129).[25] While granting a genuine thirst to acquire and preserve knowledge *per se* in many cases, therefore, one may wonder whether scholarship can ever be pure.[26] The phrase 'a useful past' in the title of this chapter implies a commitment to the notion that the Icelandic historical enterprise served social purposes, and the discussion will now focus chiefly on those, moving from the more general functions of history to the more particular in an attempt to address the questions, exactly what made the Icelanders write history when they did and in the way they did; in what sense was it useful, and to whom?

INSTRUCTION AND ENTERTAINMENT

The *Hungrvaka* author adopts a common medieval topos when he offers his biographies of early Icelandic bishops as '(historical) knowledge, learning' (*fróðleikr*) which gives 'pleasure' (*gaman*). The pleasure offered by his book, he indicates, is more than a shallow type of 'quick fix' which is always followed by regret. And like any right-thinking modern academic, he devises his work not only to impart specific information but also to cultivate transferable skills in his young readership: 'There is another reason for this text: to entice the young to gain knowledge of our language and read the texts written in Norse – laws, sagas or *mannfræði* (genealogy/biography)'(*Biskupa sögur* I: 59–60).

The most basic lesson of history, perhaps, is that the judgement of society endures into the future (albeit not always unchanged), and the bestowing of fame or infamy is another very likely medieval reason for writing it. The Icelanders were particularly alive to the power of literature to confer immortality. In the 1040s, Arnórr jarlaskáld declared in his *Hrynhenda* for Magnús góði, *yppa róðumk yðru kappi . . . í kvæði fljótu* 'I mean to raise up your prowess . . . in a swift-running poem' (v. 1), *fenguð yrkisefni . . . gervi'k slíkt at mǫlum* 'you furnished matter for verse . . . I fashion such deeds into words' (v. 14), *Keppinn vannt, þat's æ mun uppi, Yggjar veðr, meðan heimrinn byggvisk* 'Daring, you fought a gale of Yggr [battle] which will always be praised aloft, as long as the world is peopled'(v. 15, *Skjaldedigtning* A I: 332 and 336; B I: 306 and 309). In the very different context of the *Njáls saga* account of Gunnarr Hámundarson's heroic last stand, characters say both of his valour and of the despicable treachery of his wife Hallgerðr that they will be spoken of (*uppi*, 'aloft') for a long time – as long as the land is inhabited in Gunnarr's case – and of course the saga author sees to that (ch. 77).

To later generations the lives commemorated are a source of moral or political education, furnishing examples of the good deeds of good men to emulate, and the bad to avoid. Bede, for instance, sees this as an important function of history, which is written *ad instructionem posteritatis* (Preface to the *Historia Ecclesiastica*, pp. 6 and 2; cf. William of Malmesbury, *De Gestis Regum Anglorum* I: 103). Similarly in the ancient world, Greek and Egyptian works about the heroic past held up standards of behaviour to societies which felt themselves to be in decline (Sparkes 1989; Baines 1989).

Much of Icelandic historiography honours great men of the past – heroes, saints, or preferably both simultaneously – whose lives have exemplary force, Oddr Snorrason's *Óláfs saga Tryggvasonar* being a classic case; but exemplary narratives can also be found outside the biographical and hagiographical works. Ari's *Íslendingabók*, short as it is, contains an embedded anecdote whose sole purpose is to demonstrate the importance of wise accommodation between factions. Þorgeirr the priest uses an *exemplum* of Danish and Norwegian kings reluctantly agreeing to peace at the bidding of the people in order to persuade the Icelanders to bury their differences and unite under Christian law (ch. 7). This reinforces the message of the importance of peaceful consensus under the law which Ari makes the burden of his brief work. On a much grander scale, Snorri Sturluson does not explicitly 'sell' his great cycle *Heimskringla* as a source of instruction, but it offers limitless lessons in practical politics, often by demonstrating what can go wrong.[27]

As for pleasure, the whole literary history of early Icelandic historiography has been characterized as a gradual shift in the balance between scholarly history and narrative verve (*frásagnargleði*, e.g. Nordal 1920: ch. 6), and this is still a reasonably acceptable model. Ari's history is certainly on the sober, even dry, side. His treatment of Hœnsa-Þórir's burning of Þorkell Blund-Ketilsson and its aftermath, for example, is summarily 'told' with an emphasis on its constitutional consequences rather than 'shown' with dialogue and detailed staging; and often we can see a story being told with increasing elaboration (even if the chronology of manuscripts does not allow the development to be fixed in time). Take, for instance, the topic of the splendid matriarch who was the daughter of Ketill flatnef 'Flat-nose', known as Auðr in some sources but Unnr in others. The brief *Íslendingabók* mentions her as the token settler in the western quarter: 'Auðr, daughter of Ketill flatnef, a Norwegian *hersir* [landed magnate], settled west in Breiðafjǫrðr; from her the Breiðfirðingar are descended.' *Landnámabók* ch. 110 gives a quite detailed account of Auðr's arrival in Iceland, and her disposition of territories to her followers; it also lavishes some attention on her death. *Laxdæla saga* ch. 7 is still more expansive, staging the death scene as a magnificent close to an impressive life.

The picture of the progressive displacement of *frœði* by *frásagnargleði* nevertheless oversimplifies, not least because austere style and apparent impartiality are not necessarily guarantees of historicity, and because *Íslendingabók* and *Landnámabók* already contain some lively narratives worthy of later sagas, and often incorporated in them. *Íslendingabók* has influenced *Hœnsa-Þóris saga*, while *Landnámabók* teems with vivid incidents, mundane or bizarre, many of which also appear in more elaborated form in the *Íslendinga sögur*. Nordal's view that the kings' sagas evolve towards a near-ideal balance between *vísindi* (science, scholarship) and *list* 'art' or *skemmtun* 'entertainment', achieved by Snorri Sturluson, has also been called into question (Nordal 1920: 128; Tómasson 1988: 193; Meulengracht Sørensen 1993: 107–8 and 133–8).

DEFINING A NATIONAL IDENTITY

'The windy edge of nowhere', a phrase used of the Faroe Islands, could equally well describe Iceland; and a vital strand in the historiography is the attempt to counter the nation's peripheral position. This, already a priority for a new and isolated nation, must have become still more urgent after AD 1000, when the Icelanders, now brought within the sphere of international Christendom, faced the task of asserting their dual identity: as an independent commonwealth of well-descended, mainly Nordic, men and women with a unique history, which was at the same time a Christian nation fully connected to mainstream European civilization.

THE WIDER WORLD

As seen above, one of the genealogies attached to *Íslendingabók* traces distinguished Icelanders back to a mythical Turkish ancestor via Nordic rulers and gods; and similarly Snorri Sturluson claimed an etymological link between the native gods – the Æsir – and Asia, the opulent and beauteous centre of the earth. Óðinn's kingdom of Ásgarðr is equated with Troy in 'Tyrkland', and Þórr is a grandson of Priam (Prologue to *Snorra Edda*, pp. 3–6). By asserting Trojan descent, Icelanders joined not only the ancient Romans but also Normans, Britons, Saxons and Franks in staking a claim to a place at the heart of the old world, not its margins. It is difficult to estimate how deeply this myth of Trojan origins penetrated Icelandic minds. It is certainly of learned, possibly Frankish, provenance, and may have remained the learned fancy of a minority. Although it finds its way into several Icelandic texts after Ari (Heusler 1908: 13–37), there is nothing in Iceland to approach the extraordinarily creative political use made of it over several centuries by the Franks and their descendants (Contamine 1996). Nor is the motif universal in learned works. *Veraldar saga*, for instance, makes no link between Troy and Scandinavia.

Nevertheless, the drive to integrate Nordic culture into the world picture is manifested in other ways too: in the indebtedness of Snorri's *Skáldskaparmál*, 'The language of poetry', to the international encyclo-paedic tradition, for example (Clunies Ross 1987: *passim*), and in the application of Latin theories of grammar and rhetoric to Norse vernacular poetics in the *Third* and *Fourth Grammatical Treatises*. *Breta sögur* substitutes Norse gods for classical ones; and Óláfr hvítaskáld, adopting the *translatio studii* topos, asserts that the Graeco-Roman poetic tradition and that brought to the North by 'Óðinn and other men of Asia' are a single art, emanating from Asia, seat of the greatest fame, power and learning in the world (*þar sem mest var frægð* [v. l, *fegurð*] *ok ríkdómr ok fróðleikr veraldarinnar*; *Third Grammatical Treatise*, ch. 10, p. 60).

ICELANDIC–NORWEGIAN RELATIONS

Perceptions of the Norwegian homeland and its rulers formed a part of the Icelandic world-view(s) which the historiography was particularly well suited to explore, not least because of the rich poetic source-materials; and the writing of Icelandic and Norwegian history run parallel, with frequent merging and overlap. The Norwegians themselves were of course not voiceless. Works celebrating the sanctity of King Óláfr Haraldsson sprang up especially in Niðaróss (Trondheim), site of his shrine and after 1152 a full archbishopric, and indeed these writings represent a crucial moment in the genesis of Nordic historiography. Latin historical surveys (Theodoricus's *Historia de antiquitate regum Norvagiensium* and the anonymous *Historia Norvegiæ*) and vernacular works including *Ágrip af Noregs konunga sögum* 'Summary of the histories of the kings of Norway' and *Fagrskinna* 'Fair vellum' were produced in the decades around 1200.[28] However, the fact remains that the great majority of the vernacular *konunga sögur* were written and preserved in Iceland,[29] and it appears that many such manuscripts were produced for a Norwegian market (Karlsson 1979). As Karlsson points out, manuscript production describes the same curve as the composition of skaldic poetry and kings' sagas: it continues to flourish among the Icelanders after it has dwindled among the Norwegians (1979: 12–13).

The earliest named Icelandic historian, Sæmundr Sigfússon, was frequently cited as an authority on Norwegian events, and among his successors the best-known all concerned themselves with both Icelandic and Norwegian history. Ari Þorgilsson by his own account composed *konunga ævi* ('kings' lives'), now lost, the scope of which has provided an inexhaustible topic of debate for literary historians,[30] and among the earliest sagas are the twelfth-century *Hryggjarstykki* and *Sverris saga*, both written by Icelanders about contemporary Norwegian events. At the end of that century, Icelandic scholars composed lives, in Latin and Icelandic, of two great missionary kings, Óláfr Tryggvason and Óláfr Haraldsson, whose careers not only impinged upon the fates of the Icelanders but also lent themselves ideally to colourful and tragic treatment (see further below). *Morkinskinna*, whose lost archetype may date from c. 1220 or earlier, then traced the story of their successors from Magnús góði ('the Good') onwards, interweaving it with tales of Icelanders at the Norwegian court.[31] This may be the work of Styrmir Kárason, cleric, law-speaker and associate of Snorri Sturluson, whose works included a redaction of *Landnámabók* and life of Óláfr helgi which are all but lost.[32] *Fagrskinna* presented a sparse but incisive survey of all the kings of Norway from the late ninth century to 1177. Building on the achievement of these and many more texts, Snorri Sturluson composed the monumental *Heimskringla*, a cycle of sagas on the kings of Norway stretching from mythical times to, again, 1177.[33] He is also widely credited with *Egils saga*, which commemorates the great Icelandic poet Egill Skallagrímsson and his turbulent relationships with Norwegian kings, while in *Snorra Edda* he rescues from oblivion the rich heritage of myth, poetic diction and metre which is common to the two nations. Similarly, Snorri's nephew Sturla Þórðarson deployed his considerable skill in poetry and prose narrative on both sides of the Norwegian Sea. One of the last-recorded of the Icelandic skalds to serve at the Norwegian court, he also composed a saga about Hákon Hákonarson (r. 1217–63), commissioned by his son Magnús shortly after his death. It was compiled from eyewitness accounts and royal documents, though perhaps written with gritted teeth, given Sturla's many reasons for animosity against the king. He also wrote a saga about Magnús, now only fragmentarily preserved. That such sagas were a vital part of the royal reading-matter and presumably of the royal propa-ganda-machine is suggested by the fact that Hákon is depicted as commanding 'accounts of kings (*konunga tal*) about Hálfdan the Black (*svarti*), and then about all the kings of Norway in succession' to be read to him on his death-bed. Vernacular saints' lives were also read, but Latin texts were too taxing for the ailing king (*Hákonar saga*, ch. 329).

Reasons for the Icelandic enthusiasm for Norwegian history are not hard to find. Firstly, Norway is the homeland, with a shared past and a language almost identical to Icelandic up to *c.* 1100. Contact was maintained by voyages which Hastrup argues were first undertaken not merely for material advantage (trade or the pursuit of inheritance claims) but also in pursuit of 'roots' – specific genealogical knowledge and (ethno-) historical identity (1985: 223). Only later did trade become a specialized occupation in the hands mainly of professional Norwegian merchants, whose visits could generate considerable tension, leading, for instance, to violent exchanges involving the Oddaverjar about which Snorri Sturluson had to negotiate on his first visit to Norway in 1218–20. The deal he struck – that Norway would not invade Iceland but that he would urge acceptance of Norwegian sovereignty on his countrymen – shows the strength of the Norwegian ambitions in that direction in the early thirteenth century.[34] Nevertheless, the importance of shared Nordic origins not only continued to be emphasized at the expense of others, especially Celtic, in redactions of *Landnámabók*, but also must have been a major factor in the writing of the kings' sagas. As Sverrir Tómasson puts it, Snorri intended, in *Heimskringla*, to write a universal history, an *origo gentis*, of the Nordic people (1988: 288).

Secondly, Norwegian history goes further back in time and provides the 'kings and battles' type of material which, however outmoded now, makes 'rattling good history'.[35] Some Icelanders, moreover, became part of that history. They made almost a profession of praising and commemorating Norwegian rulers in verse, and skalds and non-skalds alike found in the service of foreign rulers an opportunity to trade skills in war and diplomacy for kudos and remuneration. Although the importance of these men may be over-rated in Icelandic sources, the tales (*þættir*) and sagas about the *útanferð* 'travels abroad' of dynamic young Icelanders reveal the importance of this wider, more stratified theatre in the Icelandic imagination, and show how inextricably the histories of Norwegian kings and Icelanders are interwoven. Indeed, one theory of the origins of the *Íslendinga sögur* sees them as growing out of tales of court appearances within the *konunga sögur* (e.g. Danielsson 1986).

In the representation of the Norwegian past, as of the Icelandic, the conversion and the kings who presided over it assume gigantic and pivotal importance. Óláfr Haraldsson was celebrated as a Christian saint and martyr soon after his fall at Stiklastaðir in 1030, and, despite suspicions about his territorial and fiscal designs on Iceland, was commemorated in a great deal of skaldic verse and in sagas including some of the earliest, longest and greatest. His canonization provided Iceland with the nearest thing to a native saint until their own Þorlákr was recognized as such in 1199.[36] The fame of his short-lived namesake Óláfr Tryggvason (d. 1000) may have flourished especially through his typological casting as John the Baptist to Óláfr Haraldsson's Christ (*Saga Óláfs Tryggvasonar*, p. 1), but he is gratefully represented in *Íslendingabók* (ch. 7) and throughout the Icelandic tradition, as the missionary king who spread Christianity, by means which today would be considered foul as well as fair, to Norway and its former colonies. Certain other monarchs perceived as benefactors of the Icelanders tended also to attract interest, for instance Haraldr Sigurðarson harðráði ('Hard-ruler'), a great patron of poets, whose portrayal is colourful if not always flattering.

The histories of Norwegian kings, and of Icelanders in their domain, therefore provided materials which, fascinating in themselves, also allowed the Icelanders to explore their own situation, present and past, vis-à-vis the nation which was undoubtedly closest and most important to them, of all. As one looks at the range of texts, attitudes towards Norway and its rulers seem to shift and shade rather like the aurora borealis, mingling respect, affection and dependency with a strong need for independence and self-assertion; but an underlying set of oppositions can also be discerned (Clunies Ross 1999).

ORIGINS OF A NATION

Much of the historical endeavour, however, comes closer to home, as we have seen by glancing at *Íslendingabók* and *Landnámabók*. It seems from the epilogue to the Þórðarbók manuscript of *Landnámabók* that those who wrote about the settlement of Iceland had to justify themselves: 'Many people say that it is an uncalled for [use of] scholarship to write about the settlement (*Þat er margra manna mál, at þat sé óskyldr fróðleikr at rita landnám*)[37] – perhaps because religious subjects were considered a more appropriate use of vellum. The writer points out the importance of deploying historical and genealogical lore to refute 'foreigners, who accuse us of being descended from slaves and criminals'. He also sees comprehensive knowledge of origins as being a characteristic of wise nations. It would be fascinating to know exactly which foreigners are meant here. Certainly, the foreign disdain cannot have been invented, and it is expressed in the Norwegian *Konungs skuggsjá* 'The King's Mirror' (mid-thirteenth century), according to which the unstable geology of Iceland, with its erupting volcanoes and geysers, anticipates the pains of Hell (pp. 17–20). On the other hand, both Adam of Bremen, writing his *Gesta* in the late eleventh century, and the writer who appended a sketch of the Britannic islands to it a century or so later, portrayed the Icelanders as good Christians, who manage to live in 'holy simplicity' despite the geographical and climatic pecularities of the land (ed. Schmeidler, pp. 272 and 286; trans. Tschan p. 217, p. 228 and n. 1).

But if *Landnámabók* is an attempt to promote a certain national image, we might ask for whose consumption it and other historical writings were intended. The use of the vernacular not only excludes non-Nordic speakers, but also imposes a more precise kind of parochialism, especially by the use of pronominal and adverbial elements such as *ossa landa* 'us countrymen'; *á pvísa landi* 'in this land', *út hingat* 'out here' (examples from *Íslendingabók*). Certain larger scale features also imply an informed 'home' audience, for instance the lack, in *Íslendingabók*, of the conventional description of the land, and the assumption that 'Sæmundr' and his journey to 'Frakkland' will be familar. Of the main historical themes treated in Icelandic writings, it seems that only the lives and miracles of native bishops and of Norwegian martyr-kings attracted treatment in the international medium of Latin to any great extent, and even then the texts were often translated into the vernacular afterwards (see Cormack and Kirby in this volume).[38]

Nevertheless, the celebration of native bishops in saga was an attractive means of nurturing national pride and confirming the dignity of the Icelandic church (an objective clear from the *Hungrvaka* prologue, *Biskupa sögur* I: 59), and in ways recognizable to the international community. The first native bishop, Ísleifr, is said to have presented a Greenlandic polar bear to Heinrekr, Emperor of Saxony, and was consecrated on Whit Sunday by Archbishop Adalbertus of Bremen, at the behest of Pope Leo (*Biskupa sögur* I: 61–2). His son and successor Gizurr was 'both king and bishop over the land as long as he lived' (*Biskupa sögur* I: 67). As well as consorting internationally with the great and good, Icelandic bishops are frequently compared in their sagas with, among others, Martin of Tours, and may have modelled themselves on hagiographical prototypes in 'real life'.[39] The holy bishop Þorlákr Þórhallsson seems to have answered a positive craving for a native-born saint, and the epilogue to *Hungrvaka* claims that Þorlákr can justly be called 'a sunbeam or jewel of the saints, both in Iceland and elsewhere in the world' (*Biskupa sögur* I: 86). Qualifying this trend are the passages in which the chill light of international disdain is allowed momentarily to play upon these native treasures. The stock anti-Icelandic jibe about suet-eating, which appears quite frequently in *útanferðar þættir* (stories of [Icelanders'] travels abroad), underlies a miracle-story of St Þorlákr, who has to chastise an English priest in Norfolk for abusing a statue of himself (*Biskupa sögur* I: 357). *Guðmundar saga* similarly does not flinch from portraying the condescension bestowed by the archiepiscopal establishment in Niðaróss upon the rustic bishop Guðmundr inn góði (e.g. *Biskupa sögur* I: 573). In such cases, the disparagement is there to be punished or proved wrong, but it is there nevertheless.

A UNIQUE LAW AND CONSTITUTION

The oddity of Iceland's status as a community which lacked not only a king but also a centralized state of any sort was registered both abroad and at home. Adam of Bremen wrote in 1080 that the Icelanders regarded their bishop as king, and accepted his scriptural pronouncements as law; or (in a scholion) that 'they have no king, except the law' (*Apud illos non est rex, nisi tantum lex*; ed. Schmeidler p. 273; trans. Tschan p. 217). Modern ethnographers, meanwhile, have to go as far afield as the Pacific islands, South-East Asia and the North-West coast of America to find closely comparable 'non-state' societies (Pálsson 1992: 6).[40] A slight hankering to have a king like other nations might be detectable in the Icelandic fascination with the Norwegian monarchy, and in the way that certain prominent Icelanders were regarded, albeit more or less figuratively, as kings.[41] The example of Gizurr Ísleifsson has already been mentioned, and in the secular sphere Jón Loptsson is referred to as the foremost chieftain in Iceland in several texts, and as *princeps* in a Latin fragment about St Þorlákr (*Biskupa sögur* I: 398), while his royal descent as a grandson of Magnús berfœttr is celebrated in the genealogical poem *Nóregs konunga tal* (*Skjaldedigtning* A I: 579–89, B I: 575–90).

Íslendingabók traces the institution in AD 930 of Iceland's unique republican constitution, – the division into four quarters, and the vesting of judicial, though not executive, power in a national assembly (*Alþingi*) comprising at first thirty-six chieftains or *goðar* under the presidency of a law-speaker (*lǫgsǫgumaðr*). These things, are, however, given surprisingly slight coverage in *Íslendingabók* and later sources, whereas the fundamental importance of law to the fabric of society is constantly underlined. Ari tells how one Ulfljótr devised a law-code which was based on the Norwegian Gulaþingslög, but was also the first departure from Norwegian law (ch. 8). The conversion to Christianity appears above all as an affirmation of the need for nationally agreed laws, and the importance of wisdom and the rule of law comes over with some urgency, which may reflect circumstances at the time of writing. This was, indeed, a period when the old consensus of clerical and secular chieftains under the law (achieved especially through the powerful personality of Bishop Gizurr Ísleifsson) was seriously under threat, and when the feud later documented in *Þorgils saga ok Hafliða* presented Ari with a dilemma of split loyalties. In retrospect, it appears as a chilling foretaste of the Sturlung Age some decades later, and like other medieval historians, Ari stopped his narrative a little short of his own present,[42] mentioning Hafliði only in connection with the codification of the law.

A CHRISTIAN NATION

One of the vital tasks facing those who shaped Icelandic tradition, whether oral or written, was to register the radical change of religion which dominated the country's short history, and to do so in a way that validated the present without negating a cherished past. The early settlers, according to *Landnámabók*, included pagans, Christians, those who hedged their bets, and those who worshipped no gods, trusting instead in their own might and main. The worship of Þórr, Óðinn and others in the Norse pantheon must have dominated, and by the late tenth century Christianity was very thinly represented in Iceland.

From any point of view, but especially from the stance of those devoted by profession to learning and religion more than to sheep-farming, the *siðaskipti* (lit. 'change of customs'), the conversion of Iceland around the year 1000, was the most significant event since the settlement itself; and it is natural that the strongly clerical *Íslendingabók* gives it more elaborate treatment than any other topic. As Joseph Harris puts it, 'the general nature of early Christian conception must have provided the model for the Icelandic view in terms of two great epochs separated by the radical intervention of God in history' (1986: 195). The importance of the change of religion to the entire population, meanwhile, is suggested by its centrality in many of the *Íslendinga sögur* (Harris 1986, esp. pp. 193–7), though the details of the conversion process are far from clear or unanimously agreed among texts.[43]

The conversion, according to Ari's account, was followed by a long period of peaceful co-operation between Church and people. Skálholt was established as the episcopal see by Gizurr Ísleifsson after his consecration as Iceland's bishop in 1082. Tithe regulations were accepted (1097) and embedded in the lawcode *Grágás*. The final landmark is the written codification of the law in *Hafliðaskrá* (1117–18).[44] Later texts, on the other hand, depict severe clashes of interest between clerical and secular authority, such as the *staðamál*, a long-running battle over ecclesiastical estates, which began during the episcopacy of Þorlákr Þorhallsson, 1178–93.

Meanwhile, partly because literacy and literary production were not exclusively in the hands of cathedrals and monasteries, a certain *pietas* towards the pagan past survived. It may indeed have been positively cultivated in some chieftainly circles *c.* 1200, where status was felt to have its roots in paganism, and it may have offered a marker of group identity with which to defy political encroachment by the Church (Meulengracht Sørensen 1993: 58), and perhaps also the Norwegian imperialism with which it was closely connected.

It is, naturally, difficult to detect in the early writings any hint of resentment about the globalizing cultural effects of institutional Christianity, or of anxiety about its effects on the vernacular heritage. Nor, at the other extreme, is there an obliteration of the culture of the pagan past on the same scale as was seen in Anglo-Saxon England, although Bishop Jón Qgmundarson did eradicate the names of pagan deities from the names of the days of the week in the early twelfth century as part of a campaign against the more unwholesome of the old ways (*Biskupa sögur* I: 237). Demonizing of pagans largely takes the restricted form of condemning pagan magic put to evil ends, while the category of the noble heathen brings esteemed ancestors within the Christian pale.[45] The law-speaker Þorkell máni is said in *Landnámabók* (S9) to have been counted 'one of the noblest heathens that ever lived' (*er einn heiðinna manna hefir bezt verit siðaðr*). As he died, he had himself moved into the sun, and commended himself to the God who created the sun; he had lived as purely (*hreinliga*) as the best Christians. Heathen practices are sometimes also seen as analogues to Christian ones. Where Ørlygr commits his voyage and settlement to God, St Patrick and St Columba (S15, H15), Ingólfr entrusts his high-seat pillars, and hence his future dwelling-place, to the gods; and when his brother Herjólfr meets a violent end at the hands of slaves Ingólfr reflects that no good comes of people who refuse to sacrifice to the gods (S8, H8). This looks like a genuinely sympathetic effort of historical imagination, such as is also discernible in S197, H164 where Kráku-Hreiðarr draws back from violence out of common-sense and a belief that it is Þórr's will. Though sympathetic, however, these views of the pagan past are mostly anachronistic – a variety of *interpretatio christiana*.

FACTIONAL IDENTITY AND INTERESTS

So far the historical traditions have been discussed as though they belong equally to the whole Icelandic nation, and to some extent they clearly do. It is time, however, to consider which particular sections of society, in terms of class, ethnicity and gender, they serve. To put it simply, whose history is this?

The historiography of past ages is often, and often rightly, characterized as élitist and conservative, a story told by victors. Or as Vincent puts it,'The past is incorrigibly male, as it is incorrigibly aristocratic, incorrigibly religious, incorrigibly unfair' (1995: 11). The extent to which this applies to Iceland is obviously limited by the fact that settlement involved no conquest of indigenous population, that justice was managed by local and national assemblies (*þing*), dominated by a few dozen chieftains (*goðar*) who were technically equal among themselves, and *primi inter pares* in their individual communities of freeholding farmers. In the society depicted, therefore, differences of wealth and status are less extreme than elsewhere in Europe, the production of literature is not restricted to courtly and ecclesiastical environments, and the subjects of genealogy are similarly broader than elsewhere in Europe. Snorri Sturluson, despite some condescension towards farmers' assemblies and their dependence on aristocratic leaders and spokesmen, 'presents . . . popular interests in such a concrete way and so frequently refers to the people and their opinions that he clearly represents a different and more "democratic" historiography than the one current in contemporary Europe' (Bagge 1991: 139). In these respects one might accept, and extend to the historical writings, Meulengracht Sørensen's cheerful view of the sagas, that they are 'in the proper sense of the word popular literature: the literature of all the people' (1993: 133). However, as far as the sagas are concerned, assuming that the audience at communal readings included servants and even vagrants receiving hospitality, one wonders how included or excluded they would have felt by narratives about families and classes not their own, whose portrayal of the poor is frequently stereotypical and negative.[46] As for the historiography, some of it is so learned and Latin(ate) that it must at least in part have a different kind of audience from the 'farmers and farmhands, women and men, learned and illiterate' Meulengracht Sørensen envisages for the sagas (1993: 105–6). Moreover, producing vellum and writing on it implies resources far above subsistence level, and it is probably true in Iceland as elsewhere that the historical record, like other forms of power, was mainly in the hands of secular and ecclesiastical magnates. The greatest names in Icelandic historiography were raised among some of the most notable clans in Iceland – Ari Þorgilsson among the Haukdœlir, Snorri Sturluson and his nephew Sturla Þórðarson among the Oddaverjar and Sturlungar – as well as enjoying links by birth, marriage and friendship with other chieftains and churchmen. Ari's academic mentor Sæmundr was father of the Loptr who married a grand-daughter of King Magnús berfœttr of Norway; Jón, son of Loptr (1124–97), was foster-father to Snorri Sturluson; and so on. Many of those who recorded events also took a prominent part in shaping the veents of their own time, and, correspondingly, original historical composition (as opposed to copying, compiling and editing) dwindled soon after the end of the commonwealth (1262–64), when Norwegian (and later Danish) royal officials replaced independent chieftains as the oligarchy in Iceland. For all these reasons, it is unsurprising that a chieftainly bias seems to be detectable in major historical works. Sturla Þórðarson's *Íslendinga saga*, for instance, carefully preserves details of Icelandic legal procedures which were a valuable source of income to chieftains (Grímsdóttir 1988).

It is also true that large sections of the community are seriously underrepresented in the literary records. Slaves, insofar as they appear at all, are usually portrayed as dealing in shabby behaviour and receiving peremptory treatment. In *Landnámabók*, Bjǫrn, a thieving thrall of the great Geirmundr heljarskinn, is quickly dismissed (S115, H87). Skorri, a freedman of Ketill gufa, 'settled the land in Skorradalr, above the lake, and was killed there' (S31), while Ketill's slave Flóki (again no patronymic) suffered the same unexplained fate (S34; see also S125, H97).

Many of the slaves must have been of Celtic origin, from Western Scotland and the Isles or more especially from Ireland, and the representation of this ethnic group is also slight and uncomplimentary. Ari fróði, despite his ancestors' associations with the British Isles, gives the false impression that the settlers were exclusively *norrænn* (see further Hermann Pálsson 1970: 79–91). It is left to *Landnámabók* to tell stories such as that of the slaying of Herjólfr by Irish slaves (S8), or Hǫskuldr's purchase of the captive Melkorka, daughter of King Myrkjartan of Ireland (S105). As in these instances, Celts are frequently stereotyped either as treacherous cowards if male or as daughters of Irish kings if female – presumably because the latter became the ancestors of several prominent Icelanders. In the *Íslendinga sögur*, slaves of Celtic origin are often represented as dark or ugly, either by means of direct description or through (nick)names such as Svartr or Ljótr (Jochens 1997: 316–17). Celts constitute ten per cent of the 270 persons of specified origin in *Landnámabók* (Meulengracht Sørensen 1993: 8 and chapter 1 of this volume), whereas research into the genetic typology of twentieth-century Icelanders reveals that in terms of blood groupings and other genetic indicators such as skull measurements, they correlate strongly with the population of modern Ireland, so that estimates of the Celtic share of the medieval population range from fourteen to forty per cent (Benediktsson, *Íslendingabók* p. cxxxii; Sigurðsson 1988: 35–40). The picture is not, however, entirely negative, and from a broader anthropological view the degree of interbreeding between Celt and Norse is striking. Some male slaves are of royal parentage, and some distinguished Celts emigrated to Iceland independently and uncoerced (Jochens 1997: 315).

As for women, some are portrayed as skilled in diplomacy or the interpretation of dreams, and many form links in a genealogical chain, but it is usually only the most exceptional who figure prominently in early Icelandic historiography, except as links in a genealogical chain, and it is noticeable that the name of even the formidable daughter of Ketill flatnef referred to above is unstable in the tradition, coming out as Auðr (variants Qðr/Oðr) or Unnr. Like the Southampton schoolboy asked as part of a questionnaire exercise if he could name important women in the past, we might shake our heads thoughtfully and answer, 'No there were only men'(Emmott 1989: 25).[47]

FAMILY INTERESTS

It would be difficult to find a text touching on Icelandic history in which genealogy (tracing both agnatic and cognatic links) is not fundamental. *Landnámabók* is the classic case, and the different redactions of the work often show a preoccupation with tracing lines down to the redactor's own family.[48] As well as providing individuals with roots, families with group identities, and communities with rationales for continuing alliances or enmities,[49] genealogical lore self-evidently underpins claims to hereditary property, and hence has vital contemporary relevance to landholding groups in any culture.[50] Thus, 'the genealogy is able to be a legal title, a political weapon, and an expression of learning' (Dumville 1977: 84).

Landnámabók, with its careful documentation of settlers and distinction between the ways of obtaining land – by taking virgin territory, by gift, by dowry, by seizure – is a natural test-case for an examination of the possible motives for historical endeavour. The view that this 'Domesday book of Iceland' (as Collingwood called it (Collingwood and Steffánson 1902: 4)), whether or not it started off with a purely historical viewpoint,[51] had ulterior motives, is far from new, but it has steadily gathered momentum in recent decades. More and more doubts have been voiced about the factual reliability of *Landnámabók*, and although this is not in itself proof of ulterior motives, it starts to look like proof insofar as the implausibilities have an underlying rationale. Vilmundarson, for instance, has brought to light many instances where 'ancestors' and their deeds seem to have been extrapolated from place-names for which more plausible explanations are to hand (e.g. 1971, esp. p. 583 on the unreliability in this respect of *Landnámabók*). The etymological anecdote attached to the settlement at Brynjudalr, mentioned above, is a case in point (Vilmundarson 1980: 73–4). Further, although *Íslendingabók*'s claim that the land was *albyggt*, 'completely settled', in the sixty years beginning *c.* 870 tallies well with modern tephrochronological and archaeological evidence, the traditional model of the process of settlement has been questioned. *Landnámabók* pictures a relatively small number of mighty individuals claiming large tracts of land whose outlying parts they then distribute among dependants or latecomers; but this seems to underplay the element of gradual expansion away from the most favourable centres and increasing domination of lesser farmers by greater. It also seems a suspiciously convenient model for the legitimizing of the rights of the descendants of those mighty individuals.[52]

TOWARDS A CONCLUSION

Icelandic historical writing comes about through the confluence of two streams: a clerical, international, Latin one which contributed specific historiographical techniques, international and chronological perspectives; and a popular, native, vernacular one which emphasized narratives rooted in genealogy, family feuds, local landmarks and place-names. The force of foreign example is striking in Ari fróði's *Íslendingabók* (*c.* 1122–33), the earliest and most clearly historiographical prose work from early Iceland. After Ari, *Landnámabók* undergoes a long process of maturation, but otherwise historical writing makes slow progress until the later twelfth century, when translations of foreign historiography, Latin writings on Nordic themes, and sagas of Norwegian rulers all flourished. External prompts, meanwhile, helped the Icelanders to overcome their reticence and commemorate themselves in vernacular prose. Foreign hagiography was an important facilitator for the *Biskupa sögur*, as also for the *konunga sögur*; while the great *Íslendinga sögur* owe their being at least in part to short stories (*þættir*) about the adventures of Icelanders abroad which were attached to the konunga sögur. Nevertheless, a truly vernacular literary culture gathers strength. The *Íslendinga sögur* and *Sturlunga saga*, though not untouched by the foreign learning available to Icelandic intellectuals, are uniquely and resolutely Icelandic in both style and content. Uninhibited by the lack of a monarchy or centralized state, Iceland commemorates the lives of its greatest sons, even though this means focussing on conflicts between individuals and families rather than events of national or international significance. The ascendancy of certain great chieftainly families, and the shadow of Norwegian dominance may well have sharpened the appetite for this national literature.

Concerning the purpose of the historical writings, one may wonder whether there is such a thing as disinterested history, written in the pursuit of truth and with the promise of entertainment, or whether it is always partisan, promoting prejudices and vested interests. The either/or formulation of the question, however, is clearly unhelpful. The Icelanders seem to have had a genuine curiosity about the past, and not just their own, and history was an important source of entertainment and of moral and political example. However, if it had not also served present needs it would not have taken the form it did, and in some cases it might not have been written at all. If one were to choose a single proof of the usefulness of Icelandic historical writing, it would probably be the dominance of genealogical lore – surely the classic case of information for a purpose, since to remember chains of names without good reason would be difficult, pointless and dull. But good reasons are plentiful, from the legitimizing of claims of birth and landholding to the reassuring sense of a place in the flow of generations. Genealogy, together with narratives of Norwegian roots, of the settlement of Iceland, the founding of its unique constitution, and its development as a Christian nation, provided important frameworks within which people could live, and the stances taken in relation to pagan ancestors enabled them, on the whole, to be harmonized with the new world-view. Perhaps the single most important 'use' of historical writing in Iceland, then, was to foster national self-definition, at least among those of perceived social and economic consequence. Although every text must have served a unique configuration of needs (as determined by author, audience and, if any, patron), this element of self-definition seems a likely highest common factor. Literacy and membership of an international network of learning must have brought a sense of belonging coupled with a sharp awareness of difference, a need to assert both at home and abroad, and the means to do so in written prose, in Latin or the vernacular. The fact that the vernacular prevailed overall suggests that speaking to a home audience was by far the most urgent priority. It is appropriate to give the last word to an Icelandic intellectual, writing about the problem of maintaining Icelandic identity and independence whilst responding to a changing and increasingly international world.

> The Icelanders themselves seldom realize that their history is an adventure. The adventure is fascinating because it is incredible. It is instructive because it is true. Both because it is fascinating and incredible, it must never come to an end. An understanding by the nation itself of the essence of this adventure provides the greatest impulse for it to continue to be Icelandic . . . In an attempt to solve this problem, it is an invaluable support for the nation to understand thoroughly the honour of being an independent and civilized nation. (Gíslason 1973: 8)

NOTES

1 Kurt Schier finds the 'awareness of standing at a beginning, of having created something entirely new' one of the strongest reasons for the Icelanders' remarkable propensity for developing, preserving and handing down traditions (1975: 180).

2 It is not, however, the earliest manuscript. *Íslendingabók* is preserved complete in two seventeenth-century copies (AM 113 a & b) made by Jón Erlendsson, under commission from Bishop Brynjólfur Sveinsson, and apparently working from a copy made c. 1200. Copies of extracts are also preserved.

3 It is *várt mál* 'our language' (*First Grammatical Treatise* 215, 219), as distinct from the general Nordic *dönsk tunga*, lit. 'Danish tongue'. This is especially striking given that *norræna* or *norrænt mál* 'Norse, Nordic language'

continued to be used of Icelandic and Norwegian throughout the medieval period (Karlsson 1979: 1 and references).

4 Sigfússon believed that this practice emanated from Oddr and Gunnlaugr, monks of Þingeyrar (1944: 114). Tómasson suggests that the attachment of the nickname *fróði* to particular Icelandic authors may be a vernacular response to the foreign custom of citing *auctoritates* (1988: 225).

5 The *formáli* (Prologue) to *Sturlunga saga* implies that *Íslendinga saga* was intended to complement other sagas in the collection which cover earlier periods (*Sturlunga saga* I: 115).

6 Stefán Karlsson adduces strong reasons to connect Sturla with the compilation of *Resensannáll*, a set of annals to 1295 (1988: 47–50). To what extent the Icelandic annals pre-date the time of Sturla and rest on traditions independent of the sagas is disputed; the debate is summarized by Benediktsson; (1993).

7 Little is known about Latin-based learning in medieval Iceland. Tómasson gives a useful review, including references to Icelanders studying abroad (1988: 19–35). Jóhannesson gives a brief résumé of foreign contacts (1974: 156–60).

8 Brief introductions to these and other works mentioned may conveniently be found in Pulsiano 1993 and in the multi-volume *Kulturhistorisk Leksikon for nordisk middelalder*.

9 The Icelandic *tíðendi* similarly implies both happenings and news or discourse about them.

10 The term occurs within the famous account of saga performances at the Reykjahólar wedding, which also interestingly mentions that even some wise people were taken in by fantastical tales, *Sturlunga saga* I: 27.

11 See further Meulengracht Sørensen's discussion of the opposition between *fræði* and *saga* (1993: 107–8).

12 E.g. 'Histories are intentional only insofar as they – exactly like coins, account books, charters or whatever – had a practical context' (Goffart 1988: 16; cf. Geary 1994, esp. p. 159 on dragons and charters).

13 Those that do are most conveniently accessible in vols. I–II of *Diplomatarium Islandicum*.

14 Concepts of truth in medieval historiography and literature are explored by Tómasson (1988: 189–94) and Meulengracht Sørensen (1993: 133–8).

15 See Byock 1992, who inveighs against the way in which the 'nationalist' Icelandic school, while discrediting traditional uses of the sagas as historical sources, closed off other approaches.

16 Tómasson points out that Snorri's use of the word *skemmtan* 'entertainment' in connection with old poems might imply that some of his contemporaries thought them untrue (1988: 214–15).

17 Compare Inuit society, in which the passing of names down the generations 'signifies the importance of this system in preserving the past on an intimate daily level. It also carries with it the necessity of repeating an oral history, and

causes our people to relate to the figures who throughout time have held this name' (Anawak 1989: 45).

18 This is the provisional conclusion of a study by Chris Callow of Birmingham University (p.c.), to whom I am very grateful for this information.

19 This topos (and a textual problem at this point) is discussed by Tómasson (1988: 258–89).

20 There is debate as to whether these genealogies are original and integral to *Íslendingabók* or its lost first edition. Sigfússon thought not (1944: 60–2), but probably a majority accept that they are (Jakob Benediktsson, introduction to *Íslendingabók*, 1968: xiii and xv). An early genesis is convenient but not essential to the point being made here, that the genealogies encapsulate vital aspects of the world-view of the Icelanders.

21 Jóhannesson 1941 is still the classic discussion of the textual relationships.

22 Some of these 'great settlements' in the *Landnáma* account may have been enlarged through interpolations (e.g. Skalla-Grímr's, under influence from *Egils saga*; Rafnsson 1974: 233).

23 The Hauksbók text of *Landnámabók* makes more of royal connections than Sturlubók (Pálsson and Edwards 1972: 7).

24 Local bias is also detectable in the contents of the different redactions of *Landnámabók*, as when the Hauksbók text is fuller for the section between Kjalarnes and Akranes.

25 Cf. 'Memory . . . depends upon selection from the original multiplicity of actions of those that represent useful responses to the environment' (Young 1987: 456).

26 Cf. Goffart, writing of Jordanes, Gregory of Tours, Bede and Paul the Deacon: "Though more often honest and high-minded than not, their endeavours were never innocent' (1988: 16). A brief review of possible motives for medieval historiography is offered in Whaley (1991: 129–30); Bagge offers a useful discussion of 'The purpose of history' centring on Snorri's *Heimskringla* (1991: 201–8); and Tómasson (1988: 81–148) surveys the statements made in prologues about the motives which occasion Icelandic historical writings (*tilefni*), and their purpose(s) (*tilgangur*).

27 See especially Bagge 1991 and 1992. Bagge emphasizes that, although *Heimskringla* does offer ideological explanations, especially as one strand in his portrayal of the fall of Óláfr helgi, 'Snorri and his contemporaries thought in terms of individual men and conflicts between them rather than in social groups or opposed ideologies' (1992: 67).

28 Bjarni Einarsson envisages *Fagrskinna* as having been written by an Icelander or Norwegian, probably working in Trondheim to a commission from Hákon Hákonarson (*Fagrskinna*: cxxvii–cxxxi).

29 Brief surveys of the sagas of kings are given in Knirk 1993 and Whaley 1993a.

30 A convenient summary of the debate about these and other lost lives is given by Andersson 1985: 200–11.

31 Such *þættir* were evidently included in the original, lost, ms. of *Morkinskinna*, but more were added to the later, extant, version so that it is now difficult to recover the exact scope of the original.

32 Gade (1998) argues strongly for Styrmir's authorship of *Morkinskinna*. I am grateful to the author for making this paper available to me.

33 For an introduction, see Whaley 1991, esp. 63–77 on written sources.

34 *Hákonar saga Hákonarsonar*, ch. 59; *Íslendinga saga*, esp. chs 35 (40), 38 (43) and 41 (46).

35 'My argument is that War makes rattling good history; but Peace is poor reading', says the Spirit Sinister in Hardy's *The Dynasts*, p. 88.

36 Cormack gives details of his *cultus* in Iceland, including thirty-five church dedications and another twenty-four shared with another saint (1994: 138–44, esp. 138–9).

37 Printed in *Íslendingabók*, cii. Þórðarbók is seventeenth century, but the epilogue is thought to go back to Styrmir Kárason, in the early thirteenth (Jóhannesson 1941: 302–5, and Jakob Benediktsson, *Íslendingabók*, cii). Still earlier origins cannot be ruled out.

38 Tómasson reviews the Latin writings known or produced in medieval Iceland (1988: 36–44).

39 A verse attributed to Kolbeinn Tumason in 1208 scoffs at Guðmundr Arason's aspirations to power like that of the *hǫfðingi* (chieftain) Thomas à Becket *(Skjaldedigtning* B II: 48, v. 6).

40 Durrenberger emphasizes that Iceland's status as a 'stratified but stateless society' implies that a different set of concepts is required for the understanding of its literature and culture (1989, esp. p. 242).

41 Ármann Jakobsson argues that the Icelanders not only had an interest in kingship but a need for it, long before the acceptance of Norwegian rule in 1262–64 (1994).

42 'Bede and Paul [the Deacon] drew a veil over their own generation. Conceivably, the importance of current events to them was in inverse ratio to the space those events occupy in their writings' (Goffart 1988: 17).

43 The main sources are *Íslendingabók* 7; *Kristni saga*; *Njáls saga*, chs. 100–5; and *Þorvalds þáttr víðfǫrla*.

44 Benediktsson points out that Ari does not claim that this was the first time law had been written down, and thinks this unlikely (*Íslendingabók* 24, n. 8).

45 See Lönnroth 1969 and Weber 1981. Harris 1986 provides a useful résumé of these, adding further thoughts on the representation of the old and new religions.

46 'In truth the sagas are a deeply reactionary literature that stresses the predominant views of a small upper-class stratum of chieftains in thirteenth century Iceland' (Lönnroth 1986: 305).

47 The question was part of a survey of attitudes among Southampton school-children to the past. The researchers suggested that the significantly greater

proportion of 'don't know' answers given by girls to the questionnaire might reflect 'a sense of lack of involvement in history' (Emmott 1989: 25).

48 Rafnsson reckons that Melabók contains forty genealogical 'tables', Hauksbók ten and Sturlubók eleven (1974: 233). The lines in Sturlubók are often traced to Sturla's grandparents, Sturla and Guðný of Hvammr, while Melabók forty-three times traces a line to the wife of parents of Snorri Markússon á Melum, d. 1313 (Jakob Benediktsson, introduction to *Land-námabók*, lxxxiii).

49 'Genealogies validate present relationships; these relationships prove the genealogies; and the form of the genealogy is modelled on the form of present relationships' (Bohannan, quoted in Dumville 1977: 86).

50 Cf. a recent study from north-west Portugal, which discovered among other things that genealogical knowledge was stronger and deeper among property-owning households than among the poor (Pina-Cabral 1989: 63–4).

51 Jóhannesson inclined to think that the *söguleg sjónarmið* was the initial motive for the *Landnáma* venture (1941: 220).

52 Guðmundsson (1938) and Rafnsson (1974) present detailed arguments for seeing the justification of family landholdings as a driving force in *Landnáma* (though Jóhannesson countered some of Barði's claims, 1941: 212–20). Líndal (1969) and Meulengracht Sørensen (1974) also question the veracity of *landnám* narratives from various perspectives. Stefánsson points out that some of the largest estates were not founded until the ninth or tenth centuries (1993: 311). Vésteinsson (1998) argues for a two-phase settlement. In the first, groups of families work large estates in well-favoured sites by wetlands, while the second consists of planned settlement of smaller, more regular estates on secondary land with limited, but roughly equal, access to resources.

REFERENCES

Primary literature

Note: abbreviated forms of reference in the text of the chapter appear in square brackets.

[Adam of Bremen, *Gesta Hammaburgensis Ecclesiæ Pontificum*] Schmeidler, Bernard (ed.) 1917, *Adam von Bremen, Hamburgische Kirchengeschichte*. 3rd edn. Hanover & Leipzig: Hahnsche Buchhandlung.

Tschan, Francis J. (ed.) 1959, *Adam of Bremen. History of the Archbishops of Hamburg-Bremen*. New York: Columbia University Press.

Ágrip af nóregskonunga sögum. Fagrskinna – Nóregs konunga tal. Einarsson, Bjarni (ed.) 1984, ÍF 29, pp. 1–52.

[Bede, *Historia Ecclesiastica Gentis Anglorum*] Colgrave, B. and Mynors, R. A. B. (eds.) 1969, *Bede's Ecclesiastical History of the English People*. Oxford: Clarendon.

Bede, *Vita Sancti Cuthberti*. In Colgrave, B. (ed.) 1940, *Two Lives of Saint Cuthbert*. Cambridge: Cambridge University Press.

Biskupa sögur. gefnar út af hinu íslenzka bókmentafélagi 1858–62, 2 vols. Copenhagen: Möller.

Diplomatarium Islandicum. Íslenzkt fornbréfasafn, I: 834–1264, Sigurðarson, Jón (ed.) 1857–76; II: 1253–1350, Þorkelsson, Jón (ed.) 1893. Reykjavík: Hið íslenzka bókmentafélag.

Egils saga Skalla-Grímssonar. Nordal, Sigurður (ed.) 1933. ÍF 2.

Fagrskinna. In *Ágrip af nóregskonunga sígum. Fagrskinna – Nóregs konunga tal*. Einarsson, Bjarni (ed.) 1984. ÍF 29, pp. 55–364.

First Grammatical Treatise, The. Benediktsson, Hreinn (ed.) 1972. Reykjavík: Institute of Nordic Linguistics.

Hákonar saga [Hákonarsonar].Vigfusson, Gudbrand (ed.) 1887, *Icelandic Sagas* II, Rolls Series 88. London: HMSO.

Hardy, Thomas. *The Dynasts*. (ed. Harold Orel) 1978. London: Macmillan.

Hauksbók. Jónsson, Eiríkur and Jónsson, Finnur (eds.) 1892–6. Copenhagen: Thiele.

Heimskringla I–III. Aðalbjarnarson, Bjarni (ed.) 1941–51. ÍF 26–8.

Hungrvaka. In *Biskupa sögur* I, pp. 59–86.

[ÍF] Íslenzk fornrit. Reykjavík: Hið íslenzka bókmenntafélag.

Íslendinga saga. In *Sturlunga saga* I, pp. 229–534.

Íslendingabók. In *Íslendingabók. Landnámabók*. Benediktsson, Jakob (ed.) 1968. ÍF 1, 1–2, pp. 1–28.

Konungs skuggsjá. Holm-Olsen, Ludvig (ed.) 1945. Oslo: Norsk historisk kjeldeskrift-institutt.

Kristni saga. Kahle, B. (ed.) 1905. Altnordische Saga-Bibliothek, 11. Halle: Niemeyer.

Landnámabók. In *Íslendingabók. Landnámabók* [above], pp. 29–397. [In references to chapters, S = Sturlubók, H = Hauksbók.]

[*Landnámabók*] *The Book of Settlements: Landnámabók*. Trans. Pálsson, Hermann and Edwards, Paul. 1972, Winnipeg: University of Manitoba Press.

Laxdœla saga. Sveinsson, Einar Ól. (ed.) 1934. ÍF 5.

Morkinskinna. Jónsson, Finnur (ed.) 1932. Samfund til udgivelse af gammel nordisk litteratur, 53. Copenhagen: Jørgensen.

[Oddr Snorrason] *Saga Óláfs Tryggvasonar af Oddr munk*. Jónsson, Finnur (ed.) 1932. Copenhagen: Gad.

[Saxo] *Saxonis Gesta Danorum*. Olrik, Jørgen and Raeder, H. (eds.) 1931. I. Copenhagen: Levin and Munksgaard.

Skjaldedigtning: Den norsk-islandske skjaldedigtning. Jónsson, Finnur (ed.) 1912–15. 4 vols. Copenhagen: Gyldendal; repr. Rosenkilde & Bagger, 1967 and 1973.

[*Snorra Edda*] *Snorri Sturluson. Edda. Prologue and Gylfaginning*. Faulkes, Anthony (ed.) 1982. Oxford: Clarendon.

Sturlunga saga. Jóhannesson, Jón, Finnbogason, Magnús and Eldjárn, Kristján (eds.) 1946. 2 vols. Reykjavík: Sturlunguútgáfan.

Sverris saga. Indrebø, Gustav (ed.) 1920, repr. 1981. Kristiania (Oslo): Dybwad.

[Theodoricus] *Theodrici Monachi, Historia de Antiquitate Regum Norwagiensium.* In Storm, G. (ed.) 1888, *Monumenta Historica Norvegiæ.* Kristiania (Oslo): Brøgger, pp. 1–68.

[*Third and Fourth Grammatical Treatises*] *Den tredje og fjærde grammatiske afhandling i Snorres Edda.* Ólsen, Björn Magnússon (ed.) 1884. Samfund til udgivelse af gammel nordisk litteratur. Copenhagen: Knudtzon.

Veraldar saga. Benediktsson, Jakob (ed.) 1944. Samfund til udgivelse af gammel nordisk litteratur, 61. Copenhagen: Luno.

Willelmi Malmesbiriensis Monachi, de Gestis Regum Anglorum Libri Quinque. Stubbs, William (ed.) 1887–89. 2 vols. Rolls Series 90. London: Eyre & Spottiswoode for HMSO.

Þorgils saga ok Hafliða. In *Sturlunga saga* I, pp. 12–50.

Þórvalds þáttr víðförla. In Jónsson, Þorleifur (ed.), *Fjörutíu Íslendinga-þættir,* 1904. Reykjavík: Sigurður Kristjánsson, pp. 477–502.

Secondary literature

Anawak, Jack 1989, 'Inuit perceptions of the past' in Layton, pp. 45–50.

Andersson, Theodore M. 1985, 'Kings' sagas (*Konungasögur*)', in Clover, Carol J. and Lindow, John (eds.) *Old Norse-Icelandic Literature: a Critical Guide.* Ithaca and London: Cornell University Press, pp. 197–238.

Bagge, Sverre 1991, *Society and Politics in Snorri Sturluson's Heimskringla.* Berkeley and Los Angeles: University of California Press.

1992, 'From sagas to society: the case of *Heimskringla* ', in Pálsson, Gísli, pp. 61–75.

Baines, John 1989, 'Ancient Egyptian concepts and uses of the past', in Layton, pp. 131–49.

Bekker-Nielsen, Hans 1965, 'Frode mænd og tradition', in Bekker-Nielsen, Hans, Olsen, Thorkil Damsgaard and Widding, Ole (eds.), *Norrøn fortællekunst.* Copenhagen: Akademisk forlag, pp. 35–41.

Benediktsson, Jakob 1993, 'Annals. 2. Iceland and Norway', in Pulsiano, pp. 15–16.

Byock, Jesse 1992, 'History and the sagas: the effect of nationalism', in Pálsson, Gísli, pp. 43–59.

Clunies Ross, Margaret 1987, *Skáldskaparmál: Snorri Sturluson's ars poetica and Medieval Theories of Language.* The Viking Collection, 4. Odense: Odense University Press.

1999, 'From Iceland to Norway: essential rites of passage for an early Icelandic skald', *alvíssmál* 9: 55–72.

Collingwood, W. G. and Stefánsson, J. 1902, *The Life and Death of Cormac the Skald.* Ulverston. Repr. Lampeter: Llanerch, 1991.

Contamine, Ph. 1996, 'Trojanerabstammung (der Franken)', in *Lexikon des Mittelalters* VIII: 5. Munich: Lexma Verlag, col. 1041.

Cormack, Margaret 1994, *The Saints in Iceland*. Brussels: Société des Bollandistes.

Danielsson, Tommy 1986, *Om den isländske släktsagans uppbygnad*. Stockholm: Almqvist & Wiksell.

Dumville, David N. 1977, 'Kingship, genealogies and regnal lists', in Sawyer, P. H. and Wood, I. N. (eds.), *Early Medieval Kingship*. Leeds: School of History, University of Leeds, pp. 72–104.

Durrenberger, E. Paul 1989, 'Perspectives on the Commonwealth period', in Durrenberger, E. Paul and Pálsson, Gísli (eds.), *The Anthropology of Iceland*. Iowa City: University of Iowa Press, pp. 228–46.

Einarsson, Bjarni 1993, 'Íslendingadrápa', in Pulsiano, p. 333.

Emmot, Kathy 1989, 'A child's perspective on the past: influences of home, media and school', in Layton, pp. 21–44.

Gade, Kari Ellen 1998, 'A Riddle Unravelled: the Identity of the Author of Morkinskinna'. Unpublished paper presented at the annual conference of the Society for the Advancement of Scandinavian Study, Tempe, Arizona.

Geary, Patrick J. 1994, *Phantoms of Remembrance*. Princeton: Princeton University Press.

Gíslason, Gylfi Þ. 1973, *The Problem of being an Icelander, Past, Present and Future*. Reykjavík: Almenna bókafélagið.

Goffart, Walter 1988, *The Narrators of Barbarian History (AD 550–800): Jordanes, Gregory of Tours, Bede and Paul the Deacon*. Princeton: Princeton University Press.

Grímsdóttir, Guðrún Ása 1988, 'Um sárafar í Íslendinga sögu Sturlu Þórðarsonar', in Grímsdóttir, Guðrún Ása and Kristjánsson, Jónas (eds.), *Sturlustefna*. Rit 32. Reykjavík: Stofnun Árna Magnússonar, pp. 184–203.

Guðmundsson, Barði 1938, 'Uppruni *Landnámabókar*', *Skírnir* 112: 5–22.

Guðnason, Bjarni 1978, *Fyrsta sagan*. Studia Islandica, 37. Reykjavík: Menningarsjóður.

Halvorsen, E. F. 1957, 'Breta sögur'. *Kulturhistorisk Leksikon* II, cols. 220–3.

Harris, Joseph 1986, 'Saga as historical novel', in Lindow, John, Lönnroth, Lars and Weber, Gerd Wolfgang (eds.), *Structure and Meaning in Old Norse Literature*. Odense: Odense University Press, pp. 187–219.

Hastrup, Kirsten 1985, *Culture and Literature in Medieval Iceland*. Oxford and New York: Oxford University Press.

Heusler, Andreas 1908, *Die Gelehrte Urgeschichte im altisländischen Schrifttum*. Abhandlungen der königlich preussischen Akademie der Wissenschaften, philosophisch-historische Classe, Abh. III. Berlin: Verlag der königlichen Akademie der Wissenschaften.

Jakobsson, Ármann 1994, 'Nokkur orð um hugmyndir Íslendinga um konungsvald fyrir 1262.' In *Samtíðarsögur / The Contemporary Sagas. Níunda alþjóðlega fornsagnaþingið. Forprent*. Akureyri; pp. 31–42.

Jochens, Jenny 1997, 'Race and ethnicity among medieval Norwegians and Icelanders', *Sagas and the Norwegian Experience*, Senter for Middelalder studier, Trondheim, pp. 313–22.

Jóhannesson, Jón 1941, *Gerðir Landnámabókar*. Reykjavík: Félagsprentsmiejan.

1974 (trans. Bessason, Haraldur) *A History of the Old Icelandic Commonwealth*. Winnipeg: University of Manitoba Press.

Karlsson, Stefán 1979, 'Islandsk bogeksport til Norge i middelalderen'. *Maal og minne*, 1–17.

1988, 'Alfræði Sturlu Þórðarsonar', in Grímsdóttir and Kristjánsson, pp. 37–60.

Knirk, James 1993, 'Konungasögur', in Pulsiano, pp. 362–6.

Kulturhistorisk leksikon for nordisk middelalder I–XXII. 1956–78. Copenhagen: Rosenkilde & Bagger.

Layton, Robert (ed.) 1989, *Who Needs the Past? Indigenous Values and Archaeology*. London: Unwin Hyman.

Líndal, Sigurður 1969, 'Sendiför Úlfljóts'. *Skírnir* 143: 5–26.

Lönnroth, Lars 1969, 'The noble heathen: a theme in the sagas', *Scandinavian Studies* 41: 1–29.

1986, 'Indoctrination in the Icelandic saga', in Andersen, Frank Egholm and Weinstock, John (eds.), *The Nordic Mind*. Lanham: University Press of America; pp. 305–18. [Written 1968.]

Louis-Jensen, Jonna 1974, 'Trójumanna saga'. *Kulturhistorisk Leksikon* XVIII, cols. 652–5.

Meulengracht Sørensen, Preben 1974, 'Sagan um Ingólf og Hjörleif', *Skírnir* 148: 20–40.

1993, (trans. Tucker, John), *Saga and Society*. Odense: Odense University Press. [Revised, English, version of *Saga og Samfund*. Copenhagen: Berlingske forlag, 1977.]

Nordal, Sigurður 1920, *Snorri Sturluson*. Reykjavík: Helgafell. Repr. 1973.

Pálsson, Gísli 1992, 'Text, life, saga.' Introduction to Pálsson, Gísli (ed.), *From Sagas to Society: Comparative Approaches to Early Iceland*. Enfield Lock: Hisarlik, pp. 1–25.

Pálsson, Hermann 1970, *Tólfta öldin*. Reykjavík: Prentsmiðja Jóns Helgasonar.

Perkins, Richard 1989, 'Objects and oral tradition in medieval Iceland', in McTurk, Rory and Wawn, Andrew (eds.), *Úr Dölum til Dala. Guðbrandur Vigfusson Centenary Essays*. Leeds: Leeds Texts and Monographs, n.s. 11, pp. 239–66.

Pina-Cabral, J. de 1989, 'The valuation of time among the peasant population of the Alto Minho, northwestern Portugal', in Layton, pp. 59–68.

Pulsiano, Phillip and Wolf, Kirsten (eds.) 1993, *Medieval Scandinavia: an Encyclopedia*. New York and London: Garland.

Rafnsson, Sveinbjörn 1974, *Studier i Landnámabók*. Lund: Gleerup.

Sagas and the Norwegian Experience / Sagaerne og Noreg. 10th International Saga Conference. Preprints. 1997. Trondheim: Senter for middeladerstudier.

Schier, Kurt 1975, 'Iceland and the rise of literature in "Terra Nova"', *Gripla* 1: 168–81.

Sigfússon, Björn 1944, *Um Íslendingabók*. Reykjavík: Víkingsprent.

Sigurðsson, Gísli, 1988, *Gaelic Influence in Iceland. Historical and Literary Contacts: a Survey of Research.* Studia Islandica, 46. Reykjavík: Bókaútgáfa menningarsjóðs.

Sparkes, Brian 1989, 'Classical Greek attitudes to the past', in Layton, pp. 119–30.

Stefánsson, Magnús 1993, 'Ísland', in Pulsiano, pp. 311–20.

Tómasson, Sverrir 1988, *Formálar íslenskra sagnaritara á miðöldum.* Rit 33. Reykjavík: Stofnun Árna Magnússonar.

Vésteinsson, Orri 1998, 'Patterns of settlement in Iceland: a study in prehistory'. *Saga-Book of the Viking Society* 25: 1–29.

Vilmundarson, Þórhallur 1971, '-stad (-staðr, -staðir). Island', in *Kulturhistorisk Leksikon* XVI, cols. 578–83.

    1980, *Grímnir* I. Reykjavík: Örnefnastofnun Þjóðminjasafns.

Vincent, John 1995, *An Intelligent Person's Guide to History.* London: Duckworth.

Weber, Gerd Wolfgang 1981, 'Irreligiosität und Heldezeitalter. Zum Mythencharakter der altisländischen Literatur', in Dronke, Ursula, Helgadóttir, Guðrun, Weber, Gerd Wolfgang and Bekker-Nielsen, Hans (eds.), *Speculum Norrœnum: Norse Studies in Memory of Gabriel Turville-Petre.* Odense: Odense University Press, pp. 474–505.

Whaley, Diana 1991, *Heimskringla: an Introduction.* London: Viking Society for Northern Research.

    1993a, 'The kings' sagas'. In Faulkes, Anthony and Perkins, Richard (eds.), *Viking Revaluations.* London: Viking Society for Northern Research, pp. 43–64.

    1993b, 'Nicknames and narratives in the sagas', *Arkiv för nordisk filologi* 108: 122–46.

    1993c, 'Sæmundr Sigfússon', in Pulsiano, pp. 636–7.

White, Hayden 1978, 'The historical text as literary artifact', in his *Tropics of Discourse: Essays in Cultural Criticism.* Baltimore and London: Johns Hopkins University Press, pp. 81–100.

Young, J. Z. 1987, 'Memory', in Gregory, Richard L. (ed.), *The Oxford Companion to the Mind.* Oxford and New York: Oxford University Press, pp. 455–6.

8

Sagas of the Icelanders (*Íslendinga sögur*) and *þættir* as the literary representation of a new social space

JÜRG GLAUSER

translated by John Clifton-Everest

INTRODUCTION

The following chapter, which examines the *Íslendinga sögur* and *þættir* in their role as literary representatives of a new social space, calls first of all for a brief introductory description of the objects of enquiry.[1]

The *Íslendinga sögur*, some forty in number, and the *þættir*, of which there are more than a hundred, are Old Icelandic prose narratives which were composed in their surviving forms between *c.* 1220–30 and *c.* 1400 on the basis of oral traditions and literary models, and form one of the chief types of medieval saga literature. For the most part they are preserved on parchment from the period between the late thirteenth and the fifteenth centuries and in paper manuscripts dating from the sixteenth to the early twentieth centuries. Their contents treat chiefly of the conflicting struggles of individuals (both men and women) and groups (associated families, allies) for wealth, prestige and power. These conflicts are described against the setting of emigration by Norwegian chieftain families to a newly discovered Iceland in the later part of the ninth century, of settlement of the most important parts of the country, depicted as it were as an unpeopled land, in this context of its seizure, and of the establishment of a new social, political, economic and cultural order. The *Íslendinga sögur* and *þættir* are normally set in the ninth, tenth and eleventh centuries, and the action largely takes place in Iceland and Norway, though sometimes in other geographical regions familiar to the northern peoples in the Viking Age. In the fictional worlds of these texts a course of history is established which is essentially

203

defined by their retrospective view of the origins of the Icelanders, by their contradictory and often hostile attitude to the old Norwegian motherland, by Iceland's adoption of Christianity, portrayed as peaceful and successful, and generally by the emergence of specifically Icelandic attributes, and of a conscious, incipiently perhaps even a national, identity. Much space is filled in the *Íslendinga sögur* and *þættir* by descriptions of the Old Icelandic legal system, on which the feuds forming a major constituent of the action closely depend.

The differentiation of three chronological levels is accordingly of significance for this preliminary characterization of the *Íslendinga sögur* and *þættir*. Firstly there is the 'saga era' (ninth to eleventh centuries), the period of the fictional events; secondly the 'writing era' (thirteenth and early fourteenth centuries), the time of the initial recording in writing of individual texts, and of the formation of genres; and thirdly the 'era of memory' (fourteenth to early twentieth centuries), being the time of the transmission of the texts. A central aspect of all the *Íslendinga sögur* and *þættir* is this coming to terms with the past, this construction, and therefore interpretation, of history and cultural memory. These concepts are a leading theme in this study, which seeks to investigate the question of the representative quality and function of the *Íslendinga sögur* and *þættir* in new social spaces.

While early research into the sagas, up to the 1920s and 1930s of this century, dealt primarily with the first phase, treating the *Íslendinga sögur* in general as reliable sources for the period of the settlement, interest was subsequently focussed more and more on the so-called Sturlung age, the period in Icelandic history at the end of the twelfth and in the thirteenth centuries which ended with the acceptance by the Icelanders in the years 1262–64 of the overlordship of the Norwegian crown, and which is regarded by many researchers as the immediate cultural and social backdrop of the *Íslendinga sögur* (Clover 1985). By way of contrast, the third phase of the development of the sagas suggested here, following 1262–64, has become a focus of interest only recently, and for that very reason will receive greater emphasis than usual in the following discussion.

My arguments rest upon a number of studies and essays[2] which, for all their differences, have in common the fact that they more or less explicitly, and to a varying extent, thematize the picture of history and the relationships to the past that are drawn in Old Icelandic prose literature as constructed entities. In the present study, following these works, I shall attempt to apply to the *Íslendinga sögur* and *þættir* the concept of cultural memory developed first and foremost by the German Egyptologist Jan Assmann (1997), a concept which has only occasionally been adopted hitherto in saga-research (cf. in particular Fechner-Smarsly 1996: 194–5). But in incorporating into my arguments at the same time the conclusions of more recent Icelandic researchers on the significance of the late medieval transmission of the saga texts, I shall lay greater emphasis on the 'post-classical' texts and on the transmission phase of the fourteenth and fifteenth centuries.[3]

A REPRESENTATIVE TEXT: THE STORY OF BRÁK

A brief example from one the best-known Icelandic sagas serves to illustrate the argument and at the same time conveys an impression of the narrative style and rhetorical methods that these texts use.

Chapter 40 of *Egils saga Skalla-Grímssonar*, about the middle of this extensive narrative, recounts the following events. At the age of seven, Skalla-Grímr's son Egill, with the help of his friend Þórðr Granason, kills Grímr Heggsson, some three or four years his senior, as a result of a quarrel during a ball-game. This first killing, leading to greater conflicts which then result in seven further deaths, is allowed by his father to pass without comment. But Egill is praised for it by his mother Bera, who sees in her son a promising Viking destined to command warships one day. In an improvised strophe Egill takes up this praise (*lausavísa* 7).

Thereafter the narrative jumps over an interval of about five years, to continue with the description of a new ball-game:

> Þá er Egill var tólf vetra gamall, var hann svá mikill vexti at fáir váru menn svá stórir ok at afli búnir, at Egill ynni þá eigi flesta menn í leikum; þann vetr, er honum var inn tólfti, var hann mjǫk at leikum. Þórðr Granason var þá á tvítugs aldri; hann var sterkr at afli; þat var opt, er á leið vetrinn, at þeim Agli ok Þórði tveimr var skipt í móti Skalla-Grími. Þat var eitt sinn um vetrinn, er á leið, at knattleikr var at Borg suðr í Sandvík; þá váru þeir Þórðr í móti Skalla-Grími í leiknum, ok mœddisk hann fyrir þeim, ok gekk þeim léttara. En um kveldit eptir sólarfall, þá tók þeim Agli verr at ganga; gerðisk Grímr

þá svá sterkr, at hann greip Þórð upp ok keyrði niðr svá hart, at hann lamðisk allr, ok fekk hann þegar bana; síðan greip hann til Egils. Þorgerðr brák hét ambátt Skalla-Gríms; hon hafði fóstrat Egil í barnœsku; hon var mikil fyrir sér, sterk sem karlar ok fjǫlkunnig mjǫk. Brák mælti: 'Hamask þú nú, Skalla-Grímr, at syni þínum.' Skalla-Grímr lét þá lausan Egil, en þreif til hennar. Hon brásk við ok rann undan, en Skalla-Grímr eptir; fóru þau svá í útanvert Digranes; þá hljóp hon út af bjarginu á sund. Skalla-Grímr kastaði eptir henni steini miklum ok setti milli herða henni, ok kom hvártki upp síðan; þar er nú kallat Brákarsund. En eptir um kveldit, er þeir kómu heim til Borgar, var Egill allreiðr. En er Skalla-Grímr hafði sezk undir borð ok alþýða manna, þá var Egill eigi kominn í sæti sitt; þá gekk hann inn í eldahús ok at þeim manni, er þar hafði þá verkstjórn og fjárforráð með Skalla-Grími ok honum var kærstr; Egill hjó hann banahǫgg ok gekk síðan til sætis síns. En Skalla-Grímr rœddi þá ekki um, ok var þat mál þaðan af kyrrt, en þeir feðgar rœddusk þá ekki við, hvárki gott né illt, ok fór svá fram þann vetr. (Nordal 1933: 101–2)

(When Egil was twelve, he was so big that few grown men were big and strong enough that he could not beat them at games. In the year that he was twelve, he spent a lot of time taking part in games. Thord Granason was in his twentieth year then, and strong too. That winter, Egil and Thord often took sides together in games against Skallagrim.

Once during the winter there was a ball-game at Borg, in Sandvik to the south. Egil and Thord played against Skallagrim, who grew tired and they came off better. But that night, after sunset, Egil and Thord began losing. Skallagrim was filled with such strength that he seized Thord and dashed him to the ground so fiercely that he was crushed by the blow and died on the spot. Then he seized Egil.

Skallagrim had a servant-woman called Thorgerd Brak, who had fostered Egil when he was a child. She was an imposing woman, as strong as a man and well versed in the magic arts.

Brak said, 'You're attacking your own son like a mad beast, Skallagrim.'

Skallagrim let Egil go, but went for her instead. She ran off, with Skallagrim in pursuit. They came to the shore at the end of Digranes, and she ran off the edge of the cliff and swam away. Skallagrim threw a huge boulder after her which struck her between the shoulder blades. Neither the woman nor the boulder ever came up afterwards. That spot is now called Brakarsund (Brak's Sound).

Later that night, when they returned to Borg, Egil was furious. By the time Skallagrim and the other members of the household sat down at the table, Egil had not come to his seat. Then he walked into the room and went over to Skallagrim's favourite, a man who was in charge of the workers and ran the farm with him. Egil killed him with a single blow, then went to his seat. Skallagrim did not mention the matter and it was left to rest afterwards, but father and son did not speak to each other, neither kind or unkind words, and so it remained through the winter.) (Scudder 1997: 78)

A year and a half later Egill contrives to make his older brother Þórólfr take him along on his ship to Norway. The chapter ends with a short genealogical list.

The text of *Egils saga* in this form presumably dates from about 1220, which would make it one of the oldest Icelandic sagas. The important chapter in question, chapter 40, exhibits a series of characteristics that are specific to this saga. First of all there is the markedly psycho-social discourse: as can clearly be seen in this small excerpt, the text defines itself consistently by means of fundamental conflicts within the generations of the family, both between the father and one of his sons, Egill, and between the two unequal brothers Egill and Þorsteinn.[4] It is certainly no coincidence that the boy whom Egill kills in the first part of the text bears the same name as Egill's own father. Jón Karl Helgason (1992) showed with reference to Freud's analysis of the *Doppelgänger*-phenomenon how in such passages, and numerous other ones, the text of the saga generates uncertainties as to the identity-limits of individual characters through metonymical merging in the mind of the reader. In the first ball-game Grímr Heggsson takes the place of Skalla-Grímr, in a certain sense substituting for him, and so it is hardly surprising that he becomes precisely in this capacity an object of aggression for the still child-like Egill. The psycho-social discourse, more suggested than actually carried out, and therefore realized predominantly in the sub-text, is in its turn couched in a typical feud-discourse.[5] The preliminary short sequence of vengeful and feuding actions is set in train by the conflict between Egill Skalla-Grímsson and his opponent Grímr. The text is concerned primarily with establishing the personal and social relationships necessary for drawing the character of Egill and therefore focusses its account on the development of this figure. The feud arising from this killing by Egill, leading to a battle between two parties, therefore receives less attention from the narrative and is dealt with comparatively briefly. The text relates Egill's conflict with his father (Skalla-) Grímr, following the jump in time, in much greater detail. Once more it is third parties that are affected by the antagonism between father and son. In his berserk fury the older man kills not only Egill's friend but also his foster-mother, another person closely related to Egill and introduced by the text as a substitute in the very last moment before the son is killed. Egill's only possible countermove, given that patricide is inconceivable in this particular universe, is to kill somebody else close to Skalla-Grímr. He accordingly kills his farm manager.

The theme of the journey to Norway in the last third of the chapter, anticipating the resumption of another thread of the plot, namely the conflict between Kveld-Úlfr, Skalla-Grímr and Egill and the Norwegian kings Haraldr and Eiríkr, introduces here an important political discourse, constituting the principal element of many *þættir*. And with the genealogy at the end of the chapter the text finally embarks on a discourse of power and memory that is definitive of the genre of the *Íslendinga sögur*.

The 'Brák-episode', forming the middle part of chapter 40, was cited here in its entirety on account of its precision and the power of its testimony. In a manner quite typical of the sagas it provides, in the boundless, abandoned fury of Skalla-Grímr after sunset, a reference to an archaic mode of behaviour associated in the text with the werewolf-attributes of the heads of this family, a point further alluded to in the name of his father Kveld-Úlfr – 'evening-wolf'. In the overall narrative of *Egils saga* these attributes and forms of behaviour are construed as the dominating characteristics of a time past, which the present has 'over-come',[6] and which have left no more than traces in the real landscape outside the literary text. The theme of the werewolf introduces a mythological–magical discourse that is central to the text and which also embraces a field as dominant as poetry (cf. above all Clunies Ross 1998: 173–9). Just as in the case cited of the strong slave Brák with her magic powers, this magical element is opposed most of all when it has connotations of the female (Kress 1996: 91–3). For in the figure of Brák, a whole culture with 'female/matriarchal', 'heathen' and 'oral' charac-teristics is subjected to a remorseless process of exclusion and destruc-tion by a 'patriarchal', 'Christian' and 'written' principle, one that has triumphed by a process of recording, codifying and theologizing the ancient stories.[7] The narrative intention conveyed by the specific receptive and representational perspective of the sagas in the High and Late Middle Ages arises then from a typical colonial situation, in which the land-taking in Iceland was portrayed as a male action with respect to a land construed as female. As the sagas tell it, cultural paradigms are brought by the land-taking men from the society they have left, and are transferred, as 'other', to an alien nature (landscape, femaleness).

Traces of the superseded culture, introduced here in concrete and overt form, are inscribed in the landscape through its place-names. The semioticization of the landscape, previously empty and undescribed, and therefore meaningless and without sense, proceeds in a manner not dissimilar to modern stories and legends. In the Icelandic sagas, written texts from the High and Late Middle Ages in Iceland, one constantly finds at crucial points a 'mapping', a descriptive record of the landscape and of nature. In the text following the quotation above, there is for instance a statement that the ship anchored 'in Brákarsund'. By narrative means, a place-name is thus established to whose literary description the fiction immediately following it can refer repeatedly. The brief narrative also shows how a transformation of nature into culture occurs, in that nature – in the concrete form of the Icelandic landscape surrounding the community – is 'described' by the sagas, i.e. endowed with signs and so filled with significance. This 'locating' of culture, a semioticization of the landscape such as is found at this point of *Egils saga Skalla-Grímssonar*, forms a trope of memory.

THE ICELANDIC SAGAS AS A MEDIUM OF CULTURAL MEMORY

In a still very valuable survey of research on the genre of *Íslendinga sögur*, Clover (1985: 254) examined the various possibilities of treating these texts as the expression of a 'reality', thus concentrating on the problem of representation, and in this context highlighted their significance as 'some imaginative version of their pagan past to which the medieval Icelanders collectively subscribed'. In looking to the realms of the 'imaginary', the 'past' and the 'collective memory', she applies key concepts of cultural-memory research. But notwithstanding the state of research described by Clover ('critical commonplaces'), which regarded the thirteenth century in a quite one-sided way as the principal, or indeed the only place from which to achieve an interpretation of the sagas about the period of settlement (1985: 267), an approach founded on culture and memory theory opens up quite varied possibilities of interpretation.

For example, Ólason's monograph (1998) on the *Íslendinga sögur* works with the concept of a 'dialogue', which in literary texts such as the sagas is conducted both with and about the past, and shows some features of New Historicism.[8] According to Ólason, in this dialogical model it is not the free state which forms 'the immediate historical background for many of the *Íslendingasögur*', but memory and ideas in the last three decades of the thirteenth century. In Ólason's view (1998: 35) it was therefore the time *following* the Icelanders' loss of so-called national independence in which the social energy behind the cultural symbolism of these texts mainly evolved. The following argument owes much, *inter alia*, to the work of Jan Assmann, which utilizes the concepts of 'forming tradition', 'relationship to the past', 'written culture' and 'formation of identity' for its theoretical definition of cultural memory. In the case of the Icelandic sagas all four of these elements are conspicuously present (Assmann 1997: 301).

The most important reference made in Icelandic literature, and specifically, and above all, in the *Íslendinga sögur*, *þættir*, *fornaldarsögur* and *samtíðarsögur*, is to a fictional owning of the past, in which the representation of history and pre-history is achieved principally through genealogical accounts, as Clunies Ross (1993, esp. pp. 382–5; 1998) has shown in various contexts. Genealogies are among the most characteristic and original forms of cultural memory techniques; in such accounts there is frequently a direct leap from mythological beginnings to the present (Assmann 1997: 49–50). The dynastic interests of individual texts or groups of texts (mostly crossing the boundaries of genre without problems) formed as early as the thirteenth century in Iceland, can even lead, through the systematic application of genealogical modes of narrative during the fourteenth and fifteenth centuries, to the phenomenon of 'family ownership of the past' described by Clunies Ross (1998: 113–21). Texts from the thirteenth century, like *Egils saga Skalla-Grímssonar*, *Landnámabók* or the *forn-*

aldarsögur about the so-called Hrafnistumenn, and tales from about 1300 such as *Grettis saga Ásmundarsonar,* allow a privileged status to individual chieftain families, which is provided principally by genealogical links to prominent Norwegian dynasties; for 'lordship requires lineage' (Assmann 1997: 71). In the large compendium-manuscripts of the fourteenth century (primarily in those manuscripts which, like *Möðruvallabók* and *Vatnshyrna,* contain sagas of Icelanders, but also in extensive compilations like *Flateyjarbók, Hauksbók* or *Bergsbók,* which contain a variety of genres), this literary construction of the past is subjected to a further process of selection and codification, which once again exhibits traces of a perception and representation focussing on the family origins of the patron or his wife and their social, economic and above all mythological status.

Clunies Ross, too, sees both in the *Íslendinga sögur* and in the *fornaldarsögur* and the *samtíðarsögur* stories intended to narrate the legendary past of individual families, reaching back to a time before the great ancestor of the family emigrated from Norway to settle in Iceland and covering the development of Icelandic society from the early age of settlement down to the immediate past of the eleventh and twelfth centuries (1998: 93). As a result of this narrative process the Icelandic chieftains in the Middle Ages 'recreated the past as saga literature' and 'literature became history for them'.[9]

However here one must differentiate. The past exists because one refers to it, so that memory is a reconstructed past. Assmann contrasts the concept of 'tradition', which signifies continuity, a continuation through writing and cultural maintenance, with 'memory', which is only made possible through the awareness of historical difference. To achieve consciousness and a creation of the past, a break is needed. 'Tradition', on the one hand, does not concern itself with matters like reception, and reaching back to traverse the breaks, nor with the process of suppression and forgetting. 'Cultural memory' on the other hand arises rather from an affective, creative approach to memories, and brings about a conscious relationship with the past by overcoming the break (cf. Assmann 1997: 31–4). For the present case of the *Íslendinga sögur* as a group of texts, this means that they only become an instrument of cultural memory in Iceland after the break of '1262–64'. Without the period following the loss of the Icelanders' independence (if indeed there is any point at all in giving so much weight to this event) there would be no Icelandic past-awareness in the form found in the *Íslendinga sögur*.

Seen from this point of view, the *Íslendinga sögur, þættir, fornaldar-sögur, samtíðarsögur*, texts like Ari's *Íslendingabók* and the various versions of *Landnámabók* are components of the 'great narration' of the Icelanders' pre-history, their exodus, immigration and settlement, and their change of faith. This meta-text revokes the contingencies of historical development to present us with a decisive sequence of events that is to a certain extent logical and consistent.[10] The view of history created in these texts and resting on a basis of fiction, can thus be assumed into cultural memory as a well-structured narrative unit, due to the texts' ability to substantiate and give meaning to that view. While communicative memory retains events from a recent past of up to some forty years, cultural memory focusses on fixed points of the past, and can justify the identity of the remembering group through its own particular relations with the past.[11] This is just what happens in the *Íslendinga sögur* of the late thirteenth, the fourteenth and fifteenth centuries, when the Icelandic chieftains with social and political origins in the oligarchy of the period of the *goðar* of the eleventh and twelfth centuries had their past symbolically recorded.[12]

Not just the thirteenth, but also the fourteenth and fifteenth centuries remain indispensable agents in the further transmission of the texts, of the genres, and of the historical images they project, as well as in the continued debate they conduct in this way with the past. At times when, for reasons of historical development, the tradition becomes less self-evident, there is an increased need for explanation. This can lead to a codification of knowledge about the past,[13] a process which can be clearly discerned in the Icelandic compendia of the fourteenth and fifteenth centuries. As in many similar cultures, the period of the writing down of the sagas in Iceland is followed by one of codification, having some features of a process of active canon formation. The transmission of the texts first written down in the thirteenth and early fourteenth centuries, extending as it does over a long period, and quantitatively extensive as it is, should in no circumstances be characterized as a matter of mere reproduction.[14] The diachronic dimension implicit in the circumstances of the transmission of the Icelandic sagas through the medium of the manuscripts defines such crucial aspects as variation, changes of medium, re-oralization and the time-depth of the transmission. But on a synchronic level it is repeatedly apparent that the conventional boundaries of the genres – between the *Íslendinga sögur* and the *fornaldarsögur* or the *riddarasögur* for instance, but also between the *Íslendinga sögur* and works with an immediate historical intention like *Landnámabók* – are undergoing dissolution. Yet on the diachronic level too the firm boundaries of single texts in the variable manuscript transmission can be seen to be undergoing dissolution, as older versions are replaced by newer ones, so that one text becomes simply a matter of the collection of its variants, or merely the result of the possibilities inherent in their intertextuality.[15] From a cultural–historical point of view the specific character of medieval Icelandic literature resides precisely in this late and post-medieval stage of the transmission process.

At this juncture it is necessary to point to the writing down of the tradition, brought about by the codification of the *Íslendinga sögur*, as being an important pre-condition of their formation of the past.[16] Only 'the advent of literacy gave Icelandic writers the freedom to recreate the past, incorporating oral traditions'.[17] However, only the mediating achievements brought by writing made possible the poetics of intertextuality which is so characteristic of the *Íslendinga sögur* and their related genres, and so allowed the emergence of a range of coherent narratives dealing with the past which had an identifying and validating function for individual groups in Icelandic society of the High and Late Middle Ages.

In the developing perceptions of those medieval Icelanders who for a variety of reasons had an obviously very considerable interest in the writing down and transmission of the texts, one can discern a progression from myth, via literature, to history, when tales of mythological type about origins and descent are first constructed, then – transmitted in the form of sagas – are accepted as past, and are duly passed on as such. Emigration and land-taking are striking tropes in the Icelandic cultural memory, though it is of course not their historicity but rather the functions of these historical constructions which are crucial in the memory process. For the remembered past is represented in the narrative form of the prose texts precisely because it is seen as important. Land-taking by the ancestors of the dynasty is thus the defining action which serves to bestow a founding identity on the group.[18] In contrast to those processes of mythologizing in which a timeless myth is derived from an historical event, one might perhaps speak in the case of Icelandic literature of the thirteenth and fourteenth centuries of a process of historicization. In the form of the sagas, this process inseparably embraces both myth and history, of course (Assmann 1997: 75–8).

The *Íslendinga sögur*, the *þættir* and other genres may be characterized as formative texts in the sense intended by Assmann. They provide an answer to the question: Who are we? And they do this by conveying information which, as was shown, also confirms identity. Resort to myth makes an important contribution to these narratives of identification. The impulses derived from them Assman (1997: 142) calls 'Mythomotorik' (myth-dynamism). Thus there is a close connection between the sagas and ethnogenesis in Iceland.[19]

In the 'interested remembering' recorded in these Icelandic tales a so-called 'hot' memory finds expression, while a 'cold' historical memory provides forms of chronological checking (cf. Assmann 1997: 237–8). The literary tradition of the north is quite precisely described by means of this paired concept: in Norway and the rest of the medieval north, forms of texts arise in which the past is dealt with much less creatively, with few exceptions, such as *Guta saga*, for instance. In Iceland, a productive approach to the past leads to a semioticization of history, resulting in the genre of the saga. Only the fact that the literature of the sagas becomes the chief medium for the cultural memory of Iceland, makes possible their manuscript tradition down to the beginning of the modern age at the start of this century (Glauser 1994; Driscoll 1997).

It is not merely the fact that the view of their national history formed from the ninth to the eleventh centuries in the fictional texts of the Icelandic Middle Ages was taken over and hypostasized by the Icelanders of the waning Middle Ages and the early modern period which speaks for the thorough-going success of the construction attempted by the *Íslendinga sögur*. Philological research of the late nineteenth and the twentieth centuries, pursuing a national–romantic ideology,[20] also felt driven to take up these images and narratives on account of their supposedly realistic and neutral narrative modes, and to construct from them notions of an original reality behind the fictions of the text.

The Danish historiographer Saxo Grammaticus was in error when he asserted in his *Gesta Danorum*, written about 1200, that the Icelanders remembered the great deeds of other peoples to compensate for the lack of their own, as Weber (1987: 95) has observed, for the ambitious reconstructions of Iceland's past which led to the emergence of literary genres like the *Íslendinga sögur* and the *þættir* refute Saxo's verdict with as much clarity as anyone could wish for. In these stories, representing with their particular fictionality new social spaces, there is recorded a self-constructed memory of the emigration, the settlement, the re-building of a society and a religious conversion which are epoch-making events for the Icelanders. In this manner the *Íslendinga sögur* treat of notable, that is to say memorable, deeds that are their own, as is evidenced by the active and productive use made of the stories long after the time they were first written down. By bridging the gap brought about through the historical events of the thirteenth century, the sagas become a decisive element in forming the cultural memory of medieval Iceland. However, without the late medieval reception and the subse-quent productive transmission of the texts in manuscript and semi-oral form in the early modern age, this recollection of their history as determined through literature would not have become so firmly established and fixed in the collective consciousness of the Icelanders as to provide over the centuries justification, not only of a great tale of a mythical descent and origins, but also of their present sense of identity.

NOTES

1 For the terminology cf. e.g. Schier 1970, Clover 1985, Ólason 1993, Pulsiano and Wolf 1993, Ólason 1998. Recent attempts to define the Icelandic sagas as a genre are to be found in Tómasson 1998 and Clunies Ross 1998, esp. pp. 97–121, the last of whom stresses the heterogeneity of genre manifest above all in the numerous intertextual relationships apparent at quite varied discursive levels between the *Íslendinga sögur*, the *samtíðarsögur*, the *fornaldar-sögur* and in the latter phases partly even in the *riddarasögur*. *Íslendinga sögur* and *þættir* are heterogeneous both as to theme and time, so that they remain generically open kinds of texts, over and above the plurality of discourses

found in individual sagas (cf. e.g. Ólason 1998: 190 on *Grettis saga Ásmundar-sonar*).

2 Cf. Schier 1975, Weber 1981, Hastrup 1990a (esp. pp. 67–135), Meulengracht Sørensen 1993, Fechner-Smarsly 1996, Clunies Ross 1998, Ólason 1998. At this point attention is particularly drawn to the excellent report on the state of research in Clover 1985, since for reasons of space the older scholarly literature cannot be examined here. Clunies Ross 1993 and 1998 (esp. pp. 76–96) presented a notable analysis of the central function that genealogical narrative modes have in forming cultural memory in Iceland (see below).

3 On the reasons for the importance of this late medieval transmission cf. Glauser 1998 and the literature listed there.

4 Cf. the psycho-social arguments of Tulinius 1995 (esp. pp. 230–42), who views the pattern of patricide and fratricide in *Egils saga* against a background of a whole collection of socio-historical events in Iceland in the thirteenth century.

5 Cf. particularly the work of Byock, who *inter alia* developed the structuralistically oriented concept of the 'feudeme', a pattern of feuding activity (vengeance followed by counter-vengeance) with precise social implications that is virtually ubiquitous in saga literature and thereby serves to define the genre (Byock 1982; 1984–85; 1988).

6 Cf. Ólason 1998: 191–7. Ólason suggests that in the sequence of generations from Skalla-Grímr Kveld-Úlfsson through Egill Skalla-Grímsson to Þorsteinn Egilsson one can see a growing civilization and domestication of wild elements, and that the 'wild' period of the settlers finally comes to an end with Egill's son Þorsteinn. The semioticization of the law, which can be seen in numerous ancient high cultures as a linking of text, law, memory and history (cf. Assmann 1997: 230–58), is a central element in Icelandic sagas too. Old Icelandic mythological narratives such as the stories of the poetic mead, of the building of the wall round Ásgarðr, or of Týr and the Fenriswolf, involve the breaking of contracts or laws. In sagas such as *Bandamanna saga*, *Hænsa-Þóris saga*, *Egils saga* or *Njáls saga*, the law is interpreted in the context of the narrative.

7 In certain texts, *Vatnsdœla saga* for instance, one finds over and above the exclusion and eradication of the magical and the female the similarly uncanonical Irish element. Clunies Ross 1998: 122–57, ch. 6, 'Myth of settlement and colonisation', deals with various aspects of settlement ideology in a broader context and discusses the various paradigms of land-taking.

8 Cf. also Greenblatt's (1988: 1) well-known summary of the aim of New Historicism: 'I began with the desire to speak with the dead.'

9 Cf. Clunies Ross 1998: 50, who on this point refers to Meulengracht Sørensen 1993.

10 Cf. esp. Weber 1981 and 1987. Clunies Ross 1998: 189 and elsewhere shows

how, for example, in the context of settlement the finding of a suitable place for establishing a new home in Iceland takes an altogether mythological course (divine power, rites of passage, signs of the numinous).

11 Cf. Assmann 1997: 49–53, who pursues among other things Jan Vansina's concept of the 'floating gap' in historical tradition.

12 Ólason 1998 repeatedly observes in the *Íslendinga sögur* this same recording of forms of the past used to define groups of people.

13 On this see Assmann 1997: 181–2, with examples from early high cultures (Babylonia, Egypt, Israel and Greece).

14 Such is one of the theories of Hastrup 1990b. This essay accordingly views with great scepticism Hastrup's variously formulated theory of decline, which claims that in the early modern period in Iceland (*c.* 1400–*c.*1800) an actual 'cultural deconstruction' occurred (e.g. Hastrup 1990a: 184–200). Such a picture of the development of Icelandic cultural history seems to me too closely tied to the traditional self-images and national–romantic myths of the nineteenth and early twentieth centuries to have any literary–historical value.

15 This understanding of the saga texts is in stark contrast to the position adopted most typically by the Icelandic literary scholar Einar Ólafur Sveinsson in a way typical of the New Criticism of his time and with specific reference to *Njáls saga*. For Sveinsson this saga was a work created by one author, and defined as a great work of art by its hermetically contained aesthetics and its thematic unity, whose subsequent manuscript variations counted for little (e.g. Sveinsson 1933). One of Sveinsson's books about the saga was accordingly titled: *Njáls Saga: a Literary Masterpiece* (Sveinsson 1971; cf. also Ólason 1993).

16 Cf. Assmann 1997: 99 101. Bachmann-Medick 1996: 15 was critical, from an ethnological–cultural point of view, of such an assessment of the text as a privileged, revolutionary vehicle of culture. This criticism, quite justified in the face of the absoluteness with which Assmann presented his theory, is also valid for much 'literacy'-research of the type carried out by Walter J. Ong or Jack Goody.

17 Clunies Ross 1998: 82, with subsequent reference to Brian Stock, among others.

18 Assmann 1997 investigated this using the example of the exodus of the Israelites. There have been frequent references to the correspondences between national myths of foundation such as are found in the Old Testament (esp. in the Pentateuch) and the tradition of the Icelandic sagas (though also for instance in Virgil) (cf. Schier 1975). One should add here that the imagination of the Icelanders also contains in a certain form the notion of 'chosenness' or 'otherness', similar to that in the Jewish foundation-myth (cf. Assmann 1997: 30). However, in the Icelandic case it is not defined by the religious element, and is largely restricted to the separation of Iceland

from Norway. As has been stated, it is of literary relevance in a long series of *þættir*.

19 Cf. Assmann 1997, esp. pp. 272–80, on Homer and Greek ethnogenesis. Here too there are numerous parallels between the Homeric epics analysed by Assmann and the Icelandic sagas, particularly with regard both to Homer's position in a time of change from a 'loose society' to a 'tight society', (a time just like that which has been described for northern society in the transition from the Viking Age to the Middle Ages) and the dynamics of the colonizing movement.

20 Cf. Assmann 1997, esp. pp. 79–80. The *Íslendinga sögur* and the image they advance of the origins of the Icelanders were still creating a myth of foundation in the nineteenth century. But the reality of experience of the Icelanders in the nineteenth century fell far short of the expectations of this myth. So the past became a social and political utopia to strive for.

REFERENCES

Assmann, Jan 1997, *Das kulturelle Gedächtnis. Schrift, Erinnerung und politische Identität in frühen Hochkulturen*. Second, rev. edn, Munich: Verlag C. H. Beck.

Bachmann-Medick, Doris (ed.) 1996, *Kultur als Text: die anthropologische Wende in der Literaturwissenschaft*. Frankfurt am Main: Fischer Taschenbuch Verlag.

Byock, Jesse L. 1982, *Feud in the Icelandic Saga*. Berkeley, Los Angeles and London: University of California Press.

1984–85, 'Saga Form, Oral Prehistory, and the Icelandic Social Context', *New Literary History* 16: 153–73.

1988, *Medieval Iceland: Society, Sagas, and Power*. Berkeley, Los Angeles, London: University of California Press (paperback printing 1990).

Clover, Carol J. 1985, 'Icelandic Family Sagas (*Íslendingasögur*)', in Clover, Carol J. and Lindow, John (eds.), *Old Norse–Icelandic Literature: a Critical Guide*. Islandica, 45. Ithaca and London: Cornell University Press, pp. 239–315.

Clunies Ross, Margaret 1993, 'The Development of Old Norse Textual Worlds: Genealogical Structure as a Principle of Literary Organisation in Early Iceland', *Journal of English and Germanic Philology* 92: 372–85.

1994, *Prolonged Echoes: Old Norse Myths in Medieval Northern Society*, I: *The Myths*. The Viking Collection. Studies in Northern Civilization, 7. Odense: Odense University Press.

1998, *Prolonged Echoes: Old Norse Myths in Medieval Northern Society*. II: *The Reception of Norse Myths in Medieval Iceland*. The Viking Collection. Studies in Northern Civilization, 10. Odense: Odense University Press.

Driscoll, Matthew J. 1997, *The Unwashed Children of Eve: the Production, Dissemination and Reception of Popular Literature in Post-Reformation Iceland*. Enfield Lock, Middlesex: Hisarlik.

Fechner-Smarsly, Thomas 1996, *Krisenliteratur: Zur Rhetorizität und Ambivalenz in der isländischen Sagaliteratur*. Texte und Untersuchungen zur Germanistik und Skandinavistik, 36. Frankfurt am Main: Peter Lang.

Glauser, Jürg 1994, 'The End of the Saga: Text, Tradition and Transmission in Nineteenth- and Early Twentieth-Century Iceland', in Wawn, Andrew (ed.), *Northern Antiquity: the Post-Medieval Reception of Edda and Saga*. Enfield Lock, Middlesex: Hisarlik, pp. 101–41.

1998, 'Textüberlieferung und Textbegriff im spätmittelalterlichen Norden: Das Beispiel der Riddarasögur', *Arkiv för nordisk filologi* 113: 7–27.

Greenblatt, Stephen 1988, *Shakespearean Negotiations: the Circulation of Social Energy in Renaissance England*. The New Historicism, 4. Berkeley and Los Angeles: University of California Press.

Hastrup, Kirsten 1990a, *Island of Anthropology: Studies in Past and Present Iceland*. The Viking Collection. Studies in Northern Civilization, 5. Odense: Odense University Press.

1990b, *Nature and Policy in Iceland 1400–1800: an Anthropological Analysis of History and Mentality*. Oxford: Clarendon.

Helgason, Jón Karl 1992, 'Rjóðum spjöll í dreyra: Óhugnaður, úrkast og erótík í Egils sögu', *Skáldskaparmál. Tímarit um íslenskar bókmenntir fyrri alda* 2: 60–76.

Kress, Helga 1996, *Fyrir dyrum fóstru. Konur og kynferði í íslenskum fornbókmenntum. Greinasafn*. Reykjavík: Háskóli Íslands, Rannsóknastofa í kvennafræðum.

Meulengracht Sørensen, Preben 1993, *Fortælling og ære. Studier i islændingesagaerne*. Aarhus: Aarhus University Press.

Nordal, Sigurður (ed.) 1933, *Egils saga Skalla-Grímssonar*. Íslenzk fornrit II. Reykjavík: Hið íslenzka fornritafélag.

Ólason, Vésteinn 1993, 'The Sagas of Icelanders', in Faulkes, Anthony and Perkins, Richard (eds.), *Viking Revaluations: Viking Society Centenary Symposium, 14–15 May 1992*. Viking Society for Northern Research, University College London, pp. 26–42.

1998, *Dialogues with the Viking Age: Narration and Representation in the Sagas of the Icelanders*. Translated by Andrew Wawn. Reykjavík: Heimskringla, Mál og menning Academic Division.

Pulsiano, Phillip and Wolf, Kirsten (eds.) 1993, *Medieval Scandinavia: an Encyclopedia*. Garland reference library of the humanities, 934. Garland encyclopedias of the Middle Ages, I. New York and London: Garland.

Schier, Kurt 1970, *Sagaliteratur*. Sammlung Metzler, 78. Stuttgart: J. B. Metzlersche Verlagsbuchhandlung.

1975, 'Iceland and the Rise of Literature in "terra nova": Some Comparative

Reflections', *Gripla* 1: 168–81; repr.: Schier, Kurt, *Nordlichter. Ausgewählte Schriften, 1960–1992*. Strerath-Bolz, Ulrike, Würth, Stefanie and Geberl, Sibylle (eds.), Munich: Diederichs, 1994, pp. 140–53.

Scudder, Bernard (trans.) 1997, *Egil's saga* in Hreinsson, Viðar (ed.), *The Complete Sagas of Icelanders, Including 49 Tales*. 5 vols. Reykjavík: Leifur Eiríksson, I, pp. 33–177.

Sveinsson, Einar Ólafur 1933, *Um Njálu*, I. Reykjavík: Menningarsjóður.

1971, *Njáls Saga: a Literary Masterpiece*. Schach, Paul (ed. and trans.). With an introduction by E. O. G. Turville-Petre. Lincoln: University of Nebraska Press. [Icelandic Original: *Á Njálsbúð. Bók um mikið listaverk*. Reykjavík: Hið íslenzka Bókmenntafélag, Félagsprentsmiðjan, 1943.]

Tómasson, Sverrir 1998, '"Ei skal haltr ganga": Um *Gunnlaugs sögu ormstungu*', *Gripla* 10: 1–22.

Tulinius, Torfi H. 1995, *La 'Matière du Nord': Sagas légendaires et fiction dans la littérature islandaise en prose du XIIIe siécle*. Voix Germaniques. Paris: Presses de l'Université de Paris-Sorbonne.

Weber, Gerd Wolfgang 1981, 'Irreligiosität und Heldenzeitalter. Zum Mythencharakter der altisländischen Literatur', in Dronke, Ursula, Helgadóttir, Guðrin, Weber, Gerd Wolfgang and Bekker-Nielsen, Hans (eds.), *Specvlvm Norroenvm: Norse Studies in Memory of Gabriel Turville-Petre*. Odense: Odense University Press, pp. 474–505.

1987, 'Intellegere historiam: Typological Perspectives of Nordic Prehistory (in Snorri, Saxo, Widukind and others)', in Hastrup, Kirsten and Meulengracht Sørensen, Preben (eds.), *Tradition og historieskrivning. Kilderne til Nordens ældste historie*. Acta Jutlandica, 43. Humanistisk Serie, 61. Aarhus: Aarhus University Press, pp. 95–141.

9

The contemporary sagas and their social context

GUÐRÚN NORDAL

Sturlunga saga falls within the category of medieval *historia*; it is a carefully constructed version of political events in Iceland from the latter half of the twelfth century to the end of the third quarter of the thirteenth century. The work is a compilation of the so-called contemporary sagas, edited and adapted around the year 1300 by an Icelander, probably the lawman Þórðr Narfason (d. 1308; Nordal 1992).[1] Þórðr Narfason's sources were a number of separate sagas of unequal length written for the most part by unknown writers shortly after the events took place. We can therefore expect *Sturlunga saga* to contain a relatively faithful chronicle of historical events. The reality is more complex and the edited version by Þórðr is indicative of the social and literary currents at play in thirteenth-century society in Iceland.

Only one of Þórðr's sources, *Hrafns saga Sveinbjarnarsonar*, is known in an extant version outside the compilation, and by comparing it to Þórðr's version in *Sturlunga saga* it is possible to gauge his intention in writing the compilation. It is clear that he understated and even omitted overtly religious elements that we can see are more prominent in the independent *Hrafns saga Sveinbjarnarsonar* and chose instead to highlight a more pronouncedly secular point of view in his narrative (Tranter 1987; Bragason 1988). In spite of this editorial policy, events in *Sturlunga saga* are interpreted and foreshadowed according to the recognized traditions of historiography in the thirteenth century: human life was to be understood and interpreted in terms of a larger religious and moral framework (Ward 1982: 201–2; Weber 1987: 125). An interplay between the telling of facts in a *historia* and Christian symbolism and typology is therefore a poignant possibility in a work of such planning and scope as *Sturlunga saga.*

Sturlunga saga is our only source for many of the crucial events in the history of Iceland, culminating at the point when the Icelandic aristocracy made a pact with the Norwegian king in 1262–64, accepting Norwegian sovereignty in return for certain concessions. Consequently the saga has become an indispensable source for this important period in the history of the country. Moreover, the saga itself has supplied the social context for the world of thirteenth-century sagas of Icelanders and has furthermore provided the details of the lives of many of the known writers of the period, including Snorri Sturluson (1179–1241), Ólafr Þórðarson (d. 1259) and Sturla Þórðarson (1214–84), who was himself the author of the greater part of *Sturlunga saga*. *Sturlunga saga* commands, therefore, an important position in medieval Icelandic culture. Notwithstanding the direct relevance of this work to our appreciation of thirteenth-century Iceland, the saga must be treated with care as a historical source, and with clear acknowledgement of the social and literary context within which it was written and conceived. The artificial construction of the saga is in itself suggestive of the ideology of the writers who produced it and its inherent propaganda value for its intended audience, the ruling class, should not be underestimated.

This chapter is devoted to a study of the social background against which the representation of political developments in twelfth- and thirteenth-century Iceland must be placed. An explication of this social context is not only important as far as *Sturlunga saga* is concerned, but for our understanding of intellectual life in thirteenth-century Iceland. I wish to suggest to the reader the ideological framework within which a work of this kind operates. The themes chosen for discussion in the chapter are introduced in the opening *þáttr* of the compilation and developed throughout the work: the myth of the settlement, the aristocratic background of the ruling class, the importance of kinship and Christian values, and the role of the poet and writer in this society.

THE SOCIAL CONTEXT

Scholars have stressed that Iceland's small population in the Middle Ages, probably around fifty or sixty thousand, formed a homogeneous society in which the division between different social groups was not as strictly drawn as in the larger countries in Europe (Foote 1974: 43). This notion is commonly sustained by the kind of society represented in sagas of Icelanders, the 'saga society' as William Ian Miller has called it (1990: 8), in which workers, farmers and chieftains seem to interact on an equal footing and are even presented as social companions. The discussion of this concept of 'saga society' has inevitably involved the society in which many of the authors of the sagas of Icelanders lived, that of the twelfth and thirteenth centuries as it is depicted in *Sturlunga saga*. In spite of the apparent structural parallels between the idealized society of the sagas of Icelanders and the historical reality of *Sturlunga saga*, the differences must not be ignored. They manifest themselves in the latter above all through a more precise definition of the different social classes, particularly the ruling class (G. Nordal 1998).

It is evident from *Sturlunga saga* that Iceland was a rigorously class-divided society in the thirteenth century. The gap and the possible interaction between the illiterate and powerless majority on the one hand, and the group which controlled the growing textual culture and held positions of power in the thirteenth century (the ruling class and the clergy) on the other, is difficult to measure. However, *Sturlunga saga* is a product of aristocratic culture in Iceland and depicts events from the point of view of people occupying the seats of power. Our estimation of the presentation of historical fact in the compilation must inevitably be tempered by this hierarchical perspective. The scale and grandeur of the Icelandic ruling class may be smaller than that of its counterparts in Europe, but its class symbols refer to a recognizably similar cultural and social milieu.

The organization of the separate sagas within *Sturlunga* reveals a strongly aristocratic ideology which is directed towards bringing one man to the centre of the saga. This man is Gizurr Þorvaldsson (1209–68), who was to become the first Earl of Iceland in 1258. The editorial discrimination evident in *Sturlunga saga* anticipates his ascendancy to the Icelandic 'throne', even though some of the editor's primary sources clearly contradicted his endeavours, notably Sturla Þórðarson's *Íslendinga saga*, the largest saga in the compilation. Sturla's depiction of the crucial events in Gizurr Þorvaldsson's life is laced with serious criticism of his actions in achieving the earldom, yet it is Gizurr whom Þórðr Narfason presents as the hero.

Sturlunga saga is an intricate work, with a large number of characters and a complex web of narrative threads. By focussing on the editor's historical perspective and the hierarchical patterns which dictate his organization of the material in the compilation we can conveniently divide the work into five parts. The editor's sources are noted in brackets.

1 The myth of the settlement and the ideal of Christian morals in the running of society (*Geirmundar þáttr heljarskinns* and *Þorgils saga ok Hafliða*).
2 The genealogical material (*Ættartǫlur* and *Sturlu saga*).
3 The local disputes *c.* 1180–1217 (*Formáli, Guðmundar saga dýra, Prestssaga Guðmundar Arasonar, Hrafns saga Sveinbjarnarsonar, Íslendinga saga*).
4 The heroes in the battle for the favours of the Norwegian king.
    a 1217–38: Sturla Sighvatsson and Gizurr Þorvaldsson (*Haukdæla þáttr* and *Íslendinga saga*).
    b 1238–58: Gizurr Þorvaldsson, Þórðr kakali Sighvatsson and Þorgils skarði Bǫðvarsson (*Íslendinga saga, Þórðar saga kakala, Þorgils saga skarða* and *Svínfellinga saga*).
5 The Icelandic poet at the Norwegian court (*Sturlu þáttr*).

These five parts correspond roughly with the structure of a typical saga of Icelanders written in the thirteenth century and dealing with persons and events of the settlement age and the period immediately afterwards. *Sturlunga saga* opens with the myth of the settlement and a cautionary tale which foreshadows the matter at hand (Part 1). The introduction of the genealogy of the main antagonists follows (Part 2). The development of the plot is marked by a description of petty disputes and local quarrels reminiscent of the sagas of Icelanders, which underpin power patterns in the country and throw into relief the dominant figures who will be the main contestants for control over Iceland (Part 3). The actual confrontation between the Icelandic chieftains in *Sturlunga saga* is over the favours of the Norwegian king (Part 4). The final section brings one of the losers to the Norwegian court, where he wins the ultimate victory by controlling the products of textual culture and the presentation of historical material (Part 5).

THE MYTH OF THE SETTLEMENT OF ICELAND

The myth of the settlement of Iceland *c.* 870–930 pervades Icelandic story-telling. The majority of the sagas of Icelanders begin in Norway, and depict the migration from the old country which led to a new beginning in the promised land in the north. One of the basic features of this popular myth is to make a genealogical connection between those who settled Iceland and the Norwegian aristocracy, thereby emphasizing that they belonged to the same cultural milieu. The importance of this settlement myth in Icelandic historiography, both in a chronological and a mythological sense, is brought home by its direct relevance to the political history of Iceland in the twelfth and thirteenth centuries, some three hundred years after the settlement of the country. The beginning of *Sturlunga saga* in the settlement period places the saga firmly within the framework of Icelandic historiography as we know it in Ari Þorgilsson's *Íslendingabók* ('The Book of Icelanders'), the many versions of *Landnámabók* ('The Book of the Settlement') and the sagas of Icelanders.

Sturlunga saga opens in the ninth century at the court of King Hjǫrr, the son of Hálfr Hálfsrekki (see *Hálfs saga*), in an undisclosed land east of Norway. *Geirmundar þáttr* is a classical revelation tale of the importance of kinship and rank. Hjǫrr's wife gives birth to two ugly and dark-skinned sons while her husband is away. The queen does not like the look of her two boys, Geirmundr and Hámundr, and swaps them with a beautiful boy born to a slave-woman at the court. However, the true kinship of the boys cannot be hidden: *bregzt því meir hverr til síns ætternis* ('each shows more clearly the true nature of his kinship'). The queen does not dare to tell the truth, until the arrival of the poet Bragi Boddason at the court, whose perceptive and intuitive gifts unveil the queen's deceptive plan and release her from the lie.

The story of Geirmundr is also found in Sturla Þórðarson's and Haukr Erlendsson's versions of *Landnámabók*, where it is stated that he was believed by wise men (*vitrir menn*) to have been the most distinguished of the settlers (Benediktsson 1968 1: 115–16).[2] This estimation of Geirmundr was widely accepted in the thirteenth century and certainly known to Þórðr Narfason, who was a close friend of Sturla Þórðarson. The beginning of *Sturlunga saga* thus endorses Geirmundr's singularity among the settlers, but for a reason. *Íslendingabók* was written for the bishops at Skálholt and lists only four settlers who could claim one of the bishops among their descendants: Ketilbjǫrn gamli, Auðr djúpúðga, Hrollaugr and Helgi magri. *Sturlunga saga* is, by contrast, a political saga, written for the Icelandic chieftains and their prototype is the noble and courageous son of a viking king whose ancestry is recounted in one of the *fornaldarsögur*. Geirmundr is the only settler who is unquestionably the son of a king. Some of the settlers are married to princesses, usually of Irish descent (H11; S83; S84, H72; S208, H175), others trace their kinship to kings (S96, H83; S205, H172; S184, H151; S305, H26; S366, H321) or are possibly princes (S140, H112) but their royal lineage is not documented as widely in Icelandic saga literature as that of Geirmundr. Geirmundr is exceptional and his story serves to lay the groundwork for the aristocratic perspective dominant in the compilation.

The emphasis on Christian temperance and moderation is touched on in *Geirmundar þáttr*. The pagan Geirmundr is sensitive to the coming of Christianity, and belongs to the group of noble chieftains in the sagas of Icelanders, such as Ingimundr the old in *Vatnsdæla saga* and Gestr Oddleifsson in *Laxdæla saga*, who recognize the force of the new religion before the official conversion in Iceland (Lönnroth 1969). Geirmundr has an intuition about the supernatural quality of the grassy slope where a church will be built after the conversion and the next section in *Sturlunga saga* takes up this religious thread. The saga of Þorgils Oddason and Hafliði Másson, two chieftains from the beginning of the twelfth century, is a Christian parable proclaiming that Christian morality, moderation and wisdom will be the yardstick by which social behaviour will come to be measured (Brown 1952: l–lii). There is no question about the Christian perspective of the writers of *Sturlunga saga*, and towards the end of the saga the compiler inserts yet another parable, the saga of the Svínfellingar family, which reiterates the importance of peaceful settlements and the mediation of the clergy in political disputes.

THE IMPORTANCE OF KIN

One of the messages of *Geirmundar þáttr* is the importance of kin. True kinship cannot be hidden from the watchful eyes of the wise men in society, such as Bragi Boddason, who here plays the role of the archetypical poet in Icelandic saga society, a role also associated with wisdom and authority (Clunies Ross 1993b). The compiler gives great importance to kinship throughout the compilation and uses symbols of kinship to drive this message home.

Geirmundr heljarskinn ('dark skin') notices the light which shines above the rowan tree that grows on a *hvammr* ('grassy slope') on his land:

> sá er einn staðr í hvamminum, at ávallt, er ek lít þangat, þá skrámir þat ljós fyrir augu mér, at mér verðr ekki at skapi. Ok þat ljós er ávallt yfir reynilundi þeim, er þar er vaxinn einn samt undir brekkunni. (*Sturlunga saga* I 9 [6/6])[3]

> (there is one place on the grassy slope such that,whenever I look upon it, a light gleams into my eyes, which is not to my liking. And this light is always just above the rowan tree, which grows there by itself under the lip of the slope.)

Geirmundr forbids all usage of the *hvammr*. The chapter concludes on the note that the church at Skarð was built on the spot where the rowan tree had grown. This may be inferred to be holy ground. This depiction of the rowan tree as sacred has been associated with the pagan god Þórr, since the rowan tree was associated with him in a myth recounted by Snorri Sturluson in his *Edda* (*Skáldskaparmál* chapter 27, Jónsson 1931: 105–10) and presumably widely known in Iceland. The Christian symbolism of this passage, however, cannot be ignored. The tree and the radiant light clearly denote the advent of Christianity. The tree is furthermore a powerful symbol of kinship and genealogy in medieval historiography (Bloch 1983: 87–91) and its appearance at the very beginning of the compilation suggests the importance of lineage in *Sturlunga saga*. Geirmundr is intimidated and awed by the tree. He is sensitive to its power even though he is not able to grasp its spiritual significance.

We are reminded of this episode in a narrative assigned to the year 1238. The reminder occurs in the imagery of Sturla Sighvatsson's dream before his final battle at Örlygsstaðir where he, his father and three of his brothers will be killed. Sturla tells his cousin, Sturla Þórðarson and the author of the saga at this point, the details:

> 'Mik dreymði þat,' sagði Sturla, 'at ek var í Hvammi á föðurleifð minni, ok þar várum vér allir fyrir handan ána upp frá Akri. Kross stóð hjá oss á holtsmúlanum, hár ok mikill. Þá þótti mér hlaupa skriða mikil ór fjallinu, ok var smágrjót í ok allt nema einn steinn. Hann var svá mikill sem hamarr hlypi at oss, ok þótti mér undir verða margt várra manna, ok margt komst undan. En Vigfúss Ívarsson varð undir, svá at ek kennda, en þá vaknaða ek,' sagði hann. (*Sturlunga saga* I 422 [134/284] 1238)

> ('I dreamt . . . that I was at Hvammr at my father's home, and that we were all on the other side of the river above Akr. A cross, high and grand, stood near us on a crag. Then it seemed to me that a great avalanche was running down the mountain and it was all small gravel, except for one stone. This was as huge as an anvil-crag, and crashing against us, and it seemed to me that many of our men were buried underneath it, though many escaped. But I noticed that Vigfúss Ívarsson was hit, but then I woke up,' he said.)

The dream upsets Sturla and he pushes the compelling thought away by saying: *[o]ft verða sveipr í svefni* ('often incredible things happen in sleep') (*Sturlunga saga* I 422 ([134/284] 1238). Glendinning suggests in his study of dreams in *Íslendinga saga*, that Sturla's dream can be seen as God's judgement on his arrogant actions, and that Sturla understands the meaning of it (Glendinning 1974: 212). He will be killed by the avalanche. This is not, however, the only message of this dream. The setting of the dream carries a more poignant significance. Sturla finds himself at Hvammr, his paternal estate, the symbol of the Sturlungs' authority and the avalanche occurs precisely at their power base. The crushing of their family power is sanctioned by the Church, betokened in the dream by the large cross. This combined symbolism of kinship and Christianity is sustained in a dream experienced by Sturla's opponent in the fight at Örlygsstaðir. On the morning of the fight, Gizurr Þorvaldsson tells of a dream he had during the night. It seemed to him that his deceased uncle, Bishop Magnús Gizurarson of Skálholt, appeared before him and said: *Standið þér upp frændi . . . ok skal fara með yðr* ('Kinsman, stand up and I shall go with you'). This dream fills

Gizurr with confidence: *[b]etra þykkir mér dreymt en ódreymt* ('I find it better to have dreamt this than not') (*Sturlunga saga* I 429 [137/287] 1238). Gizurr is blessed in his political endeavours, whereas Sturla Sighvatsson is doomed. The two dreams demonstrate the underlying patterns of kinship against which political events in *Sturlunga saga* must be interpreted and reveal the Christian perspective of the whole work.

The main narrative of *Sturlunga saga* clearly begins at the end of *Þorgils saga ok Hafliða* by enumerating, and thus distinguishing, the genealogies of seven of the most powerful families that will dominate the political scene in the twelfth and thirteenth centuries: the Odda-verjar, Sturlungar, Ásbirningar, Svínfellingar, Seldælir, Vatnsfirðingar and Hítdælir. The Haukdælir, the family of Gizurr Þorvaldsson, victor in the rivalry between the chieftains in the thirteenth century, is the one significant omission from this list. In spite of the apparent importance of the seven families, the compiler, by delaying the presentation of the Haukdælir, places a greater emphasis on them at the very beginning of *Sturlunga saga*. His reasons will become evident as the saga draws to a close. A whole *þáttr* (*Haukdæla þáttr*), inserted into *Íslendinga saga* just before Gizurr Þorvaldsson's birth, is devoted to their genealogy, settle-ment myth, family history and an account of the workings of fate (*forlǫg*) which bring about the marriage of Gizurr's parents, Þorvaldr Gizurarson and Þóra Guðmundardóttir.

The genealogies of the powerful families are not traced back to the settlement period, as in Gizurr's case in *Haukdæla þáttr*, but to impor-tant ancestors in Iceland. The connections of the first and the last family listed in the section, the Oddaverjar and Hítdælir, suggest a royal lineage for the Icelandic aristocracy. The first family is the Oddaverjar and their genealogy commences with Sæmundr Sigfússon the learned and his son Loftr Sæmundarson, who married Þóra, the daughter of King Magnús berfœttr. This royal connection was important for their family ideology, as we will note below. The forefather of Ketill Þorláksson, the thir-teenth-century chieftain of the Hítdælir family, reckoned through his mother, was held to be the East Anglian king St Eadmund (*Sturlunga saga* I 56 [7/43]), whose death in 870 (or 869) was used by Ari Þorgilsson in *Íslendingabók* to mark the settlement of Iceland (Lindow 1997: 456). The notice taken of this royal connection is an indication of the implicit links between different works of Icelandic history.

The chapter on the genealogies is followed by the saga of Sturla Þórðarson, the father of Þórðr, Sighvatr and Snorri Sturlusynir. Sturla was an upstart from the west of Iceland and a newcomer in the aristocratic milieu. *Sturlu saga* falls into two parts, the first describing Sturla's success in local disputes and the second showing how his arrogant behaviour earned him the opposition of the clergy and the main chieftains in the country. Þórðr Narfason does not suppress the negative aspect of Sturla's character and his life anticipates in part the failed actions of his younger kinsmen in gaining political power. The Sturlungs' more lasting success lay in their control of Icelandic textual culture. This was secured when the most powerful man in Iceland in the twelfth century, Jón Loftsson, from the eminent seat of learning at Oddi, agreed to foster Sturla Þórðarson's son Snorri Sturluson there in 1182.

THE QUEST FOR AN EARLDOM

Prestssaga Guðmundar góða, Guðmundar saga dýra, Hrafns saga Svein-bjarnarsonar, and parts of *Íslendinga saga* relate events which happen simultaneously (*samtíða*) in the late twelfth and the early thirteenth centuries. The compiler thus has the difficult task of amalgamating them in the saga. A short section, with the deceptive name *Formáli* ('Prologue'; see Meulengracht Sørensen 1993: 93) follows *Sturlu saga* in the compilation, in which the editor's techniques in dovetailing these sources into a unified whole are explained. In the second part of the Prologue the compiler refers to *Íslendinga saga* in particular and notes Sturla Þórðarson's authorship and his sources as follows:

> vísindi af fróðum mönnum, þeim er váru á öndverðum dögum hans, en sumt eftir bréfum þeim, er þeir rituðu, er þeim váru samtíða, er sögurnar eru frá. Marga hluti mátti hann sjálfr sjá ok heyra, þá er á hans dögum gerðust til stórtíðinda. Ok treystum vér honum bæði vel til vits ok einurðar at segja frá, því at hann vissa ek alvitrastan ok hófsamastan. Láti guð honum nú raun lofi betri. (*Sturlunga saga* I 115 [1/81])

> (knowledge from learned men, who lived in his youth, but some parts from letters written by those who were contemporary with those who are depicted in the sagas. He saw and heard many things, which were

the greatest events in his time. And we trust both his wisdom and steadfastness to tell this story because we knew him to be the wisest and most moderate of men. May God grant that reality serve him better than praise.)

This section shows that the writing of the saga is authenticated by those who controlled Icelandic textual culture, those who were learned and could read and write. The compiler does not mention the testimony of poets, even though skaldic poetry played a significant role in thirteenth-century society, as will become apparent at the end of the chapter.

It has been noted that Gizurr Þorvaldsson is the hero of *Sturlunga saga*. He is the only character in the saga to be introduced with a special *páttr*. *Haukdœla páttr* is a key episode in *Sturlunga saga*. It begins with the settlement of Ketilbjörn Ketilsson, of the family of the earls of Hlaðir. The family ancestry of the Haukdælir is intimately connected with the beginning of Christianity in Iceland (Heinrichs 1994). Sturla Sighvatsson is Gizurr's main adversary in *Íslendinga saga*, and it is their dealings that produce some of the finest moments in Sturla Þórðarson's *Íslendinga saga*. The entrance of Sturla Sighvatsson into the political arena happens precisely in the year 1217, when Hákon Hákonarson becomes king in Norway; the quest for the earldom coincides with Hákon's kingship.

Sturlunga saga is a political history in the sense that it documents the reasons for and consequences of political manoeuvrings in Iceland in the twelfth and thirteenth centuries. The traditional conflicts of the Icelanders were transformed by the return of Sturla Sighvatsson from Norway in 1236. His confident and ill-fated ambition to control the country was spurred on by the Norwegian king, who manipulated such ambitions to bring Iceland under the rule of the Crown. From that date most powerful Icelandic chieftains became royal retainers and Gizurr Þorvaldsson was the victor in their contest for power. The compiler does not criticize the chieftains' royal connections or regret their inevitable, and historically logical, subjection to the Norwegian king, but reproaches them instead for their moral failings, character short-comings and unscrupulousness in achieving this end.

Sturla and Gizurr are depicted as opposites and the main rivals for the earldom. The descriptions of their characters are complicated by analogies with two dominant figures of Norse mythology, Óðinn, to whom Gizurr is likened, and Freyr, who is seen to be analogous with Sturla. The likening of historical characters to pagan gods is a means of representing particular human attributes in thirteenth-century Christian writing. It is worth noting, too, that Freyr and Óðinn are depicted as members of different families in the mythological writings of Snorri Sturluson. It is Óðinn of the Æsir family who gains control over the Vanir, the family to which Freyr belongs; it is Gizurr, of the Haukdælir family, who achieves the Sturlungar's ambition and wields the royal sword Brynjubítr (Nordal 1998: 55–8).

It is a convention in the family sagas and the kings' sagas to shed light on the hero's character by depicting him as a young man in action, thereby supplying a more rounded, anticipatory view of the character he will have as an adult (*Egils saga* 80–3 [31], 98–103 [40]; *Grettis saga* 36–42 [14]). Likewise *Prestssaga Guðmundar góða* includes a scene in which a future bishop, Guðmundr Arason, and a future chieftain, Qgmundr sneis Þorvarðsson, play with a crook and sword that are symbols of their future roles in society (*Sturlunga saga* I 123 [4/85]).

This technique is also brought into use in the portrayal of Sturla. Sturla's 'initiation' into society throws into relief the differences between his character and fortune and those of Gizurr Þorvaldsson. Here also symbols with royal and Christian connotations suggest the significance of the action. Þorvarðr Qrnólfsson, a neighbour of Sturla Sighvatsson's father at Miklagarðr in Eyjafjǫrðr, has promised to lend his valuable sword Brynjubítr to the eighteen-year-old Sturla. It is noted that Sigurðr grikkr had brought it from Miklagarðr (Constantinople) and then it had been passed on to Sveinn Jónsson, who died a martyr's death at Hólar in 1209. The sword is clearly associated with religious service, Sigurðr's journey to Constantinople, and Sveinn's support of Bishop Guðmundr.

Sturla becomes too impatient to wait for Þorvarðr to give him the sword and hurries to Miklagarðr to claim it:

> Þá var Sturla átján vetra gamall, er hann fór upp í Miklagarð, ok tveir eyfirzkir menn kómu í ferð hans. Þeir riðu at durum, ok gekk Sturla inn, en hinir sátu á baki úti. Sturla gekk til rúms bónda ok tók sverðit ok gekk í anddyri ok ætlaði at sjá ok bregða. Þá kom prestr ok þreif sverðit ok vildi eigi bregða láta. Kallaði hann þá á heimamenn. Kom þá at Þorvarðr bóndi ok bað hann eigi taka sverðit. Sturla bað hann ljá

sér. Þorvarðr kvað hann eigi svá með fara, at þess væri ván, ok kvað hann með engu móti skulu fá þat. Drifu þá at heimamenn, konur ok karlar ok vildu allir á sverðinu halda ok reitti þá þvöguna út at durunum. Var þá snarat af honum sverðit. (*Sturlunga saga* I 261 [32/ 182] 1217)

(Sturla was eighteen at the time he went to Miklagarðr, and two men from Eyjafjǫrðr accompanied him. They rode to the front door, and Sturla went in, but the others waited on horseback outside. Sturla went to the farmer's bed and took the sword and went into the entrance hall and intended to look at it and hold it. Then a priest arrived and grabbed the sword and would not have him unsheath it. Then he called out for the household. Þorvarðr the farmer arrived and asked him not to take the sword. Sturla asked him to lend it to him. Þorvarðr said that he did not know how to handle it in such a way that this would be likely, and said he should not have it by any method. Then members of the household, men and women, came to the scene and all wanted to hold the sword and the group moved towards the door. Then the sword was taken from him.)

In his anger Sturla almost kills Þorvarðr with his axe Sveðja. In spite of the apparent vehemence of Sturla's reaction, his attack on Þorvarðr is awkward and clumsy: *hann gáði eigi, hvárt fram horfði á ǫxinni, ok kom hamarrinn í hǫfuð Þorvarði* ('he did not consider which way the axe was turned, and the back part struck Þorvarðr in the head') (*Sturlunga saga* I 261 [32/182]1217). This is a comic blunder that heroes such as Grettir Ásmundarson or Egill Skalla-Grímsson would not have made, even in their early youth.

This scene illuminates the way the compiler expands on a minor incident to deepen the reader's perception of the action. Sturla's conduct at Miklagarðr shows his lack of political shrewdness, since just before his uncontrolled outburst it is mentioned that Sighvatr has had a mixed reception in the district of which he has just become a chieftain. Sturla displays total ignorance of the volatile political situation.

The episode at this particular farm may also have been chosen deliberately by the compiler to foreshadow Sturla's future. The farm's name, Miklagarðr, is the same as the Old Icelandic name for Constantinople, and thus connotes this great Christian city and pilgrim destination. Hence the scene hints at the uncontrollable ambition of Sturla Sighvatsson which was to break all moral codes of Christian conduct and ultimately ensure that he would not prove worthy as the King's *sverðtakari* ('sword-carrier'). But the significance of Sturla's hapless visit cuts deeper. The incident takes place in 1217, in the year King Hákon Hákonarson ascended the throne of Norway, and it marks the beginning of an unbroken sequence of *Íslendinga saga* in the *Sturlunga* compilation which lasts until 1242. The sword Brynjubítr in the context of *Íslendinga saga* symbolizes royal power that is blessed by divine will, as can be deduced from other stories about kings, such as King Arthur and Charlemagne. In *Hirðskrá*, commissioned by King Hákon's son Magnús Lawmender, it is stated that the king handed his earl a sword and the earl should *vid þui i kennazt at hann hælldr þan iarldom af konongdomenum oc er han sværðtakare* ('thereby recognize that he has received the earldom from the kingdom and that he is his sword-carrier') (Keyser and Munch 1848: 404). Sturla hopes to snatch the sword from its rightful owner, but he is caught in the act. He has not the patience and wisdom to wait till it is rightfully his. The sword's true owner, as the saga later reveals, is Gizurr Þorvaldsson, the truly appointed Earl of Iceland and Sturla's main rival in the saga.

The significance of the sword metaphor in *Íslendinga saga* cannot be appreciated until later in the saga, when Gizurr is attacked at Flugumýrr thirty-six years afterwards. When the attackers approach, Gizurr's wife Gró hands him *sverðið Brynjubít ok spretti friðböndum ok fekk Gizuri. Brá hann þá sverðinu* ('the sword Brynjubítr, unfastened the sheath ties and and gave it to Gizurr, who then drew the sword') (*Sturlunga saga* I 487 [172/411] 1253). The attackers never see Gizurr and he never parts with the sword. When he is cornered in an outbuilding, he first takes care of the sword, then of himself: *hleypti hann sverðinu Brynjubít ofan í skyrit, svá at þat søkk upp um hjǫltin* ('he ran his sword Brynjubítr down into the curds so that it covered the hilt') (*Sturlunga saga* I 492 [174/413] 1253). Gizurr survives the burning of Flugumýrr, but he loses his wife and sons. His only possession is the sword as he runs out of the ruins of his farm. The sword is mentioned for the last time in the saga when Gizurr avenges the brutal killing of his family. He kills seven arsonists in a furious attack, among them Kolbeinn grǫn Dufgussson. Brynjubítr is introduced when Gizurr lays his eyes on Kolbeinn: *Ok er Gizurr sá Kolbein, brá hann sverðinu Brynjubít ok þótti eigi svá skjótt unnit á Kolbeini sem hann vildi, ok spurði, hví þeir væri nú svá lathendir* ('And when Gizurr saw Kolbeinn, he drew the sword Brynjubítr and thought that Kolbeinn was not beaten as soon as he wanted, and asked why they were so slow to act'; *Sturlunga saga* I 499 [176/416] 1254). Kolbeinn is the only one of the seven victims named in Gizurr's verse after his successful revenge and he is the only Sturlung, which indicates that Kolbeinn was his most important target.

The Byzantine sword is a poignant symbol of royal power, which adds a distinct colour to the contrast drawn between Sturla Sighvatsson and Gizurr Þorvaldsson in the saga. Sturla desires the sword, but loses it on account of his own recklessness. Gizurr, however, carries it with confidence and the sword seals his victory over the Sturlungs. In the context of the saga, Brynjubítr is a symbol of royal approval in the aristocratic world of Icelandic chieftains in the thirteenth century and it is Gizurr who proves to be the true sword-carrier of King Hákon in Iceland, after he has overcome the bid by two Sturlungs, Sturla Sighvatsson's brother, Þórðr kakali Sighvatsson, and his cousin, Þorgils skarði Bǫðvarsson to become Earl of Iceland.

THE ROLE OF THE POET IN SOCIETY

Sturlunga saga ends with *Sturlu þáttr*, which relates Sturla Þórðarson's travels to Norway and his acceptance by the Norwegian king. The *þáttr* begins in 1263, when Gizurr Þorvaldsson, the Earl of Iceland, has had Sturla cheated out of power in the Sturlung's home territory so he is driven out of the country after disputes with his former ally Hrafn Oddsson. Before Sturla sets sail the text quotes the second half of a stanza in which Gizurr Þorvaldsson is likened to Óðinn. The Sturlungar family were out of favour with King Hákon Hákonarson, and therefore it is not inappropriate to compare Sturla's excursion to Norway to Egill Skallagrímsson's visit to Eiríkr Bloodaxe in York (Meulengracht Sørensen 1977: 118–19; 1993: 68–9). Like Egill with his friend Arinbjǫrn, Sturla also had a good friend at the court, Gautr af Meli, who proves an invaluable help.

We noted at the beginning of the chapter that *Geirmundar þáttr* belonged to the world of the *fornaldarsögur*, but in *Sturlu þáttr* the poet uses the telling of a *fornaldarsaga, Huldar saga*, to open his way to the court. The queen hears of Sturla's story-telling abilities and gets him to tell the story to the King and herself. Sturla's poetic skill and the queen's persistence ultimately secure him Magnús's friendship. Sturla is then given the task of writing the saga of King Hákon and of King Magnús himself, as well as of composing a number of poems about the king and other dignitaries.

Skaldic verse was worthy of royalty. The professional poets earned their living through their verse-making at the courts of Scandinavia and the British Isles, according to the kings' sagas and *Skáldatal*. Leaving aside the historical reliability and authenticity of this verse, the poets are clearly presented in thirteenth-century sources as reliable witnesses to royal history, recording the achievements of kings and earls in elaborate praise poems and eulogies. Snorri's *Prologue* to *Heimskringla* endorses this view. The court poet provided the earl or the king with elaborate poems and this profession was highly respected from the ninth to the beginning of the fourteenth century. Sturla Þórðarson is cast in the role of the court poet known from many of the *Íslendinga þættir* (Harris 1972). In the late twelfth century there was, however, a detectable expansion in the audience of the court poet. The new audience was in Iceland.

Before this time there is little evidence of praise poems and eulogies for Icelanders. Two poems are mentioned in *Eyrbyggja saga*, *Illugadrápa* by Oddr skáld (Sveinsson 1935: 31 [17]) and Þormóðr Trefilsson's *Hrafnsmál*, where the cleverness and cunning of Snorri goði Þorgrímsson is praised (Sveinsson 1935: 124 [44], 156 [56], 168 [62]). A memorial poem by Arnórr jarlaskáld in honour of Gellir Þorkelsson is noted at the end of *Laxdœla saga* (Sveinsson 1934: 229 [78]). Two poems are composed in honour of dead friends or relatives: Egill Skalla-Grímsson (the manuscript provenance is complicated) composed *Sonatorrek* after the death of the poet's sons, Bǫðvarr and Gunnarr (Nordal 1933: 24–256 [78]), and Þormóðr Kolbrúnarskáld his *Þorgeirs-drápa* in memory of his foster-brother Þorgeirr Hávarsson (Þórólfsson and Jónsson 1943: 152 [7], 156 [8], 181 [12], 209 [17]). Egill and Þormóðr are not composing in the service of these men. The poems are personal in their expression of praise and lament after the death of a loved one.

In the late twelfth century Icelandic chieftains assumed the role previously occupied by foreign dignitaries in having verse composed for them. Why did the poets regard the Icelandic chieftains as worthy receivers of their art? It is difficult to chronicle all the shifts of emphasis in ideology and cultural life but it seems that the emergence of this new audience coincided with the leaning of the Icelandic ruling families towards aristocratic codes of behaviour. But is there a connection between the two?

Icelandic chieftains began to identify themselves with European aristocrats in the twelfth century, and particularly in the thirteenth century, through the writing of royal *historiae*, genealogies, the myth of the settlement and skaldic poetry. The Oddaverjar linked their lineage directly to Norwegian dynasties. The poem *Nóregs konunga tal*, composed for Jón Loftsson *c.* 1180 and preserved in conjunction with *Snorra Edda*, links the family at Oddi with Magnús berfœttr, the grandfather of Jón. If scholars are right in associating works such as *Skjǫldunga saga* and *Vǫlsunga saga* with Oddi, it would be a further indication of that family's interest in their heroic and royal past (Guðnason 1969). Gizurr Þorvaldsson, the first Earl of Iceland, had the privilege of calling King Hákon Hákonarson his *frændi* ('kinsman'), on account of his kinship with the Oddaverjar (*Sturlunga saga* 493). This association by blood with King Hákon is emphasized in *Sturlunga saga*, probably due to endeavours on the part of the writer to substantiate the legitimacy of Gizurr's earldom. His family was 'royal' in an Icelandic context, as is also attested by *Hungrvaka* (Jakobsson 1994). The genealogy of the Sturlungs, probably not written till the thirteenth century and preserved in conjunction with *Skáldatal* in the Codex Upsaliensis, is an explicit gesture of a preoccupation of the Sturlungar with the noble origin of their family. Genealogies carry with them knowledge and a recognition of the past and this substrate may even have been 'fundamental to the development of epic narrative in Iceland' (Clunies Ross 1993a: 377; Meulengracht Sørensen 1993: 109).

The Oddaverjar, Haukdælir and Sturlungar were the three families most overtly engrossed in their relationship with the Norwegian royal house in the thirteenth century. The Haukdælir and Sturlungar were in direct competition for the earldom in Iceland. The fourth family of note was the Seldælir, the descendants of Hrafn Sveinbjarnarson. Hrafn Sveinbjarnarson was not considered to be of royal descent but his saga depicts him as an overtly religious man, almost a saint-like figure, commanding the divine gift of healing presented to his great-grandfather through the intermediary of King Óláfr Haraldsson, or St Óláfr. Hrafn Oddsson, Sturla Sighvatsson's son-in-law, became the most powerful man in Iceland after the death of Gizurr Þorvaldsson. The fifth family is the Hítdælir, the family of the compiler Þórðr Narfason, who traced their ancestry to St Eadmund. The preservation of skaldic verse in thirteenth-century sources serves to contribute to the image of the new aristocracy in Iceland, for they even keep their own court poets in the same way as their counterparts in Scandinavia (Nordal forthcoming). Skaldic verse and its association with myth became one of the important tools in the endeavours of the ruling families to create an aristocratic image for themselves.

The contrast between the authenticating signs associated with the verse of the élite and the anonymity of the poetry associated with the general public throws into relief the cultural divide between these groups in thirteenth-century Iceland. The authors of the sagas in *Sturlunga saga*, in particular, make extensive use of anonymous verse to cloak their commentary on the unfolding action. The dream stanzas are of particular importance. Unknown people, usually of the lower classes or of little means, are visited in a dream by persons who recite a stanza, either in skaldic or eddic metre (Nordal 1990; Kristjánsdóttir 1990). The effect of this technique is that the illiterate general public is entangled in the web of battles and conflicts woven by the ruling families while it is temporarily given a voice which is not its own. Moreover, this technique provides the compiler with a neutral platform from which to voice his comments.

The citation of skaldic verse in thirteenth-century sources is a highly political act; it contributes to the presentation of historical material. The choice of verse in the kings' sagas, such as in *Hákonar saga Hákonarsonar*, does not represent the skaldic activity around Hákon along the lines suggested by *Skáldatal*. Sturla Þórðarson chooses instead to cite mostly his own verse and that of his brother Óláfr Þórðarson. Skaldic verse-making becomes in Sturla's hands a conscious semantic layer in the writing of historical works: the poet and the writer are the same man. *Sturlu þáttr* in *Sturlunga saga* symbolizes the Sturlungs' ultimate manipulation of the medium of skaldic poetry and historical writing in the thirteenth century. In this sense, they were the lasting victors in the political disputes of thirteenth-century Iceland.

NOTES

1 In this chapter it will be assumed throughout that Þórðr Narfason was the compiler of *Sturlunga saga*, in accordance with the argument presented in Nordal 1992.

2 Sturla's version is referred to by S followed by the chapter number, and Haukr's by H and the chapter number. All citations are from Benediktsson's 1968 edition. The story of Geirmundr is in S115, H87.

3 The citations from *Sturlunga saga* are from the 1946 edition of *Sturlunga saga* by Jóhannesson Eldjárn and Finnbogason, the chapter number is noted in brackets and the second number is a reference to the most recent edition of the saga by Kristjánsdóttir *et al.* 1988. The year of the event is noted if known. All English translations are my own.

REFERENCES

Benediktsson, Jakob (ed.) 1968, *Landnámabók*. Íslenzk fornrit, I 1 and 2. Reykjavík: Hið íslenzka fornritafélag.

Bloch, R. Howard 1983, *Etymologies and Genealogies: a Literary Anthropology of the French Middle Ages*. Chicago: University of Chicago Press.

Bragason, Úlfar 1988, 'The Structure and Meaning of *Hrafns Saga Sveinbjarnarsonar*', *SS* 60: 267–92.

   1990, 'Um hvað fjallaði *Huldar saga*', *Tímarit Máls og menningar* 51: 76–81.

Brown, Ursula (ed.) 1952, *Þorgils saga ok Hafliða*. Oxford: Oxford University Press.

Clunies Ross, Margaret 1993a, 'The Development of Old Norse Textual Worlds: Genealogical Structure as a Principle of Literary Organisation in Early Iceland', *Journal of English and Germanic Philology* 92: 372–85.

   1993b, 'Bragi Boddason', in Pulsiano, Phillip and Wolf, Kirsten (eds.), *Medieval Scandinavia: an Encyclopedia*. New York and London: Garland, pp. 55–6.

Foote, Peter 1950–51. 'Sturlusaga and its Background', *Saga-Book of the Viking Society* 13: 207–37.

   1974, 'Secular Attitudes in Early Iceland', *Mediaeval Scandinavia* 7: 31–44.

Glendinning, Robert J. 1974, *Träume und Vorbedeutung in der Islendinga saga Sturla Thordarsons. Eine Form- und Stiluntersuchung*. Kanadische Studien zur deutschen Sprache und Literatur, 8. Berne and Frankfurt.

Guðnason, Bjarni 1969, 'Gerðir og ritþróun *Ragnars sögu loðbrókar*', in Guðnason, Bjarni, Halldórsson Halldór and Kristjánsson, Jónas (eds.) *Einarsbók: Afmæliskveðja til Einars Ól. Sveinssonar 12. desember 1969*. Reykjavík: Nokkrir vinir, pp. 28–37.

Harris, Joseph C. 1972, 'Genre and Narrative Structure in Some *Íslendinga þættir*', *Scandinavian Studies* 44: 1–27.

Heinrichs, Anne 1994, 'Die jüngere und die ältere Þóra: Form und Bedeutung einer Episode in *Haukdæla þáttr*', *alvíssmál* 5: 3–28.

Jakobsson, Ármann 1994, 'Nokkur orð um hugmyndir Íslendinga um konungsvald fyrir 1264', in *Samtíðarsögur. The Contemporary Sagas. Preprints* I. Níunda alþjóðlega fornsagnaþingið. Akureyri 31.7. – 6.8. 1994, pp. 31–42.

Jóhannesson, Jón, Eldjárn, Kristján and Finnbogason, Magnús (eds.) 1946, *Sturlunga saga*. 2 vols. Reykjavík: Sturlunguútgafan.

Jónsson, Finnur (ed.) 1931, *Edda Snorra Sturlusonar udgivet efter håndskrifterne*. Copenhagen: Gyldendalske Boghandel.

Jónsson, Guðni (ed.) 1936, *Grettis saga Ásmundarsonar*. Íslenzk fornrit, 7. Reykjavík: Hið íslenzka fornritafélag.

Keyser, R. and Munch, P. A. (eds.) 1848, *Hirðskrá*, in *Norges gamle love indtil 1387* II. Christiania (Oslo): Grøndahl.

Kristjánsdóttir, Bergljót S. 1990, ' "Hvorki er eg fjölkunnig né vísindakona . . ." Um konur og kveðskap í Sturlungu', *Skáldskaparmál* 1: 241–54.

Kristjánsdóttir, Bergljót S. *et al.* (eds.) 1988, *Sturlunga saga. Árna saga biskups. Hrafns saga hin sérstaka*. Reykjavík: Svart á hvítu.

Kålund, Kr. (ed.) 1906–11, *Sturlunga saga efter membranen Króksfjarðarbók udfyldt efter Reykjarfjarðarbók*. 2 vols. Copenhagen: Gyldendal.

Lindow, John 1997, '*Íslendingabók* and Myth', *Scandinavian Studies* 69: 454–64.

Lönnroth, Lars 1969, 'The Noble Heathen: a Theme in the Sagas', *Scandinavian Studies* 41: 1–29.

Meulengracht Sørensen, Preben 1977, *Saga og samfund: En indføring i oldislandsk litteratur*. Copenhagen: Berlingske forlag.

    1993, *Fortælling og ære. Studier i islændingesagaerne*. Aarhus: Aarhus University Press.

Miller, William Ian 1990, *Bloodtaking and Peacemaking: Feud, Law and Society in Saga Iceland*. Chicago and London: University of Chicago Press.

Nordal, Guðrún 1990, ' "Nú er hin skarpa skálmöld komin" ', *Skáldskaparmál* 1: 211–25.

    1992, 'Sagnarit um innlend efni: Sturlunga saga', in Nordal, Guðrún, Tómasson, Sverrir and Ólason, Vésteinn (eds.), *Íslensk bókmenntasaga* I. Reykjavík: Mál og Menning, pp. 309–44.

    1998. *Ethics and Action in Thirteenth-Century Iceland*. The Viking Collection, II. Odense: Odense University Press.

    forthcoming, *Tools of Literacy: the Role of Skaldic Verse in Icelandic Textual Culture of the Twelfth and Thirteenth Centuries*.

Nordal, Sigurður (ed.) 1933, *Egils saga Skalla-Grímssonar*. Íslenzk fornrit, 2. Reykjavík: Hið íslenzka fornritafélag.

Seelow, Hubert (ed.) 1981, *Hálfs saga ok Hálfsrekka*. Rit, 20. Reykjavík: Stofnun Árna Magnússonar á Íslandi.

1994, 'Der Geirmundar þáttr heljarskinns in der Sturlunga saga.' *Samtíðarsögur. The Contemporary Sagas. Preprints* II. Níunda alþjóðlega fornsagnaþingið. Akureyri 31.7. – 6.8. 1994, pp. 698–711.

Sveinsson, Einar Ól. (ed.) 1934, *Laxdæla saga*. Íslenzk fornrit, 5. Reykjavík: Hið íselnzka fornritafélag.

(ed.) 1935, *Eyrbyggja saga*. Íslenzk fornrit, 4. Reykjavík: Hið íslenzka fornritafélag.

Tranter, Stephen Norman 1987, *Sturlunga Saga: the Role of the Creative Compiler*. European University Studies Series 1, German Language and Literature, 941. Frankfurt: Peter Lang.

Þórólfsson, Björn K. and Jónsson, Guðni (eds.) 1943, *Fóstbræðra saga*. Íslenzk fornrit, 6. Reykjavík: Hið íslenzka fornritafélag.

Ward, Benedicta 1982, *Miracles and the Medieval Mind: Theory, Record and Event 1000–1215*. Philadelphia and London: University of Pennsylvania Press and Scolar Press.

Weber, Gerd Wolfgang 1987, 'Intellegere historiam: Typological Perspectives of Nordic Prehistory (in Snorri, Saxo, Widukind and others)', in Hastrup, Kirsten and Meulengracht Sørensen, Preben (eds.), *Tradition og historieskrivning. Kilderne til Nordens ældste historie*. Acta Jutlandica 63:2. Humanistisk Serie, 61. Aarhus: Aarhus University Press, pp. 95–141.

10

The *Matter of the North*: fiction and uncertain identities in thirteenth-century Iceland

TORFI H. TULINIUS

How and why did sophisticated prose fiction appear in medieval Iceland? It is tempting to seek the answer to this question by comparing it with the nearly contemporary development of fiction in the vernacular elsewhere in the West during the High Middle Ages. In this chapter, I will look at the development of literature in Iceland as a result of an historical and cultural evolution similar to that of the rest of Europe. This shows how the literature of Iceland was an intrinsic part of Western medieval literature and also provides improved insights into why it developed in its own way. It is important to consider the saga corpus as a whole, especially the role of a group of sagas hitherto only accorded a marginal role in the appearance of literary fiction in Iceland, the *fornaldarsögur Norðurlanda*.

This will show us how the various types of sagas expressed various aspects of contemporary culture in different ways. It will in particular enable us to understand better the special nature of the most celebrated saga genre, the family sagas. As I will show, these seem to deal more than others with uncertain identities, a feature which is of particular importance in understanding the relationship between literary development and social change in medieval Iceland.

FORNALDARSÖGUR

Carl Christian Rafn coined the term *fornaldarsögur Norðurlanda* in 1829 as a title for his three-volume edition of sagas, *þættir* and fragments telling of Nordic heroes of old. By doing so, he was bringing together a wide variety of narrative texts of diverse origin, structure, theme and tone, into what has since been considered a special saga genre. In fact there are quite a few arguments against this grouping: some of the narratives are pseudo-historical while others are purely fictional, some are genealogical in their structure while others focus on individuals, some are based on ancient heroic poetry while others seem more inspired by myth, folklore or even continental romance. This disparity is reflected in the English terminology, since they have alternately been called legendary sagas and mythical–heroic sagas.

Despite the differences, scholars have continued to use this blanket term *fornaldarsögur Norðurlanda*, probably because there is a rationale both for the term and the grouping together of these texts. *Fornaldarsögur* means tales of the distant past, i.e. before the settlement of Iceland at the end of the ninth century. *Norðurlönd* points to the Nordic countries. The *fornaldarsögur* tell of heroes who are said to have lived in a distant legendary past and are more or less connected with the Nordic countries.

The criteria which have been used to establish the grouping are therefore spatial and temporal, not literary. However, similar criteria were also used in the Middle Ages by the *trouvère* Jean Bodel, who, in his *Chanson des Saisnes* from around 1200, classified vernacular romances into three groups. These reflected the geographical settings of the stories and the provenance of the material they were based on: the *matières* of France, Rome and Britain. Inspired by this, Henry Goddard Leach (1921: 162) drew an interesting parallel between the *fornaldarsögur* and the translated continental romance. Studying the introduction of this literary form into Old Norse, he proposed that *fornaldarsögur* were the Norse response to romance and that they constituted what could be called the 'Matter of the North'.

Leach seems only to have had in mind the kind of *fornaldarsögur* to which the term 'adventure tales' has been applied by Hermann Pálsson, who divides *fornaldarsögur* into two categories, 'heroic legend' and 'adventure tales'. The former are based on the same ancient heroic tradition in the tragic mode as the lays of the Edda and have links with similar traditions in other Germanic languages. They are believed to have appeared earlier than the 'adventure tales' which are stories that usually end well about heroes undertaking a quest or series of quests. The former open a 'window on a remote pagan past', the latter invite the audience 'to escape from the harsh realities of its everyday struggle by making imaginary journeys to the world of fantasy and romance' (Pálsson 1985: 138).

I consider that the scope of Leach's concept of a 'Matter of the North' can be extended to the whole group of texts, and not only the adventure tales. Indeed, the idea of a 'Matter of the North' can be taken still further and be understood to imply a comparison between the rise of fiction in the French-speaking world during the twelfth century and in the North one or two generations later. The conditions that are thought to have fostered this development in Western Europe were in many ways similar in Norway and Iceland.

With an improving climate and greater peace, Europe entered a period of economic growth in the late eleventh century, which continued at least to the end of the thirteenth (Duby and Mandrou 1968: 74–94). This resulted in an increase in the general population, which led in turn to a greater social complexity. Town-dwellers, mainly tradesmen and craftsmen, became visible. Society became increasingly layered, even within the aristocracy, among whom it was now possible to distinguish between a *nobilitas* of royal blood and a lower aristocracy of *milites* or fighting men, small landholders who owed service of arms to the higher aristocrats. This composite social class had a complex relationship with the clergy, whose members were usually recruited from the aristocracy, the latter undergoing the civilizing influence of the former. While the clergy civilized the aristocracy, the latter also had numerous and deep-seated conflicts with the Church, resisting its endeavours to regiment laymen's behaviour and disputing the respective prerogatives of lay aristocrats and the higher clergy.

This opposition resulted in the emergence of a distinct aristocratic culture which had access to writing but chose to express itself more often in the vernacular than in Latin, the language of the Church. This culture, an important element of which was literature, seems to have appeared first in the aristocratic courts of Southern France but was refined in the ducal and royal courts of Northern France, Flanders and England. From there, it spread all over Europe and became a sign of distinction adopted by aristocrats to indicate who they were: laymen and not clerics, of noble as opposed to undistinguished birth.

A complex social system in which the respective hierarchical positions of its actors was determined by their genealogical links to past royalty was bound to foster an intense interest in the past. Indeed, in a sort of cultural 'trickle-down effect', genealogical tables, which already existed for royalty, now started to appear for increasingly lower ranks of society (Duby 1961 and 1968). Genealogies played an important role in the rise of vernacular literature (Duby 1967). The Matter of Britain owes its migration from oral tradition to literature mainly to the efforts of Geoffrey of Monmouth to create a past for the kings of England by using legendary and mythical material of Celtic origin in his *Historia regum Britanniae*, whose Old French adaptation, *le Roman de Brut*, is one of the earliest examples of the romance genre.

What we know of the genesis of vernacular literature in twelfth- and thirteenth-century Iceland seems consistent with these historical developments. Of the four existing types of writings in Icelandic mentioned by the First Grammarian around the middle of the twelfth century, two can be related to them. The existence of genealogies (*áttvísi*) most likely royal, indicates that, despite their not having sworn allegiance to a king, Icelanders were already influenced by the developing ideology of the monarchy. The fact that these genealogies established links between royal dynasties and Icelandic families also indicates that leading Icelanders sought to enhance their position, at home and abroad, by highlighting these links (Clunies Ross 1993: 375–7). Ari Þorgilsson's *spaklig frœði*, that is, writings of a historical character such as his *Íslendingabók* and possibly an early version of *Landnámabók*, concurred in grounding the legitimacy of the leading Icelandic families in the past. The composition of kings' sagas from the late twelfth century onwards is witness to the growing fascination of Icelanders with kingship, a fascination not free from worry about the consequences of a strengthened monarchy for the freedom of action of the local aristocrat.

The 'Matter of the North' slowly coalesced in a cultural atmosphere in which ancient lore acquired new value through what might be called a socio-politically grounded antiquarianism. Icelanders earned the reputation of being specialists in this field. One of them, Arnaldus Tylensis, as Saxo calls him, is the latter's main source of information about the earliest kings of Denmark, giving the Danish royal dynasty a longer history and therefore increased legitimacy. Probably in the last decades of the twelfth century the Icelandic author of *Skjǫldunga saga* wrote a vernacular history of the same dynasty, also freely using myth and legend to enrich the distant past. In the 1220s, Snorri Sturluson uses a skaldic genealogical poem, *Ynglingatal*, to compose a prose pseudo-history of the Swedish Yngling dynasty, ancestors of the Norwegian kings: *Ynglinga saga*, the first part of his *Heimskringla*. Skaldic praise poetry also became an important source of information for the historians of Nordic kings, and therefore the knowledge of pagan myths necessary to understand it acquired value. Thus, Snorri composed his *Edda* around 1225 for those who wished to understand the ancient poetry, but also for those who wanted to compose poetry themselves, for skaldic verse had again become a tool of political advancement.

The ideological underpinnings of these literary developments must not make us forget that they also had considerable entertainment value: in addition to that of the reciting of poetry, which was a courtly pursuit, one could mention the telling of stories such as those *Þorgils saga og Hafliða* says guests were treated to at a wedding uniting offspring of prominent families in 1119 (*Sturlunga saga*: 22). Likewise, Sturla Þórðarson is said to have entertained the Norwegian court with a *Huldar saga* in 1263 (*Sturlunga saga*: 765–6). Both examples indicate that literature and its enjoyment was a sign of social distinction.

Skjǫldunga saga is now lost but there exists a seventeenth-century retelling of it as well as fragments of the original saga which have been incorporated into other texts. It is an example of the evolution described here. The saga-writer worked on the basis of *Langfeðgatal*, a genealogical poem in honour of the Oddaverjar, the most prominent aristocratic family in the late twelfth and early thirteenth centuries, who claimed descent from the Danish Skjǫldung dynasty. The writer also enriched his material with elements from heroic poetry and legends.

Though it is now lost, scholars have shown that *Skjǫldunga saga* was used by the authors of a great many preserved texts. Among them the most prominent was Snorri Sturluson. In both *Ynglinga saga* and his *Edda* he used fragments of the saga for the specific purposes, in one case for information on the Swedish dynasty, in the other to elucidate kennings. But the saga also served as an inspiration to writers composing in the late thirteenth and the fourteenth centuries. They amplified the stories told there, either by enriching them with material from heroic legend and myth or by embroidering them with material from continental romance. An example of this is the fragment *Sögubrot af fornkonungum* which was included in Rafn's 1829 edition. It is believed to be what is left of an expanded version of *Skjǫldunga saga* from the late thirteenth century (Guðnason 1963: 96–113). Another is *Hrólfs saga kraka* which may be from the fourteenth, and is a fanciful enlargement of the part of the saga which deals with this most famous of ancient Danish kings. Still another scion of the Skjǫldung dynasty, Ragnarr loðbrók, inspired more than one version of his saga in the thirteenth century, integrating different aspects of a rich tradition associated with him and his sons.

A FICTIONAL APPROACH

Genealogy seems to have been a major organizing principle in the 'Matter's' transition from oral to written forms of expression as well as from poetry to prose. Thus the heroic poems contained in the Codex Regius manuscript are arranged as much as possible in genealogical order. Around 1260, possibly earlier, a saga-writer adapted this poetry to prose and wrote a history of the legendary Vǫlsung dynasty (Finch 1993). How he worked helps understand how the antiquarian and historical attitude to the material is permeated by a developing fictional approach.

The writers of *fornaldarsögur* such as *Vǫlsunga saga*, *Hervarar saga ok Heiðreks* and *Hálfs saga og Hálfsrekka* not only subjected the material at their disposal to genealogical ordering, but also made an effort (whether conscious or unconscious) to give it meaning by adding new material to it and by arranging the existing material in order to suggest interpretation. We can see this in *Vǫlsunga saga*. Here the author seems more or less solely responsible for the first eight chapters. Not only does he adapt motifs from a variety of sources, among which there is a *lai* of Marie de France (Clover 1986), but he also crafted his work in such a way as to draw attention to his interpretation of the tradition conveyed by eddic poetry (Tulinius 1995: 125–41). This interpretation in turn influenced the way he retold the narrative contained in the poetry. An analysis of the saga shows that its major theme is betrayal. This is developed on the basis of a double set of oppositions, on the one hand betrayal of family ties versus betrayal of contractual obligations, on the other hand intentional versus unintentional breaking of these ties or obligations. The stories of Sigmundr and Signý respectively explore these oppositions, Sigmundr unintentionally causing harm to his son Sinfjǫtli twice, Signý betraying her marital obligations in revenge for the slaying of her blood family. These oppositions throw light on the characters of Guðrún, Brynhildr and Sigurðr in the next generation and allow the author to make sense of some of the contradictions in his poetic sources, especially concerning the behaviour of Sigurðr (Tulinius 1995: 129–33).

Thus it can be said that the author proceeded in very much the same way as Chrétien de Troyes says he did in the prologues to his twelfth-century romance: from a *matière* he extracted *sen* (a meaning) by giving it a *conjointure*, or a certain way of arranging its different aspects in order to give it beauty and meaning (Zumthor 1972: 362). This meaning was probably something which preoccupied early thirteenth-century Icelanders of the chieftain class living in the period of composition of *Vǫlsunga saga*. Indeed, they most certainly felt the conflicts between faithfulness to the family, in particular in matters of the collective honour of the lineage, and the obligation to respect contractual engagements, such as marriage agreements and sworn fidelity to equals or superiors. The authors of *Hervarar saga ok Heiðreks, Hálfs saga ok Hálfsrekka* and *Ragnars saga loðbrókar* organize their subject matter similarly, bringing together a wide variety of material of different age and provenance along a chronological and intergenerational structural backbone to reflect tensions in Norwegian and Icelandic society (Tulinius 1995: 67–101).

FORNALDARSÖGUR AND FAMILY SAGAS

It may be argued that the *fornaldarsögur* are born of a certain socio-historical configuration, and that they also reflect in many ways the tensions, preoccupations, and mental attitudes that accompany the changes going on in Icelandic and Norwegian society at the time of their appearance. Interestingly, when one looks at the earliest of the major family sagas from the same perspective, tantalizing parallels with the *fornaldarsögur* come to light.

Let us consider *Vǫlsunga saga* and *Ragnars saga*, which follow each other in their main manuscript (Ny. kgl. saml. 1824b, quarto). This is not mere chance because in this version of *Ragnars saga*, Áslaug, the mother of Ragnarr's younger sons, is said to be the daughter of Sigurðr and Brynhildr of *Vǫlsunga saga*. The ordering is therefore genealogical and the sagas in their major preserved versions may have been composed together. *Vǫlsunga saga* may have been originally written as a preamble to *Ragnars saga* since no other version of it survives or is known to have existed (Guðnason 1969: 30). It is therefore interesting to note striking similarities between the general structure of the two sagas taken together and that of the family saga *Laxdæla saga*. This similarity does not lie in the fact that both the family saga and the two *fornaldarsögur* are genealogically ordered, for this is a major character-istic of Icelandic prose literature of the Middle Ages, especially in its beginnings (Clunies Ross 1993: 377). It lies rather in the juxtaposition of almost the same two plots.

Long ago scholars recognized that *Laxdæla saga* owes a lot to the heroic lays about Sigurðr, Guðrún and Brynhildr (*Laxdæla saga*: xlv, n. 3). Guðrún is in the same situation as Brynhildr, having been tricked out of her expected marriage to Kjartan, a Sigurðr-like hero in his perfection, and having to settle for the second best, Bolli. However, she has not forgotten him and in the end she goads her husband, Kjartan's cousin and foster-brother, into attacking and killing him, just as Hǫgni and Gunnar kill their sworn-brother and brother-in-law Sigurðr.

There is another less obvious similarity between the two sagas. The Melkorka episode in *Laxdæla saga* and the Kráka episode in *Ragnars saga* both have in common the situation of the young woman who is a princess who has been taken into slavery. Because of her great beauty, she is desired by an aristocrat, with whom she has a son or sons but to whom she also later proves the nobility of her birth. The unique combination of illegitimacy and noble origin, which is the shared situation of Óláfr Hǫskuldsson in *Laxdæla saga* and the sons of Ragnarr and Kráka in the *fornaldarsaga*, is a major theme in the family saga. The saga as a whole can be seen as a drama about how the introduction of royal blood into a lineage via the fruit of an illegitimate union causes strife in later generations and ultimately a weakening of its place within Icelandic society. This thematic combination does not, however, exist in *Vǫlsunga saga* as an independent text but is produced by its connection to *Ragnars saga* in the former saga's only preserved manuscript.

A LITERARY SYSTEM

The result of such analyses is a fresh view of what was going on in Icelandic literature during the first decades of the thirteenth century, when the fictional treatment of the 'Matter of the North' seems to have experienced a first flowering. Instead of the *fornaldarsögur* appearing later, when the family sagas were already an established genre, it seems that at least the ones which Hermann Pálsson classifies as heroic legend appear more or less at the same time as the *Íslendingasögur*, along with other well-crafted historical fictions, such as *Færeyinga saga* and *Jómsvíkinga saga*. They may even have appeared somewhat earlier than the family sagas, thus paving the way for the creation of meaningful narratives out of more or less historical material concerning the first generations of Icelanders.

Be that as it may, putting the *fornaldarsögur* alongside the family sagas in the development of literary fiction in the thirteenth century can give a better general picture of the generic system of medieval Icelandic writing. We can thus better understand the specificity of each genre and see what individual works meant for their authors and first audience. Indeed, genres are an important element in the communication between authors and readers, since generic markers tell the reader into what kind of world he is being led and – in consequence – how he is to interpret the work (Todorov 1970: 12). The notion of 'world' is important in this context and has been elaborated upon by several literary theorists (Eco 1979; Pavel 1986). Each genre evolves in a different 'possible' (Eco) or 'fictional' (Pavel) world. As soon as the reader commences reading he more or less unconsciously interprets the generic signs which tell him what kind of world he is in and thus what to expect. For example if he is reading a *fornaldarsaga* he will expect to find supernaturally strong characters developing in a world of wonders, whereas if he is reading a historical account, as in *Sturlunga saga*, he will expect people like him acting in the same world as his own.

These are only two of the infinite number of possible worlds, but the notion is intimately related to that of genre and can throw light on how genres interact in a literary system, which can in many ways be compared to a language. In the same way as in the latter, the difference between its elements – phonemes or words – signifies: in a system of synchronic genres the differences between them can also engender meaning, when there is any kind of interaction between them. This interaction can be of different types: narrative structures originating in one of the genres can be adapted to the world of another, there can be a coexistence of different worlds within the same work and there can be intertextual allusions within one genre to the world of others. We have already seen an example of the first type in how the principal plot of *Laxdæla saga* seems to have been borrowed from heroic legend, making the characters and their destiny slightly 'larger than life'. Chapter 5 of the family saga *Bjarnar saga Hítdælakappa* gives us an example of the second, when during his travels abroad Bjǫrn encounters a dragon which he kills with one blow of his sword. This shows what a hero he is and puts his subsequent not so glorious life in Iceland into strange perspective. An example of the third can be found in the contemporary saga *Íslendinga saga*, when one of Snorri Sturluson's men compares him to Hrólfr kraki in a verse, implicitly drawing a comparison between the legendary king who was betrayed by his son-in-law and Snorri, whose men were complimenting him on how powerful his own sons-in law were (*Sturlunga saga*: 305).

An interesting feature of these three genres is that they are genealogically ordered and that many thirteenth-century Icelanders claimed descent from characters in the two other saga groups (Clunies Ross 1993: 382). Despite this fact, the world of the *fornaldarsögur* is not the same as the world of family sagas, which in turn is not the same as that of the contemporary sagas.[1]

The worlds of these three genres are however not the only ones in the literary system. There are several others, including the world of romance, which began to be known at the latest in the third decade of the thirteenth century via the translation of *Tristrams saga* in 1226. Here genealogical ordering does not apply. Instead, a kind of geographical organization can be perceived. Despite structural and thematic similarities between the romantic *fornaldarsögur* (the adventure tales, sometimes called *lygisögur*) and romances, there seems to have been an awareness that the worlds of these two genres were not quite the same, and that different things happened in the two worlds to different characters. *Samsons saga fagra* is a romantic saga from the fourteenth century which reveals this awareness in an interesting way, because the author plays on the difference between the *matière de Bretagne*, which provides the setting for the main story, and the Matter of the North, which provides very different themes and situations for a trip undertaken to the North by one of its main characters (Tulinius 1990: 147–8).

Still other textual worlds were part of the literary system, those of pagan mythology as well as of hagiography and Scripture, these last two being of considerable importance, since narrative structures were borrowed from saints' lives and allusions could be made to biblical stories or themes. Icelandic authors and readers would have been particularly prepared for intertextual play between different textual worlds, because part of their poetic heritage, skaldic poetry, was based on just such interplay, mainly between the world of the skald and that of Norse mythology, but also that of Christian thought and symbolism (Clunies Ross 1987: 93; Tulinius 1995: 204–9).

For several decades scholars have been accustomed to using Sigurður Nordal's chronological division of the corpus of prose narrative literature into *samtidssagaer*, *fortidssagaer* and *oldtidssagaer* (Nordal 1953: 181). Taking into account this interplay between the different genres, I believe the saga corpus could be described in a more dynamic way as a generic system organized according to five principles. As will be seen, the first two, genealogy and geography, are spatio-temporal and therefore quite concrete, whereas the three remaining principles are less tangible: religion, the supernatural and social status.

The genealogical principle results from the chieftain class's endeavour to ground its identity in the past. It is implicitly a chronological one like Nordal's, since genealogy is a way of structuring time, but it is through genealogy that the passing of time is perceived rather than through a more chronologically based time-reckoning such as ours. The geographical principle separates *fornaldarsögur* from romances, that is, the Matter of the North from the other *matières*, but also kings' sagas from family sagas, their respective geographical locations being Norway or Denmark for the former and Iceland for the latter. A combination of the genealogical and geographical underlies the usual classification of sagas into *samtíðarsögur*, *biskupasögur*, *konungasögur*, *Íslendingasögur*, *fornaldarsögur* and *riddarasögur*.

ONTOLOGICAL UNCERTAINTY

The third organizing principle is religious, embracing the world of pagan myth on the one hand, and Christian stories of conversion, saints and miracles on the other. *Fornaldarsögur* and myths happen in a heathen world, *vitae* of saints, bishops and missionary kings in a Christian one. Paganism is absent from the world of the contemporary sagas except through accounts of dreams and intertextual allusions in poetry. However, the world of the kings' sagas and the family sagas is interesting because it represents a transition from one of these worlds to the other, from paganism to Christianity.

The religious principle highlights the 'in-between-ness' of these two groups of sagas. They take place in a transitory period between paganism and Christianity and they are constantly, often discreetly though, being opposed in the texts. From a literary point of view, this is particularly interesting in the case of the family sagas. The fact that their textual world is a world in transition results in what could be called an ontological uncertainty about the characters they portray. Some remain pagan all their lives but can be what Lars Lönnroth (1969) has called 'noble heathens', people who have a natural understanding of Christianity without having been exposed to the Gospel. Some pagans are converted, but in a more or less ambiguous way. The case of Egill Skalla-Grímsson is very interesting from this point of view, because he is not quite a convert and not quite a heathen either, having been prime-signed and his earthly remains taken from a pagan burial mound and moved to hallowed ground after the Conversion (Tulinius 1997). Hallfreðr is a convert but has many relapses and is only redeemed by the mutual bond between him and King Óláfr Tryggvason (Kalinke 1997). While Njáll and Þorsteinn Egilsson can be seen as unambiguous converts to Christianity, a figure such as Guðrún Ósvífrsdóttir is interesting because she is portrayed as a convert who learns to feel deep contrition for her past sins.[2] Finally, the life of Grettir Ásmundsson, though only a child when Iceland was converted to Christianity, takes place in an ambiguous transitory period where, as is said in the saga itself, 'many vestiges of heathendom remained' (*Grettis saga*: 245).[3]

The nature of Grettir's world is therefore not quite that of the author of the saga, which brings us to the fourth organizing principle of the literary system: the representation of the supernatural. There is a distinct difference between the way the supernatural appears in *fornaldarsögur* on the one hand and contemporary sagas on the other. The latter are historical chronicles and it is rare to read about anything outside the realm of the natural. This does not mean that thirteenth-century Icelanders had the same attitude to the supernatural as we do (Bayerschmidt 1965: 39–53). Medieval Christianity certainly allowed for the intervention of the supernatural in human affairs, divine or diabolical, and there were also many surviving beliefs from pagan times which people probably did not know whether to classify under the former or latter category (Tulinius 1999). When the supernatural intervenes in the contemporary sagas, however, it is usually in the form of dreams or visions, and its direct impact on human affairs is very rare.

In the *fornaldarsögur*, on the other hand, direct contact with the supernatural is the rule. The same applies to the world of the adventure tales, whether they are *riddarasögur* and exploit the matters of the South or younger *fornaldarsögur* building on that of the North. Despite the differences between the two, the supernatural seems to be handled in the same way. In the world of religious texts, the supernatural also intervenes freely. Here, however a distinction must be made, because in these texts its presence is characterized as either divine or diabolical, while in the pagan world of the *fornaldarsögur*, these categories seem rarely to apply.

This distinction must however be qualified for the *vitae* of more recent saints, whose miracles were considered a proof of their holiness. Here, the supernatural is in general less spectacular and treated in a more circumspect way. This is probably due to the fact that the cult of the saints had economic and political outcomes. Everybody wanted his saint and the Church had to institute a system of verification in which accounts of the life and miracles of the proposed saints were investigated (Geary 1983). This fostered a debate in medieval society – not on whether miracles happened, which no one seems to have doubted, but on whether individual accounts were true or not.

This questioning may have been encouraged by political uses of 'proofs' of sanctity current in Norway and Iceland in the late twelfth and early thirteenth century (Foote 1974). It can be seen in a dialogue between Sighvatr Sturluson and Arnórr Tumason reported in *Íslendinga saga*. Arnórr tells his brother-in-law that he had been sick all winter until he was asked to take part in the battle in which they were engaged, at which moment his illness suddenly disappeared. In an implicit mockery of their opponents, Bishop Guðmundr's men, who were convinced of his ability to work miracles, Sighvatr asks whether he believes this to be a miracle. Arnórr answers: 'I call this an event and not a miracle' (*Sturlunga saga*: 261; Foote 1974: 43–4).[4] This same attitude can also be seen in the way King Sverrir (d. 1202), in one of his speeches, ridicules the archbishop's promise to King Magnús's men that those who would fall in the battle against Sverrir would immediately enter Paradise (*Sverris saga*: 42–3; Foote 1974: 38–41).

In their representation of the supernatural, the family sagas again seem to occupy an intermediate position in the generic system. The fact that the sagas take place in historical time and in places their authors knew seems often to have inhibited them from allowing such events in their stories, even though they are more frequent than in contemporary sagas and there are distinct differences in this matter between individual sagas. But there remains a reluctance to describe direct contact with the supernatural.

An example of this attitude is the account of Þórólfr bægifótr's haunting in *Eyrbyggja saga*. He is never shown actively pursuing his victims. We are only shown the effect of his activity and the fact that his remains have become hideous to look at (*Eyrbyggja saga*: 94–5). The literary result of this reluctance to describe direct contact is that the accounts become more compelling than in the *fornaldarsögur*. Blanks are left for the imagination to fill in, as in a modern horror film. This technique is mastered to perfection in the chapters on Glámr in *Grettis saga*, whose author was obviously inspired by the tale of Þórólfr bægifótr. He likewise delays describing direct contact with Glámr, progressively increasing the tension by showing what the ghost can do to men and animals, until Grettir is alone with him, making this one of the most genuinely hair-raising episodes in the family sagas (Tulinius 1999).

Eyrbyggja and *Grettla* contain more than an average amount of supernatural material. Elsewhere this element can be more discreet but still has to be accounted for. *Hrafnkels saga* may be one of the family sagas with the least interest in such things. However, one should consider carefully the mysterious disappearance of the flock of sheep and the subsequent tempting of young Einarr by the only horse he was not allowed to ride. Indeed, Freyfaxi holds unnaturally still while all the other horses, who are usually very tame, cannot be caught. There is a definite suggestion that there might be something out of the ordinary going on – possibly related to the pagan god to whom the horse is consecrated (*Hrafnkels saga*: 101–3).

In the same way as with the religious principle, the supernatural is used to show ontological uncertainty. This trait can be seen in the way Glámr is portrayed in *Grettis saga*. The author creates a hestitation in his reader's mind about the nature of Glámr's haunting of Forsæludalur. Is he a ghost, originating in pagan times, like the *vættir* he was killed fighting, or is he diabolical? This, in turn, leads to doubt about the status of Grettir himself (Tulinius forthcoming). Just as enigmatic though less overtly involving the supernatural is the description of Skalla-Grímr's death in chapter 58 of *Egils saga*. The upright position of the body and the way Egill avoids looking his dead father in the eyes while taking him out of the house through a hole in the wall, strongly suggests he is trying to prevent his returning as a ghost. This aspect must be taken into account when interpreting the saga.

SOCIAL AMBIGUITY

This ontological uncertainty in the family sagas can be extended to other fields, the most interesting one being that of social status, the fifth principle organizing the literary system. Characters in legendary fiction, be it those of *fornaldarsögur*, chivalrous tales or even hagiography, are ideal figures who are representatives of a certain social status which is revealed in how they look or what they do. A good example of this is Áslaug in *Ragnars saga*, who becomes a ravishing beauty despite her step-mother's efforts to make her ugly. At the other end of the spectrum, characters in the contemporary sagas are also determined by their social status, even when they are not ideal representatives of their class. The family sagas seem however rather to focus on characters with changing or unclear social status. *Hrafnkels saga* is one example among many, being the story of its eponymous hero's fall from his position of *goði* of Hrafnkelsdalur and his reclaiming of it. *Gísla saga* is another, the main hero losing his status of free farmer to become a hunted outlaw. *Egils saga* is of particular interest here because it deals in so many respects with degraded or threatened social status: the regional kings of Norway who must submit to Harald Fine-Hair, the sons of Hildiríðr who do not receive what they consider their rightful inheritance, Egill himself whose claims to wealth and status are threatened by Berg-Ǫnundr's allegations that his wife Ásgerðr is illegitimate, Þorsteinn Egilsson's dealings with Steinarr Sjónason whose ultimate goal was to supplant his neighbour's position as chieftain of their area. In many of these cases the rightful positions of the respective protagonists are unclear.

If the genealogical principle organizing the literary system of medieval Iceland places the family sagas in a central position situated between the distant and highly stylized past and the present in all its complexity and opacity, the following three: religion, the supernatural and social status, bring to light their intermediary character. Indeed, they are set in a period when heathen times, as they are represented with their cluster of themes which belong to the 'Matter of the North', meet the new era of Christianity, and when the supernatural intrudes into a world almost identical to that of the authors and audience of the sagas. This creates a hesitation about the ontological status of what is portrayed, which seems also to apply to the social position of the protagonists.

We can now take another look at the principle of geographical organization, according to which the family sagas are not intermediary but are placed on one of the extremities of the scale, nearest to their authors and audience: home. Indeed, they are about the ancestors of leading Icelandic families and must therefore have something to do with who they are. It is very tempting to link this uncertainty about identities in the family sagas with some kind of ambiguity, questioning or doubt concerning the identity of the social class which seems to have created them: the leading families of early thirteenth-century Iceland.

Indeed, when we look at a variety of sources, we see evidence that the identity of this ruling class was being questioned, especially in Norway. A significant example is the taunting of Páll Sæmundarson in Bergen in 1216 (*Sturlunga saga*: 254–5). He was the eldest son of the leading family in Iceland at the time, the Oddaverjar, a family which prided itself on links with the Skjöldung dynasty and on close family ties with the Norwegian royal house, since Páll's great-grandmother was said to have been a daughter of King Magnús Barefoot. When Páll arrived in Bergen the merchants there made fun of him, pretending to believe that he was going to make a claim to the Norwegian throne. Implicit in their mockery is doubt concerning the truth of the Oddaverjar's nobility, since Páll is allusively being compared to a number of royal pretenders of questionable birth who arrived in twelfth-century Norway from countries across the sea. Among these was King Sverrir himself, grandfather of the then reigning king, Hákon Hákonarson.

Another sign of this questioning may be found in the historical synopsis of Norwegian history, *Historia Norwegiae*, which probably dates from the same period (Santini 1993). It is manifestly Norwegian and gives a different account of the settlement of Iceland from Icelandic sources: the first settlers had to flee Norway because they had committed murder ('ob reatus homicidiorum patriam fugentes', *Historia Norwegiae*: 92–3). What appears to be a response to this is to be found in the version of *Landnámabók* attributed to Styrmir Kárason (*c.* 1170–1245) and thought to date from the same period (*Landnámabók*: civ). In its epilogue it gives as reason for composing such a work the necessity to answer foreigners who call Icelanders descendants of criminals and slaves ('at vér séim komnir af þrælum ok illmennum', *Landnámabók:* cii–ciii). Whether or not these two texts and the Bergen incident are directly linked, they bear witness to a debate about the origins of the Icelandic aristocracy in the first decades of the thirteenth century, the exact period when literary fiction is flowering.[5]

It may be that doubts about the legitimacy of the aristocracy's claim to supremacy were also shared by Icelanders themselves. *Sturlunga saga* tells us that in 1255 farmers in Eyjafjörður and Skagafjörður said, when asked to accept Þorvarðr Þórarinsson and Þorgils skarði as *hǫfðingjar* or overlords of their districts, that it would be best to have none at all (*Sturlunga saga*: 706–7).[6] This might not mean that they doubted the legitimacy of the two's identities but it does imply a doubt about the *hǫfðingjar*'s usefulness as a class.

It would not come as a surprise to find that the increased complexity of Icelandic society from the mid-twelfth century onwards, when aristocrats with pretensions to overlordship lifted themselves above the ranks of a former class of *goðar*, created friction within society. In a recent thesis Orri Vésteinsson has shown that Bishop Þorlákr in the late twelfth century and Bishop Guðmundr in the early thirteenth were both members by birth of the ruling class but were marginalized by poverty in the case of Þorlákr and illegitimacy in Guðmundr's (Vésteinsson 1996: 254–8). It is tempting to consider the two bishops' respective attacks on the aristocracy's authority in the late twelfth and early thirteenth centuries as having not only been motivated by Church policy but also by their own backgrounds. As powerless members of the ruling class, they had grudges against those who wielded power. Whether this explanation is correct or not, Vésteinsson convincingly shows that by the last third of the thirteenth century, the Icelandic higher clergy had established a separate identity, distinct from that of the lay aristocracy it had been part of since the beginnings of Christianity in the country (Vésteinsson 1996: 260–91).

Vésteinsson's thesis also shows that while some of the former *goðar* families disappeared during the period in which *hǫfðingjar* flourish, others maintained local authority and rose to influence again after the weakening of the aristocratic families in the conflicts of the Sturlung age (Vésteinsson 1996: 304). This class shared ancestry and a similar culture with the *hǫfðingjar* and had more or less the same values and ideas about itself. It did not however have the family links to royalty most of the latter claimed to have, which were a key aspect of aristocratic identity. Indeed, both the Oddaverjar and the Haukdælir were blood-relations of Norwegian kings. It is possible that Sturla Sighvatsson's marriage to Solveig Sæmundardóttir of the Oddaverjar family was important in making him eligible to become Earl of Iceland. This seems to have been a condition of the deal he struck with King Hákon if he managed to bring the country under Norwegian rule (*Hákonar saga*: 91).

Though more research has to be done on this issue, it seems that there were a number of social actors in medieval Iceland who could question the identity of the families in power in the late twelfth and early thirteenth centuries. This scepticism would also have fostered a critical attitude towards – or at least doubt about – the tales of the past which established this identity. It is therefore interesting to consider the remarks of the author of *Þorgils saga og Hafliða* in the often cited description of literary entertainment at the wedding feast at Reykja-hólar. It is said that the stories of Hrómundr Gripsson were called *lygisögur* (fictional tales) by King Sverrir but nevertheless people claimed descent from this hero of ancient times (*Sturlunga saga*: 22).[7] Though *Þorgils saga* is now thought to date from after 1237 (Brown 1952: xxix), this split attitude about the truth of the 'Matter of the North' seems somewhat older. It is tempting to connect such ambiguity with the changes going on in Icelandic society during the whole period.

CONCLUSION: FICTION AND UNCERTAINTY

Uncertain ontological status is perhaps a common feature of sophisti-cated fiction in the Western tradition. Chrétien's romances have been read as the expression of an identity crisis of the knightly class in the second half of the twelfth century (Köhler 1956). The fictions of Cervantes in early seventeenth-century Spain show an interest in ambiguities of social position and the gap between ideological represen-tations and reality. Nineteenth-century French novels, from Balzac to Proust, deal with the instability of the social order after the Revolution and the uncertainty of identities after the downfall of the *Ancien Régime* and the rise of a bourgeois industrial society. The most important novels of our century are grounded in metaphysical doubt which affects not only individual identities but also the nature of perception, memory and even the coherence of the self. It could be said that the evolution of narrative fiction has accompanied changes in Western humankind's perception of itself and the world, from a mythical–religious world-view necessarily founded on some metaphysical truth to an open and scientific attitude which has learned to live with ontological uncertainty.

It is therefore interesting to note that the rise of fiction in early thirteenth-century Iceland seems intimately linked to a crisis in the identity which had been established by historiographers of the pre-ceding century, an identity in many ways built on an image of the distant past constructed through the 'Matter of the North'. As its treatment became more elaborate and thus more fictional, two genres appeared more or less simultaneously. The *fornaldarsögur* are set in a mythical prehistorical world where ideal figures play out the fears and preoccupations of thirteenth-century Icelanders. The family sagas take place in the same physical world as theirs but during the Conversion period two centuries before the appearance of the genre, an age of transition and shifting identities in which authors and audience seem to have believed their social world originated. The characters represented are religiously, socially and morally ambiguous, which is what makes them so interesting as creatures of fiction. Examples are the main characters of *Egils saga*, perhaps the first major family saga. As settlers they founded Icelandic medieval society but they also had blood-ties with Norwegian nobility, with whom they had shared roots in the pagan past. They are ambiguous for they belong to two different worlds, the one of the saga's audience and the other of the 'Matter of the North'.

Contemporary interest in ambiguities of identity might be the reason for the international success of the family sagas over the last century and a half. With them we are already in the world of the novel, because saga society is much like ours: a stratified yet mobile society where identities are unstable and where there is an ongoing struggle between individuals climbing the social ladder. Such a premature development of novelistic discourse is due to an unusual historical situation: political instability in Norway during most of the twelfth century allowed the ruling class of Iceland to use medieval humanism to forge its own identity as an independent aristocracy through the constitution of genealogies and historiography. The strengthening of the royal state, however, attracted the Icelandic aristocracy into the king's orbit, provoking competition for status. This new situation acted so as to reveal tensions within the upper layers of society and led to a symptomatic questioning of the ideological foundations of the social system. This questioning is at the heart of the genre which is closest to the identity of authors and audience of saga literature: the family sagas.

With renewed stability in the early fourteenth century, what was left of the aristocracy, as well as descendants of old *goðar* families and new social actors, achieved social position through royal office. Questioning about the origin of social identity had disappeared and so did the family sagas. However, *fornaldarsögur* continued to be written for many centuries but progressively lost the strong links with the distant past of the leading families of Iceland and therefore their sense of identity. The world of the *fornaldarsögur* became a world of pure fiction, not without links with the social and cultural realities of their time of writing, but links of a different kind, which need further study to elucidate.

NOTES

1   Pálsson and Edwards (1971: 8–13) attempt to classify Icelandic medieval literature according to a system based on the nature of the hero, rather than, as here, the nature of the world in which he evolves.

2   That is the sense of the Herdís Bolladóttir's dream near the end of the saga (*Laxdæla saga*: 224). The bones of the *völva* who comes to visit her are burned by Guðrún's tears. As Bjarni Guðnason has elucidated in an as yet unpublished work, this confirms that they are signs of true contrition, holy and therefore active against pagan remains.

3   'En þó at kristni væri á landinu, þá váru þó margir gneistar heiðninnar eptir.' The English version is taken from Bernard Scudder's translation (*The Complete Sagas of Icelanders* 1997 II: 168).

4   'Slíkt kalla eg atburð en ekki jartegn'.

5   In a recent article Grímsdóttir (1995: 50) discusses the origin of this supposed epilogue to Styrmir's version of *Landnámabók* and comes to the conclusion that it is more likely to be from the seventeenth century because of flimsy manuscript evidence and similar statements in *Crymogæa* by Arngrímur Jónsson (1568–1648). She therefore believes this epilogue to be more consistent with seventeenth-century attitudes she describes in the article than what can be known of medieval attitudes. She does not however make the connection with *Historia Norwegiae*.

6   See also the debate about how to interpret this refusal between Gunnar Karlsson (1972 and 1980) and Helgi Þorláksson (1979 and 1982).

7   'En þessari sögu var skemmt Sverri konungi og kallaði hann slíkar lygisögur skemmtilegar. Og þó kunna menn að telja ættir sínar til Hrómundar Gripssonar.'

REFERENCES

Primary literature

Brennu-Njáls saga, Sveinsson, Einar Ól. (ed.) 1954. Íslensk fornrit XII. Reykjavík: Hið Íslenzka fornritafélag.

Eyrbyggja saga, Sveinsson, Einar Ól. and Þórðarson, Matthías (eds.) 1935. Íslensk fornrit IV. Reykjavík: Hið íslenzka fornritafélag.

Fornaldarsögur Norðurlanda, Rafn, Carl Christian (ed.) 1829–30. 3 vols. Copenhagen: Popp.

Hákonar saga Hákonarsonar, Mundt, Marina (ed.) 1977. Norrøne skrifter, 2. Oslo: Norsk historisk kjeldeskriftinstitut.

Historia Norwegiae in *Monumenta Historica Norvegiae,* Storm, Gustav (ed.) 1880. Kristiania (Oslo): Brøgger.

Hrafnkels saga in *Austfirðinga sögur.* Jóhannesson, Jón (ed.) 1959. Íslensk fornrit XI. Reykjavík: Hið íslenzka fornritafélag.

Laxdæla saga, Sveinsson, Einar Ól. (ed.) 1934. Íslensk fornrit III. Reykjavík: Hið íslenzka fornritafélag.

Sturlunga saga, Thorsson, Örnólfur *et al.* (eds.) 1988, 3 vols. Reykjavík: Svart á hvitu.

Sverris saga etter Cod. AM 327 quarto, Indrebø, G. (ed.) 1920. repr. 1981. Kristiania (Oslo): Dybwad.

Secondary literature

Bayerschmidt, Carl F. 1965, 'The Element of the Supernatural in the Sagas of Icelanders,' in Bayerschmidt, Carl F. and Friis, Erik J. (eds.), *Scandinavian Studies: Essays Presented to Dr. Henry Goddard Leach on the Occasion of His Eighty-fifth Birthday.* Seattle: University of Washington Press, pp. 39–53.

Brown, Ursula (ed.) 1952, *Þorgils saga ok Hafliða.* Oxford: Oxford University Press.

Clover, Carol J. 1986, 'Völsunga saga and the Missing Lai of Marie de France', in Simek, Rudolf, Kristjánsson, Jónas and Bekker-Nielsen, Hans (eds.), *Sagnaskemmtun. Studies in Honour of Hermann Pálsson.* Vienna, Cologne and Graz: Böhlaus, pp. 79–84.

Clunies Ross, Margaret 1987, *Skáldskaparmál: Snorri Sturluson's* Ars Poetica *and Medieval Theories of Language.* The Viking Collection, 4. Odense: Odense University Press.

1993, 'The Development of Old Norse Textual Worlds: Genealogical Structure as a Principle of Literary Organization in Early Iceland', *Journal of English and German Philology* 92: 372–85.

Duby, Georges 1961, 'La noblesse dans la France médiévale', *Revue historique* 226: 1–22.

1967, 'Remarques sur la littérature généalogique en France aux XIe et XIIe siècles', *Académie des Inscriptions et Belles-Lettres, Comptes rendus des séances de l'année 1967.* Paris: Klincksieck, pp. 335–45.

1968, 'Les origines de la chevalerie', *Ordinamenti militari in Occidente nell' alto medioevo.* Spoleto: Presso La Sede des Centro, pp. 739–61.

Duby, Georges and Mandrou, Robert 1968, *Histoire de la civilisation française.* Paris: Armand Colin.

Eco, Umberto 1979, *The Role of the Reader: Explorations in the Semiotics of Texts.* Bloomington: Indiana University Press.

Finch, R. G. 1993, 'Vǫlsunga Saga', in Pulsiano, Phillip and Wolf, Kirsten (eds.), *Medieval Scandinavia: an Encyclopedia.* New York and London: Garland, p. 711.

Foote, Peter G. 1974, 'Secular Attitudes in Early Iceland', *Mediaeval Scandinavia* 7: 31–44.

Geary, Patrick 1983, 'Canonization', *Dictionary of the Middle Ages*, III, New York: Scribner, pp. 67–9.

Grímsdóttir, Guðrún Ása 1995, 'Fornar menntir í Hítardal: Eilítið um íslenska tignarmenn og ættartölurit á 17. öld', *Ný Saga* 7: 43–52.

Guðnason, Bjarni 1963, *Um Skjöldunga sögu.* Reykjavík: Menningarsjóður.

1969, 'Gerðir og ritþróun Ragnars sögu loðbrókar', in Guðnason, Bjarni, Halldórsson, Halldór and Kristjánsson, Jónas (eds.), *Einarsbók. Afmæliskveðja til Einars Ól. Sveinssonar 12. des. 1969.* Reykjavík: Nokkrir vinir, pp. 28–37.

Kalinke, Marianne E. 1997, '*Stæri ek brag*: Protest and Subordination in Hallfreðar Saga', *Skáldskaparmál* 4: 50–68.

Karlsson, Gunnar 1972, 'Goðar og bændur', *Saga* 10: 5–57.

1980, 'Völd og auður á 13. öld', *Saga* 18: 5–30.

Köhler, Erich 1956, *Ideal und Wirklichkeit in der hofischen Epik: Studien zur Form der fruhen Artus- und Graldichtung.* Beihefte zur Zeitschrift für Romanishce Philologie, 97. Tübingen: Niemeyer.

Leach, Henry Goddard 1921, *Angevin Britain and Scandinavia.* Cambridge Mass.: Harvard University Press.

Lönnroth, Lars 1969, 'The Noble Heathen: a Theme in the Sagas', *Scandinavian Studies* 41: 1–29.

Nordal, Sigurður 1953, *Sagalitteraturen [Nordisk Kultur VIII:B. Litteraturhistorie. Norge og Island].* Stockholm, Oslo and Copenhagen: Bonnier, pp. 180–274.

Pálsson, Hermann 1985, 'Fornaldarsögur Norðurlanda', *Dictionary of the Middle Ages*, V. New York: Scribner, pp. 137–43.

Pálsson, Hermann and Edwards, Paul 1971, *Legendary Fiction in Medieval Iceland.* Studia Islandica, 30. Reykjavík: Menningarsjóður.

Pavel, Thomas G. 1986, *Fictional Worlds.* Cambridge, Mass. and London: Harvard University Press.

Santini, Carlo 1993, 'Historia Norwegiae', in Pulsiano, Phillip and Wolf, Kirsten (eds.), *Medieval Scandinavia: an Encyclopedia.* New York and London: Garland, pp. 284–5.

Todorov, Tzvetan 1970, *Introduction à la littérature fantastique.* Paris: Editions du Seuil.

Tulinius, Torfi H. 1990, 'Landafræði og flokkun fornsagna', *Skáldskaparmál* 1: 142–56.

1993, 'Kynjasögur úr fortíð og framandi löndum', in Guðmundsson, Böðvar, Tómasson, Sverrir, Tulinius, Torfi H. and Olason, Vésteinn (eds.), *Íslensk bókmenntasaga*, II. Reykjavík: Mál og menning, pp. 165–245.

1995, *La 'Matière du Nord': Sagas légendaires et fiction dans la littérature islandaise en prose du XIIIe siècle*. Paris: Presses de l'Université de Paris-Sorbonne.

1997, 'Le statut théologique d'Egill Skalla-Grímsson', in Lecouteux, Claude (ed.), *Hugr. Mélanges d'histoire, de littérature et de mythologie offerts à Régis Boyer pour son soixante-cinquième anniversaire*. Paris: Presses de l'Université de Paris-Sorbonne, pp. 279–88.

1999, 'Framliðnir feður: Um forneskju og frásagnarlist í Eyrbyggju, Eglu og Grettlu', in Hafstað, Baldur and Bessason, Haraldur (eds.), *Heiðin minni*. Reykjavík: Heimskringla, Mál og menning, pp. 283–316.

Þorláksson, Helgi 1979 'Stórbændur gegn goðum. Hugleiðingar um goðavald, konungsvald og sjálfræðishug bænda um miðbik 13. aldar', in *Söguslóðir. Afmælisrit helgað Ólafi Hanssyni*, Reykjavík: Sögufélagið, pp. 227–50.

1982, 'Stéttir, auður og völd á 12. og 13. öld,' *Saga* 20: 63–113.

Vésteinsson, Orri 1996, *The Christianisation of Iceland: Priests, Power and Social Change 1000–1300*. Ph.D. thesis (History), University of London.

Zumthor, Paul 1972, *Essai de poétique médiévale*. Paris: Editions du Seuil.

II

Romance in Iceland

GERALDINE BARNES

In something of a parallel with its development in England, medieval romance in Iceland comes in two sequential categories – translations or adaptations from French or Anglo-Norman and independent narratives – known collectively to modern scholarship as *riddarasögur* ('sagas of knights') but often distinguished as 'translated' and 'independent' (or 'Icelandic') *riddarasögur*.[1] The translated *riddarasögur* comprise Old Norse prose versions of French epic and romance, among them Marie's *lais* (in *Strengleikar*); Thomas's *Tristan* (*Tristrams saga*); and three Arthurian narratives by Chrétien de Troyes, *Erec et Enide* (*Erex saga*), *Yvain* (*Ívens saga*), and *Perceval* (*Parcevals saga* and *Valvens þáttr*); produced in Norway, probably from Anglo-Norman exemplars (Leach 1921), for the court of King Hákon the Old (r. 1217–63). These sagas are, for the most part, preserved in Icelandic manuscripts and generally presumed to have reached Iceland soon after their composition. The independent *riddarasögur*, which are the focus of this discussion, appear in Iceland around the beginning of the fourteenth century. Frequently dismissed as the inferior, 'escapist', dreary, and depressing products of a gloomy period in Iceland's history following the surrender of its autonomy to Norway in 1262–64 and subsequent deterioration in its economic and political status, the *riddarasögur* have proved the least appealing form of Old Icelandic prose narrative to modern scholarship, which has tended to regard them as something of an embarrassment to the Old Norse literary corpus. The view which Henry Holland expressed, in his 'Preliminary Dissertion' to Mackenzie's *Travels in the Island of Iceland*, of the fifteenth century as a time when 'genius and

literature disappeared . . . and the wretched remnant of the Icelanders
. . . sunk into a state of apathy, superstition, and ignorance' (1812: 53),
has been the prevailing one.[2]

Economic decline and loss of political identity do not, however,
necessarily entail literary poverty. In her seminal *Romance in Iceland*
(1934), Margaret Schlauch took a more positive view of the independent
riddarasögur as narratives, probably of clerical authorship, which draw
upon an impressive range of learned foreign sources, including lapid-
aries, bestiaries, and classical geography. If, in her opinion, these were
intended as tales of mere 'escapism', then they would have to be
regarded as 'a sort of intellectual narcotic' (1934: 11). Schlauch modestly
classified her pioneering study as 'in many respects a mere preliminary
survey of a vast field which still awaits detailed investigation' (Preface),
but the surge of *riddarasögur* scholarship which she intended the book
to generate (*ibid.*) was unforthcoming for more than a generation. The
last thirty years, however, have seen a revival of interest in romance in
Iceland. Subsequent to Einar Ól. Sveinsson's discussion of the style,
provenance, and interrelationship of the *riddarasögur* in his introductory essay to Jónas Kristjánsson's edition of *Viktors saga ok Blávus*
(1964), monographs have been published on *riddarasögur* motifs (Van
Nahl 1981), the centrality of the bride quest in Icelandic romance
(Kalinke 1990), and the audiences and ideology of medieval (Glauser
1983, 1990) and post-Reformation (Driscoll 1997) *riddarasögur*.

Romance took a different course in fourteenth- and fifteenth-
century Iceland from England and continental Europe in the same
period. Fourteenth-century Middle English verse romance followed
the tradition of the Anglo-Norman romances composed in England in
the previous two centuries by embracing the ideology of the barony,
according to which the interests of the hero – the restoration, defence,
and preservation of land and family – are coterminous with those of
the nation (Crane 1986: 217–18). Wolfram von Eschenbach in
Germany and composers of prose romance in thirteenth-century
France and fifteenth-century England focussed on the religious dimension of chivalry in their continuations of the Grail quest initiated in
Chrétien's *Perceval*. Through the story of Lancelot and Guinevere, they
explored the implications of the conflict between love and loyalty for
the Arthurian world. The principal narrative motifs of the *riddarasögur*

– bride quests; the restoration of patrimony; the validation of identity – are themselves part and parcel of European folktale and romance. The *riddarasögur* are also rich in the surface attributes of romance: the marvellous, the exotic, the mysterious, the improbable, and the hyperbolic. Their underlying ethos, however, radically differs from the idealistic values of European chivalric romance, since the *riddarasaga* hero has little sense of obligation beyond his own self-interest. Typically he is a king's son, from Western or Eastern Europe, and the story chronicles his accession to the throne and the extension of his power, processes which entail either or both the restoration of his patrimony and the quest for a bride, travel to distant lands, battles against monstrous and human opponents, and the acquisition of new kingdoms.

The absence of an independent Norse Arthurian cycle comes as no surprise, given that feudal chivalry took only tenuous hold in medieval Norway and Iceland. There was some flirtation with chivalric terminology and ritual in the reign of Magnús Hákonarson (r. 1263–80), king of Norway and Iceland, who, in 1277, substituted the titles *barrun* ('baron') and *riddari* ('knight') for *lendr maðr* ('landed man') and *skutilsveinn* ('page'), but no *barrunar* were created after 1308, and only sixty-five *riddarar* dubbed between 1277 and 1310 (Löfqvist 1935: 112–52). Traces of feudal ritual in the organization of the Norwegian court are found in Mágnus's *Hirðskrá* ('Court Law'), where the initiation of the *hirðmaðr* ('retainer') entailed kneeling before the king, the clasping of hands, and an oath of loyalty (Meissner 1938: 12, 16, 31). The use of the king's consecrated sword in that part of the ceremony known as the *sverðtaka* ('swordtaking') introduced an echo of the religious ritual which had dominated the dubbing ritual in continental Europe since the mid-twelfth century (Bloch 1961: 314–16). On the other hand, the Round Table, the defining symbol of the Arthurian world and inspiration for tournaments in England and continental Europe in the twelfth and thirteenth centuries, was virtually unknown in medieval Scandinavia (Reichert 1986).

This chapter will consider the audience, authorial voice, genealogy, and ideology of the *riddarasögur*. It will argue that their literary models are to be found not in the chivalric romances of Europe but in the sagas of the legendary history of Scandinavia known as *fornaldarsögur* ('sagas of olden days'), and that their ethos is in many ways antithetical to that of traditional chivalric narrative.

AUDIENCE

The time of composition of the independent *riddarasögur*, the late thirteenth to the fifteenth century, coincides with a period of economic and constitutional change in Iceland: from wool to fish as the chief export and from free to subject state. The export of dried codfish (*skreið*) to Norway, which began at the end of the thirteenth century, brought an increase in economic prosperity and remained brisk until the outbreak of the Black Death there in 1349 (Gelsinger 1981: 183–4, 189). The constitutional changes of 1271 and 1281, codified in the text known as *Jónsbók*, eliminated the offices of *goðar* and *hofðingjar* ('chieftains'), who had held political authority in the Icelandic commonwealth (Karlsson 1977), and replaced them with fifteen positions of royal administration in Iceland: twelve sheriffs (*sýslumenn*), two lawmen (*lögmenn*), and the *hirðstjóri*, the leader of the royal retinue (Sigurðsson 1995). New families who became prominent after 1300 included a small number of men made wealthy through the burgeoning fishing industry. Thus two new socially élite groups, with overlapping interests and membership, appear in post-commonwealth Iceland: those successfully engaged in the *skreið* trade and descendants of the former chieftain class co-opted into the vice-regal retinue.

Are the patrons and audience of the *riddarasögur* to be identified with these newly prominent families? Whereas we can, on the basis of the colophon to *Tristrams saga*, prologue to *Strengleikar*, and last words of *Ívens saga*, all of which make attribution to King Hákon, identify with a degree of confidence the circumstances of the composition of the translated *riddarasögur* (Tómasson 1977), the independent *riddarasögur* offer little tangible or credible internal evidence of their audience. In *Ectors saga*, for instance, a story whose hero is a descendant of the Trojan prince Hector, seven Icelandic names appear among Ector's *hesta strakar* ('horse-boys') in what may be a reference (Dodsworth 1962: 171), and perhaps a jesting one, to members of the writer's audience or to his circle. The unnamed commissioners of the *riddarasögur* manuscripts must, however, have been people of means, and in the first part of the fourteenth century, these were the entrepreneurs of the fishing industry (Glauser 1983: 77–8). Several *riddarasögur* manuscripts come from the rich fishing area of the Vestfirðingafjörðungur, where, from 1300, there was the greatest concentration of manors (*höfuðból*) (Glauser 1983: 75–6), the residences of the post-commonwealth aristocracy, that is, 'the families of chieftains who were in power when Iceland became part of the kingdom of Norway, and the families used by the king for his local administration of Iceland after 1262/64' (Sigurðsson 1995: 153 n.3). The ribaldly flippant invitation at the conclusion of *Vilmundar saga viðutan* (Loth 1962–5 (henceforth *LMIR*) *IV*: 200–1) to readers, listeners, and 'those who are not so wealthy that they have to pay taxes to our king' (*þeir sem eigi eru suo rikir at þeir eigi kongi uroum skatt at giallda*), to kiss the backside of a servant woman called Qskubuska may have humorous application to an audience, in whole or in part, of *skáttbœndir* ('landowners liable to tax'), the equivalent of the franklin class in England.

This suggested *riddarasögur* audience – of the well-to-do and élite of Icelandic society – is not dissimilar to that of Middle English verse romance, which is likely to have been a combination of the mercantile and an essentially administrative knightly class, the latter's numbers swelled through necessity in the fourteenth century by the admission of lowlier members of the landowning classes to the 'parliamentary gentry' (Butt 1989: 254). Similarly in Iceland, the need to expand the royal retinue made upward mobility possible for those who were not descendants of the *hǫfðingjar* and *goðar* of the previous age, but who had 'an acceptable economic and social background' (Sigurðsson 1995: 158). We can therefore postulate a *riddarasögur* audience consisting of the 'establishment', those aspiring to join it, and wealthy entrepreneurs: in other words, a largely *nouveau riche* fraternity, motivated not by ideals of feudal service but by aspirations to social and material advancement.

THE AUTHORIAL VOICE

As Schlauch (1934) and Glauser (1983: 77) suggest, the wealth of Latin learning in the *riddarasögur* is strongly suggestive of clerical composition, but the authorial voice wears its learning with a degree of insouciance. Whereas the translated *riddarasögur* eliminate Chrétien's loquacious and witty narrators (Barnes 1993), an assertive authorial persona in the independent *riddarasögur* expresses itself as conscious of the literary narrative as the product of individual creative imagination, of the text as artefact, and the narrative stage as boundless. The self-defining compositional persona (*sá, er söguna setti saman*; 'he who composed the saga') actively engages in expression of opinion, confessions of non-omniscience or inadequacy, allegations of 'truthfulness', and references to patently spurious sources and circumstances of discovery (Barnes 1990: 11–16). *Konráðs saga*, for instance, is said (Vilhjálmsson 1954a: 344) to have been discovered by a cleric 'written in a street' (*skrifaða á stræti*). The authenticity of the Latin source for *Klári* (*Clári*) *saga*, allegedly found in France by Jón Halldorsson (I, 1), the bishop of Skálholt from 1322 to 1339, is doubtful. *Ectors saga* refers several times to a dubious authority called *meistarinn*, who is named at the end of the saga as 'Master Galterus'. A group that might be called the 'graffiti sagas' are said to have been found written on stone walls (*á steinvegginum*): *Sigurðar saga fóts* in Cologne (*LMIR III*: 233); *Jarlmanns saga ok Hermanns*, found by a 'Master Virgilius', in Lisbon (*LMIR III*: 3) and *Vilhjalms saga sjóðs* in Babylon (*LMIR IV*: 3). Although such allegations of unlikely provenance are themselves a medieval literary convention (Amory 1984: 515–16), in the *riddarasögur* they also serve to reinforce the impression of witty complicity between author and audience established, for example, by the invocation to readers, listeners, and the tax-liable in *Vilmundar saga viðutan* and, more particularly, by the often irreverent and self-assertive authorial voice which is disposed to wry or sardonic comments on the action.

The author–narrator of *Vilhjálms saga sjóðs* twice expresses his consciousness of the text as material artefact: first, there is the claim that his source was written on stone; second, there is not, he says, enough parchment (*bókfell*, p. 98) to describe the extent of the vileness of the forces of two kings from the Caucasus. Nevertheless, whereas some components of its story might exceed the capacity of the tools of literary construction, the saga's narrative framework extends to the furthest reaches of the earth. Its geographical range, as announced in the opening words, extends to the world's end (*heims enda*, p. 3): from England to Saxland, Greece, Africa, the city of Nineveh, and the

Caucasus. *Sigurðar saga pögla*'s account of Blankiflúr's conversion of Flóres, which derives from the translated *riddarasaga* of *Flóres saga ok Blankiflúr*, provides an interesting example of the extension of geographical boundaries in the independent *riddarasögur*. In *Flóres saga ok Blankiflúr* (Kölbing 1896: XXIII: 10–13), Blankiflúr takes Flóres on a tour of the churches of Paris, whereas in the retelling of the conversion of Flóres in *Sigurðar saga pögla*, he travels as far as the Holy Land (*af hennar aaeggiann for kongrinn Flores wt yfir hafit til Jorsala*, p. 102; 'through her urging King Flóres travelled across the sea to Jerusalem').

Nitida saga (*LMIR V*) provides the most extensive demonstration of the global consciousness of the *riddarasögur*. Near the beginning of the saga, a lush island called Visio, located at the end of the earth, is said to contain four magic stones, through which the whole world (*allar haalfur veralldarinnar*, p. 6) can be seen. Later, Nitida, queen of France, uses them to show the hero, Liforninus, every corner of the world: from France to Greece; the North (Norway, Iceland, the Faroes, the Hebrides, the Orkneys, Sweden, Denmark, England, Ireland); the East; and everywhere else (pp. 30–1). At the saga's conclusion, when three marriages are celebrated with lavish festivities, the author disparages his native tongue and his geographical isolation in relation to the rest of the world in a rhetorical gesture of modesty about his compositional talents: *er og ei audsagt med öfrodre tungu í utledgumm veralldarinnar . . . hvor fogndur vera munde i midiumm heimenum af sliku hoffolke samannkomnu* (p. 36) ('It is not easy to say, with an unlearned tongue, in the backblocks of the world . . . what joy there would have been at the centre of the world from such a courtly gathering').

Generally speaking, Scandinavia is implicitly relegated to the narrative fringes of the *riddarasögur*, where reminders of its existence are restricted to the occasional eruptions of vikings and berserkers. At the conclusion of *Viktors saga ok Blávus*, however, the story is abruptly integrated into the legendary Scandinavian context: the sons of Viktor and Blávus ultimately forfeit their lives in battle with a King Geirmínir of Denmark and thereby provide a link with an incident which is preserved in the seventeenth-century *Hrómundar saga* (*LMIR I*: 49).

Controlled by an authorial voice which is learned, playful, and artistically self-conscious, the *riddarasögur* constitute a veritable *summa* of the tools of fictional composition, from encyclopedic learning to oral tradition, in which language itself is acknowledged as the primary resource. The travellers who activate the flying carpet in *Viktors saga ok Blávus* by reading the gold letters on its sides (*LMIR I*: 9, 38, 39, 47) pointedly demonstrate the creative power of the written and spoken word. More generally, the interest expressed throughout the *riddarasögur* in the desirability of foreign-language acquisition (Kalinke 1983) demonstrates an awareness on the part of their authors of the capacity of language to facilitate the travels of their heroes in unfamiliar territory, to construct worlds untrammelled by human limitation, and to enhance the pleasure of the text for their audiences. Luxuriating in hyperbolic description and action and in breadth of narrative canvas, the *riddarasögur* persuade us exuberantly of the capability of language, like the magic stones of Visio in *Nitida saga*, to conquer the bounds of geography and transport its readers and listeners from the margins of the world to its centre and beyond.

LITERARY GENEALOGY

There is little in the development of the *Íslendingasögur* to prepare us for the *riddarasögur*. They did not, however, abruptly displace other forms of saga composition. Some of the most famous *Íslendingasögur*, *Njáls saga* and *Grettis saga* for example, were written at the end of the thirteenth century and the beginning of the fourteenth, when the composition of *riddarasögur* is generally assumed to have begun. The concluding sections of the late thirteenth-century *Eiríks saga rauða*, where, in the course of the quest for Vínland, a member of Þorfinnr Karlsefni's company is killed by a uniped (*einfœtingr*), and the rest of the company sight and briefly entertain the prospect of journeying to *Einfœtingaland* ('Unipedland') (ch.12), point that saga in the direction of the fantastic adventures characteristic of the *riddarasögur*. On the grounds of their structural affinities with folktale and native oral tradition, some scholars (Hume 1980; Weber 1986) see the *riddarasögur* as a primarily indigenous phenomenon; others see them as imitative or derivative of continental romance, through the medium of the 'translated' *riddarasögur* and other written sources (Kalinke 1983: 852, 861; Mitchell 1991: 27).

The independent *riddarasögur* do occasionally acknowledge a debt to specific translated *riddarasögur*. *Sigurðar saga þǫgla*, for example, whose female protagonist, Sedentiana, is said to be the daughter of Flóres and Blankiflúr, makes explicit reference to the events of *Flóres saga ok Blankiflur* (*sem segir j sogu hans*; 'as it says in his [Flóres's] saga') (*LMIR II*: 99), the Norse version of the twelfth-century *Floire et Blanchefleur*. *Ectors saga* cites *Trójumanna saga*, which ultimately derives from the Latin *De excidio Troiae*, as one of its sources (*LMIR I*: 185). *Samsons saga fagra* concludes (Vilhjálmsson 1954a: 401) with a reference to *Mǫttuls saga* ('Skikkju saga'; 'the saga of the cloak'), an adaptation of the Old French *lai*-cum-*fabliau*, *Le mantel mautaillié*.

More common is the silently borrowed motif. *Vilmundar saga viðutan*, for instance, has elements of the stories of *Parcevals saga* (Schlauch 1934: 166–7) and *Tristrams saga*. Like Isolt, Princess Sóley changes identities with a serving-woman, Ǫskubuska, to circumvent a bargain with an unwanted lover. Like Perceval, Vilmundr is the son of parents who live *langt j burt fra audrum monnum* (p. 152) ('far away from other people'), is possessed of great physical strength and well-versed in shooting and fencing, but is unable to recognize the funda-mental structures of society, including the monarchy itself. Vilmundr does not know what a king is, for he has led an entirely isolated life: *heyrt hefi eg kong nefnndan . . . enn ecki veit eg huad þat er. þviat eg hefi eigi menn sed fyri utan fodr minn og modur* (p. 160) ('I have never heard [the word] "king" uttered . . . and I don't know what that is, because I have not seen people apart from my father and mother'). Unlike *Parcevals saga* and *Tristrams saga*, however, which incorporate these folktale–romance motifs into narratives that engage with the wider issues of chivalric education, obligation, and morality, the ethical dimensions of *Vilmundar saga* are restricted to the wish-fulfilling pattern of folktale: Vilmundr, the country-bred, socially inexperienced, but capable and prodigiously strong hero eventually finds himself married to Sóley, solely by virtue of his muscle power.

It is, as Weber (1986) argues, largely in terms of surface motif that the influence of the translated *riddarasögur* manifests itself in independent Icelandic romance. Athough the former continued to be copied in Iceland in the fourteenth and fifteenth centuries, these sober and restrained narratives exerted little influence on the development of native literature in the later Middle Ages. Moreover, contrary to the translated *riddarasögur*, the independent *riddarasögur* founded a literary dynasty of their own, in the form of *rímur* (narrative poems) and post-Reformation *riddarasögur*, works which remained popular well into the nineteenth century (Driscoll 1997).

The literary model for indigenous Icelandic romance is more immediately traceable to a group of *fornaldarsögur*, tales of the legendary North which draw upon the resources of folklore and foreign and native literature. Usefully defined by Stephen Mitchell as 'Old Icelandic prose narratives based on traditional heroic themes, whose numerous fabulous episodes and motifs create an atmosphere of unreality' (1991: 27), the *fornaldarsögur* share a number of stylistic, thematic, and codicological affinities with the independent *riddara-sögur* (Kalinke 1990: 6–13; Mitchell 1991: 19–32; Driscoll 1997: 5–6).

Although the majority of *fornaldarsögur* date from the fourteenth and fifteenth centuries, they are, if we accept the argument of Torfi Tulinius, likely to have been composed as early as the first half of the thirteenth and thus to constitute the first manifestation of a consciously fictional mode in Icelandic prose literature (Tulinius 1995). Tulinius argues that, in their celebration of the deeds of legendary ancestors for an audience of *höfðingjar* and their followers, the *fornaldarsögur* consider in a deliberately fictionalized fashion many issues also of interest to *Íslendingasögur* authors, such as a concern with inheritance and lineage. The *fornaldarsögur*, he argues, have topical social relevance for their audiences: marriage as means of upward social mobility for the hero is a goal in the *fornaldarsögur*, just as it was for young men in thirteenth-century Iceland (1995: 163–8). Like the *riddarasögur*, many *fornaldarsögur* have a predilection for stories of bride quests, a fascination with royal power, a geographical range which extends to India, and an assertive and sometimes playful narrator. The defence of the questionable truthfulness of *Hrólfs saga Gautrekssonar* (*Hvárt sem satt er eða eigi, þá hafi sá gaman af, er þat má at verða* (Jónsson 1954: 142); 'whether it is true or not, may he who can derive pleasure from it'), for example, is, suggests Tulinius, 'une sorte de justification ludique' (1995: 156), which has its parallel in the tongue-in-cheek discussions of veracity and provenance in some of the *riddarasögur*. Generally speaking the *fornaldarsögur* incline either to the 'heroic–tragic' (e.g. *Ragnars saga loðbróka, Vǫlsunga saga*) or 'adventurous–comic' (e.g. *Bósa saga; Gǫngu-Hrólfs saga*) mode (Mitchell 1991: 43; Tulinius 1995: 20). Two late-thirteenth-century *fornaldarsögur – Qrvar-Odds saga*, in which the hero fulfils a prediction that he will spend his long life wandering the world (ch. 2), and *Hrólfs saga Gautrekssonar*, which entails four separate bride quests – are, Tulinius argues, the turning points in the development of the genre from the heroic to the adventurous.

If one subscribes to Tulinius's *fornaldarsögur* dating, the appearance of the *riddarasögur* coincides with the shift in mode in *fornaldarsögur* from the heroic–tragic to the comic–adventurous towards the end of the thirteenth century, a shift which coincides with the political transformation of Iceland from free to subject state. That chronology presents us with the possibility that, at this transitional point in their development, *fornaldarsögur* gave rise to a new kind of saga, in which interest in royal power and the quest to extend one's sphere of power and authority, which Tulinius identifies as important concerns in the *fornaldarsögur* (1995: 262–4), are recast in a pseudo-chivalric context for the Icelandic subjects of the king of Norway.

IDEOLOGY

For those disinclined to dismiss the *riddarasögur* simply as 'escapist' literature, the transfer of audience taste from *Íslendingasögur* to *riddarasögur* continues to be a source of puzzlement and speculation. Kathryn Hume (1980: 22–3) suggests that 'the political changes that made the experiences depicted in the family sagas unreal to later Icelandic audiences' were a critical factor. Jürg Glauser argues that those same constitutional changes actively inspired *riddarasögur* writers to endorse the exercise of royal power. His thesis is that the *riddarasögur* show how a powerful monarch can destroy hostile alien or marginal forces – women, monsters, vikings – and restore stability to his subjects (Glauser 1983: 229–33). Sverrir Tómasson (1986) also sees a political ethic, which underscores personal loyalty to the king, in *Adonias saga*. The prevailing ideology of the *riddarasögur* is fundamentally secular. With exceptions such as *Mírmanns saga* and *Bærings saga*, confrontations between Christians and Saracens have more to do with the restoration of patrimony or the securing of a bride than with the reconquest of the Holy Land or the glorification and propagation of the Christian faith (Schlauch 1934: 169; Glauser 1983: 189–90). The ultimate aim in the *riddarasögur* is the acquisition, extension, and legitimization of power, through marriage, conquest, and the validation of the hero's identity, which may be obscured by the circumstances of his birth (*Adonias saga*), enchantment (*Ala flekks saga*), usurpation (*Adonias saga*; *Bærings saga*; *Sigrgarðs saga ok Valbrands*), or abduction (*Flóres saga konungs ok sona hans*).

Although the validation and restoration of identity are primary concerns of medieval European romance, the independent *riddarasögur* diverge from the mainstream of romance tradition in their total lack of chivalric idealism. Physical prowess rather than statesmanship is the defining element of kingship (Hughes 1978), and those concepts fundamental to the courtly ideal, 'refinement of the laws of combat, courteous social intercourse, service of women' (Auerbach 1957: 117), are conspicuously absent. 'Chivalry', in the sense of noble, self-sacrificing conduct and service – to God, lord, and lady – is little more than a matter of terminology, armorial decoration, and displays of swordsmanship. Whereas 'courtly' love is, at most, a superficial and occasional embellishment – it is for example, said in *Sigrgarðs saga ok Valbrands* of Sigrgarðr's reaction to the description of a princess whom he has never seen, that *fagre fuglenn Venus* ('the fair bird Venus') has shot her *astar ør* ('love-arrow ') into his heart (*LMIR V*: 132) – misogyny underpins the *riddarsögur* to the extent that Glauser ranges women with trolls and berserkers as inimical forces in need of the hero's subjugating hand.

Women function principally in the *riddarasögur* not as the objects of love quests but as the powerful and often misogamous begetters of the hero's heirs. The underlying agenda here is a concern with family inheritance which also appears in the translated *riddarasögur*. Although the heroes of twelfth-century French romance tend to be childless, *Erex saga* and *Flóres saga ok Blankiflúr* do not conclude before the hero's kingdom has passed to the succeeding generation. *Erex saga* ends with a three-generational overview: Erex and Evida have two sons, one of whom is said to have been named after Evida's father, and the other after Erex's; they jointly inherit Erex's kingdom (p. 106). When the hero and heroine of *Flóres saga ok Blankiflúr* turn seventy, they divide their kingdom among their unnamed and unnumbered sons and retire to the religious life (Kölbing 1896: XXIII: 16). In *Sigurðar saga þǫgla*, the lineage of Flóres and Blankiflúr extends over four generations: from themselves to their daughter, Sedentiana, who marries Sigurðr þǫgla ('the silent') and has a son, Flóres, who fathers children. In *Tristrams saga ok Ísoddar*, a fifteenth-century narrative independent of the thirteenth-century translated *Tristrams saga*, Tristram has a son and grandchildren.

Whereas Tristram's marriage, following his banishment from the court of King Markis in *Tristrams saga* is unconsummated, in *Tristrams saga ok Ísoddar* the union of Tristram Kalegrasson with Ísodd svarta ('the dark'), a Spanish noblewoman, brings him the kingship of Spain and is blessed with issue, a handsome son named Kalegras, upon whom King Móroddr, husband of Ísodd hin fagra ('the fair') eventually bestows the throne of England. A knight without peer, Kalegras also becomes an ideal king. In the last chapter of *Tristrams saga ok Ísoddar* Kalegras Tristramsson undertakes a mission which is a paradigm of an obstacle-free bride-quest romance. He travels to Saxland to press his suit, successfully, for the emperor's daughter, Lilja, surpassed in beauty only by Ísodd the Fair, and they produce three accomplished children: two sons and a daughter. The concluding allegation that there is a *mikil saga* ('great saga') about the sons of Kalegras (Vilhjálmsson 1954b: 145) implies that Tristram's line continued successfully. In becoming something of a dynastic chronicle, *Tristrams saga ok Ísoddar*, along with *Sigurðar saga þǫgla*, reflects vestiges of the genealogical interests integral to Icelandic prose narrative in general (Clunies Ross 1993).

Since marriage is not the consummation of idealized desire, as in *Erex saga* or *Ívens saga*, but the means of acquiring political and dynastic power, relations between the sexes in the independent *riddarasögur* are unencumbered by the notion of chivalry as a code of behaviour dedicated to the protection of the weak, the transformation of the sexual impulse into noble deeds, and the attempted resolution of the problems of allegiance posed by the 'courtly dilemma', those characteristic concerns of the twelfth-century *roman courtois* which are preserved, even in attenuated form, in the translated *riddarasögur*.

What, in fact, we get in many of the independent *riddarasögur*, and in a number of *fornaldarsögur*, is a complete reversal of the conventions of wooing in continental romance. Pivotal to this is the figure of the *meykóngr* ('maiden king'), a *riddarasögur* phenomenon related to the tradition of the 'maiden warrior' (*valkyrja*; *skjaldmær*) found in eddic and saga literature (Andersen 1993). The aggressive misogamy of those *meykóngur* sought in marriage by the hero frequently entails the reciprocal degradation of suitor and intended. The wooing of Se-dentiana, who becomes absolute ruler of France after Flóres and Blankiflúr take their monastic vows in *Sigurðar saga þǫgla*, by Hálfdan, Vilhjálmr and their eventually successful younger brother, Sigurðr, is typical. Not only, as Tulinius points out, do these unorthodox wooings comically transgress the clearly defined and socially highly sensitive boundaries of gender roles in medieval Iceland (1995: 158), they also flaunt the generic proprieties of chivalric romance, in which the hero may suffer humiliation in the name of love but never retaliates in kind. Lancelot's self-abasement, at Guinevere's bidding, in a tournament in Chrétien's *Lancelot* (Kibler 1981: ll. 636–706), for example, is a volun-tary public atonement for his momentary reluctance to sacrifice knightly honour by riding in a tumbrel on his quest to rescue her from her abductor, Meleagant. The calculatedly brutal and grotesque humi-liation of male by female, and vice versa, in the course of bride quests for *meykóngur* in *Klári saga*, *Dínus saga dramblāta*, and *Sigurðar saga þǫgla* is, on the other hand, part of a ritual of contest for sexual and political ascendancy. Similarly, in contrast to the promiscuous, emotionally uninvolved, but ever 'courtly' Gauvain of twelfth- and thirteenth-century French verse romance, Sigrgarðr, the hero of *Sigrgarðs saga frækna* ('the valiant') (*LMIR V*) is a heartless Casanova. The woman who eventually becomes his bride, another *meykóngr*, takes vengeance on his sexual arrogance and predacity by drugging him into insensibility in the pre-marital bed and subsequently mocking his alleged lack of virility.

Riddarasögur heroes are typically introduced as exemplars of royal and chivalric virtue, endowed with beauty, nobility, scholastic attain-ments, refined manners, and strength. Although these are traditional endowments of the romance hero, the subsequent conduct of *riddara-sögur* protagonists tends to belie all but the last of these attributes. Whereas the hero of *Vilmundar saga sjóðs*, son of King Ríkaðr of England, is a model of conscientiousness who rejects the offer of the throne when his father is abducted and instead sets out to find him, Viktor, heir to the throne of France in *Viktors saga ok Blávus*, is something of a *rex inutilis* who brings the country to ruin within three years of his succession. In another reversal of the standard gender roles in European chivalric narrative, Viktor's mother, the wisest of women (*hin uitrazta fru*) (*LMIR I*: 5), proves to have the talent for ruling which her son conspicuously lacks. When he abandons his kingdom without explanation – although the reader is left to infer that it is to replenish its coffers – she serves competently as regent. After twelve years of adventures, Viktor returns to France with treasure won from two berserkers. In the second part of *Viktors saga ok Blávus*, Viktor suffers humiliation at the hands of Fulgida, the *meykóngr* of India whom he eventually weds. The eponymous heroes of *Jarlmanns saga ok Hermanns* (*LMIR III*) are said to be without peer in their chivalric and scholarly qualifications; but Hermann, another king of France, is twice guilty of poor judgement. Unjustifiably untrusting and jealous of his loyal foster-brother, Jarlmann, Hermann misplaces his faith in a mysterious group of masons, who build him a splendid new hall in which to celebrate his marriage, and this leads directly to the kidnapping of his bride, Rikílát, on their wedding night. Distraught, Hermann takes to his bed and neglects his kingdom (*legzt hann j reckium. ok gaer eigi rikis sins*, p. 39). As Kalinke (1990: 177) comments, 'King Hermann appears not to be as *djúpvitr* ["profoundly wise"] as he had been portrayed at the outset.' In *Sigurðar saga fóts*, two kings, Ásmundr – who, like Hermann, thinks of marriage entirely in terms of its capacity to enhance his own prestige – and Sigurðr fail to live up to their exemplary reputations. Ásmundr is said to be wise and prudent (*uitr . . . ok raduandr*, *LMIR III*: 234) but, inexplicably, he surrenders his intended bride, Signý, to Sigurðr. Sigurðr, famed for his invincibility (p. 236), is defeated in single combat by Ásmundr.

Such discrepancies between introductory portrait and subsequent conduct raise the question of whether the *riddarasögur* should be regarded, collectively, as a 'reply' to the translated *riddarasögur* and their exemplary heroes, in the same way as a number of thirteenth-century French verse romances can be read as 'replies' to the perceived over-idealization of chivalric life in the twelfth-century *roman courtois* (Wolfzettel 1981). It has, for example, been argued (Schach 1960) in the case of the two Norse versions of the Tristan legend, which offer the only instance of 'companion' translated and independent *riddarasögur*, that the independent *Tristrams saga ok Ísoddar* deliberately burlesques the translated *Tristrams saga*. Whether or not this is so, some individual *riddarasögur* do seem to be engaged in a form of dialogue with each other. *Nitida saga*, for example, has been read as a 'reply' to *Klári saga*, whose avaricious and sadistic *meykóngr* protagonist is the antithesis of the exemplary Nitida; and *Jarlmanns saga ok Hermanns* to *Konráðs saga*, which are tales of foster-brothers. As Paul Bibire puts it: 'In both cases, the second saga takes the same situation and examines it from an opposed viewpoint, as if to provide a commentary upon the first saga' (1982: 70).

The late fifteenth-century Middle English *Squyr of Low Degre* provides an interesting text for comparison here. Hyperbolic in style and exotic in setting (Hungary), the *Squyr* is a self-consciously fictional narrative which makes explicit allusion to other romances. Its attitude towards chivalry is, arguably, more materialist than idealistic, and its treatment of gender roles unconventional. The heroine, the daughter of the king of Hungary, takes charge of the course of her squire–suitor's wooing – and, in the process, the course of the narrative – by drawing up the itinerary for his quest to prove his love and worthiness. Later, in an erotically ghoulish sequence, the naked princess picks up a corpse which she mistakes for the squire's, disembowels, embalms, inters, and keeps it in a marble casket beside her bed, and kisses it every day for seven years, until it turns to dust. The otherwise breathless pace of the action is frequently interrupted by descriptive catalogues, of exaggerated length, of the trappings of aristocratic life. The critically contentious issue of the work is whether the *Squyr* is (Kiernan 1973) or is not (Fewster 1987; Spearing 1993) a deliberate parody of Middle English verse romance. Either way, in its excesses of style and conduct, the work is generally closer in register to the *riddarasögur* than to other Middle English romances.

In medieval Iceland, as Bibire shrewdly observes (1982: 73), 'the true functions of European romance . . . [c]hivalric honour, tragic love, or transcendent religious understanding' remain the province of the *Íslendingasögur*. The ultimate concerns of the *riddarasögur*, which demonstrate a love for the showy externals of chivalry but little understanding of its ethos, are the establishment of royal dynasties and the extension of estates. In this materialistic 'might is right' context the chivalric and heroic ideal of altruism is transformed into an egocentric ethic, where the goal is domination: sexual, martial, and political.

Whereas the *fornaldarsögur* can be read as a form of 'cultural revitalization' of the legendary North (Mitchell 1991: 132–6) in the lean times of the fourteenth and fifteenth centuries, the *riddarasögur* of this period address political reality through the medium of fiction by relating the (often rapacious) deeds of foreign kings. Glauser (1983) makes a forceful case for a close ideological connection between *riddarasögur* and their original audiences in his argument that these sagas demonstrate the victory of 'courtly' over 'non-courtly' forces and show that stability and order are to be found under the rule of a powerful and capable king. If, however, we shift the perspective slightly and extend the timeframe, possibilities for ironic readings open up. Iceland became progressively more distanced from its offshore monarchs after 1319, when the joint Norwegian–Swedish monarchy was established and the king for the most part resided outside Norway, and after 1380, when a weakened Norway entered a union with Denmark. By the mid-fourteenth century, royal rule in Iceland had resulted in a situation whereby it was 'only a minor player within the Norwegian kingdom, and by mid-century (1349), the governorship . . . was routinely sold to the highest bidder . . . a system that invited abuse and led to severe taxation and economic oppression' (Mitchell 1991: 128). In addition to the element of comic discrepancy in the accounts of kingly conduct demonstrated in *Viktors saga ok Blávus*, *Jarlmanns saga ok Hermanns*, and *Sigurðar saga fóts*, the narrator's address in *Vilmundar saga viðutan* to those who pay taxes to the king is couched in less than dignified terms. In this underlying seam of irreverence towards kingly authority, the *riddarasögur* maintain a narrative custom established in many of the foreign episodes in the thirteenth-century *Íslendingasögur* and the short works known as *þættir*: the refusal of Icelanders to be overawed by the office of royalty.

Schlauch's concession that the *riddarasögur* might have served as an intellectual narcotic has its appeal, and Glauser's argument for the *riddarasögur* as fictional endorsements of the immediate post-commonwealth monarchy is powerfully sustained. The injection of the element of literary and political subversion for which I have argued merely adds a little piquancy to both viewpoints. From this third perspective, the *riddarasögur* offer both an Icelandic reading of monarchal power, with ludic overtones, and a sophisticated reading of chivalric romance which provides its audiences with wish-fulfilment and surface glamour but simultaneously encodes an underlying critique of the conventions of the genre. In so doing, the *riddarasögur* move beyond the traditional boundaries of medieval romance into the realm of literary experiment, to explore the process of composition and the fabric of fiction itself.

NOTES

1 The term *lygisögur* ('lying sagas') is occasionally used of the independent *riddarasögur*.
2 For a review of scholarly opinion, see Weber 1986: 415–20.

REFERENCES

Amory, Frederic 1984, 'Things Greek and the *Riddarasögur*,' *Speculum* 59: 509–23.
Andersen, Lise Præstgaard 1993, 'Maiden Warriors', in Pulsiano, Phillip and Wolf, Kirsten (eds.), *Medieval Scandinavia: an Encyclopedia*, New York and London: Garland, pp. 403–4.
Auerbach, Erich 1957 (trans. Trask, Willard), *Mimesis: the Representation of Reality in Western Literature*. Garden City, NY: Doubleday.
Barnes, Geraldine 1990, 'Authors, Dead and Alive, in Old Norse Fiction,' *Parergon*, n.s. 8(2): 5–22.
    1993, '*Riddarasögur* (TRANSLATED),' in Pulsiano, Phillip and Wolf, Kirsten (eds.), *Medieval Scandinavia: an Encyclopedia*, New York and London: Garland, pp. 531–3.
Bibire, Paul 1982, 'From *Riddarasaga* to *Lygisaga*: the Norse Response to Romance', in Boyer, Régis (ed.), *Les Sagas de Chevaliers: Riddarasögur*. Paris: Presses de l'Université de Paris-Sorbonne, pp. 55–74.
Bloch, Marc 1961 (trans. Manyon, L. A.), *Feudal Society*, II. Chicago: University of Chicago Press.
Butt, Ronald 1989, *A History of Parliament: the Middle Ages*. London: Constable.
Cederschiöld, Gustaf (ed.) 1907, *Clári saga (Klári saga)*. Altnordische Saga-Bibliothek, 12. Halle: Niemeyer.
Clunies Ross, Margaret 1993, 'The Development of Old Norse Textual Worlds:

Genealogical Structure as a Principle of Literary Organisation in Early Iceland', *Journal of English and Germanic Philology* 92: 372–85.

Crane, Susan 1986, *Insular Romance: Politics, Faith, and Culture in Anglo-Norman and Middle English Literature*. Berkeley, Los Angeles, London: University of California Press.

Dodsworth, J. B. 1962, English Résumé of *Ectors Saga*, Loth 1962–65 XX: 81–186.

Driscoll, Matthew 1997, *The Unwashed Daughters of Eve: the Production, Dissemination and Reception of Popular Literature in Post-Reformation Iceland*. Enfield Lock: Hisarlik.

Fewster, Carol 1987, *Traditionality and Genre in Middle English Romance*. Cambridge: D. S. Brewer.

Gelsinger, Bruce E. 1981, *Icelandic Enterprise: Commerce and Economy in the Middle Ages*. Columbia, SC: University of South Carolina Press.

Glauser, Jürg 1983, *Isländische Märchensagas: Studien zur Prosaliteratur im spätmittelalterlichen Island*. Basel and Frankfurt: Helbing and Lichtenhahn.

   1990, 'Romances, *Rímur*, Chapbooks: Problems of Popular Literature in the Late Medieval and Early Modern Scandinavia', *Parergon*, n.s. 8(2): 37–47.

Holland, Henry 1812, 'Preliminary Dissertation', in Mackenzie, Sir George Steuart, *Travels in the Island of Iceland During the Summer of the Year MDCCCX*. 2nd. edn. Edinburgh: Constable.

Hughes, Sean 1978, 'The Ideal of Kingship in the *Riddarasögur*', *Michigan Academician* 10: 321–36.

Hume, Kathryn 1980, 'From Saga to Romance: the Use of Monsters in Old Norse Literature', *Studies in Philology* 78: 1–25.

Jónsson, Guðni (ed.) 1954, *Hrólfs saga Gautrekssonar*. Fornaldarsögur Norður-landa, 4. Reykjavík: Íslendingasagnaútgáfan.

Kalinke, Marianne E. 1983, 'The Foreign Language Requirement in Medieval Icelandic Romance', *Modern Language Review* 78: 850–61.

   1990, *Bridal-Quest Romance in Medieval Iceland*. Islandica, 46. Ithaca and London: Cornell University Press.

Karlsson, Gunnar 1977, '*Goðar* and *Höfðingjar* in Medieval Iceland', *Saga-Book of the Viking Society* 19: 358–70.

Kibler, William W. (ed. and trans.) 1981, *Lancelot or, The Knight of the Cart (Le Chevalier de la Charrete)*. New York and London: Garland.

Kiernan, K. S. 1973, '*Undo Your Door* and the Order of Chivalry', *Studies in Philology* 70: 345–66.

Kölbing, Eugen (ed.) 1896, *Flóres Saga ok Blankiflúr*. Altnordische Saga-bibliothek, 5. Halle: Niemeyer.

Leach, Henry Goddard 1921, *Angevin Britain and Scandinavia*. Cambridge, Mass.: Harvard University Press.

Löfqvist, Karl-Erik 1935, *Om riddarväsen och frälse i nordisk medeltid*. Lund: Ohlsson.

Loth, Agnete (ed.) 1962–65, Late Medieval Romances I–V. Editiones Arnamagnænæ, series B, vols. XX–XXIV. Copenhagen: Munksgaard.

Mead, William Edward (ed.) 1904, *The Squyr of Low Degre: A Middle English Metrical Romance*. Boston: Ginn.

Meissner, Rudolph, (ed.) 1938, *Hirðskrá: Das norwegische Gefolgschaftsrecht*. Weimar: H. Böhlaus.

Mitchell, Stephen A. 1991, *Heroic Sagas and Ballads*. Ithaca and London: Cornell University Press.

Reichert, Hermann 1986, 'King Arthur's Round Table: Sociological Implications of its Literary Reception in Scandinavia', in Lindow, John, Lönnroth, Lars and Weber, Gerd Wolfgang (eds.), *Structure and Meaning in Old Norse Literature*. The Viking Collection, 3. Odense: Odense University Press, pp. 394–414.

Schach, Paul 1960, 'The *Saga af Tristram ok Isodd*: Summary or Satire?', *Modern Language Quarterly* 21: 336–52.

Schlauch, Margaret 1934, *Romance in Iceland*. Princeton and New York: Princeton University Press, American–Scandinavian Foundation.

Sigurðsson, Jón Viðar (1995), 'The Icelandic Aristocracy after the Fall of the Free State', *Scandinavian Journal of History* 20: 153–61.

Spearing, A. C. 1993, *The Medieval Poet as Voyeur: Looking and Listening in Medieval Love-Narratives*. Cambridge: Cambridge University Press.

Sveinsson, Einar Ól. 1964, '*Viktors saga ok Blávus*. Sources and Characteristics', in Kristjánsson, Jónas (ed.), *Viktors Saga ok Blávus*. Reykjavík: Handritastofnun Íslands, pp. cix–ccix.

Tómasson, Sverrir 1977, 'Hvenær var Tristrams saga snúið?', *Gripla* 2: 47–78.

1986, 'The "fræðisaga" of Adonias,' in Lindow, John, Lönnroth, Lars and Weber, Gerd Wolfgang (eds.), *Structure and Meaning in Old Norse Literature*. The Viking Collection, 3. Odense: Odense University Press, pp. 378–93.

Tulinius, Torfi 1995, *La <matière du Nord>: Sagas légendaires et fiction dans la littérature islandaise en prose du XIIIe siècle*. Paris: Presses de l'Université de Paris-Sorbonne.

Þórðarson, Matthías (ed.) 1935, *Eiríks saga rauða*. Íslenzk fornrit, IV. Reykjavík: Hið Íslenzka fornritafélag.

Van Nahl, Astrid 1981, *Originale Riddarasögur als Teil altnordischer Sagaliteratur*. Frankfurt: Peter Lang.

Vilhjálmsson, Bjarni (ed.) 1954a, *Riddarasögur III* [includes *Konráðs saga*, *Samsons saga fagra*]. Reykjavík: Íslendingasagnaútgáfan and Haukadalsútgáfan.

(ed.) 1954b, *Riddarasögur VI*. [includes *Tristrams saga ok Ísoddar*]. Reykjavík: Íslendingasagnaútgáfan and Haukadalsútgáfan.

Weber, Gerd Wolfgang 1986, 'The Decadence of Feudal Myth – Towards a Theory of *Riddarasaga* and Romance,' in Lindow, John, Lönnroth, Lars and Weber, Gerd Wolfgang (eds.), *Structure and Meaning in Old Norse Literature*. The Viking Collection, 3. Odense: Odense University Press, pp. 415–54.

Wolfzettel, Friedrich 1981, 'Arthurian Adventure or Quixotic "Struggle for Life"? A Reading of some Gauvain Romances in the First Half of the Thirteenth Century', in Varty, Kenneth (ed.), *An Arthurian Tapestry: Essays in Memory of Lewis Thorpe*. Glasgow: International Arthurian Society, pp. 203–13.

12

The Bible and biblical interpretation in medieval Iceland

IAN KIRBY

The Bible is of fundamental significance in the medieval period in Iceland. Substantial parts of it were translated, in some cases more than once; passages long and short are incorporated into almost all the religious literature that has survived. This chapter will survey both the translated materials and the quotations, commenting where appropriate on the individual authors' approach to their texts.

Although the conversion of Iceland to Christianity took place at the very end of the first millennium, the earliest known translation of the entire Bible into Icelandic is that of Guðbrandur Þorláksson, which dates from 1584. Four decades earlier, Oddur Gottskálksson had translated the New Testament, which Guðbrandur incorporated largely unchanged into his work. But we know of no medieval Icelandic version of either Testament. On the other hand, parts of the Old Testament, and the historical material in the Apocrypha, were translated in the medieval period, and it is highly probable that at any rate the Gospels were too, both individually and in the form of a single harmonized version of the texts of the four Evangelists, or Gospel harmony.

The Old Testament historical material has been edited under the title *Stjórn* by C. R. Unger (1862): but it is not a homogeneous work, and in fact this material, covering the period from the Creation to the Exile, has come down to us in three separate and distinct versions. Taking them in biblical order: the historical material from Genesis 1 to Exodus 18 (Unger 1862: 1–299) represents one version, the rest of the Pentateuch (300–49) a second, while the material from Joshua to the Exile

(349–654) reflects a third. But this biblical order is not that of the chronological order of the versions.

It seems likely that the earliest of these versions is the text of the latter part of the Pentateuch, from Exodus 19 to the end of Deuteronomy. This survives in only one manuscript, AM[1] 226 folio; it is written in a hand probably from the late fifteenth century, and the folios on which it is written were inserted into the manuscript to supply the gap in the Bible story. But examination of the text strongly suggests that the scribe copied this material from a very much older exemplar, going back at any rate to the first part of the thirteenth century (Kirby 1986: 56–60; Benediktsson 1994: 449–53). This version, which must certainly have comprised the Pentateuch and may also have included the post-Pentateuchal historical material, is a relatively straightforward translation of the Scriptures, though in much abbreviated form: while the historical material of this latter section of the Pentateuch is often translated quite closely, the passages concerned with Jewish law in Leviticus and Deuteronomy are heavily summarized. There is very little additional material. The author, most probably an Icelander, is unknown.

By contrast, the post-Pentateuchal material which survives does so in a version which is reflected in a number of manuscripts and manuscript fragments. The oldest of these manuscripts is AM 228 folio, generally dated to the first quarter of the fourteenth century; AM folios 226 and 227, from about the middle of the century, also have this version, except that the AM 226 text of the Book of Joshua is a different version, based not directly on the Vulgate but on Peter Comestor's *Historia Scholastica*. This version's treatment of the Bible text is like that of the first-mentioned version in so far as it keeps close to the Vulgate, and frequently omits or summarizes; but it also makes use of alliteration and shows a moderate amount of writing-up, with interpretative comment and the incorporation of material from other sources, notably the *Imago Mundi* and *Speculum Ecclesiae* of Honorius Augusto-dunensis and Richard of St Victor's *Liber Exceptionum*. There is furthermore a tendency towards a saga-style elaboration of Bible incidents, not unlike that found in Icelandic saga literature. It is most probable that this version also comprised a text of the Pentateuch: apart from the likelihood that a translator of the Old Testament material would not undertake to render the post-Pentateuchal material without first having translated the Pentateuch, there is extant a fragment of a translation of Genesis which, though it does not correspond with that in *Stjórn*, is closely comparable in a number of respects to the post-Pentateuchal translation.[2] The author of this version, again, is unknown; but Brandr Jónsson, Bishop of Hólar, translator of *Gyðinga saga* and *Alexanders saga*, has been considered a likely candidate.

Finally, the first part of the Pentateuch. This version appears in AM folios 226 and 227, and is also reflected in two small manuscript fragments. According to its Prologue it was produced at the command of Hákon Magnússon, King of Norway 1299–1319; and, although this attribution is called into question by some scholars, it seems certain that it was made in the late thirteenth or early fourteenth century.[3] It is in essence a compilation which takes its origin in three major sources and a number of minor ones, principally the Church Fathers, who are quoted sporadically. The major sources are mentioned in the Prologue: the Vulgate text, Peter Comestor's *Historia Scholastica*, and the *Speculum Historiale* of Vincent de Beauvais. The author, and his nationality, are unknown, though Bergr Sokkason, Abbot of Munkaþverá (in Iceland), has been suggested.

From the above, the following pattern of translation of the historical material of the Old Testament would seem to emerge. The earliest version, which was almost certainly in existence in the first part of the thirteenth century and may well be considerably older, was in the main a close translation of the Pentateuch and possibly the later books from Joshua to the Exile, with virtually no extraneous material. It emphasized the specifically historical material, omitting or summarizing the laws which make up a substantial part of the Pentateuch, and therefore functioned essentially as an account of the early history of the world as reflected in the Bible. This version was probably used by the author of the second version, which comprised the post-Pentateuchal books and almost certainly the Pentateuch, and was produced some time around the middle of the thirteenth century: he modified and augmented it by developing Bible incidents into full-scale narratives, perhaps under the influence of Icelandic saga literature, and including references to the Church Fathers and a number of other works, notably those of Honorius and Richard of St Victor. Finally, some time around 1300 another unknown author produced a new version of the Pentateuch as far as Exodus 18 in which, as in Comestor's *Historia Scholastica*, close translation went hand in hand with commentary, and very substantial use was made of other writers.

In addition to the Old Testament historical material, there is extant an Icelandic version of the Apocryphal books of the Maccabees, which also formed part of the Vulgate Bible, and which is part of a work generally entitled *Gyðinga saga*.[4] It is found in full in the manuscript AM 226 folio, and there are also a number of fragments, of which two, AM 655 quarto XXV and AM 238 folio XVII, are generally dated *c.* 1300 and are thus about half a century older than 226. At the end of the text in 226 it is stated that the author of the work was Brandr Jónsson, later Bishop of Hólar, and that he undertook the work at the request of Magnús of Norway, who was named king in 1257. Brandr died in 1264, so if the statement is reliable – and there seems no reason why it should not be – the work can be dated to this eight-year period. It is a composite work, of which the first part only is derived from the Books of the Maccabees, which are parallel, not consecutive, accounts of this period of Jewish history; and Brandr based his treatment on the first book, with additions from the second.

In analysing this treatment, we have to note that there are some differences between the overlapping parts of the fragments in 655 and 238 and the full text in 226. The 655 text in particular is close to the Bible, while the 226 text seems to have been modified and shortened somewhat; and since the 655 text was copied only a few decades after the death of Brandr it seems probable that it represents his work, while the 226 text has been adapted by a later reviser. However, the overall similarity of the texts suggests that the treatment of the Bible text by Brandr is in general reflected in 226. This treatment is akin to that of the post-Pentateuchal material in *Stjórn*: though close to the Bible text in general, there is a certain amount of saga-style rewriting, and alliteration is common.

Apart from the Old Testament and Apocryphal historical material, no part of the Bible has survived as translation proper into medieval Icelandic. However, the existence of one or more translations of the Book of Psalms, whether the Bible version or the liturgical Psalter, and of the Gospels, individually or as a harmony, can be deduced.

In the so-called Vienna Psalter, a thirteenth-century Latin Psalter which may have originated in England, there is an interlinear Icelandic gloss copied into it in the second half of the sixteenth century. Examination of this gloss has shown that it is not an *ad hoc* version, but rather part of a close Icelandic translation which is likely to date back to the last century before the Reformation.[5] We can therefore say with confidence that, as in other European countries, the Psalms were translated into the vernacular in the medieval period. Furthermore, although no other manuscript evidence has survived, it would seem probable that the Psalms were translated at an early date. Heiko Uecker has pointed out that the language of the Vienna Psalter gloss is, apart from modernizations, much earlier than the sixteenth century. Comparison of quotations from the Psalms extant in the religious literature from the thirteenth century shows a degree of similarity which is unlikely to be fortuitous (Kirby 1986: 92–3). And interest in the Psalms is attested, among other things, by the existence of a commentary on the Penitential Psalms, reflected in the early thirteenth-century fragments AM 655 quarto XXIII and 696 quarto XXIV (Kirby 1980: 93–4, 97–9).

As to the Gospels: towards the end of the thirteenth century, Grímr Hólmsteinsson compiled a saga of John the Baptist (see Unger 1874: 849–931). At the beginning of the letter to Abbot Rúnólfr of Ver which is prefixed to the saga, he reminds the abbot that he had asked him to take his material from the Gospels, as well as from homilies of the Church Fathers; and it is demonstrable that Grímr used an Icelandic translation of the Gospels as his source. Comparison between the text of Oddur Gottskálksson's New Testament of 1540 and that of Grímr shows a considerable degree of correspondence; and the only reasonable deduction from this is that both were using a medieval Icelandic translation which must thus have been in existence by the late thirteenth century (Kirby 1986: 100–1, 164–6). This does not mean, of course, that this or another translation was not in existence much earlier; but evidence of this is less certain. However, the fifteenth-century manuscript AM 672 quarto contains two Norse passages from different Gospels which were apparently inserted into the manuscript to fill vacant space at two points: one tells the Parable of the Sower in the version of Luke (chapter 8), the other the story of Thomas's doubts and post-Resurrection experience as recorded at John 20.24–31 (Kirby 1976: 242, second passage, and 321–3). Such insertions may perhaps suggest a degree of familiarity with Norse gospels.

In the Middle Ages, then, parts of the Bible were directly translated into Icelandic. But the Bible was also translated indirectly in various ways. Thus, it has been demonstrated that, apart from translations of individual gospels, Tatian's *Diatessaron* was also known and used in Iceland in the Middle Ages (van Arkel and Quispel 1978); and there are traces of the use of a gospel harmony in Bible quotations in Icelandic texts. One such harmonization is incorporated into the 'Old Icelandic Homily Book' (Stock. Perg. quarto, no. 15), which is, with the 'Old Norwegian Homily Book' (AM 619 quarto), one of the two oldest Norse sermon collections (*c.* 1200): it takes the form of a Passion History; it is based on John's Gospel, with additions from the synoptics; and it is almost certainly translated from an existing Latin history (see Kirby 1980: 59–60).

At the end of the twelfth century there appeared one of the most influential works of the entire Middle Ages, Peter Comestor's *Historia Scholastica*. This is a Bible text with substantial commentary: and there are abundant traces of its use in Icelandic texts from the thirteenth century onwards. These include evidence of the translation of Comestor's Bible text. Mention has already been made of the substitution in AM 226 folio of a Comestor-based text of the Book of Joshua, contrasting with the Vulgate-based text of AM 227 folio. In addition, Brandr Jónsson seems to have used Comestor for the second part of *Gyðinga saga*; and there is a Norwegian fragment extant, AM 1056 quarto IV, which has a text related to I Samuel 22.20–3 but which is taken from the Comestor Bible account. All these texts use the Comestor Bible account, but largely omit his commentaries.[6]

From the above survey there would seem to emerge a pattern of translation practice in the Christian Middle Ages in Iceland. In the first place, no attempt seems to have been made to produce a translation of the entire Bible. However, in the period before about 1200 relatively straightforward translations appear to have been made of certain parts of the Bible: of these, part of the Pentateuch survives, and we can reasonably deduce the existence of a translation of the remainder of the Pentateuch, the post-Pentateuchal historical books of the Old Testament, the Book of Psalms, and the Gospels. This is readily explained: in the first two centuries after the Christianization of the country the young Church of Iceland would have needed a vernacular version of the essential texts concerning the biblical history of the world, the Gospel story, and the Psalms, which play a significant part in the liturgy of the church. And this pattern is comparable with that of other countries: in England, France and Germany these are also the parts of the Bible which figure most prominently in early translation (Kirby 1986: 8–16).

. Around the middle of the thirteenth century, Brandr Jónsson translated the Apocryphal historical material, and perhaps also the Old Testament historical material. This latter seems to have been an adaptation of the older translation; its most distinctive feature is that it contemporized the older work as and where possible along the lines of the then current saga literature of Iceland. Thus, in paragraph 230 (Unger 1862: 458–9), the episode of David's fight with the bear and the lion, to which he alludes in his conversation with Saul in I Samuel 17, is developed into a full-scale narrative and incorporated into the initial description of David in I Samuel 16. The purpose of this, again, seems clear: it is to provide an account which, while remaining true to the essential Bible story, will appeal to the people of the time, who, as Grímr Hólmsteinsson was to comment in his letter to Abbot Rúnólfr (Unger 1874: 849) were no doubt far more interested in *skröksögur*, 'fables', than the noble deeds of the servants of God. In this respect he was following in the footsteps of the Anglo-Saxon poet Cædmon and his imitators, and was succeeded in the twentieth century by Dorothy Sayers (*The Man Born to be King*), 'Godspell', and 'Jesus Christ Superstar'.

In contrast with what has gone before, the youngest, partial, translation of the Old Testament historical material is directed, we are informed in the Prologue (Unger 1862: 2), at the court of Hákon Magnússon, King of Norway. It is a learned work, reflecting the contemporary tendency to use works such as *Historia Scholastica* to augment the Bible story, but translated into Norse for the benefit of those at court who could not understand Latin. In this respect it is comparable with the later sagas of the apostles and saints: and as with the earlier materials, it reflects the needs and manners of its time.

In addition to translation from the Bible, a very considerable amount of citation of Bible passages, both long and short, is to be found in medieval Icelandic literature. Some of the religious literature extant, principally the homiletic material, makes occasional use of Bible quotation, frequently as an authority to justify the argument of the work; some of it, principally the hagiographical material, takes extracts from the New Testament as the basis of its accounts of, in particular, the lives of the apostles. Such materials are found throughout the medieval period. However, it must be borne in mind that in many cases the quotation is simply translated from a Latin text which is itself quoted from the Bible; and in consequence such quotations do not shed significant light on Icelandic practice. Attention must therefore be primarily focussed on works which are, or may be, essentially Icelandic in origin, whether or not they made use of Latin source material in the compilation.

The two earliest surviving manuscript fragments in Icelandic contain religious material: the first, AM 732a quarto VII, is an Easter Table compiled between 1121 and 1139, while the second, AM 237a folio, which is generally dated *c.* 1150, contains the Stave Church homily and part of a sermon which includes material from the Norse translation of Gregory's thirty-fourth homily. Both the texts in 237a contain quotations from the Bible, the latter at least at second hand. The Stave Church homily seems to be an original Norse composition, though it is likely to have made use of earlier Latin texts,[7] and it is also found, in similar form, in the Icelandic and Norwegian Homily Books. In the 237a version there are three quotations, one from John's Gospel, two from the Psalms, and also a loose reference relating to a verse in Paul's first epistle to the Corinthians. The quotations correspond quite closely to the versions in the other texts; but the homily books lack the reference from I Corinthians. Conversely, there is one quotation in the Icelandic homily book, Ephesians 2.20, which does not appear in the other texts. It would seem, then, that the 237a version had already undergone a degree of re-working in relation to the original Norse version, and that this re-working extended to the quotations from the Bible. The sermon fragment in 237a corresponds closely to the text of a sermon for Michael the Archangel's day, found in the Norwegian homily book; part of this sermon is taken from a Norse text of Gregory's thirty-fourth homily, which like some of the other homilies of Gregory is found in the early thirteenth-century manuscript AM 677 quarto. Again, therefore, 237a has a text which suggests that some of this homiletic material was in existence well before 1150, illustrating as it does the re-utilization and adaptation of source material, whether from the Bible, Gregory's homilies or other texts, which is characteristic of the medieval period in Iceland. In this connection, it may be noted that a priest was expected to know *þyding gudspialla* (so that he could preach from this material, apparently a Norse version of the Gospels) . . . *ok omílíur Gregorij* ('the meaning of the gospels . . . and the homilies of Gregory') (Kolsrud 1952: 110).

Hagiographical material is also found at an early date, for AM 655 quarto IX, a Norwegian manuscript fragment generally dated to the late twelfth century, contains passages from a version of the saga of the apostle Matthew and of the lives of the saints Blasius and Placidus. The Matthew fragment is a somewhat corrupt text of a version of the saga also found in AM 645 quarto, considered to date from the first half of the thirteenth century. All three fragments, like the 237a fragment discussed above, have brief quotations only. However, the AM 645 quarto text has survived in a much more substantial form, and it includes a version of the saga of Paul which is little more than a slightly written-up treatment of the apostle's life as it appears in the Acts of the Apostles (Unger 1874: 216–36; Kirby 1980: 25). It keeps quite close to the Bible text in general, simplifying and summarizing on occasion; one special feature is that, whereas in the latter part of the Biblical Acts account the third-person narrative gives way to a first-person account, the 645 text keeps the third person throughout. Furthermore, there is very little additional material. This version is thus comparable with the treatment of the earliest translation of the Old Testament historical material. Later versions of the lives of the apostles, like later versions of the Old Testament material, are very different in these respects. Thus, the second saga of Paul (Unger 1874: 236–79; Unger 1877: 287–309; Kirby 1980: 25–6, 49) does not seem to depend on the 645 account, but takes the form of a complete life of the apostle, making use of a number of Latin sources apart from the Vulgate Acts, principally Comestor. A similar procedure is found in the saga of Stephen, where the author uses now the Bible text, now Comestor, as he recounts the story of the saint's martyrdom on the basis of chapters 6 and 7 of the Acts of the Apostles.

This approach is closely comparable to that in the youngest version of the Old Testament historical material.

One substantial corpus of material which is uncontestably Icelandic is the sagas of the bishops of Iceland[8] – though even here the earliest known life of Jón of Hólar was written in Latin by Gunnlaugr Leifsson early in the thirteenth century, and fragments of other Latin texts are extant. There are in all a hundred or so Bible quotations or references in this material; but neither the distribution of the biblical matter nor the practice of the individual authors is uniform. Thus, the saga of Jón of Hólar contains a handful of accurate biblical quotations, each of which is accompanied by the corresponding Latin quotation, and a few loose references; the same is largely true of the sagas of Árni and Laurentius, except that they do not as a rule have an accompanying Latin text,[9] and the *Miðsaga* ('Middle Saga') of Guðmundr. By contrast, the version of the life of Guðmundr by Abbot Arngrímr of Þingeyrar has a few close quotations from the Bible, some of which reflect those in the *Miðsaga*, but it also has a considerable number of references and Latin quotations.

The most substantial representation of biblical material in the sagas of the bishops of Iceland is to be found in the life of Þorlákr. The two versions printed in *Biskupa sögur* are largely similar, and this is true of the biblical material, though occasionally a quotation or reference is found only in one of the texts. There are more than forty quotations and references in all. These are taken principally from the Psalms (a dozen), the Gospels (a score), and the New Testament Epistles (ten); but there are isolated quotations from Proverbs, Ecclesiastes and Ezekiel in the Old Testament, and from the Acts of the Apostles and the Book of Revelation in the New. Most of the quotations are accurate and close to the Bible; on no occasion is the Latin given in parallel, even though fragments of Latin material on Þorlákr are extant.[10]

The wide variety of treatment of Biblical matter in the sagas of individual bishops is reflected in the Icelandic religious literature as a whole. Some of the extant works, in many cases following and/or citing their source text, quote closely from the Bible, identifying with greater or less preciseness the location of the verse or verses quoted; others limit themselves to general references to Bible incidents or teachings. As indicated above, some works limit themselves almost exclusively to single-verse quotations; others, notably the sagas of the apostles and saints' lives, cite longer passages from the Gospels and the Acts of the Apostles *in extenso*. Although well over half the quotations and references in the Icelandic religious literature can be traced to the book of Psalms and the first five books of the New Testament, all but two of the New Testament books are represented in this literature, and most of the Old Testament books as well. And although there is much variety of treatment, a high proportion of the quotations show verbatim correspondence with the Latin source text, whether it is cited or not. The knowledge and understanding of the Bible shown by medieval Icelandic scholars is impressively high.

This last point is well illustrated by the overall accuracy of the earliest known translation of the Pentateuch, discussed at the beginning of this chapter. Comparison of, for instance, the nineteenth chapter of Exodus in the Latin Vulgate and in the Icelandic text as at *Stjórn* 300 shows total understanding on the part of the translator: the only differences result from his tendency to simplify and shorten the Latin text somewhat, principally to improve the narrative flow. It is true that he does not know all the complex terminology of later chapters, and often retains Latin words; and it is also true that there are occasional errors of translation.[11] But these are minor matters, when measured against the remarkably high degree of understanding of the Bible text shown in this version as a whole.

Other kinds of modification, and other reasons for modifying the Bible text, are now and then to be found in the work of other translators. Thus, a quotation from one of the gospels may be modified or expanded from a parallel quotation in another gospel.[12] The author of the post-Pentateuchal material in *Stjórn* uses the books of Chronicles to augment the content of his text from the books of the Kings, just as, in *Gyðinga saga*, Brandr Jónsson uses the Second Book of the Maccabees to augment his treatment of the First. Such additions are made with the intention of adding information. But occasionally the author may have other purposes.

In the saga of the apostle James there is a series of quotations, principally from the Book of Psalms, which are translated carefully from the Latin source text; but in the double saga of John and James the author has modified one of these so as to give it a New Testament emphasis. In Abdias's Apostolic History, an account is given of James's unsuccessful attempt to defend himself against the Jews by citing Old Testament passages to justify Christianity from their scriptures. Psalm 12.5 is one such passage; in Abdias, as in the Vulgate, it reads: *Propter miseriam inopum, et gemitum pauperum, nunc exsurgam, dicit Dominus.* The earliest Icelandic version is contained in AM 645 quarto, which reads: *Fyr sut aumra oc fyr vesolþ valaþra mun ec up risa qvaþ drottenn*, 'Because of the grief of the sorrowful and the misery of the poor I will rise up, said the Lord' (Unger 1874: 527); the other versions are essentially similar. But in John and James the author begins the translation as follows: *Af dauða mun ek risa, segir drottinn*, ('From death shall I rise up, says the Lord' (Unger 1874: 580)), thus transforming the passage into a reference to the Resurrection.

Such a modification does not do major violence to the Latin source text, for *exsurgam* can imply resurrection; but very occasionally an author can be shown to have misrepresented the Bible text. This is true of the author of the first saga of John the Baptist, who modifies a Gospel quotation considerably to defend the reputation of the hero of the story. At Matthew 11.11, the Vulgate text, citing the words of Jesus, reads: *Amen dico vobis, non surrexit inter natos mulierum maior Ioanne Baptista; qui autem minor est in regno caelorum, maior est illo* ('I tell you truly, among those born of women there has not arisen a greater man than John the Baptist; however, the one who is less in the kingdom of Heaven is greater than he'). In dealing with this verse at Unger 1874: 846 lines 15–23, the author of the first saga manages to turn this into a high commendation of John: *eigi reis ædri madr up Joani baptista fæddr fra karli oc konu, sa einn var ædri i himna riki, er yngri var her i heimi* ('there has not risen up a greater man than John the Baptist born of man and woman; He alone was greater in the kingdom of Heaven, who was younger here in this world').[13] Likewise, the author of the first of the Peter sagas tones down very considerably the force of Jesus's rebuke to Peter at Matthew 16.23, omitting any reference to Satan; a similar omission is found in the Andrew sagas.[14] And in the account of the appearance of the angel to Mary, at Luke 1.34 the words *quoniam virum non cognosco* ('because I do not know a man'), are further euphemized in the Bartholomew *passio* and in the Martha and Mary homily.[15]

But these are all exceptional cases. What stands out in the Icelandic religious literature is that its authors tend to quote frequently and widely from the Bible; that in the large majority of cases they quote accurately; that when they identify the quotations they usually do so correctly; that even when they are summarizing or embellishing the narrative they usually record with great care the actual words of Jesus and other speakers as they appear in the Bible; and that they have a high degree of respect for their sources, including the Bible, translating them with care and understanding.

NOTES

1 This abbreviation before a manuscript reference indicates that the manuscript in question belonged to the collection of Árni Magnússon, a seventeenth-century Icelandic scholar, who formed a major collection of Icelandic manuscripts, which he removed for safe keeping from Iceland to Copenhagen. These remained in Denmark until the second half of the twentieth century; most have now been returned to Iceland's Stofnun Árna Magnússonar, except for a small number that remain at the Arnamagnæan Institute, University of Copenhagen.

2 The fragment, AM 238 fol. XIX, makes use of *Imago Mundi*, as does this version, and like it shows a saga-style elaboration of the Bible text (Kirby 1986: 64, 69–71).

3 The use in this version of *Speculum Historiale* (completed *c*. 1254) and the ms. dates (*c*. 1350–60) are the available *termini*.

4 That is, a history of the Jews. On this, see Kirby 1986: 75–9, and the most recent edition of this work, Wolf 1995.

5 On this paragraph, see in particular Uecker 1980, especially pp. lxxxv f., and Kirby 1986: 81–2 and 92.

6 See Kirby 1986: 104–6 and the works cited there.

7 The homily was composed for the dedication festival of a distinctively Scandinavian wooden church; in it, the different parts of the church, and its contents, are enumerated and their spiritual significance explained. On this, see Turville-Petre 1972: ch. 6.

8 These sagas were edited in *Biskupa sögur* I (1858) and II (1878) by Jón Sigurðsson and Guðbrandur Vigfússon. More recent editions of some of the sagas have been published. References in this chapter are given to the 1858–78 edition, cited by volume and page numbers.

9 There is one exception to this, the second of the two quotations in Laurentius.

10 See *Biskupa sögur* (Sigurðsson and Vigfússon) I: 394–404 and Benediktsson 1969. There is no biblical matter in the Latin fragments.

11 See for instance those quoted at Kirby 1986: 59. There are also a fair number of errors in the text as it has come down to us; but these are probably due, in the main, to the copyist (see Kirby 1986: 57 and n. 30).

12 On some occasions, such a modification may indicate the use of a harmonized gospel text, rather than an *ad hoc* addition by the Icelandic translator.

13 Grímr Hólmsteinsson does not do this: in the second saga he translates the latter part of the verse correctly (see Unger 1874: 907, line 33).

14 See, respectively, Unger 1874: 6, lines 22–3 and 350, line 19.

15 These are contained, respectively, in the early ms. AM 645 quarto *(þviat ec etlag eige manne at giftasc*, 'because I do not intend to be married to a man'; see Unger 1874: 759, line 19), and in the late ms. AM 624 quarto *(því at eg em eigi manni gift*, 'because I am not married'; see Bjarnarson 1878: 156, line 5).

REFERENCES

Arkel, Andrea van and Quispel, Gilles 1978, 'The Diatessaron in Iceland and Norway', *Vigiliae Christianae* 32: 214–15.

Benediktsson, Jakob 1969, 'Brot úr Þorláksleysi', in Benediktsson, Jakob, Samsonarson, Jón, Kristjánsson, Jónas, Halldórsson, Ólafur and Karlsson, Stefán (eds.), *Afmælisrit Jóns Helgasonar. 30 júní 1969*. Reykjavík: Heimskringla, pp. 98–108.

1994, 'Fáein orð um Stjórn II', in Sigurðsson, Gísli, Kvaran, Guðrun and Steingrímsson, Sigurgeir (eds.), *Sagnaþing helgað Jónasi Kristjánssyni sjötugum 10. apríl 1994*. 2 vols. Reykjavík: Hið íslenzka bókmenntafélag, II, pp. 449–53.

Bjarnarson, Þorvaldur (ed.) 1878, *Leifar fornra kristinna fræða íslenzkra*. Copenhagen: Hagerup.

Kirby, Ian J. 1976, *Biblical Quotation in Old Icelandic–Norwegian Religious Literature*. I: *Text*. Rit, 9. Reykjavík: Stofnun Árna Magnússonar á Islandi.

1980, *Biblical Quotation in Old Icelandic–Norwegian Religious Literature*, II: *Introduction*. Rit, 10. Reykjavík: Stofnun Árna Magnússonar á Islandi.

1986, *Bible Translation in Old Norse*. Université de Lausanne: Publications de la Faculté des Lettres, XXVII. Geneva: Droz.

Kolsrud, Oluf (ed.) 1952, *Messuskýringar. Liturgisk symbolik frå den norsk–islandske kyrkja i millomalderen*. Norsk historisk kjeldeskrift-institutt, Skrifter, 57(1). Oslo: Dybwad.

Sigurðsson, Jón and Vigfússon, Guðbrandur (eds.) 1858–78, *Biskupa sögur*. 2 vols. Copenhagen: Møller.

Turville-Petre, Gabriel 1972, *Nine Norse Studies*. London: Viking Society for Northern Research.

Uecker, Heiko (ed.) 1980, *Der Wiener Psalter. Cod. Vind. 2713*. Editiones Arnamagnæanæ, Series B, 27. Copenhagen: Reitzel.

The Bible and biblical interpretation

Unger, C. R. (ed.) 1862, *Stjorn. Gammelnorsk bibelhistorie fra verdens skabelse til det babyloniske fangenskab.* Christiania (Oslo): Feilberg and Landmark.

(ed.) 1874, *Postola sögur. Legendariske fortællinger om apostlernes liv deres kamp for kristendommens udbredelse samt deres martyrdød.* Christiania (Oslo): Bentzen.

(ed.) 1877, *Heilagra manna søgur. Fortællinger og legender om hellige mænd og kvinder,* II. Christiania (Oslo): Bentzen.

Wolf, Kirsten (ed.) 1995, *Gyðinga saga.* Rit, 42. Reykjavík: Stofnun Árna Magnússonar á Íslandi.

13

Sagas of saints[1]

MARGARET CORMACK

In the name of our Saviour Lord Jesus Christ, here begins a little booklet of St Michael the Archangel, written and composed for the sole purpose that it always be read on Michael's feast-day for the enjoyment of the parishioners, especially in those places where he is patron, so that his remembrance will become all the sweeter in the thoughts of righteous men, the better known his great excellence becomes to everyone by means of this little work. (Prologue to *Michaels saga* by Bergr Sokkason)[2]

The social context of the literature about saints – hagiography, *heilagra manna sögur* – is primarily a religious one. The saints were the heroes of the Church, whose lives were illustrations of Christian perfection, and whose powers of intercession could be invoked in any conceivable emergency. Stories of the lives and miracles of holy men and women provided instruction and hope for both educated and illiterate believers. Vernacular narratives about saints, like those with secular subject matter, are known as sagas. Saints' sagas constitute the main body of Icelandic hagiography. There is in addition a limited amount of vernacular poetry, but only scattered fragments of Latin texts have survived.

The earliest sagas of saints were translations of Latin *vitae* made in the twelfth century.[3] The years around 1200 saw the composition and translation of *vitae* and miracles of two native saints, Bishop Þorlákr Þórhallsson of Skálholt and Bishop Jón Ǫgmundarson of Hólar, whose cults developed at that time. Towards the end of the thirteenth and throughout the fourteenth century, a change in literary fashion led to the revision of existing works and the composition of new ones in an ornate language called the 'florid style'; the first half of the fourteenth century saw determined efforts to promote the sanctity of another Icelander, Bishop Guðmundr Arason of Hólar. By 1400, the *terminus ante quem* of this volume, sagas in a variety of styles described the lives and miracles of over sixty saints, including the three bishops.[4]

The average Icelander would have been familiar with saints from two main sources: the major feast days of the liturgical calendar[5] and the dedication of, and images in, local churches. It is clear from church inventories (*máldagar*)[6] that the prologue to *Michaels saga* quoted above describes a common attitude: it was considered desirable for a church to own a copy of the life of its patron saint, just as the church should, if possible, display a statue of him or her. Both Latin *vitae* and vernacular sagas are mentioned in the inventories; sometimes a church would have one of each. A number of these works have survived. *Codex Scardensis*, a collection of sagas about the apostles from the church at Skarð, is probably the best known. *Helgastaðarbók* (Stock. Perg. quarto no. 16, recently published in facsimile), which contains the saga of St Nicholas, the patron saint of the church at Helgastaðir, is impressive for its copious illustrations. AM 649a quarto, a fourteenth-century manuscript from the church of John the Evangelist at Hof in Vatnsdalr, contains the saga of that saint followed by a brief list of Icelanders who were especially devoted to him.[7] In addition to the sagas of their patron saints, churches often owned volumes of saints' lives; unfortunately for scholars, the contents of such volumes are rarely listed in the *máldagar*. Several surviving fragments containing material arranged according to the Icelandic liturgical year were presumably intended to provide readings for the obligatory feasts listed in *Grágás*.

Most of the extant sagas concern saints with feast days found in Icelandic liturgical calendars. The existence of a feast day (or of a saga) did not, however, guarantee a significant *cultus*. While it is impossible to guess how many saints' sagas were lost after the Protestant Reformation, the saints whose sagas have been preserved in surviving manuscripts correspond well with those who appear to have been popular, judging by church contents recorded in the *máldagar*. The Life and Miracles of the Virgin Mary (*Maríu saga*) tops the list with fragments of thirty-seven manuscripts, and the apostles and John the Baptist are well represented. Of other universal saints, the sagas of Martin, Nicholas and Thomas à Becket exist in multiple versions, as do those of female saints such as Agatha and Catherine. From Scandinavia, St Óláfr, the Norwegian king and martyr (d. 1030), and the first Icelandic saint, Þorlákr, are met frequently both as patrons of churches and as subjects of sagas.[8]

The copying of manuscripts would presumably have taken place at ecclesiastical centres where the clergy had the time and resources for such activity. Ólafur Halldórsson (1966) has identified a group of manuscripts (including *Codex Scardensis*) produced at the monastery at Helgafell in western Iceland. Priests with ability and leisure no doubt made books for themselves and others as described in *Jóns saga* (Sigurðsson and Vigfússon 1858–78 (henceforth *BS*) I: 175). There are indications that the diocese of Hólar was especially productive of hagiographic literature. Although most saints' sagas, like secular ones, are anonymous, some translators are known by name; of those whose ecclesiastical affiliations are also known, the majority are associated with the northern quarter, in particular with the monasteries at Þingeyrar and Munkaþverá. Church *máldagar* from the diocese record twice as many saints' sagas as those from Skálholt, even though Hólar had only a third as many churches. Inefficient record-keeping by the bishops of Skálholt would hardly account for the discrepancy. There may have been a demand for such sagas outside Iceland; Karlsson (1979) has pointed out that vernacular saints' lives are well represented among the fragments of medieval manuscripts preserved in Norway.

Lay reception of saints' lives is difficult to assess. Evidence for at least a superficial familiarity with hagiographic themes is abundant. The miracles performed by the saints in Iceland resemble those recorded abroad, and motifs from saints' lives often appear in secular literature. However, the significance of this evidence is unclear. While borrowings such as those discussed by Boyer (1973) clearly indicate that authors of secular sagas were familiar with the *Dialogues* of Gregory the Great, other parallels may represent folklore motifs which could have been independently derived from oral tradition by both secular and religious authors (Foote 1994; Cormack 1994b).

Evidence for ownership of saints' sagas by individuals rather than churches is very limited. Occasionally an inventory will inform us that a saga was a gift to the church: in the fourteenth century the priest Ásgrímr Guðbjartsson gave the church at Bægisá a saga of John the

Baptist (*Diplomatarium Islandicum Íslenzkt fornbréfasafn* (henceforth *DI*) III: 519), and an otherwise unknown Skallagrímr donated a saga of St Nicholas to the church at Selárdalr (*DI* III: 92; *DI* IV: 148). We cannot, however, know whether these sagas were once part of the donors' private libraries; they may have been specially commissioned for these churches, perhaps as part of a payment owed by the donor. Donors might, however, have a vested interest in their gifts. A notice in *Codex Scardensis* (*DI* III: 658) states that the owner of Skarð had donated the manuscript to the church there in 1401. A slightly different version of the inventory[9] notes that the donation was limited: the church and the farmer at Skarð were each to own half-shares in the manuscript. This arrangement was meant to ensure that the manuscript would remain at Skarð.

The single reference to the reading of a saint's saga at the request of a layman contains no indication of the saga's owner. We are told that, a few nights before his death, Þorgils skarði was asked what sort of entertainment he would like; when he learned that a saga of Thomas à Becket was available, he chose to have it read to him, *því at hann elskaði hann framar en aðra helga menn* (Jóhannesson 1946 (*St*) II: 218; Kålund 1906–11 (K) II: 295), 'because he loved [Thomas] more than other saints'. The episode itself is clearly tendentious; a comment by Þorgils on the beauty of Becket's martyrdom prefigures his own death on the following day. That his interest in the story of the English martyr is exceptional is suggested by the prologue to *Jóns saga baptista*, in which the translator, Grímr Holmsteinsson, comments that foolish people *allt þickir þat langt, er fra Cristz kǫppum er sagt, ok skemtaz framarr med skrǫksǫgur* (Unger 1874: 849), 'think everything boring that is told of Christ's heroes, and would rather be entertained with fables'.

Although translations may have been intended primarily for the edification of the laity, the clergy benefited as well. Not all Icelandic priests were competent in Latin, and when Abbot Runólfr Sigmundarson of Þykkvabær monastery (d. 1307) requested a saga of John the Baptist which was to include glosses from the Fathers (Unger 1874: 849), he was presumably concerned with the needs of his own monks.

The cult of saints was a living entity which developed in the course of time; its growth was often directed by considerations of local pride and politics. St Óláfr, whose relics rested in Niðaróss (modern Trondheim), was the first and most important Scandinavian saint. That an Icelandic priest and poet, Einarr Skúlason, composed the poem *Geisli* in honour of the royal martyr on the occasion of the establishment of an archdiocese in Niðaróss in 1152 or 1153 serves to remind us that Niðaróss was the town in Norway to which Iceland had closest ties. Icelanders must have rejoiced that the ecclesiastical centre of the Norse–Atlantic territories was now recognized as a distinct unit in the greater world of Christendom.

The islanders would, however, have been aware that other parts of the new archdiocese had their own saints. The relics of Earl Magnús of Orkney (d. 1115) had been translated twenty years after his death, and the sanctity of the man responsible, Earl Rǫgnvaldr (d. 1158), was proclaimed in 1192. St Sunnifa had been translated from Selja to the cathedral of Bergen in 1170. Iceland, however, had no local saint. If this were not adequate grounds for an inferiority complex, Icelanders who relied on the power of St Óláfr in heaven may soon have wished to distance themselves from his representative on earth. This role was claimed by both the king of Norway and the archbishop of Niðaróss; during the last decades of the twelfth century, the archbishop displayed a regrettable tendency to insist that Icelanders conform to the ways of the Universal Church. Considerations such as these may have led two Icelandic monks to promote the sanctity of another Norwegian king, Óláfr Tryggvason, who had been responsible for the adoption of Christianity in Iceland fifteen years *before* the reign of St Óláfr.

In the first Icelandic attempt at original hagiography, Oddr Snorrason, a monk at Þingeyrar, composed a Latin life of Óláfr Tryggvason, traditionally dated *c.* 1190. Some time thereafter Gunnlaugr Leifsson of the same monastery (d. 1219) composed another *vita*. Neither work has survived; Oddr's work and some passages of Gunnlaugr's are known only from translations, which have been modified to an unknown extent. The hagiographic intent is clear, however. Óláfr Tryggvason's infancy is modelled on that of Christ, various episodes of his life are borrowed from the *Dialogues* of Gregory the Great, and the king vanishes in a beam of heavenly light in the same way as John the Evangelist (Jónsson 1932 (henceforth *OTS*) 230; Unger 1874: 454). We know nothing of the contemporary reception of the works of Oddr and Gunnlaugr, except that they were not sufficient to induce formal veneration of Óláfr. Possibly this was because he lacked two essential requirements for the establishment of a new cult: relics and miracles.

The next Icelandic attempt to acquire a local saint focussed on a very different type of candidate. In 1197, visions were reported concerning Þorlákr Þórhallsson, the recently deceased bishop of Skálholt. Rumours of his sanctity produced a spate of miracles that resulted in his translation on 20 July 1198. Visions and miracles continued to be reported, and numerous churches were dedicated to him. The spectacular success of his cult inspired the promotion of a saint for the northern diocese: Jón Ǫgmundarson, first bishop of Hólar. Although Jón never attained the popularity of Þorlákr, enough miracles were recorded to justify his translation on 3 March 1200. Both cults originated in the diocese of Hólar, where they were promoted by Bishop Brandr Sæmundarson and the priest and future bishop, Guðmundr Arason. Abbot Karl Jónsson of Þingeyrar monastery also appears to have been active on behalf of Þorlákr.

In the middle of the thirteenth century there was a renewed focus on St Óláfr. During the harsh winter of 1261, Earl Gizurr Þorvaldsson proposed a vow, which was confirmed by the populace and by the (Norwegian) bishop of Skálholt, promising to add a fast on bread and water before the saint's feast,[10] thus transforming *Ólafsmessa* into one of the highest holy days. The decision to honour a Norwegian rather than an Icelandic saint reflected the current political tendency and anticipated the acceptance by Iceland of Norwegian sovereignty a few years later.

The cult of the third Icelandic saint dates from the next century and was a Norwegian initiative. At the suggestion of King Hákon, Bishop Auðunn Þorbergsson had the bones of Guðmundr Arason placed in a prominent location in the cathedral in 1315, the year after his arrival at Hólar. By promoting the sanctity of Guðmundr and trying, less successfully, to revive interest in Jón, Auðunn may have been attempting to win popular support in his diocese and increase the prestige of his cathedral. Another Norwegian bishop, Ormr Ásláksson, repeated the process, exhuming, and washing Guðmundr's bones in 1344.

Most of these developments sparked literary activity. Dietrich Hofmann (1981) has argued that, in addition to his life of Óláfr

Tryggvason, Oddr composed a Latin text, known in translation as *Yngvars saga hins víðfǫrla*, as an apology for a missionary king who had performed no miracles; its hero, like Óláfr, is steadfast in his faith but is credited with no wonders after his death. Latin lives must also have been composed for the first native saints, Jón and Þorlákr. Translations of these works, best represented by the A versions of *Þorláks saga* and *Jóns saga*, probably date from the early years of the thirteenth century and incorporate collections of miracles that were contemporaneous with the time of writing.[11] A saga about Guðmundr Arason, known as the 'Priest's saga' because it ends with Guðmundr's departure for ordination as bishop of Hólar, may have been composed within a generation of his death in 1237. Three sagas covering his entire life (A, B, and C) date from the third and fourth decades of the fourteenth century, presumably inspired by Bishop Auðunn's activities. A collection of Þorlákr's miracles (*BS* I: 333–56) can also be dated to the first half of the fourteenth century; whether this renewed interest in Þorlákr inspired, or was a reaction to, Auðunn's promotion of Guðmundr cannot be ascertained. A new redaction of *Jóns saga* (B) in the fashionable florid style probably also dates from this time, and a third version (C) soon followed. The elevation of the bones of Guðmundr Arason in the middle of the century inspired the composition of the youngest version of *Guðmundar saga*(D) by the Benedictine monk Arngrímr, and the composition of no less than three poems, one by Arngrímr himself. Although Arngrímr clearly wrote for a foreign audience, it is unknown whether a Latin life of Guðmundr was ever composed.

Another issue which may have caused the composition and revision of hagiographic works was the struggle between ecclesiastical and secular power. An alternative explanation for the compositions about Óláfr Tryggvason and Yngvarr *hinn víðfǫrli* is that they were written with the contemporary Church–state conflict in mind. Lönnroth (1963: 90–3) and Hofmann (1981) have pointed out that their depictions of saintly kings whose bishops arc quite minor characters would have been valuable propaganda for the ideals of the Norwegian monarchy. Jón Böðvarsson (1968) has argued that the B version of *Þorláks saga* was composed during the episcopacy of Árni Þorláksson (1269–98), who battled for the control of Church property in Iceland. This version of the saga contains an episode known as the *Oddaverja páttr* which describes conflicts between Þorlákr and secular chieftains that parallel the difficulties faced by Bishop Árni. Stefán Karlsson (1973) has suggested that the three versions of the saga of Thomas à Becket were composed for bishops concerned to promote the interests of the Church. Conflict with secular authority is one of the main themes of the sagas of Guðmundr Arason. Indeed, suffering the opposition of powerful chieftains is a defining feature of sanctity for at least one hagiographer (*BS* I: 454; cf. Jørgensen 1982: 10).

Stylistic considerations might lead to the revision of existing works. The earliest sagas were translations of a single text into a straightforward form of Icelandic. In addition to adopting the new florid style, the late thirteenth century saw the appearance of sagas that are not based on a single Latin text but composed from a variety of sources, among them the liturgy, the Bible, and works such as Vincent of Beauvais's *Speculum Historiale* or the *Historia Scholastica* of Peter Comestor.[12]

The relationship between the production of hagiography and the development of secular saga literature is far too large for treatment in this chapter. Suffice it to say that Turville-Petre's dictum that the translation of saints' lives 'did not teach the Icelanders what to think or what to say, but it taught them how to say it' (1967: 141–2) has been reconsidered by Foote (1994), who points out that the early twelfth-century translation of historical materials discussed by Whaley in the present volume may have had more influence on the development of saga writing than did hagiography.

When the extant saints' sagas are compared with secular ones, two characteristic features of sagas set in Iceland or Scandinavia will be found lacking: genealogies and poetry.

One of the most characteristic features of the family sagas and *Sturlunga* is genealogy. Genealogy was, as Quinn's chapter in this volume indicates, among the earliest kinds of material to be recorded in the vernacular, and was the only form of secular learning the author of *Þorláks saga* considered worth mentioning.[13] Knowledge of genealogical connections is essential to the understanding of family sagas, kings' sagas, or *Sturlunga*.[14] Although some of the translated lives (and their Latin originals) may extend as far back in time as the grandparents of the future saint, they are more likely to begin with his parents. Some (especially those about virgin martyrs) begin the action *in medias res*.

Collings (1969) has noted that in the younger redactions of saints' lives found in the *Codex Scardensis* the translator sometimes inserts notes on the individual's kindred by way of an introduction. That the lack of such an introduction might be seen as a defect can be seen from the prologue to *Michaels saga*, in which Bergr Sokkason notes apologetically that the angelic nature of St Michael makes it impossible to describe his genealogy, kindred, or childhood.

In the sagas of the native saints, we can observe the tension between the desire to imitate foreign models and interest in family history. *Þorláks saga* provides no genealogy whatever – Þorlákr's parents are named, but without patronymics, so that the saint's nuclear family appears completely isolated from the network of kinship. The most influential figure in Þorlákr's development is his teacher, the priest Eyjólfr Sæmundarson.

In a saga probably contemporary with that of Þorlákr, Jón Qgmundarson is provided with a short but eminent lineage. Consistently with both native and Latin traditions, episodes from Jón's and his mother's childhood predict his future sanctity.[15]

In the sagas of Jón and Þorlákr, kinsmen are of little importance and the saints are portrayed, rightly or wrongly, as keeping clear of secular entanglements. Guðmundr Arason's career, however, was defined by family and ecclesiastical politics. The authors of sagas about him make the most of his struggles with secular powers, presenting him as another Becket instead of concentrating solely on his miracles, as the author of the A version of *Þorláks saga* might have done. These authors do not, however, limit themselves to the crises of Guðmundr's episcopacy. Like secular sagas, all but the youngest writings about him provide a detailed introduction to his family and relations. These include an uncle who dies in Greenland and whose body is incorrupt, another uncle who wins honour at the Norwegian court (and composes *lausavísur*), and a father who dies in Norway defending his lord. This material provides a prologue to Guðmundr's career comparable to those found in family sagas; a literary analysis of the themes it raises, and their reference to Guðmundr's life, is much to be desired. The youngest (D) version of the saga, clearly intended for foreign consumption, omits this material and instead concentrates on drawing parallels between Guðmundr and other saints.

However authors of saints' sagas felt about the inclusion of genealogy in the literature they produced, Icelanders were happy to enshrine the saints themselves in their genealogical literature as individuals with whom kinship would gladly be recognized. This can be seen in interpolations in *Landnámabók* concerning the ancestry of Jón and Þorlákr, and also in the saga of St Magnús, where the family tree of the earl of Orkney is traced to Jón Ǫgmundarson as well as to St Óláfr (Guðmundsson 1965: 337–8).

Another characteristic feature of native literature missing from sagas about saints is poetry. Neither foreign nor native saints toss off *lausavísur*, nor (as far as we know) were their doings the subject of contemporary poetic commentary. Poems were certainly written about them; the twelfth century saw the composition of a *Plácítus drápa* as well as a *Plácítus saga*, and an epilogue to the saga of John the Evangelist informs us that poems in his honour were composed by Abbot Nikulás of Munkaþverá monastery (d. 1159), the canon Gamli of Þykkvabær monastery (probably active in the second half of the twelfth century), and the chieftain Kolbeinn Tumason (1173–1208) (Unger 1874: 509–13). Of these poems, only the handful of verses quoted in the saga have survived. This is typical for the period under consideration in this volume; poetry about half a dozen other saints is known from references or fragments that can be dated prior to 1400 (Cormack 1994a: 41–3). Although poetry about Christian topics composed in the twelfth through the fourteenth centuries has been preserved (Chase 1993), most of the extant poems about saints appear to date from the fifteenth century (Helgason 1953: 162–4). The exceptions – poems from the early period which are virtually complete – are the anonymous *Plácítus drápa* from about 1200 and poetry in honour of St Óláfr and Guðmundr Arason. *Lilja* ('Lily'), from the fourteenth century, is addressed to the Virgin Mary but consists primarily of a summary of Christian history from the creation to the Last Judgement.

The poems about St Óláfr are unique in that the surviving corpus includes works composed at several periods. In the decades following the death of the saint, the court poets who had praised the king's military exploits during his lifetime composed verses which celebrated his miracles as well as his valour. A century later, the poem *Geisli*, composed at the time of the foundation of the archdiocese of Niðaróss, presents a typological comparison between Óláfr and Christ. The literary context of the twelfth-century *Plácítus drápa* is unknown. A *Plácítus saga* existed at this time, and the example of the wedding at Reykjahólar may be cited as evidence that a saga was not considered complete without acompanying poetry.[16] Three poems about Guðmundr Arason were composed in the fourteenth century in conjunction with episcopal attempts to promote his sanctity. Their authors were the lawman Einarr Gilsson, Abbot Árni Jónsson of Munkaþverá, and Arngrímr, author of the youngest of the sagas about Guðmundr, the saga in which the poetry is in fact preserved. They do not, however, appear to have been part of Arngrímr's original composition, which differs strikingly from both the secular tradition and the majority of sagas about native saints that precede it. Written in an extremely florid style and intended for a foreign audience, its presentation is thematic rather than chronological, and the saga omits the genealogical background. However, it was also copied in a version more adapted to local taste. A group of manuscripts best represented by Stock. Perg. folio, no. 5, written perhaps a decade after the saga was composed, incorporates verses that summarize or complement the action of the prose as does the poetry in secular sagas. These verses do not serve as historical evidence in the same way as the poems quoted in kings' sagas; indeed, only a handful of verses are attributed to characters in the saga and can thus lay claim to being contemporary with the events described. They are comparable to the verses composed by Sturla Þórðarson and inserted in his *Íslendinga saga*, adorning the prose without adding new information.

SAINTS AND ICELANDERS AS HAGIOGRAPHIC SUBJECTS

Although passages referring to the veneration of saints are scattered throughout Icelandic literature, the main body of evidence is found in the sagas of the three native bishops, Þorlákr, Jón, and Guðmundr. This is not because they were the most popular saints in Iceland but because the recording of miracles was necessary for the establishment and maintenance of their cults; saints already recognized by the Church did not benefit from such focussed literary activity. Only when a scribe added material of local interest at the end of his text do we learn that

Cecilia, Magnús, or the Virgin Mary performed miracles for Icelanders, or that prominent individuals composed poetry about the Apostle John. If a late version of his saga can be relied on, the Virgin Mary and St Ambrose were far more important to Guðmundr Arason than either of the Icelanders whose cult he promoted (*BS* II: 18).

The ability to call on a saint in time of need does not require sophisticated theological knowledge, or even familiarity with the saint in question. There is no evidence in Iceland at this period that saints were invoked because they specialized in specific problems.[17] On the whole, people seem to have had recourse to the saints deemed most accessible – because they were patrons of a nearby church, because their feast-day was approaching, or because they were related to the suppliant. A new saint was particularly likely to attract suppliants. Whaley (1996: 161–4) describes how the areas from which vows are recorded expands from localities (or individuals) associated with the developing cults of the three Icelandic bishops.

Whaley's study shows that the miracles in the Icelandic corpus resemble those found on the Continent in both nature and relative frequency. There are differences, such as a much higher proportion of 'first aid' miracles (i.e. cures granted at the scene of an accident, or at any rate at a distance from the cult centre). This discrepancy reflects the fact that the European miracle collections compiled at prominent shrines could afford to record only the most memorable accounts, usually cures that had been witnessed at the shrine itself: madmen who suddenly recovered their senses, or cripples who threw away their crutches after touching the tomb of a saint. While Iceland has a few such miracles, the scribes at Skálholt and Hólar could not afford to be choosy, and recorded virtually any instance of saintly intervention on behalf of humans or animals.[18]

Since the first publication of the sagas of Icelandic saints, it has been noted that the miracle collections they contain provide valuable evidence concerning the everyday life of Icelanders from all levels of society. The power of the saints was demonstrated in stories of cured children and of food supplied to impoverished households rather than chronicles of lengthy feuds. Nor do these accounts discriminate on the grounds of gender. In fact, women are far more prominent in them than elsewhere in medieval Icelandic prose. It therefore seems worthwhile to examine what the sagas of saints can tell us about contemporary ecclesiastical attitudes towards sex and women.

The first, most obvious observation that can be made is that Iceland had no female saints. The anchoress Hildr would be a good candidate; the account of her precocious asceticism in the B version of *Jóns saga* describes a devotion to the contemplative life unparalleled by any of the holy bishops. Of another ascetic, Ketilbjǫrg, who died at Skálholt, we are told that Guðmundr Arason's requiem mass over her body was so wonderful that it was thought to indicate her sanctity.[19] Neither woman, however, became an object of veneration.

The lack of female saints does not indicate an aversion to the idea of female holiness; nearly every church in Iceland had an image of the Virgin Mary, who was not only the subject of her own saga but makes occasional appearances in the sagas of other saints. The cults of St Catherine and Mary Magdalene flourished on Icelandic soil, and someone purchased for the church at Skáney an image of Margaret of Nordnes, a claimant to the Norwegian throne who had been burned as an imposter in 1301 and whose cult developed in Bergen in spite of its prohibition by the bishop. St Cecilia is credited with two miracles in Iceland (Unger 1877 (henceforth *HMS*) I: 294–7), and a vision involving St Agnes led to the addition to the ecclesiastical calendar of three new feasts (*BS* I: 420). Although virgin martyrs were hardly viable role-models for Icelandic women, the literature about them presents a coherent and positive model of female behaviour which can be contrasted with that of Eddic heroines or the 'female inciters' who promote violence in the sagas of kings and Icelanders. The violence in the sagas of Agatha, Barbara, and Cecilia is directed against the women themselves, who accept (and sometimes even actively court) it. In the lives of female martyrs, threats to the women's virginity and threats to their religion are closely intertwined – the pagan rulers whom the women defy are often sexual aggressors as well, or else use the threat of sex in an attempt to punish the woman's resistance to conversion. Since sexual violence was probably a recognized danger for Icelandic women (Jochens 1991), these sagas may have helped to convey the message that such behaviour was not approved of.

Neither the translated saints' lives nor those composed for the native saints have a misogynistic bent. Married clergy and their wives appear regularly in the miracle stories, and are in no way condemned. While the chastity of Þorlákr and Guðmundr is praised, and may well have contributed to their reputations for sanctity, St Jón had married twice, and his second wife appears to have acompanied him to Hólar in the capacity of housekeeper.[20] Only the B version of his saga goes so far as to suggest that both his marriages were chaste.[21] None of the three saints is described as struggling to overcome lusts of the flesh.

What is condemned, in no uncertain terms, is illicit sexuality, in the form of extra-marital relations or marriage within the prohibited degrees (Jochens 1980). In only one instance is the woman blamed for such activity: in a vision based on a Latin model known as *Rannveigar leiðsla*,[22] one Rannveig falls into a trance and, in the course of a stereotypical otherworld journey, is punished for having [*er þú hefir*] *lagzt undir ij presta ok saurgat svá þeirra þjónosto, ok þar með ofmetnaðr ok fègirne* (*BS* I: 452), 'slept with two priests and polluted their ministries, and in addition pride and avarice'. For the Icelandic author Rannveig's problem is her inappropriate choice of partners, not lust pure and simple.[23] The female recipient of a miracle in *Guðmundar saga* is warned against prohibited sexual relationships, but not against marriage (*BS* II: 167).

It may in fact have been difficult for Icelanders to accept contemporary teachings which portrayed women as the originators of sexual misbehaviour. As Jochens (1991) has pointed out, Icelanders were more concerned with controlling the sexuality of men than of women. In a revealing episode in *Jóns saga*, Bishop Jón is said to have prohibited the youthful Klœngr Þorsteinsson (future bishop of Skálholt) from reading Ovid, commenting that 'it was difficult enough for someone to preserve himself from bodily lust and evil passion without kindling his mind to it by . . . poetry of this sort'.[24] The only examples of aggressive and threatening female sexuality I have found in Icelandic saints' sagas are associated with the supernatural (Cormack 1996). Perhaps this is the only way that medieval Icelanders could conceive of female sexuality as representing a threat; if so, it is not clear that the Church was responsible for this attitude.

While the narrative portions of the sagas of Icelandic saints (like the secular sagas) deal primarily with the activities of men, women appear with greater frequency in the accompanying miracle collections. Diana

Whaley's study of this material reveals that men call on the saints about twice as often as women do. The saints, however, were evenhanded in dispensing aid. When one counts not supplicants but recipients of miracles, and includes unsolicited visions as well as specific prayers, men and women receive assistance from the saints with approximately equal frequency. There are, however, a number of miracles which indicate ways in which aid from the saints may have been particularly meaningful for women.

Perhaps the most intriguing piece of evidence is a pair of related miracles, the first of which concerns a labourer who swells up 'as fat as an ox' (*sva digran sem nát*) and is cured thanks to a vow made for him by the housewife on the farm (*BS* I: 339). Unfortunately, the cure excites scorn instead of piety: 'On the farm next to the one where this miracle occurred, there was a young and garrulous woman, who mocked at the event. She said that men's manners were getting perverted if people had to make vows for them as for pregnant women before they gave birth'.[25] She is punished with a horrible pain in the eyes that is not relieved until the same housewife who had invoked St Þorlákr on behalf of the labourer does so for her. While the episode centres on the nature of the man's ailment – he in fact resembles a pregnant woman – it suggests that it may have been considered a bit effeminate for men to make vows to the saints, at least for something as minor as, apparently, a bad case of colic.

While miracles resulting in successful childbirth are found throughout hagiographic literature, Iceland produced a variant on the theme that appears to be virtually unparalleled:[26] the saint not only preserves the life of mother and child, but takes the baby away when (s)he vanishes (*BS* II: 167; Unger 1871 I: 157). In a country like Iceland, whose resources could barely support the number of human beings who populated it, such an outcome must have been the desired solution to a common problem. It is worth noting in this context that the Icelandic material contains no miracles in which childless couples pray for offspring.

Women are extremely prominent in the miracles of *Jóns saga*. In the A version of the saga, St Jón's first miracles are performed for girls (*BS* I: 178), as is the first one after his translation (*BS* I: 187). The list of miracles following the translation is interrupted by a flashback to mention the only miracle to take place between his death and translation, the extermination of mice from the cell of the anchoress Hildr.[27] The final miracles in *Jóns saga* benefit women, and include the harrowing tale of a single mother named Þorfinna who is saved from both supernatural and natural hazards thanks to the intervention of no less than four different saints (*BS* I: 198–201).

A critical episode in the development of the cult of St Þorlákr is also marked by a miracle with female protagonists. Halldóra, a priest's wife, had been bedridden for three years. Another woman has a vision in which St Þorlákr suggests that Halldóra be taken to Skálholt (one might well have expected her husband, the priest, to have made this suggestion). The day after her arrival Halldóra is strong enough to walk to the altar and offer a ring. A few days later she rides to the Althing and is shown to the people as Abbot Karl of Þingeyrar proclaims the miracle. Then, we are told, Bishop Páll read out the miracles that had been recorded to date. Halldóra's cure supplied visible, public evidence of St Þorlákr's sanctity, verifiable by her husband, Abbot Karl, and Bishop Páll (*BS* I: 351–2). The feast of St Þorlákr was made obligatory throughout Iceland at the same Althing.[28]

Aside from their important positions in the sagas, perhaps the most striking feature of both these episodes is the simple fact that they are lengthy narratives about women. Rannveig's vision in *Guðmundar saga* and the account of the anchoress Hildr in the B and C versions of *Jóns saga* are comparable. Except for the expanded versions of the Sæmundr episode in the B version of *Jóns saga*, no male characters other than the saints themselves receive as much attention. The narratives about women are full of suspense, describing exciting encounters with the supernatural that do not incorporate the patterns of feud and politics which are the concern of so much saga literature. Among the sagas of the Icelanders and sagas of contemporaries the only comparable episode with female protagonists that comes to mind is the story of the two Þóras in *Haukdæla þáttr*, the culmination of a narrative which results in the marriage of Þorvaldr Gizurarson (*St* I: 60–2; and see Nordal, this volume).

There is, in addition, one small group of miracles in which women dominate: visions which contain messages from the saint for someone other than the visionary (Cormack 1996: 194). The woman who advises

Halldóra in the miracle outlined above is a case in point. This need not indicate a continuance of the belief, described by Tacitus, that Germanic women had a 'spirit of prophecy' (*Germania*, ch. 8). Rather, it reflects the disempowered status of the women (Larrington 1995), whose visions are comparable to the dreams described by Nordal in this volume.[29]

Medieval Icelandic women could not become priests, nor conduct cases at the Althing. In theory, at least, they were always under control of a male – father, brother, husband, or son. Christianity, however, taught an inversion of worldly values. It favoured the idea, commonly used to justify female visionaries, that God sometimes chose to speak through the weak and lowly when His message was being ignored by the powerful and corrupt. Women whose suggestions and advice might otherwise have been ignored became audible when they spoke the words of a saint.

If the saints chose to convey messages through women, Icelandic churchmen were ready to listen. The sagas of the Icelandic saints describe ten visions which directly promote the saint's cult and/or career. In them, women outnumber men as visionaries by two to one. The best-known example is *Rannveigar leiðsla*; the import of its message is that Guðmundr Arason would become not only bishop of Hólar but also the patron saint of Iceland.[30] *Guðmundar saga* suggests that a message from God and the Virgin Mary, conveyed through an anchoress named Úlfrún, is what finally overcomes Guðmundr's reluctance to become bishop (*BS* I: 478). Jón Ǫgmundarson appears to a 'poor and weak woman who was truthful and harmless and firm in her faith',[31] to advise the translation of his relics.

It cannot be claimed that miracle collections have preserved the voices of medieval Icelandic women across the centuries. They are found in texts prepared by scribes and authors who were presumably male (there is no evidence of literary activity emanating from Iceland's two convents). These stories do, however, provide a valuable corrective to a view of medieval Icelandic society based exclusively on legal material and literature designed for and by a male aristocracy.

NOTES

1 I would like to thank the American Scandinavian Foundation and the National Endowment for the Humanities for research grants that made it possible for me to spend the summer of 1997 at the Stofnun Árna Magnússonar in Iceland collecting material for this chapter, and to the staff of that institute for their generous hospitality. Of those who have read and commented on this work in full or in part, the following have my special gratitude: Daniel Donoghue of Harvard University, Marianne Kalinke of the University of Illinois, Philip Roughton of the University of Colorado at Boulder, and Sheridan Hough of the College of Charleston.

2   I nafni grędara varss herra Jesu Kristi byriaz her litill bæklingr heilags Michaelis hofuðengils, til þess eina skrifaðr ok samansettr, at hann iafnlega lesiz æ messuðagh Michaelis kirkiusoknar monnum til skemtanar, einkanlega i þcim stǫðum sem hann er kirkiudrottenn yfir, at þvi ǫllu sætari verðr hans minning i rettlatra manna hugrenning, sem firir þessa litlu ritning verðr ollum kunnari hans ægæta virðing (*HMS* I: 676)

3 For the Latin texts used in these translations see Widding, Bekker-Nielsen and Shook 1963 and Cormack 1994a: 239–45.

4 See Cormack 1994a: 40. This figure excludes saints known only from collections of *exempla* or who appear in the collection of miracles of the Virgin Mary in *Maríu saga*. The 'Handlist' published by Widding, Bekker-Nielsen and Shook (1963) includes these saints as well as those whose sagas were written between 1400 and 1540.

5 For a summary of the Icelandic liturgical calendar see *Kulturhistorisk leksikon for Nordsk middelalder (KLNM)* 8 col. 106 ff. and *KLNM* 4 cols. 243–5, entries 'Festum chori o, festum fori' and 'Festum terrae'. The best-known feasts would have been those whose observance (by abstaining from work and, in some cases, fasting) was required of all Icelanders. These feasts are listed in the Christian Laws Section of *Grágás* (Dennis *et al.* 1980 (*LEI*) I: 45–7); see also Cormack 1994a: 13–24.

6 A *máldagi* was a deed listing the church's endowment and other property. It was required by law that the *máldagi* be read initially at the Althing or at the local spring assembly, and annually at the church itself on a feast when attendence was greatest (*LEI* I: 32–3).

7 They are Bishop Jǫrundr Þorsteinsson of Hólar, who had been consecrated on the feast of St John, and three poets who composed verses in his honour (see below).

8 For the purpose of this chapter, all three Icelandic bishops will be considered saints, even though Guðmundr never officially attained a status higher than beatification.

9 *DI* IV: 159, an episcopal register dated 1397 but which contains younger material. It is thus unclear whether Ormr first donated a half share in the

manuscript and later renounced all rights to it, or whether both documents record the same donation. The church at Skarð was in effect an *eigenkirche* which was part of the farm on which it stood.

10 *St* I: 527/ *K* II: 311. For Gizurr's relationship with the Norwegian throne, see Nordal's chapter in this volume.

11 For descriptions of the different versions of the sagas of the native saints, see the following entries in Pulsiano and Wolf 1993:'Biskupa sögur' (pp. 45–6), 'Jóns saga ens helga' (p. 345) and 'Guðmundar sögur biskups' (pp. 245–6).

12 Studies of the styles of medieval Icelandic literature leave much to be desired. For a summary in English on the scholarship of translation style see Collings 1969: 143ff. Collings's dissertation is the most detailed study to date comparing the style of a group of Icelandic saints' sagas (those of the *Codex Scardensis*) with their Latin originals. Bekker-Nielsen (1962) contains a brief summary of the state of scholarship as applied to saints' lives, treated in more detail by Widding in Bekker-Nielsen, Foote and Olsen 1965: 132ff. For an analysis of the style of a select corpus of early saints' lives see Kristjánsson (1981). Several articles by Christine Fell (1972, 1977, 1981) analyse the sources and technique of translation of Bergr Sokkason's *Michaels saga*. The introduction to her edition of *Dunstanus saga* contains a similar analysis of the author's technique. *Nikulás saga* is also treated in detail by Sverrir Tómasson in the facsimile of *Helgastaðabók* (Jónsdóttir, Karlsson and Tómasson 1982: 161–76).

13 After a discussion of Þorlákr's education and progress through the ecclesiastical grades to the diaconate, his saga notes that in addition to his clerical education his mother taught him genealogical lore (*ættvísi ok mannfræði, BS* I: 91).

14 Knowledge of family relationships is necessary not only in order to follow the action, but because saga authors used early family history to prefigure crises in later generations. On the most basic level, tracing a lineage established continuity between the world of the saga's action and that of its audience (Hume 1973; Harris 1986: 216).

15 It could be argued that the practice of using such episodes to foreshadow the character of an individual was in fact borrowed from hagiography by the authors of secular sagas. This question raises the insoluble puzzle of saga origins, and cannot be entered into here.

16 *St* I: 27. *Þorgils saga ok Hafliða* describes a wedding which took place in 1119, about a century before the saga was composed, as mentioned in Quinn's chapter in this volume. As part of the entertainment a priest named Ingimundr told a story (*saga*) which contained verses and composed a poem to go with it. While the accuracy of the account may be questioned – indeed, the author of *Þorgils saga ok Hafliða* appears to anticipate that it will be – the association of poetry with sagas which it assumes has not been called into question.

17 Use of the saga of St Margaret as a charm for aid in childbirth appears to date from after the Protestant Reformation (Steffensen 1965).

18 Even the Icelandic authorities had their standards, however. *Jóns saga* reports that Bishop Brandr was reluctant to proclaim as a miracle the cure of a deacon's horse, because he was unsure whether it was a miracle or the result of human efforts (*BS* I: 192–3).

19 'varð sú þjónosta svá merkileg, at Gizurr váttaðe því í tölu sinne yfer gröfinne, at þeir þóttust eige slíkan líksöng heyrt hafa, ok virðo þeir henni til heilagleiks', *BS* I: 466 = *St* I: 146.

20 I take the 'widow who had directed the household' (*sú ekkja, er fyrir staðarbúi hafði ráðit, BS* I: 203), who was especially affected by Jón's death, to be none other than Jón's second wife. Nearly a century later Bishop Páll Jónsson's wife, Herdís Ketilsdóttir, is praised by the saga's author for her efficiency as housekeeper at Skálholt cathedral.

21 'and it is the opinion of many that he did not pollute himself bodily with either one' (*ok er þat margra manna ætlan, at hann hafi með hvorigri líkamliga flekkazt, BS* I: 230). Other versions of the saga state more cautiously that the author has not heard of any children who survived childhood (*BS* I: 157).

22 The visionary 'otherworld journey' is a well-known medieval genre; four-teenth-century versions of *Guðmundar saga* contain an episode, referred to as *Rannveigar Leiðsla*, in which a woman named Rannveig is the protagonist of such a journey. In his edition of *Duggals leiðsla* (the Icelandic translation of *Visio Tnugdali*), Peter Cahill (1983: liii–lviii) compares Rannveig's vision to the Latin work. He notes that while Arngrímr's version of the episode contains verbal parallels to the *Visio*, they are not to be found in earlier versions of *Guðmundar saga*.

23 *Contra* Jochens (1980) who translates *hórdómr*, 'fornication, adultery', as 'lust'. I will argue in a forthcoming article that the objectionable part of Rannveig's behaviour is the fact that she had slept with *two* priests.

24 *hverjum manni mundu ærit höfugt at gæta sín við líkamligri munnut ok rángri ást, þó at hann kveykti eigi upp hug sinn til þess meðr nè einum siðum eða þesskonar kvæðum (BS* I: 165–6).

25 *En a enom nęsta bó þvi er siá iartein gerþesc. es nv var fra sagt. var kona ein v*ŋ *oc mólǫg. hon tóc sceypiliga á of þeða atbvrþ aéan iamnsaman. oc talþe hon afleiþes þoca of kyrteise carla*ɴA. *es þa scylde sva heíta verþa firir þeim sem ohrøstom konom apr þer yrþe le[tare] (BS* I: 339–40).

26 The only comparable example I have found is the story of the nun of Watton, summarized by Constable (1978).

27 *BS* I: 194–5. In the C version of the saga, the story of Hildr is much expanded, and is preceded by another miracle in which women are the main characters (*BS* I: 203).

28 The adoption of the feast is mentioned in the annals, but not in the sagas. For the sagas, which reflect the perspective of the clergy at Skálholt, the critical

event for establishment of the feast would have been St Þorlákr's translation on July 20 of the previous year.

29 The two explanations need not be mutually exclusive. The prophetic power attributed to women is itself usually cited as evidence for the high status of Germanic women, but little in Tacitus supports this claim.

30 The author is careful to situate this episode at a point just before Þorlákr is declared a saint.

31 *kona ein fátæk ok ókröptug, sannorð og meinlaus ok trúföst* (*BS* I: 184).

REFERENCES

For a list of manuscripts containing sagas of saints, see Widding *et al.* 1963 and Cormack 1994a: 239–45. For a complete listing of saints for whom literature is attested before 1400 (including references to sagas owned by individual churches), see Cormack 1994a, where the cult of saints is also discussed in more detail.

Abbreviations

BS   Sigurðsson, Jón and Vigfússon, Guðbrandur (eds.) 1858–78, *Biskupa sögur*. 2 vols. Copenhagen: Møller.

DI   *Diplomatarium Islandicum Íslenzkt fornbréfasafn* 1857–1972. Copenhagen: Hið íslenzka bókmentafelag.

HMS   Unger, C. R. (ed.) 1877, *Heilagra manna søgur. Fortællinger og legender om hellige mænd og kvinder.* 2 vols. Christiania (Oslo): Bentzen.

K   Kålund, Kristian (ed.) 1906–11, *Sturlunga saga.* 2 vols. Copenhagen: Gyldendal.

KLNM   *Kulturhistorisk leksikon for nordisk middelalder* 1956–78. 22 vols. Copenhagen: Rosenkilde and Bagger.

LEI   Dennis, Andrew *et al.* (trans.) 1980, *Laws of Early Iceland: Grágás*, I. University of Manitoba Icelandic Studies, 3. Winnipeg: University of Manitoba Press.

OTS   Jónsson, Finnur (ed.) 1932, *Saga Ólafs Tryggvasonar af Oddr Snorrason munk*. Copenhagen: G. E. C. Gads Forlag.

St   Jóhannesson, Jón *et al.* (eds.) 1946, *Sturlunga Saga*. 2 vols. Reykjavík: Sturlunguútgáfan.

Tacitus   *The Agricola and the Germania*. See Mattingly 1970 below.

Primary literature

Cahill, Peter (ed. and trans.) 1983, *Duggals Leiðsla*. Rit, 25. Reykjavík: Stofnun Árna Magnússonar á Íslandi.

Dennis, Andrew, Foote, Peter and Perkins, Richard (trans.) 1980, *Laws of Early*

Sagas of saints

Iceland: Grágás, I. University of Manitoba Icelandic Studies, 3. Winnipeg: University of Manitoba Press.

Diplomatarium Islandicum – Íslenzkt fornbréfasafn 1857–1972. Copenhagen: Hið íslenzka bókmentafélag.

Fell, Christine (ed.) 1963, *Dunstanus saga*. Editiones Arnamagnæanæ, Series B, V. Copenhagen: Munksgaard.

Guðmundsson, Finnbogi (ed.) 1965, *Orkneyinga saga*. Íslenzk fornrit, 34. Reykjavík: Hið íslenzka fornritafélag.

Jóhannesson, Jón, Finnbogason, Magnús and Eldjárn Kristján (eds.) 1946, *Sturlunga Saga*. 2 vols. Reykjavík: Sturlunguútgáfan.

Jónsdóttir, Selma, Karlsson, Stefán and Tómasson, Sverrir (eds.) 1982, *Helgastaðabók. Nikulás saga. Perg. 4to nr. 16, Konungsbókhlöðu í Stokkhólmi.* Íslensk miðaldahandrit – Manuscripta Islandica Medii Aevi II, Reykjavík: Lögberg.

Jónsson, Finnur (ed.) 1932, *Saga Óláfs Tryggvasonar af Oddr Snorrason munk.* Copenhagen: G. E. C. Gads Forlag.

Kålund, Kristian (ed.) 1906–11, *Sturlunga saga*. 2 vols. Copenhagen: Gyldendal.

Kulturhistorisk leksikon for nordisk middelalder 1956–78. 22 vols. Copenhagen: Rosenkilde and Bagger.

Mattingly, H. (trans.) 1970 (rev. Handford, S. A.), *Tacitus: The Agricola and the Germania*. London and New York: Penguin.

Sigurðsson, Jón and Vigfússon, Guðbrandur (eds.) 1858–78, *Biskupa sögur*. 2 vols. Copenhagen: Møller.

Slay, D. (ed.) 1960, *Codex Scardensis*. Early Icelandic Manuscripts in Facsimile, 2. Copenhagen: Rosenkilde and Bagger.

Unger, C. R. (ed.) 1871, *Maríu Saga.* 2 vols. Christiania (Oslo): Brögger & Christie.

   (ed.) 1874, *Postola sögur. Legendariske fortællinger om apostlernes liv deres kamp for kristendommens udbredelse samt deres martyrdød.* Christiania (Oslo): Bentzen.

   (ed.) 1877, *Heilagra manna søgur. Fortællinger og legender om hellige mænd og kvinder*, II. Christiania (Oslo): Bentzen.

Secondary literature

Bekker-Nielsen, H. 1962, 'On a Handlist of Saints' Lives in Old Norse', *Mediaeval Studies* 24: 323–34.

Bekker-Nielsen, H., Olsen, Thorkil Damsgaard and Widding, Ole 1965, *Norrøn Fortællekunst*. Copenhagen: Akademisk Forlag.

Böðvarsson, Jón 1968, 'Munur eldri og yngri gerðar Þorláks sögu', *Saga* 6: 81–94.

Boyer, R. 1973, 'The Influence of Pope Gregory's *Dialogues* on Old Icelandic Literature', in Foote, Peter, Pálsson, Hermann and Slay, Desmond (eds.), *Proceedings of the First International Saga Conference University of Edin-*

burgh 1971. University College London: Viking Society for Northern Research, pp. 1–27.

Chase, M. 1993, 'Christian Poetry 2. West Norse', in Pulsiano and Wolf, pp. 73–7.

Collings, L. 1969, *The Codex Scardensis: Studies in Icelandic Hagiography*. Ph.D. dissertation, Cornell University.

Constable, Giles 1978, 'Aelred of Rievaulx and the Nun of Watton: an Episode in the Early History of the Gilbertine Order', in Baker, D. (ed.), *Medieval Women*. Studies in Church History Subsidia, 1. Oxford: Basil Blackwell for the Ecclesiastical History Society, pp. 205–26.

Cormack, M. 1992, '"Fjǫlkunnigri konu scallatu í faðmi sofa": Sex and the Supernatural in Icelandic Saints' Lives', *Skáldskaparmál* 2: 221–8.

1994a, *The Saints in Iceland: their Veneration from the Conversion to 1400*. Subsidia Hagiographica, 78. Brussels: Société des Bollandistes.

1994b, 'Saints Lives and Icelandic Literature in the Thirteenth and Fourteenth Centuries', in Bekker-Nielsen, Hans and Carlé, Birte (eds.), *Saints and Sagas: a Symposium*. Odense: Odense University Press, pp. 27–47.

[1994/92], 'Visions, Demons, and Gender in the Sagas of Icelandic Saints', *Collegium Medievale* 7: 185–209.

Fell, Christine 1965, 'Bergr Sokkason's *Michaels saga* and its Sources', *Saga-Book of the Viking Society* 16(4): 354–71.

1972, 'The Icelandic Saga of Edward the Confessor: the Hagiographic Sources', *Anglo-Saxon England* 1: 247–58.

1977, 'English History and Norman Legend in the Icelandic Saga of Edward the Confessor', *Anglo-Saxon England* 6: 223–36.

1981, 'Anglo-Saxon saints in Old Norse Sources and Vice Versa', in Bekker-Nielsen, Hans, Foote, Peter and Olsen, Olaf (eds.), *Proceedings of the Eighth Viking Congress*. Odense: Odense University Press, pp. 95–106.

Foote, P. 1994, 'Saints' Lives and Sagas', in Bekker-Nielsen, Hans and Carlé, Birte (eds.), *Saints and Sagas: a Symposium*. Odense: Odense University Press, pp. 73–88.

Halldórsson, Ólafur 1966, *Helgafellsbækur fornar*. Studia Islandica, 24. Reykjavík: Menningasjóður.

Harris, J. 1986, 'Saga as Historical Novel', in Lindow, John, Lönnroth, Lars and Weber, Gerd Wolfgang (eds.), *Structure and Meaning in Old Norse Literature*. The Viking Collection, 3. Odense: Odense University Press, pp. 187–219.

Helgason, Jón 1953, 'Norges og Islands digtning', *Litteraturhistorie*, Nordisk Kultur, 8 B. Stockholm: Albert Bonniers Förlag, pp. 3–179.

Hofmann, D. 1981, '*Die Yngvars saga víðfǫrla* und Oddr munkr inn fróði', in Dronke, Ursula, Helgadóttir, Guðrun P., Weber, Gerd Wolfgang and Bekker-Nielsen, Hans (eds.), *Specvlvm Norroenum, Norse Studies in Memory of Gabriel Turville-Petre*. Odense: Odense University Press, pp. 188–222.

1984, 'Die Vision des Oddr Snorrason', in Fidjestøl, Bjarne, Halvorsen, Eyvind Fjeld, Hødnebø, Finn, Jakobsen, Alfred, Magerøy, Hallvard and Rindal, Magnus (eds.), *Festskrift til Ludvig Holm-Olsen på hans 70–årsdag den 9. juni 1984*. Øvre Ervik: Alvheim and Eide Akademisk Forlag, pp. 142–51.

Hume, K. 1973, 'Beginnings and Endings in the Icelandic Family Sagas', *Modern Language Review* 68: 594–606.

Jochens, J. 1980, 'The Church and Sexuality in Medieval Iceland', *Journal of Medieval History* 6: 377–92.

1991, 'The Illicit Love Visit: an Archaeology of Old Norse Sexuality', *Journal of the History of Sexuality* 1(3): 357–92.

Jørgensen, J. 1982, 'Hagiography and the Icelandic Bishop Sagas', *Peritia* 1: 1–16.

Karlsson, Stefán 1973, 'Icelandic Lives of Thomas à Becket: Questions of Authorship', in Foote, Peter, Pálsson, Hermann and Slay, Desmond (eds.), *Proceedings of the First International Saga Conference University of Edinburgh 1971*. University College London: The Viking Society for Northern Research, pp. 212–43.

Kristjánsson, Jónas 1981, 'Learned Style or Saga Style?', in Dronke, Ursula, Helgadóttir, Guðrún P., Weber, Gerd Wolfgang and Bekker-Nielsen, Hans (eds.), *Specvlvm Norroenvm, Norse Studies in Memory of Gabriel Turville-Petre*. Odense: Odense University Press, pp. 260–92.

1979, 'Islandsk bogeksport til Norge i middelalderen,' *Maal og Minne* 1–17.

Larrington, C. 1995, '*Leizla Rannveigar*: Gender and Politics in the Otherworld Vision', *Medium Ævum*, 64(2): 232–49.

Lönnroth, L. 1963, 'Studier i Olaf Tryggvasons saga', *Samlaren* 84: 54–94.

Ólason, Vésteinn, Nordal, Guðrún, Tómasson, Sverrir and Ólason, Vésteinn (eds.) 1992, *Íslensk bókmenntasaga*, I. Reykjavík: Mál og Menning.

Ólason, Vésteinn, Guðmundson, Böðvar, Tómasson, Sverrir, Tulinius, Torfi H. and Ólason, Vésteinn (eds.) 1993, *Íslensk bókmenntasaga*, II. Reykjavík: Mál og Menning.

Pulsiano, Phillip and Wolf, Kirsten (eds.) 1993, *Medieval Scandinavia: an Encyclopedia*. London and New York: Garland.

Steffensen, Jón 1965, '*Margrétar saga* and its History in Iceland', *Saga-Book of the Viking Society* 16(4): 273–82.

Tacitus, *The Agricola and the Germania*, see Mattingly 1970.

Turville-Petre, Gabriel 1967, *Origins of Icelandic Literature*. Oxford: Clarendon. [First published 1953.]

Whaley, D. 1996[1994/92], 'Miracles in the Sagas of Bishops: Icelandic Variations on an International Theme', *Collegium Medievale* 7: 155–84.

Widding, Ole, Bekker-Nielsen, Hans and Shook, L. K. 1963, 'The Lives of the Saints in Old Norse Prose: a Handlist', *Mediaeval Studies* 25: 294–337.

Index

The following procedures have been adopted in this index for Icelandic personal names. Names of medieval and early modern Icelanders are listed in the order given name followed by patronymic and any nickname or appellation, e.g. Arnórr Þórðarson jarlaskáld. Names of modern scholars are given in the reverse order, e.g. Benediktsson, Jakob.

Index

Index

Index

Index

Index

Index

his *Íslendinga saga* 121, 189, 194, 196, 223, 224,
 229, 230, 231, 234, 251, 255, 312
his poetry 97
his *Sturlu þáttr* 46, 89, 224, 235–8
Sturlu saga 224, 230; see also *Sturlunga saga*
Sturlunga saga 68, 82, 85, 97, 105, 163, 192, 194,
 221, 250, 258; see also historical writing,
 Icelandic
 as political history 231–5, 238
 as propaganda for ruling classes 222, 223–4,
 235, 238
 protagonists analogous to Norse gods and
 heroes 231–2, 235, 251
 social context of Sturlung Age and *Sturlunga
 saga* 204, 221–5, 258
 structure of saga 224–5
Sturlungar (Icelandic family) 89, 96, 188, 229,
 230, 235, 237–8, 257–8; see also genealogies,
 importance of
Styrmir Kárason 78, 180, 196, 258, 262
Sunnifa, Norwegian saint 306
supernatural, representation of 253–4, 257; see
 also pre-Christian religion in Iceland
 female aggression in 315
Sveinn Earl of Hlaðir 78
Sveinn Eiríksson, King of Denmark 71
Sveinsson, Einar Ól. 42, 127, 156, 217, 236, 267
Sverrir Sigurðarson, King of Norway 1177–1202,
 13, 69, 83, 163, 255, 258, 260
Sverris saga by Karl Jónsson 69, 82, 83, 86, 88,
 163, 179, 255
Svínfellinga saga 224, 226; see also *Sturlunga saga*
Svínfellingar (Icelandic family) 229; see also
 genealogies, importance of

Tacitus, *Germania* 44, 318, 322
Theodoricus monachus, *Historia de Antiquitate
 regum Norwagiensium* 12, 69, 162, 179
Third Grammatical Treatise of Óláfr Þórðarson 4,
 41, 86, 96–113, 130, 142, 143
 evidence of work for Óláfr's knowledge of
 vernacular poetry 97–113, 153
 knowledge of Norse runes 97
 sources in Priscian and Donatus 96–8, 144,
 146, 147
Thomas à Becket 97, 196, 303, 305, 309, 310
Thorsson, Örnólfur 97
Tindr Halkellsson (skald) 77, 79
Todorov, Tzvetan 250
Tómasson, Sverrir 98, 99, 129, 130, 162, 165, 177,
 181, 194, 195, 196, 215, 269, 276, 320
trade as specialized occupation of Norwegian
 merchants 181
 Icelandic export of dried codfish 269–70
Tranter, Stephen 4, 113, 140, 148, 156, 157, 221
Tristrams saga 251, 266, 269, 274, 278, 281
Tristrams saga ok Ísoddar 278, 281

Troy, theory of Scandinavian emigration from
 16–17, 48–9, 178
Trójumanna saga 164, 274
Tschan, Francis 183, 184
Tulinius, Torfi 5, 121, 216, 242, 247, 248, 252, 253,
 254, 255, 256, 275, 276, 279
Turville-Petre, Gabriel 47, 52, 158, 299, 309
Turville-Petre, Joan 48

Þættir (short tales about Icelanders) 5, 68, 69, 70,
 75, 88, 104, 181, 184, 192, 196, 203–5, 208,
 215, 236, 242, 282; see also saga genre
Þiðreks saga 132
Þjóðólfr Arnórsson (skald) 74, 81, 105, 106, 107,
 108, 110, 111
 his brother Bǫlverkr 81
Þjóðólfr of Hvinir (Norwegian skald) 72, 106,
 127, 132
 his *Haustlǫng* 72, 106, 127–8, 132, 135
 his *Ynglingatal* 48, 51, 72, 73, 85, 90, 106,
 246
Þórarinn stuttfeldr (skald) 82–3
 his *Stuttfeldardrápa* 83
Þorfinnr munnr (skald) 77
Þorgils orraskáld (skald) 90
Þorgils skarði Bǫðvarsson 224, 235, 305; see also
 Sturlunga saga
Þorgils saga skarða 224
Þorgils saga ok Hafliða 105, 185, 224, 226, 229, 246,
 260, 320; see also *Sturlunga saga*
 description of entertainment at wedding feast
 45, 194, 246, 260, 312, 320
Þorlákr Þórhallsson, Bishop of Skálholt (St
 Þorlákr) 97, 184, 185, 259, 302, 304, 307, 308,
 311, 316, 317, 320
Þorláks saga 163, 308–9, 310; see also bishops and
 bishoprics, saga genre, sagas of bishops,
 saints' lives
Þorláksson, Helgi 262
Þorleifr Rauðfeldarson jarlsskáld (skald) 77,
 104–5, 108, 110, 111, 182
Þórólfsson, Björn 42, 156, 236
Þormóðr Bersason kolbrúnarskáld (skald) 78–9,
 101, 156, 236
Þorvalds þáttr víðfǫrla 196
Þórðr kakali Sighvatsson 224, 235; see also
 Sturlunga saga
Þórðar saga kakala 224
Þórðr Kolbeinsson (skald) 78, 81
Þórðr Narfason 221, 224, 226, 230, 238, 239; see
 also *Sturlunga saga*
Þrymskviða 63, 89, 90, 135

Uecker, Heiko 291, 299
Úlfr Óspaksson 81
Úlfr Uggason (skald) 72, 132
 his poem *Húsdrápa* 72, 132

CAMBRIDGE STUDIES IN MEDIEVAL LITERATURE